WATERFALLS of New York State

FIREFLY BOOKS

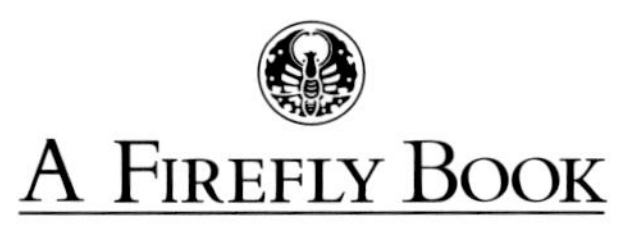

A FIREFLY BOOK

Published by Firefly Books Ltd., 2012

First printing

Publisher Cataloging-in-Publication Data (U.S.)

Ensminger, Scott A.
Waterfalls of New York State / Scott A. Ensminger ; David J. Schryver ; photographs by Edward M. Smathers.
[240] p. : photos. (chiefly col.), maps ; cm.
Includes index.
Summary: An illustrated guide to the waterfalls of New York State. Includes maps, driving and trail directions and access to the falls, descriptions of the waterfalls and their geological features and local histories.

ISBN-13: 978-1-55407-986-5 (pbk.)

1. Waterfalls – New York (State) -- Guidebooks. 2. New York (State) -- Guidebooks.
I. David J. Schryver. II. Edward M. Smathers. III. Title.
551.484 dc23 GB1425.N4.E675 2012

Library and Archives Canada Cataloguing in Publication

Ensminger, Scott A.
Waterfalls of New York State / Scott A. Ensminger, David J. Schryver, Edward M. Smathers ; photographs by Edward M. Smathers.

ISBN 978-1-55407-986-5

1. Waterfalls--New York (State). 2. Waterfalls--New York (State)--Pictorial works. 3. New York (State)--Guidebooks.
I. Schryver, David J. II. Smathers, Edward M. III. Title.
GB1425.N4E572 2012 551.48'409747 C2012-901996-8

Published in the United States by
Firefly Books (U.S.) Inc.
P.O. Box 1338, Ellicott Station
Buffalo, New York 14205

Published in Canada by
Firefly Books Ltd.
66 Leek Crescent
Richmond Hill, Ontario L4B 1H1

Printed in China

The Publisher gratefully acknowledges the financial support for our publishing program by the Government of Canada through the Canada Book Fund as administered by the Department of Canadian Heritage.

Front cover:
Watkins Glen State Park
© Edward M. Smathers

Back cover:
Hector Falls © Edward M. Smathers

Cover and interior design:
Janice McLean /
Bookmakers Press Inc.

Map design: George Walker

WATERFALLS of New York State

SCOTT A. ENSMINGER, DAVID J. SCHRYVER and EDWARD M. SMATHERS
Principal photography by EDWARD M. SMATHERS

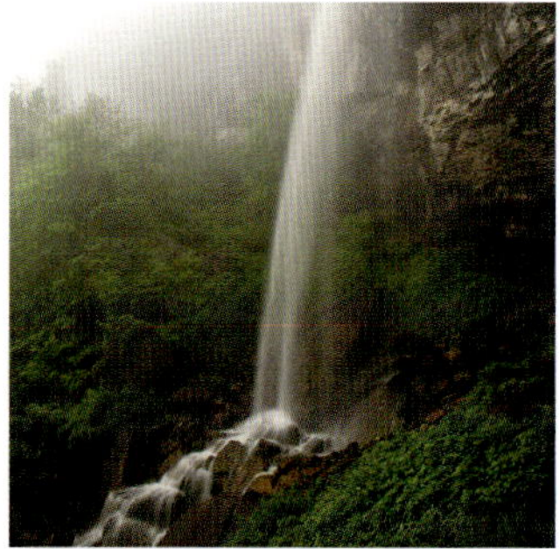
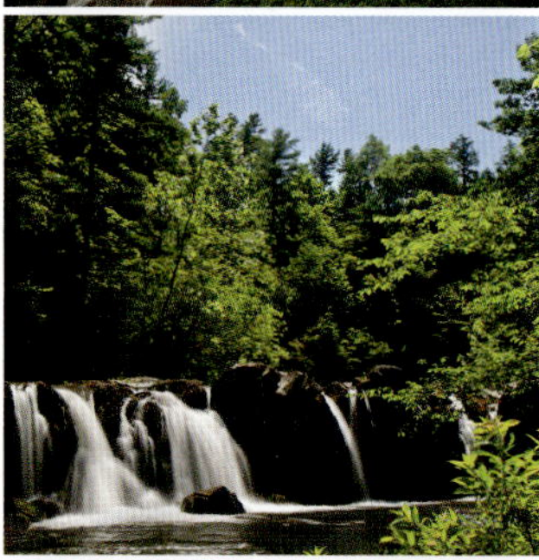
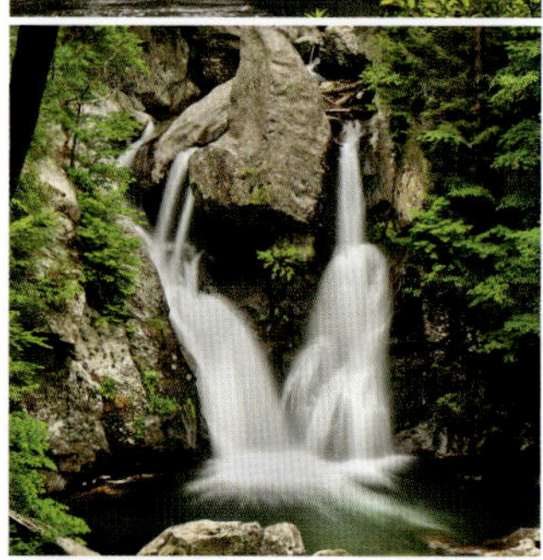
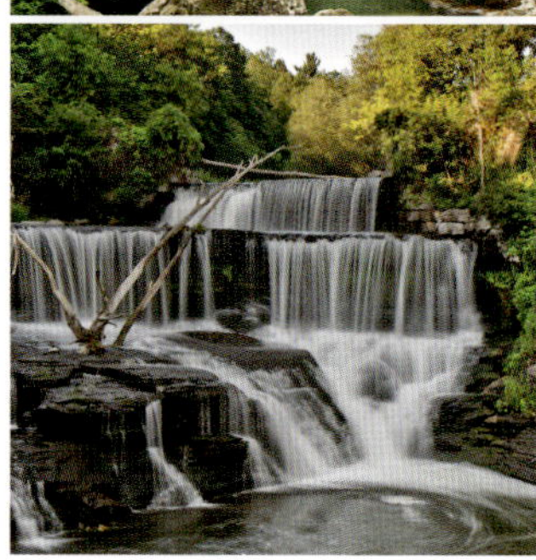

Contents

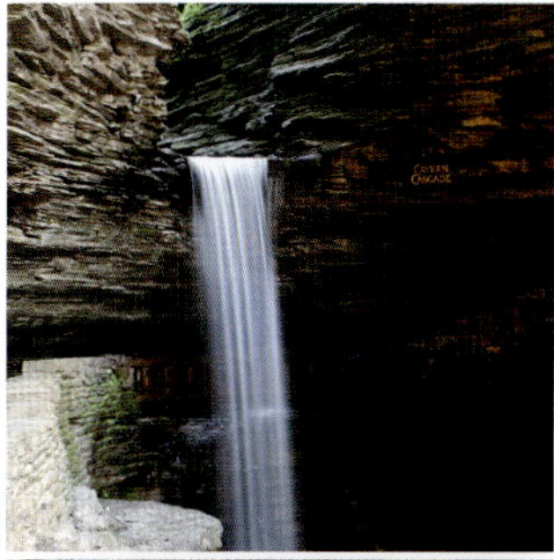

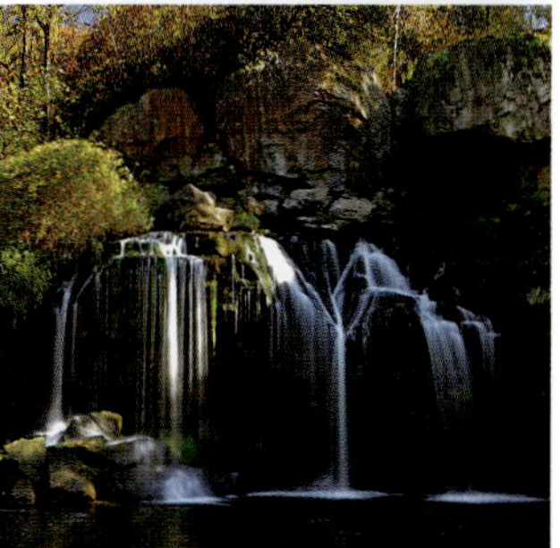

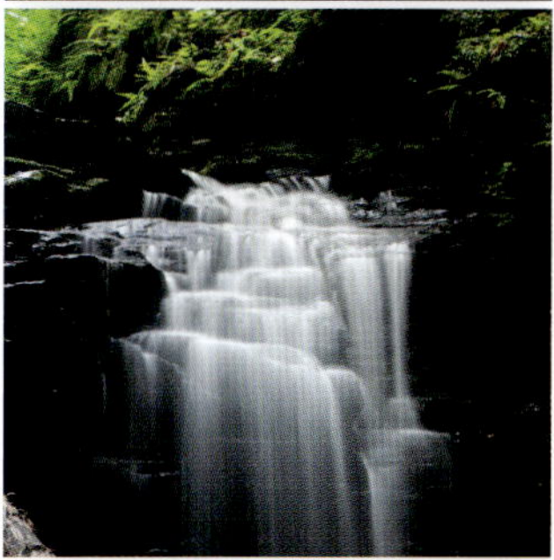

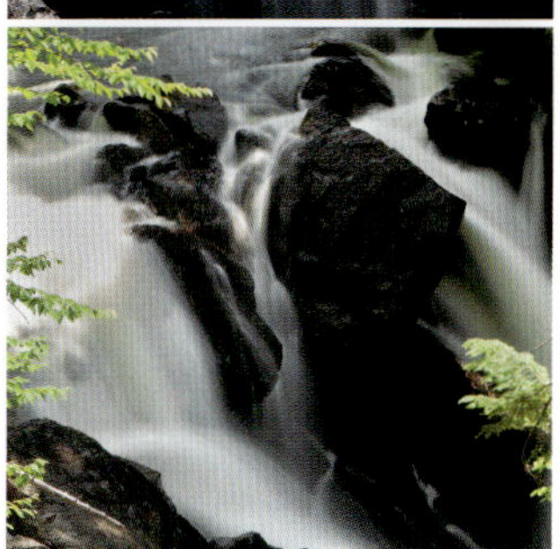

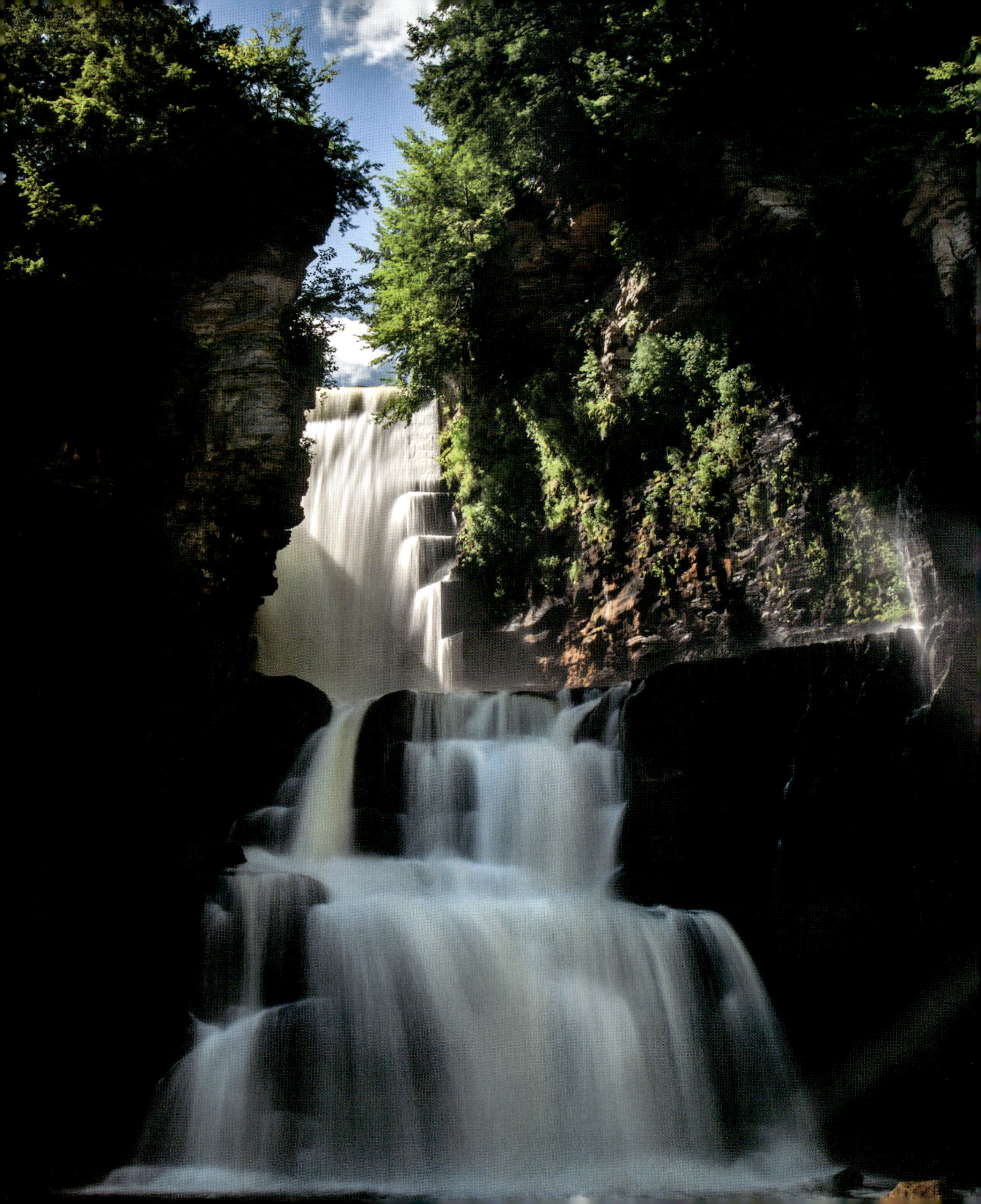

Introduction

What explains the powerful effect that waterfalls have on so many of us? Without question, there is something in the sound and sight of falling water that both refreshes and inspires us. The water's lively, relentless movement draws us closer, and the seemingly infinite flow is almost hypnotic. The gentle murmur of a wispy cascade relaxes and soothes, while the roar and power of a mighty cataract evokes feelings of respect and awe and sometimes fear.

Ranked as one of the world's top 10 waterfalls and easily the most famous falls in North America, Niagara Falls is located on the border of Ontario, Canada, and New York State. Roughly 20 million people flock to see it annually, thrilling to the magnificent power as the Niagara River rushes over the Niagara Escarpment in three distinct waterfalls. As fulfilling as that experience is, however, New York has much more to offer waterfall lovers, including a couple of waterfalls that have historically rivaled the drawing power of the great Niagara Falls.

There are more than 2,000 waterfalls in New York. In *Waterfalls of New York State*, we've gathered just over 100, in what we think is a compelling taste of what the state has to offer. These range from modest, delicate cascades to huge, thundering cataracts. The selection was made by three waterfall enthusiasts, each of whom brings his own waterfall appreciation and passion to the written descriptions. These are accompanied by photographs taken by Edward Smathers, an accomplished professional photographer who visited and photographed almost every waterfall featured here.

Each entry includes driving directions to the waterfall, as well as access points. Please note that while these directions were current at the time this book was published, waterfalls and their settings are dynamic and changeable and road and trail conditions can alter overnight as a result of severe weather. At the same time, many of these roads are closed during the winter. When you plan a visit to any of these destinations, especially the more remote ones, be sure to do your due diligence by checking the latest information about

High Falls on the Chateaugay River, North Country, page 218

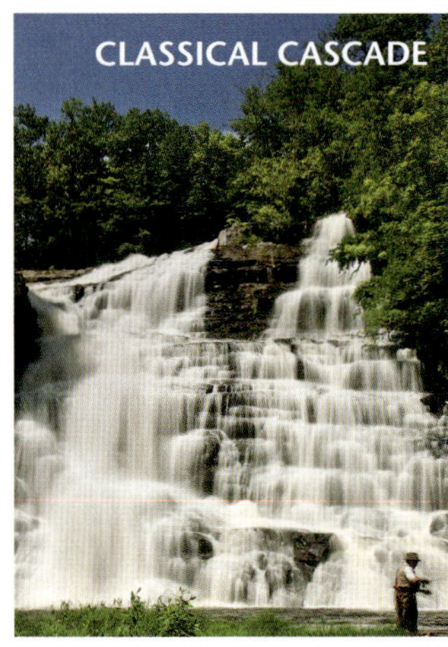
CLASSICAL CASCADE

weather and road conditions. Visit the New York State parks website at www.nysparks.com and the Department of Environmental Conservation (DEC) at www.dec.ny.gov to obtain details on waterfalls that are located on publicly managed land.

Remember that many of New York's waterfalls are on privately owned land, and access to them may be restricted by the landowner. Respect all posted and no-trespassing signs, and contact the landowner for permission to enter the property. Failure to do so may result in arrest and prosecution.

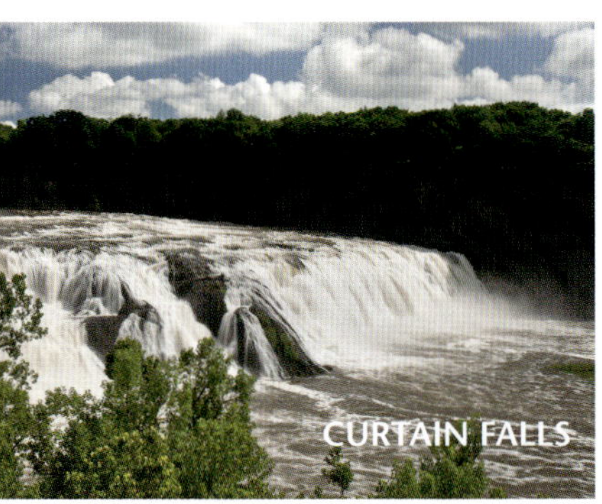
CURTAIN FALLS

UNDERSTANDING WATERFALLS

Waterfalls vary widely in their appearance and characteristics, and since there is no official international waterfall classification system, many references and websites use customized systems and terminology. We've chosen to use the system developed by members of the Western New York Waterfall Survey in 1994, which is based on the waterfall's visual appearance.

WATERFALL TYPES

By comparing the height with the width of the crest (the span of the waterway where it begins its descent), waterfalls can be divided into the following three types:

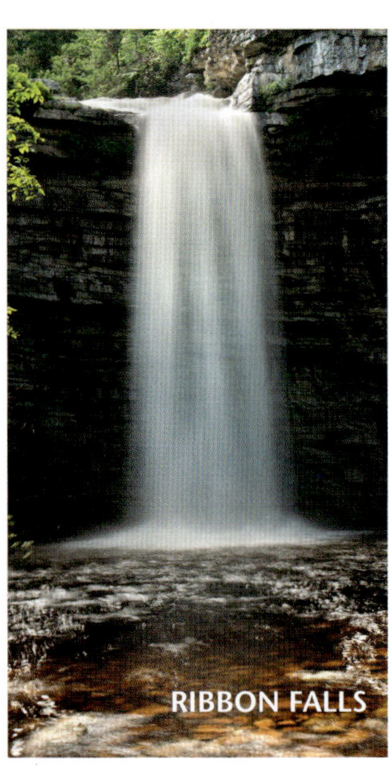
RIBBON FALLS

CLASSICAL: A waterfall whose height is slightly greater than, equal to or less than the crest width. Both of the following must be true:
(1) the height divided by 2 is smaller than the crest width; and
(2) the height multiplied by 1.5 is equal to or greater than the crest width.

CURTAIN: A waterfall whose height is notably less than the crest width. The following must be true: The height multiplied by 1.5 is less than the crest width.

RIBBON: A waterfall whose height is notably greater than the crest width. The following must be true: The height divided by 2 is equal to or greater than the crest width.

We have also placed waterfalls into one of two *classes*, based on their visual appearance and dominant feature:

CASCADE: The sudden descent of a stream, primarily over a very steep slope in its streambed. It is characterized by the stream rushing down the slope smoothly or in a series of small individual drops or both. The steepness of the descent is greater than that of rapids but less than that of a waterfall.

FALLS: The sudden descent of a stream, primarily over a vertical or an extremely steep section of the streambed. It is characterized by the stream dropping freely through the air, or very nearly so.

As you'll see later, many waterfalls combine the two classes. A waterfall may start as a gentle cascade, then fall vertically and end as an extremely steep cascade. For these, the word "complex" may appear before the type of waterfall. Remember, too, that a waterfall's appearance is very changeable, depending on water flow.

USING THIS BOOK

To organize our waterfall selection, we've divided the state into five general areas: Capital Region, Hudson Valley Region, Finger Lakes Region, Greater Niagara Region and North Country Region. A sixth region, the Southern Tier, is included on the regional map on page 11, but we do not officially represent that region in the book. Instead, due to the nature of our waterfall selection, we've shifted a handful of "outlying" waterfalls to the section that features their nearest waterfall neighbors.

As with any journey, an essential tool for planning a waterfall trip is a reliable map. With each region, we've included a map showing approximate waterfall locations, but we recommend the *New York Atlas & Gazetteer* published by DeLorme (www.delorme.com), which shows many county roads, small villages and waterways that don't appear on standard road maps. Tourism centers offer free state and county maps. You can also use an online mapping site, such as MapQuest or Google Maps. Trail maps are often available at state parks and preserves and serve as convenient guides.

SAFETY

What makes many waterfalls spectacular is often their settings, but those settings can also be incredibly dangerous. Be cautious when approaching the steep slopes and cliffs surrounding waterfalls, and remember that the rocks are often loose or covered in water or slippery algae. A plunge over the edge can be fatal, so don't stray from the established trails and keep youngsters close by. In some areas,

WATERFALL FACT BOX

Accompanying each waterfall entry is a fact box that includes the following information:

COUNTY: The name of the county/counties in which the waterfall is located.

TOWNSHIP: The name of the township(s) in which the waterfall is located.

PLACE: The closest city, village or hamlet shown on a common state road map.

WATERWAY: The name of the creek, brook, stream or river creating the waterfall.

TYPE: The type of waterfall as defined by the members of the Western New York Waterfall Survey.

HEIGHT: The vertical height of the waterfall in feet and meters. If the height has not been documented, "est." precedes the number.

TRAIL: The defining characteristics of the trail (e.g., dirt, crushed stone, blacktop or sidewalk). We also assess whether the hike is easy, moderate or difficult.

WALKING TIME: The approximate time that it takes to walk from the nearest parking area to the falls viewing area.

PEAK ACTIVITY: The months in which most people visit the waterfall. This will give you an idea of when the waterfall site is the busiest.

LATITUDE AND LONGITUDE: The location coordinates of the waterfall or of a nearby viewing area. The coordinates are given in decimal degrees (e.g., Latitude 43.0521, Longitude –78.8631), which can be entered into a handheld GPS unit or an online mapping site, such as ACME Mapper 2.0 or Google Maps, to help you locate the waterfall.

HIKING CODES OF CONDUCT

Enjoying the great outdoors is becoming a popular pastime. As more people venture outside, more pressures are put on the natural environment. It is your responsibility to take care of it. Please think about your actions, and make a conscious decision to preserve and protect this beauty so that others can also enjoy it. When hiking, keep the following points in mind:

DON'T LITTER. Trash left along trails and at viewing areas is unsightly and disrespectful to nature and other visitors. Keeping these areas litter-free is everyone's duty. Carry out all trash.

STAY ON ESTABLISHED TRAILS. Taking shortcuts contributes to erosion and to the destruction of plant life. The established trail is also the safest route.

DON'T MISTREAT WILDLIFE. All animals should be treated with respect. Don't feed the wildlife. It disrupts their eating habits and natural life cycle.

PRESERVE PLANT LIFE. Don't pick the wildflowers. Doing so deprives other visitors of enjoying their beauty.

HAVE FUN. Allow yourself enough time to fully experience the waterfall and its setting. Stop and study plants and wildlife during your hike. Find a spot to relax and savor the sights and sounds of the waterfall.

there is no fencing along cliff tops, so stay at least 6 feet (1.8 m) back from the edge. It may be hundreds of feet to the bottom. And never throw anything over a cliff. There may be visitors below.

If you plan to take the longer hikes we describe here, know your limitations and those of your companions. Keep in mind that young children may tire quickly. On the longer hikes, carry a knapsack with food and beverages. A cell phone, a compass or GPS unit, a basic first-aid kit, a flashlight, matches and a notepad and pencil are also good items to take along. Check the weather forecast for the day, and dress accordingly. And allow enough time to get back to your vehicle well before dark. In other words, be prepared.

Proper footwear is essential. Except for those few waterfalls accessible by wide paved paths or visible from the car, viewing a waterfall often requires walking along trails that can be muddy, rocky, slippery and rough. Some have stone steps. Choose shoes with good support and sturdy treads.

PHOTOGRAPHING THE WATERFALLS

These days, part of appreciating nature increasingly includes bringing back photographs that record the experience. We're not going to instruct you on how to achieve an effect with your camera — there are plenty of how-to books available on this subject — but we do have a few tips specific to waterfall shoots.

There are several things to keep in mind when trying to record the essence of any waterfall. One is to remember that no matter what its size, shape or location, a waterfall can be made to look majestic in a well-composed photo, even with very little editing.

After your camera, a tripod is probably your most important photography tool. It will help you achieve a stable, sharp image that might otherwise be blurry or soft to the eye. Not only that, but a tripod always makes a great hiking partner: It can provide a little balance when you're negotiating an uneven or sloping trail. Just don't be too rough with it.

When you arrive at the waterfall, find a safe and secure place from which to take your shots. Now consider the elements: How bright is the light? Is there enough water? Are there any distracting objects or buildings in view? Is this the best spot from which to shoot?

When faced with a waterfall with very little flow, one trick to

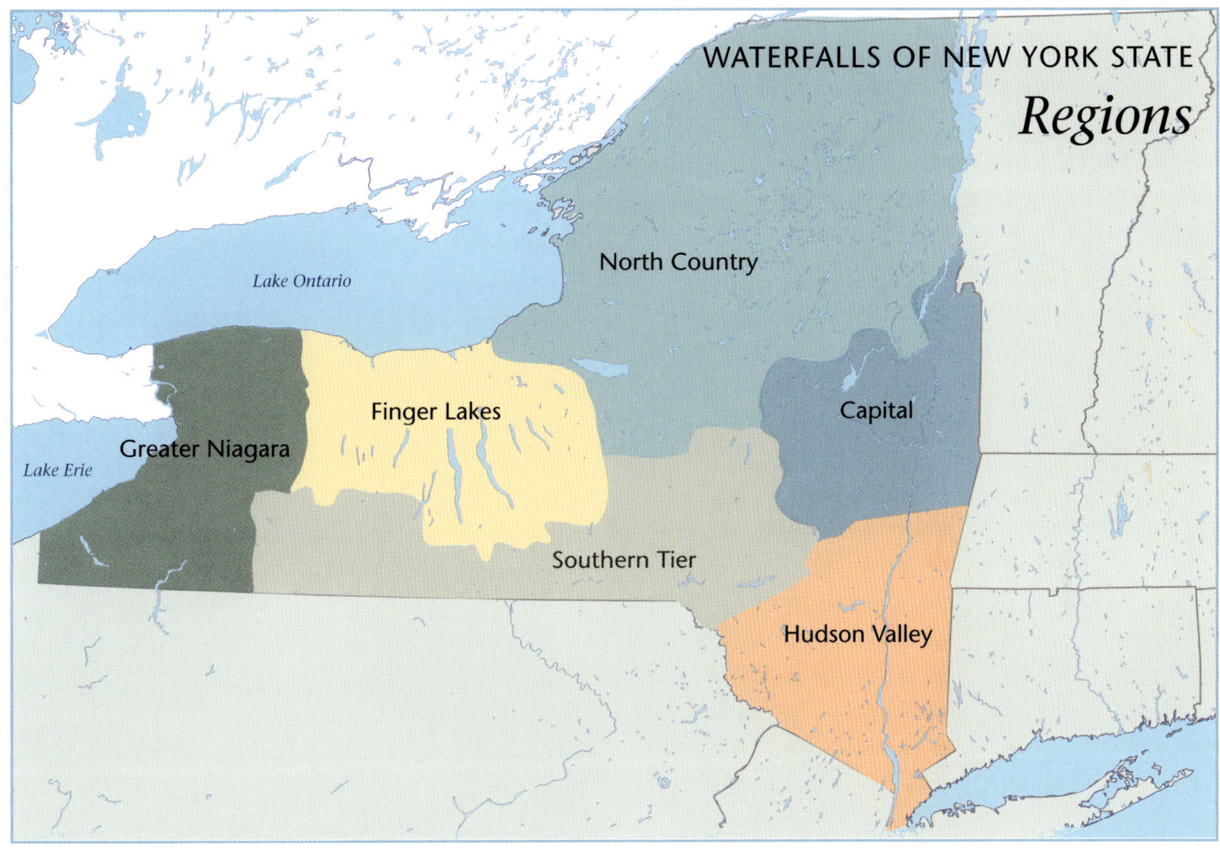

make the flow seem greater is to position yourself to the side of the falls. That way, you'll be looking across numerous little trickles, rather than one individual trickle. Tree branches and dead logs can be distracting if not handled correctly. Houses and buildings on the periphery can easily be cropped out for the most part. Leaves and foliage in the foreground nicely frame some shots and add a color contrast.

There is a solution to almost any photo situation, and all these photography details will become second nature over time. With some practice and attention to detail, you'll capture your favorite waterfall just as you wanted.

It's easy to lose yourself in the technical aspects of the photograph, but you mustn't forget that the primary reason you're here is to experience the waterfall, so don't forget to enjoy what's in front of you.

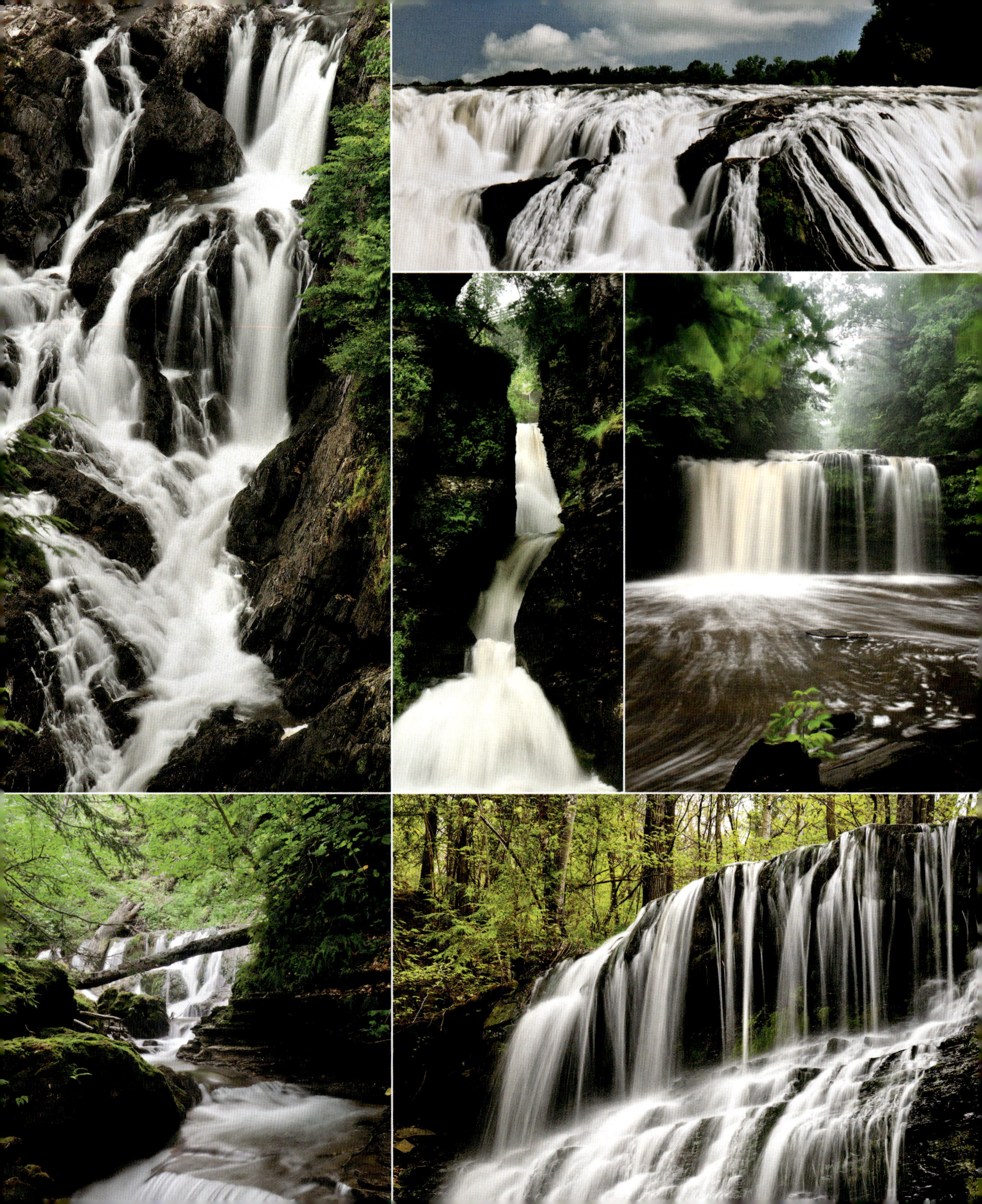

Capital

As with the rest of New York State, the geography of the Capital Region was created by advancing and retreating glaciers during the last Ice Age. These massive moving ice sheets carved out mountain ranges and great waterways such as the Hudson River and its huge tributary to the west, the Mohawk River, as well as countless smaller creeks and streams. The broad plain west of present-day Schenectady is likewise the legacy of a huge glacial lake. The sheer abundance of power-producing waterways eventually transformed the region into a transportation and manufacturing center in the 19th century, with canals, steamboats, roadways and trains moving goods in all directions.

One of the many appealing features of the area today is that it offers both access to the benefits of big-city living and proximity to natural beauty. Waterfall lovers often feel as though they are in the middle of nowhere when they are searching out new views, but at any given time, they are probably only a short distance from civilization. There are even waterfalls close to Albany, the state capital since 1797.

Although this region has a great network of well-traveled roads, it's important to note that many areas still have seasonally limited highways and single-lane dirt tracks, which can be difficult or impossible to traverse during the winter months.

Almost all the waterfalls listed in the Capital Region are located within an area that can be accessed by one means of transportation or another. We encourage you to visit all the waterfalls described here, but for the best ratio of waterfalls to hiking, don't miss John Boyd Thacher State Park, Christman Sanctuary and Plotter Kill Nature Preserve. These have varying degrees of trail difficulty while offering access to a range of diverse waterfall experiences.

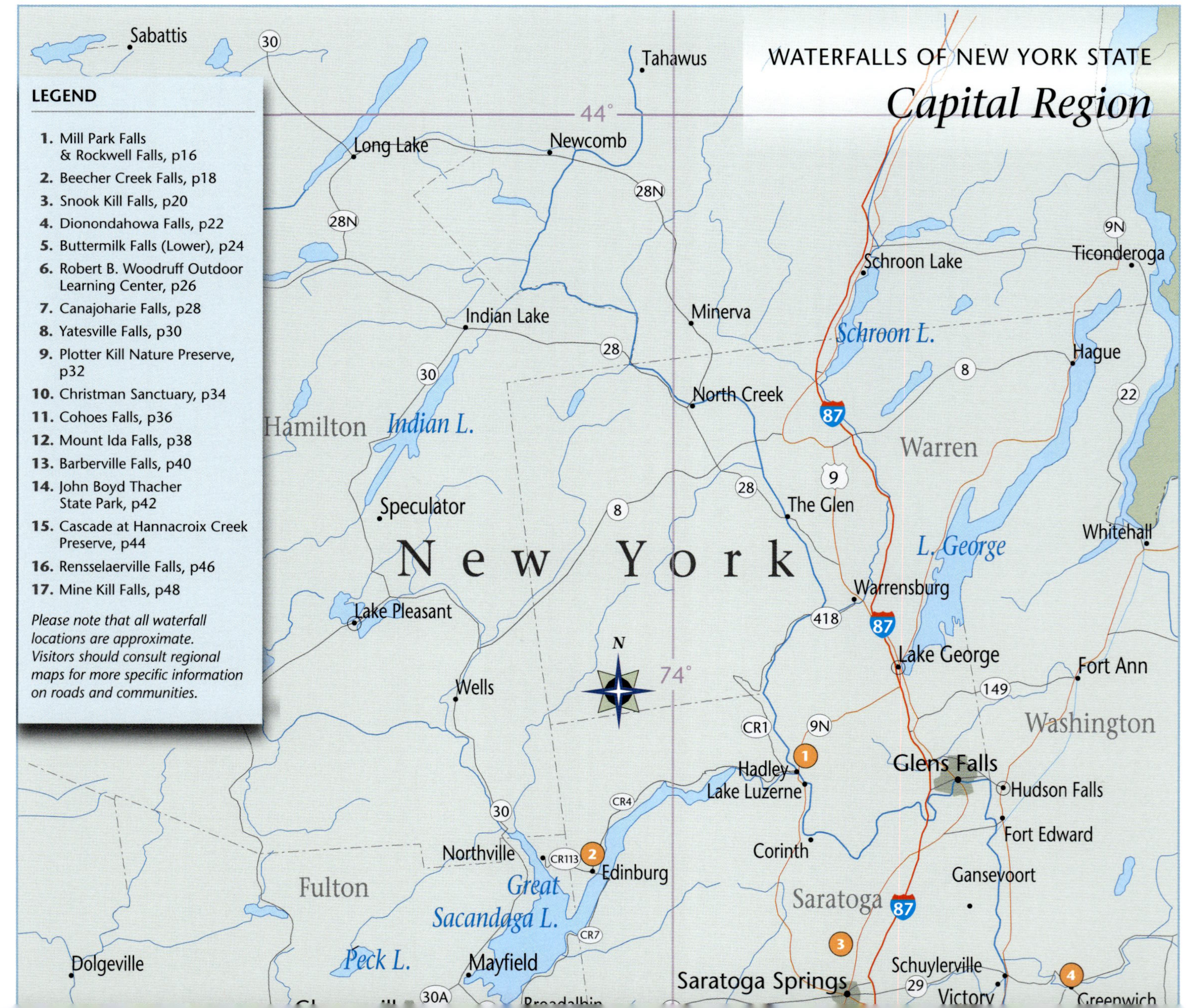
WATERFALLS OF NEW YORK STATE
Capital Region
LEGEND
1. Mill Park Falls & Rockwell Falls, p16
2. Beecher Creek Falls, p18
3. Snook Kill Falls, p20
4. Dionondahowa Falls, p22
5. Buttermilk Falls (Lower), p24
6. Robert B. Woodruff Outdoor Learning Center, p26
7. Canajoharie Falls, p28
8. Yatesville Falls, p30
9. Plotter Kill Nature Preserve, p32
10. Christman Sanctuary, p34
11. Cohoes Falls, p36
12. Mount Ida Falls, p38
13. Barberville Falls, p40
14. John Boyd Thacher State Park, p42
15. Cascade at Hannacroix Creek Preserve, p44
16. Rensselaerville Falls, p46
17. Mine Kill Falls, p48
Please note that all waterfall locations are approximate. Visitors should consult regional maps for more specific information on roads and communities.
New York
Sabattis
Tahawus
Long Lake
Newcomb
Indian Lake
Minerva
North Creek
Schroon Lake
Schroon L.
Ticonderoga
Hague
Hamilton
Indian L.
Warren
Speculator
The Glen
L. George
Whitehall
Warrensburg
Lake Pleasant
Lake George
Fort Ann
Wells
Washington
Hadley
Lake Luzerne
Glens Falls
Hudson Falls
Fort Edward
Northville
Edinburg
Corinth
Gansevoort
Fulton
Great Sacandaga L.
Saratoga
Peck L.
Mayfield
Saratoga Springs
Schuylerville
Victory
Dolgeville
44°
74°
N

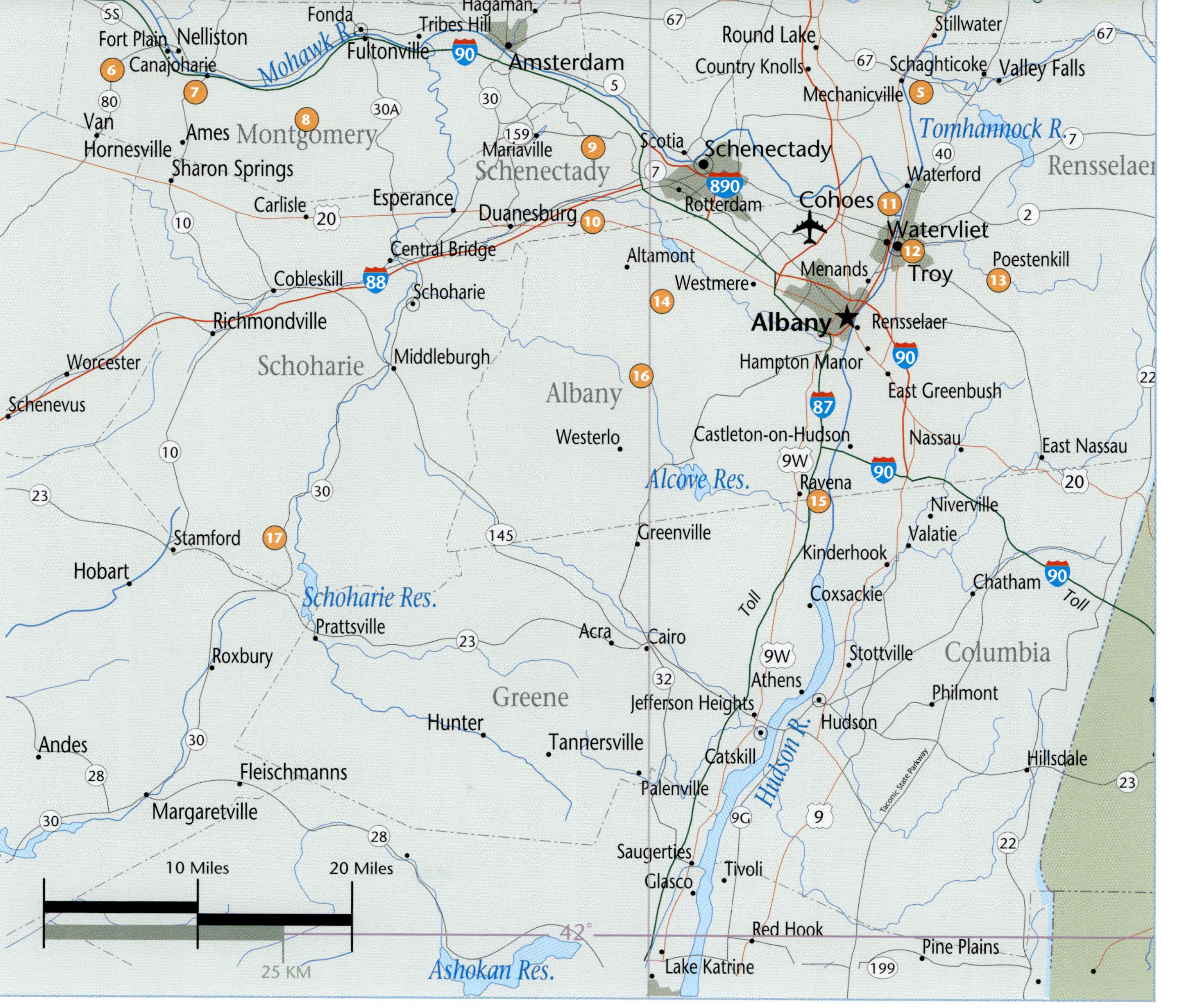
Fonda
Hagaman
Tribes Hill
Fultonville
Amsterdam
Mohawk R.
Fort Plain
Nelliston
Canajoharie
Van
Hornesville
Ames
Montgomery
Sharon Springs
Carlisle
Esperance
Mariaville
Schenectady
Duanesburg
Central Bridge
Cobleskill
Schoharie
Richmondville
Schoharie
Middleburgh
Worcester
Schenevus
Scotia
Schenectady
Rotterdam
Cohoes
Watervliet
Troy
Menands
Altamont
Westmere
Albany
Rensselaer
Hampton Manor
East Greenbush
Albany
Westerlo
Castleton-on-Hudson
Nassau
East Nassau
Alcove Res.
Ravena
Niverville
Valatie
Kinderhook
Greenville
Chatham
Toll
Coxsackie
Stamford
Hobart
Schoharie Res.
Prattsville
Acra
Cairo
Roxbury
Stottville
Columbia
Athens
Jefferson Heights
Philmont
Hudson
Greene
Hunter
Tannersville
Catskill
Hudson R.
Taconic State Parkway
Hillsdale
Andes
Fleischmanns
Margaretville
Palenville
Saugerties
Glasco
Tivoli
Red Hook
Pine Plains
Lake Katrine
Ashokan Res.
42°
10 Miles
20 Miles
25 KM
Round Lake
Country Knolls
Mechanicville
Stillwater
Schaghticoke
Valley Falls
Tomhannock R.
Waterford
Rensselaer
Poestenkill

Mill Park Falls & Rockwell Falls

The hamlet of Lake Luzerne is 5 mi (8 km) from exit 21 on I-87. Mill St. is at the north end of the hamlet, on the western side of NY 9N, across from Wayside Beach. As you turn onto Mill St., Mill Park is immediately on your left. Street parking is available, and you will see the falls area as you enter the park.

COUNTY:
Mill Park Falls: Warren
Rockwell Falls:
Saratoga and Warren

TOWNSHIP:
Mill Park Falls: Lake Luzerne
Rockwell Falls:
Hadley and Lake Luzerne

PLACE: Lake Luzerne

WATERWAY: Mill Park Falls:
Lake Luzerne outlet
Rockwell Falls: Hudson River

TYPE:
Mill Park Falls: ribbon cascade
Rockwell Falls: classical falls

HEIGHT:
Mill Park Falls: est. 25 ft (7.6 m)
Rockwell Falls: 10 ft (3 m)

TRAIL:
grass path and sidewalk; easy

WALKING TIME: 1 min

PEAK ACTIVITY: May-Sept.

LATITUDE:
Mill Park Falls: 43.3211
Rockwell Falls: 43.3182

LONGITUDE:
Mill Park Falls: –73.8392
Rockwell Falls: –73.8433

The hamlet of Lake Luzerne is located in the foothills of the Adirondack Mountains, in an area famous for its pure air, natural beauty, clear lakes and at least two picturesque waterfalls, the first of which is located on the outlet of Lake Luzerne.

As you approach Mill Park Falls, you'll see a millpond above a small dam. Below the dam is a series of steps and slides that anticipates the main drop of roughly 25 feet (7.6 m). Today, adjacent to the drop, there is a pulp mill museum, once the site of the country's "first wood pulp grinder," according to a descriptive plaque on the building. For the best views of the falls, walk downstream a bit.

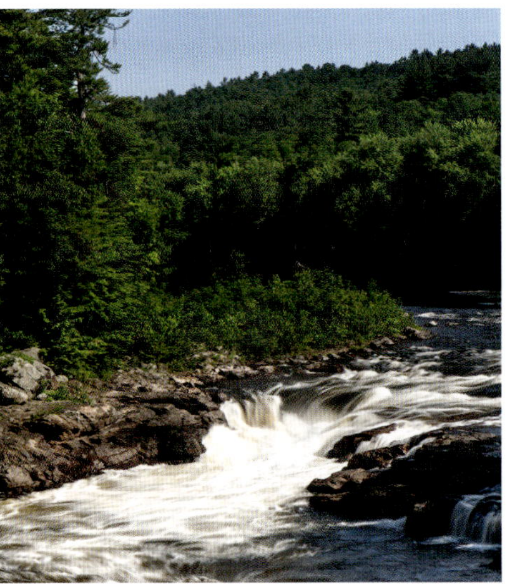

Like many waterfalls in the region, this one is technically unnamed. It is commonly known as Mill Park Falls or the Falls at Mill Park. More unusual is that the waterway is not officially named either. The outlet from Lake Luzerne to the Hudson River drops 96 feet (29.3 m) over its less than 600-yard (548.6 m) length.

After enjoying this quiet little town park, follow Mill Street west as it takes a sharp bend to the left onto Main Street. Take the first right at Bridge Street, and park on the street. It's a short walk to the bridge, where you have an excellent view of horseshoe-shaped Rockwell Falls on the right.

For the more daring or curious, it is possible to get down to a very popular swimming area at the river's edge. On a hot summer day, swimmers jump off the rock cliffs just upstream between the bridge and the waterfall and let the current carry them through the rapids that flow under the bridge.

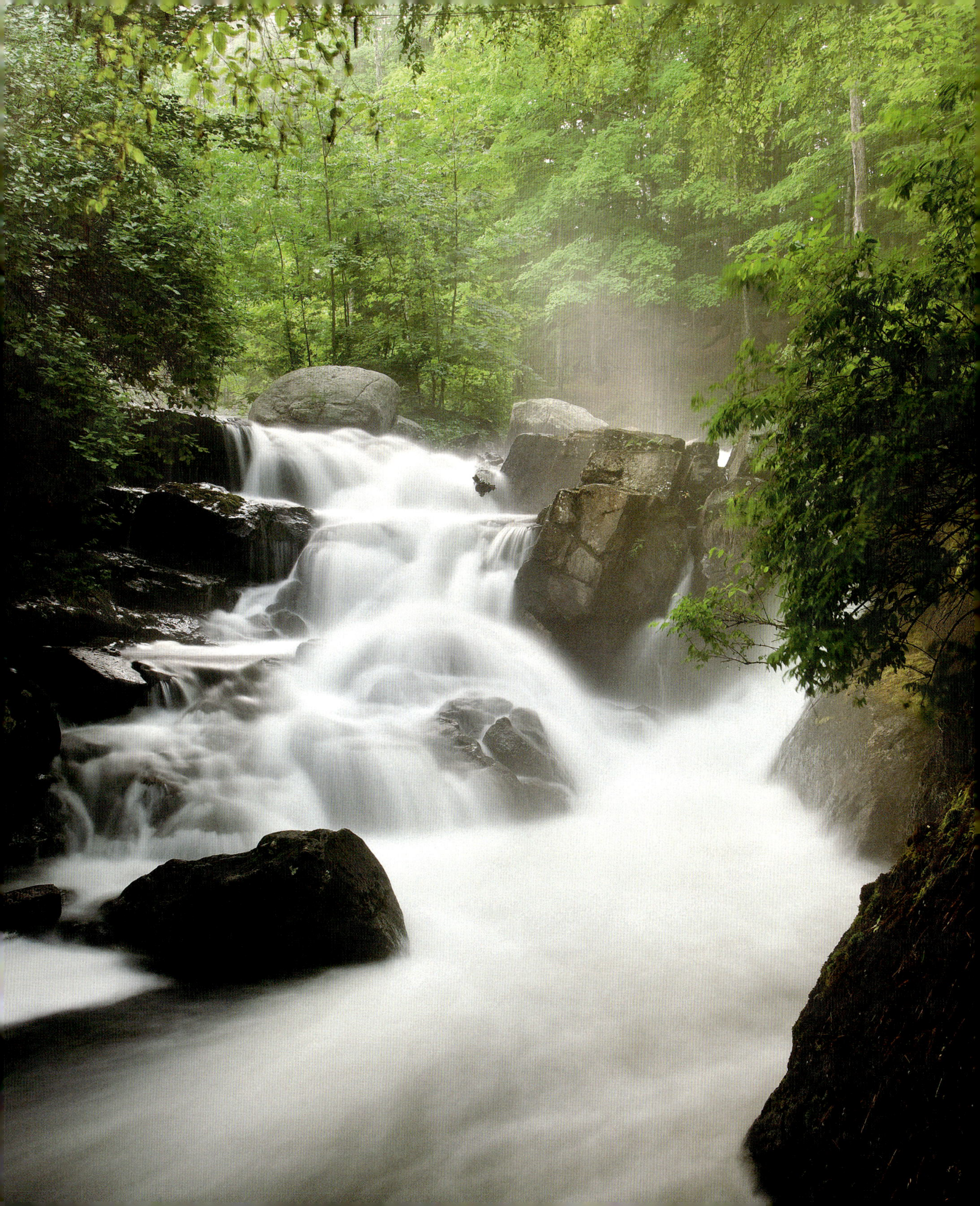

CAPITAL REGION

Beecher Creek Falls

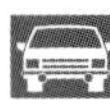 From I-90, take exit 27 and turn right onto NY 30, going north. Staying on NY 30, turn left after 9.3 mi (15 km). After 4.6 mi (7.4 km), turn right, and continue for 10.3 mi (16.6 km). Turn right onto Bridge St. In 0.7 mi (1.1 km), turn left onto Main St, then turn right onto Water St. After 0.4 mi (0.6 km), turn right at CR 149 (Ridge Rd.) and proceed for 0.8 mi (1.3 km). CR 149 turns into CR 113. Drive straight for 0.8 mi (1.3 km), then curve left and continue for another 0.7 mi (1.1 km). CR 113 becomes Northville Rd. (CR 4). Drive 1.6 mi (2.6 km), then turn left. After 0.3 mi (0.5 km), follow the road to the right for 0.2 mi (0.3 km). There is a parking area on the hill at the right side of the road.

COUNTY: Saratoga
TOWNSHIP: Edinburg
PLACE: Edinburg
WATERWAY: Beecher Creek
TYPE: classical cascade
HEIGHT: 20 ft (6.1 m)
TRAIL: footpath; easy
WALKING TIME: 3 min
PEAK ACTIVITY: June-Aug.
LATITUDE: 43.2207
LONGITUDE: –74.1005

From the roadside parking area, you can easily see all of Beecher Creek Falls, but it would be a mistake not to explore just a little farther to view the waterfall from several different perspectives.

Within a short span, Beecher Creek takes a series of drops, which classifies this waterfall as a cascade. In the past, its total height has been measured at 20 feet (6.1 m), but that can vary from year to year, depending on changes brought about by severe weather.

A short distance downstream from the waterfall is the Copeland Covered Bridge. Originally built in 1879, the bridge has been restored by the Edinburg Historic Society. Once used to take farm animals across the creek, it is suitable today only for foot traffic. Without getting your feet wet, you can enjoy the most direct views of the cascade from the bridge.

During extraordinary summer dry spells, the creek's flow may be a bit low, but that's not a common occurrence — the watersheds that feed the tributaries to this creek are robust enough to withstand the ebb and flow of the precipitation levels throughout the year.

As you walk upstream from the main falls, you'll catch a glimpse of a small yet extremely picturesque 4-foot (1.2 m) waterfall. Hiking any farther upstream will land you on private property, so be conservative in your exploration.

In the past, the creek was heavily exploited by factories and mills for its hydro power. At one time, up to nine mills operated along its banks. Many of the mills' remains have long since deteriorated beyond recognition, but you may find remnants if you stray a little off the beaten path.

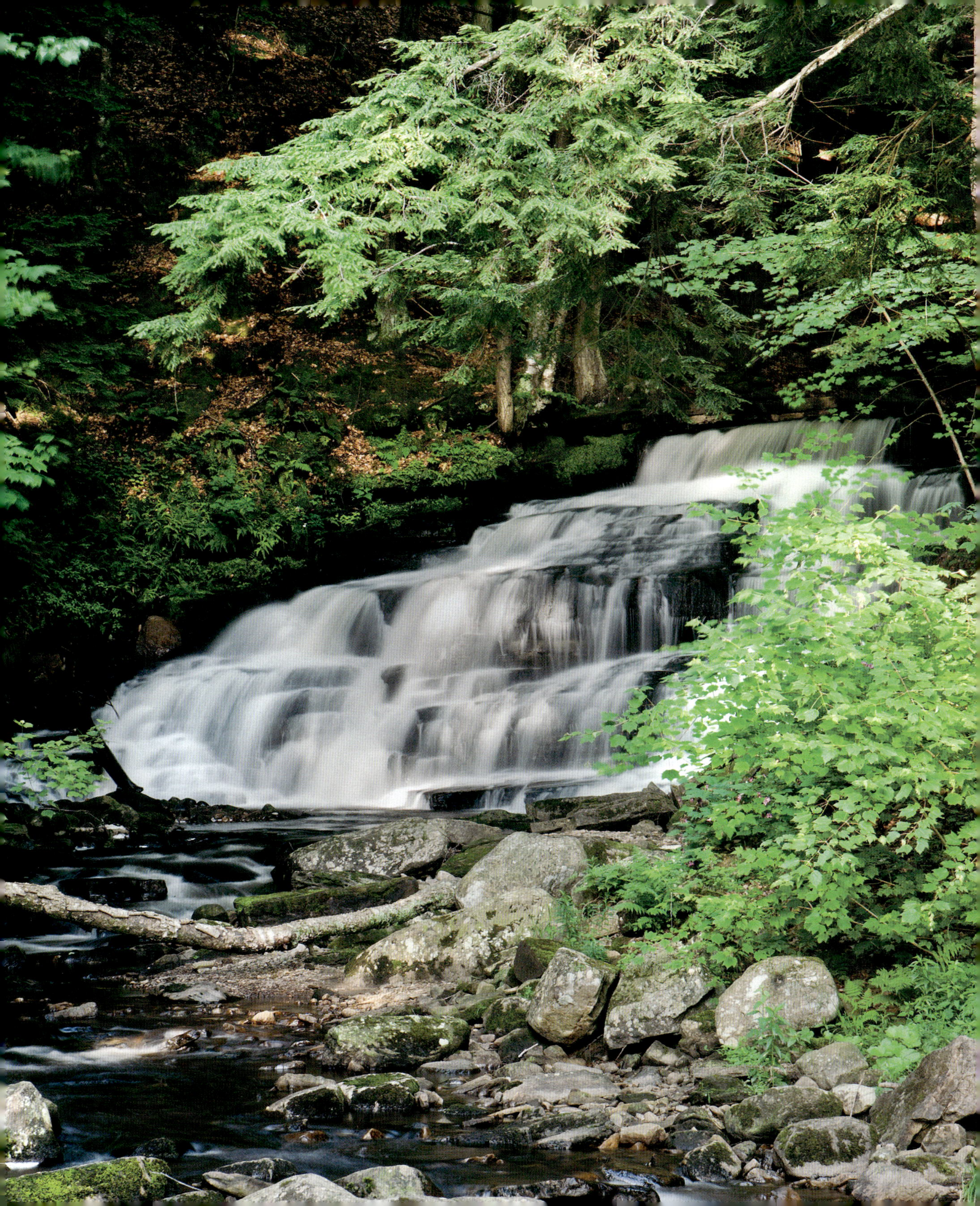

Snook Kill Falls

From the village of Saratoga Springs, where NY 9 and NY 50 divide, proceed north on NY 9. In about 3 mi (4.8 km), you'll reach an area known as Kings Station. Turn left onto CR 36 (Parkhurst Rd.). Drive about 0.25 mi (0.4 km) up the hill, then turn left onto Greenfield Rd. (CR 36). After roughly 0.4 mi (0.6 km), just before the road bends to the left, pull over and park on the shoulder on the opposite side of the road. Walk on the shoulder around the bend, and you'll find the trail to Snook Kill Falls on the left.

COUNTY: Saratoga

TOWNSHIP: Wilton

PLACE: Wilton

WATERWAY: Snook Kill

TYPE: ribbon cascade

HEIGHT: 55 ft (16.8 m)

TRAIL: dirt and rock; moderate

WALKING TIME: 30 min

PEAK ACTIVITY: May-Sept.

LATITUDE: 43.1535

LONGITUDE: –73.7734

Technically, it is unnamed, but we have dubbed this waterfall Snook Kill Falls or the Falls on Snook Kill. The word kill derives from the Middle Dutch word *kille*, meaning "water bed" or "river channel"; the modern Dutch word is *kil*. Defined in dictionaries today as a channel, creek, stream or river, the term is especially common in Delaware, Pennsylvania and New York, the three present-day states where early Dutch colonists primarily settled.

To view the falls from above, walk up the road to a culvert. To see the falls from below, find the nearby trail that leads to the stream's edge. It is a bit of a scramble because the trail is not maintained, but it's worth the effort.

The upper part of this pretty waterfall goes through several drops or slides before its final plunge of 20 feet (6.1 m) or so. The combination of the shade created by the heavy foliage and the rushing mountain stream makes this a refreshingly cool location on a hot summer day.

Just down the hill from the parking area, a historical sign marks the Battle of Wilton in 1693. In 1777, the Battle of Saratoga occurred a few miles south. The British won the first skirmish in September of that year, but the following month, a second encounter led to the surrender of British General John Burgoyne. That battle is now considered a turning point in the American Revolutionary War.

Every summer, horse-racing fans come from far and wide to take in thoroughbred racing at the world-famous Saratoga Race Course. Other attractions in the area include the Saratoga Performing Arts Center, which hosts cultural events, the Saratoga Spa State Park, with its mineral springs, and the Saratoga National Historical Park, which promotes the region's heritage.

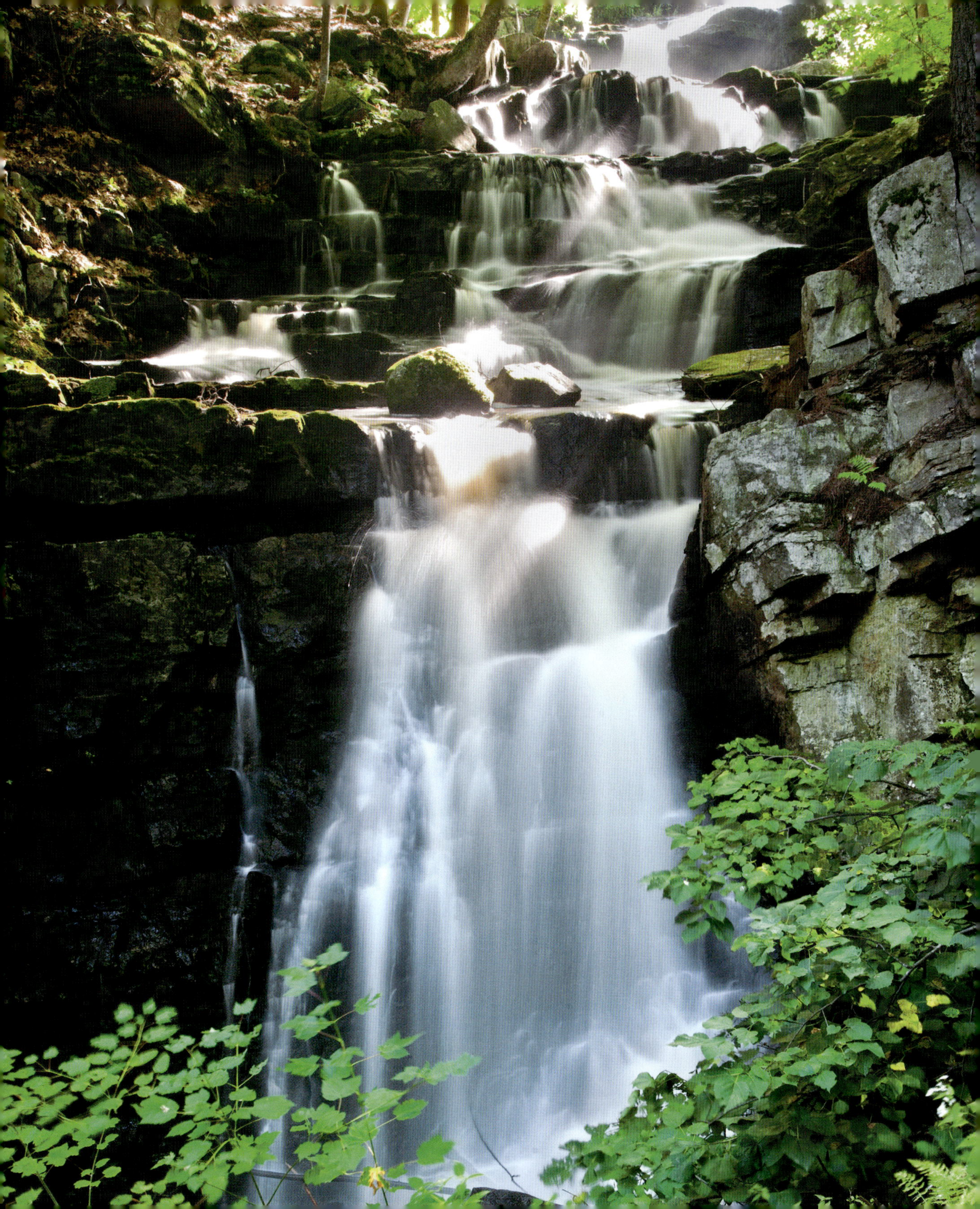

Dionondahowa Falls

From the south, take exit 14 on I-87 and merge onto NY 9P (Union Ave.), heading toward Saratoga Springs. After 0.6 mi (1 km), turn right onto Henning Rd., and continue for 0.9 mi (1.4 km). Turn right onto NY 29 (Lake Ave.). After 9.2 mi (14.8 km), turn right onto Broad St. In 0.3 mi (0.5 km), turn left onto Ferry St. (NY 29). Drive for another 2.2 mi (3.5 km) until you reach Windy Hill Rd., on your left. At about 0.5 mi (0.8 km), you'll see a parking area with a small sign for the trailhead.

COUNTY: Washington

TOWNSHIP: Greenwich

PLACE: Greenwich

WATERWAY: Batten Kill

TYPE: ribbon cascade

HEIGHT: 55 ft (16.8 m)

TRAIL: dirt; easy

WALKING TIME: 15 min

PEAK ACTIVITY: May-Aug.

LATITUDE: 43.1036

LONGITUDE: –73.5372

Located on a side road off NY 29 just outside Greenwich, downstream from Middle Falls, Dionondahowa Falls is an incredible sight. Alongside the crest of this 55-foot (16.8 m) waterfall is an old, dilapidated dam. Remnants of the factories and mills that were once powered by the water captured by this early dam and others like it are also visible near the top of the falls, although that area is closed to the public. Once nicknamed Devil's Caldron, the plunge pool at the waterfall's base has since been dubbed Hell's Hole by local residents.

From the trailhead in the parking area, follow the trail until it forks. The path to the right is the lower-trail system; the path to the left, the upper. Both offer great vantage points. From a small observation area on the lower-trail system, you can see a portion of the waterfall and the mills, along with a section of the gorge downstream. The two trails eventually meet up again.

There are two main viewing platforms on the trail system. The first is not far from where the lower- and upper-trail systems reconnect. From here, you can enjoy a lovely view of the upper half of the falls, as well as glimpses of the old mill structures across the river. The second platform is at the very end of the trail system, and here, you can see the entire waterfall and the dam.

If you're looking for more to do after visiting Dionondahowa Falls, plan your visit for the last week of August, when the Washington County Fair is held right next to Windy Hill Road. The ice-cream shop near the corner of NY 29 and Windy Hill Road is always a crowd-pleaser.

The land that encompasses the Dionondahowa Falls viewing area and Dionondahowa Park is owned by Dahowa Hydro, but the area is open to the public from dusk until dawn. The park does not have garbage receptacles, so please remember to carry out everything you bring in.

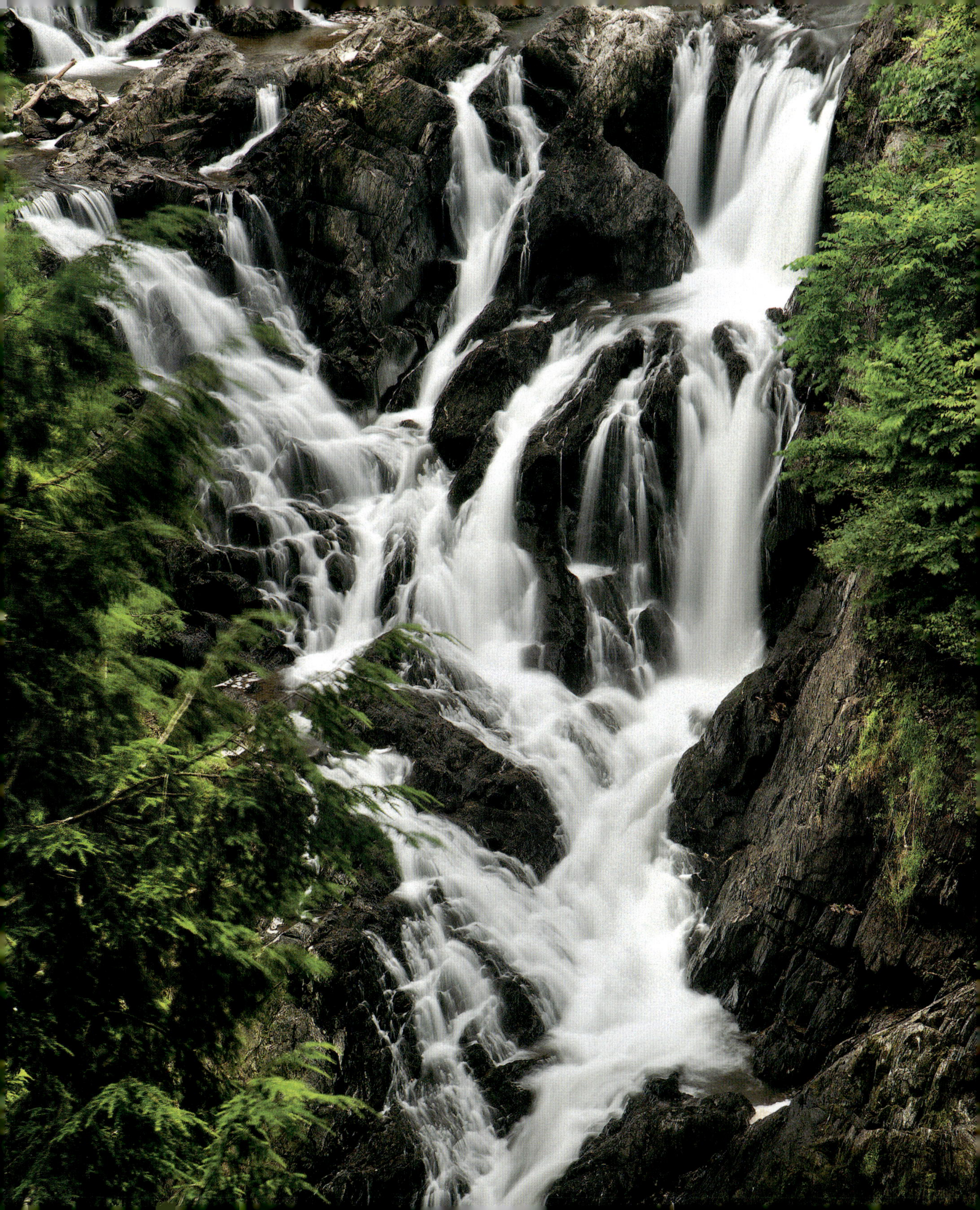

CAPITAL REGION

Buttermilk Falls (Lower)

From Albany, take I-787 north to Ontario St. in Cohoes, and turn right. Continue for 0.9 mi (1.4 km), then turn left onto 2nd Ave. After 1.1 mi (1.8 km), turn right onto 125th St. (CR 142). Proceed for 0.2 mi (0.3 km), taking a slight left and going uphill for another 0.9 mi (1.4 km). Turn left onto NY 40 (Leversee Rd.), and in 6.3 mi (10.1 km), turn left onto Bracken Rd. Follow Bracken Rd. for 0.7 mi (1.1 km), crossing the intersection onto Buttermilk Falls Rd. After about 0.8 mi (1.3 km), park on the left side of the road, just before the bridge.

COUNTY: Rensselaer

TOWNSHIP: Schaghticoke

PLACE: Schaghticoke

WATERWAY: Tomhannock Creek

TYPE: classical falls

HEIGHT: 15 ft (4.6 m)

TRAIL: roadside; easy

WALKING TIME: n/a

PEAK ACTIVITY: June-Oct.

LATITUDE: 42.8880

LONGITUDE: –73.6200

Buttermilk Falls in Rensselaer County shares its name with more than 20 other waterfalls in the state, each with its own charm. Just outside the town of Schaghticoke, this particular Buttermilk Falls offers a perfect excuse for a scenic drive along country roads, past fields and farmhouses.

There is no actual parking area at the waterfall, but you will find a place along the road. While it is possible to access Lower Buttermilk Falls from the creek, the area is a little overgrown with trees and bushes, adding to the appeal of an autumn visit. Because the waterfall is a little upstream, the narrow bridge near your parking spot offers the best straight-on vantage point for viewing and photographing.

The waterfall starts as a small cascade and gradually evolves into a full vertical drop that spans the entire creek. Even during low flow, this waterfall is beautiful. Many years ago, a mill at the side of the creek used power generated from the 15-foot (4.6 m) drop on swift-flowing Tomhannock Creek, but not even remnants of that building survive.

The private land around the falls, both upstream and downstream, is heavily posted, so you won't hear much about the other waterfalls in the immediate vicinity. But in the heart of Schaghticoke, there is a set of cascades worth visiting, easily seen from the bridge crossing into town as you travel north on NY 67 and NY 40.

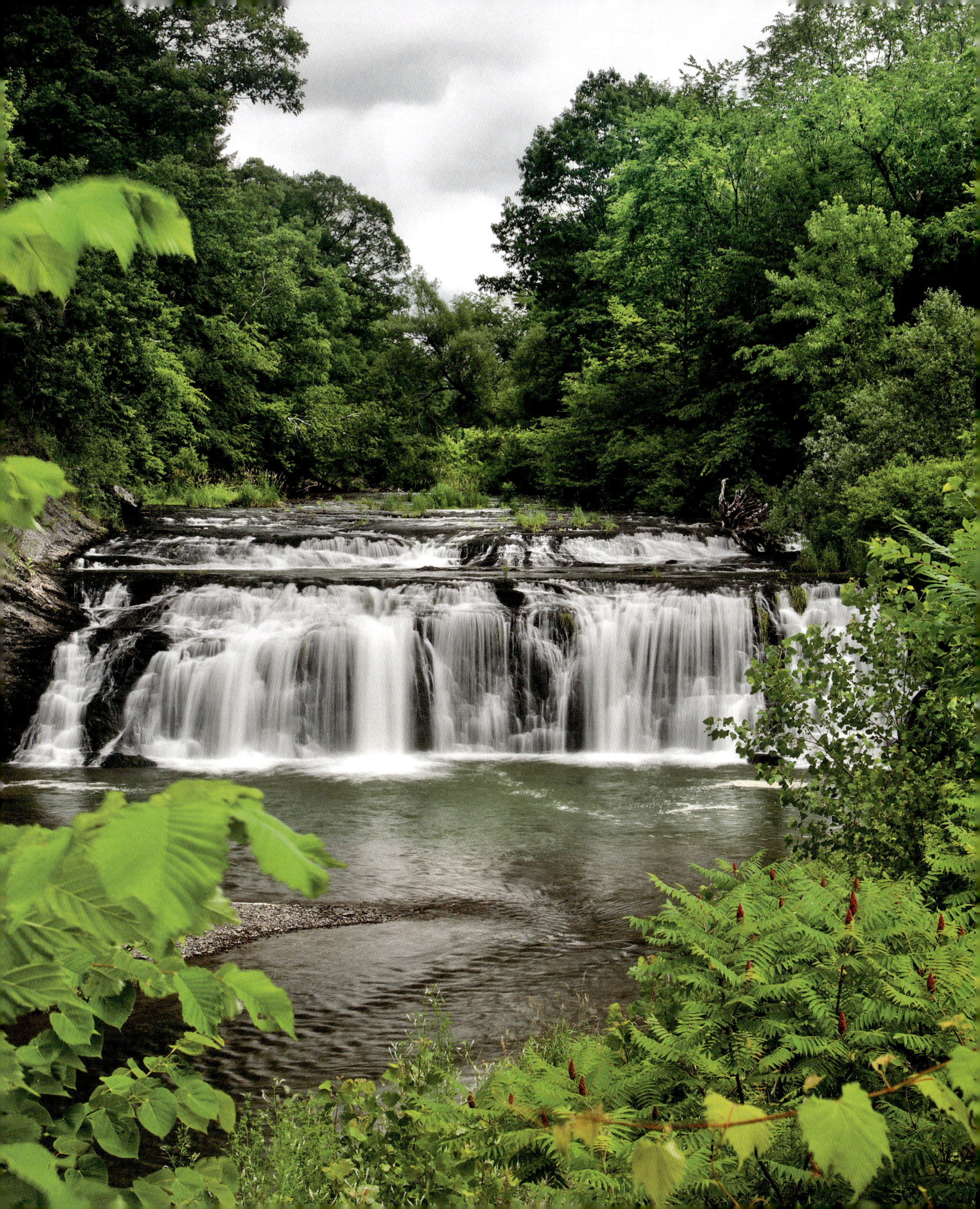

Robert B. Woodruff Outdoor Learning Center

From I-90, take exit 29, and turn right onto NY 5 south (Main St.). Drive for 3.8 mi (6.1 km) through Canajoharie into Fort Plain. At the traffic light just after the bridge, turn left onto NY 80 (Main St.), and drive 11.6 mi (18.7 km). On the left is the entrance to the main parking lot of the Owen D. Young Central School. Follow the lot down and to the left to find the trailhead.

COUNTY: Herkimer

TOWNSHIP: Springfield

PLACE: Van Hornesville

WATERWAY: Otsquago Creek

TYPE: classical falls

HEIGHT: 15 to 20 ft (4.6–6.1 m)

TRAIL: gravel; easy

WALKING TIME: 10-20 min

PEAK ACTIVITY: May-Aug.

LATITUDE: 42.8976

LONGITUDE: –74.8219

Named for a beloved former educator at the Owen D. Young Central School in Van Hornesville, the Robert B. Woodruff Outdoor Learning Center sprawls over more than 50 acres (20 ha) along the Otsquago Creek Gorge. Both the center and the adjacent school are on NY 80, once a route reportedly traveled by George Washington in the American Revolutionary War and now the link between Fort Plain and Cooperstown. Settled by the Van Horne family in the 18th century, the valley was the site of mills and factories that exploited the power of the creek to produce flour, cheese, cigar boxes, whiskey and furniture.

Nature lovers are welcome year-round to explore this beautiful natural habitat, which boasts a variety of plants and trees, rock formations and a series of waterfalls. As it rushes downhill, the Otsquago Creek cuts a path through shale cliffs on one side and limestone formations on the other. At the end of the center's main trail is a small but intriguing cave system.

In 1984, area residents began to clear paths and build bridges and amenities in the area, all in an effort to make the challenging terrain around the creek more navigable. From the center's parking area, a footbridge leads to the trailhead, where you can consult a large map of the area's extensive trail system. Signs are posted throughout, indicating landmarks and named waterfalls.

One of the more picturesque waterfalls in the area is Cheesebox Factory Falls, a pretty multitiered waterfall situated well away from regular traffic, whose crest is broken by several large boulders. Downstream, there are several other waterfalls, as well as a cave system. Its porous boulders absorb a great deal of moisture during the year, and in winter, ice columns are extruded from the rock face.

Upstream is a major waterfall, with the remains of an old mill implement near its base. Beyond the bounds of the learning center, another set of falls can be seen behind the town's feed mill. However, this waterfall is on posted land, and permission is required to gain access.

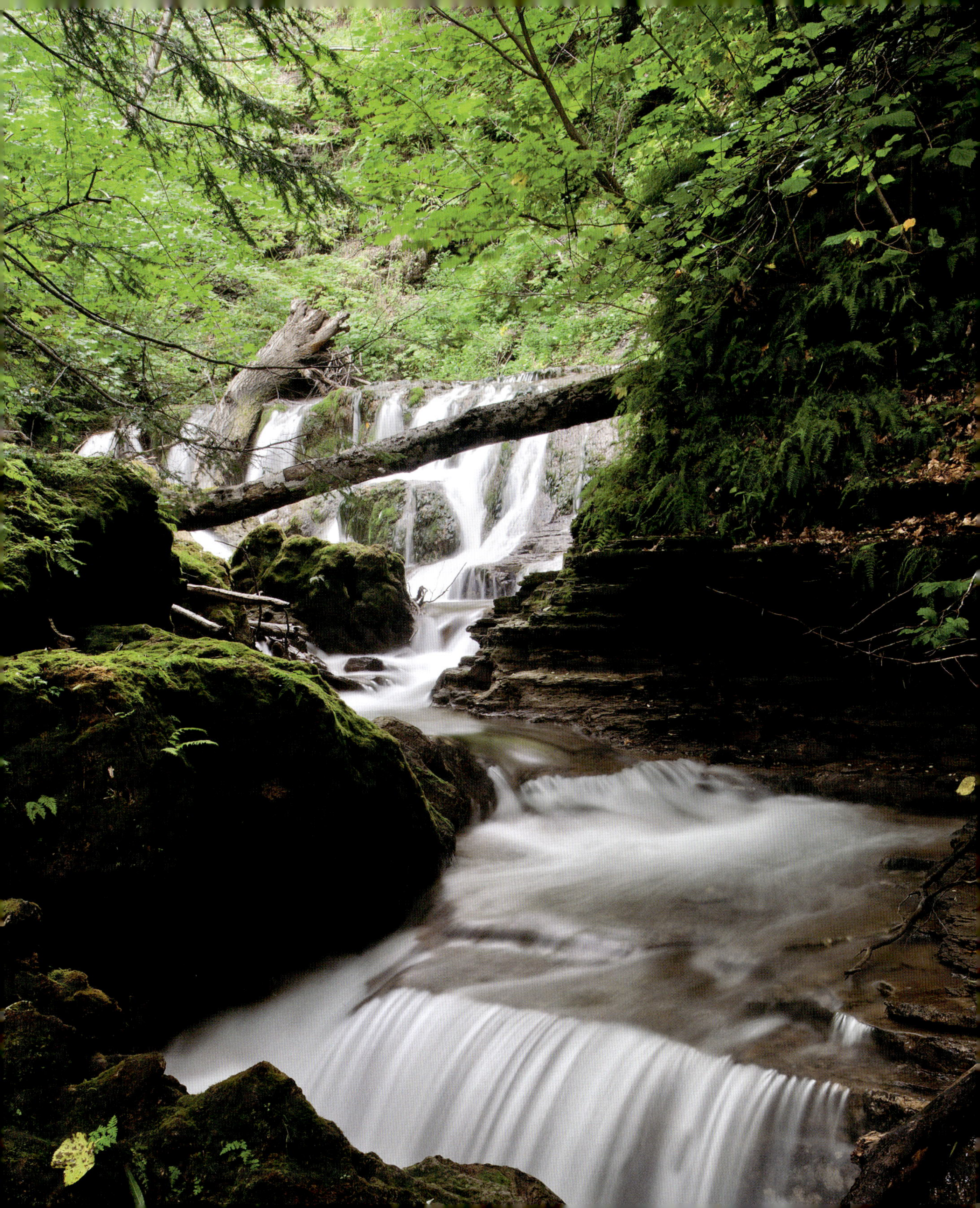

CAPITAL REGION

Canajoharie Falls

From I-90, take exit 29, and turn right onto NY 5 south (Main St.). Drive for 0.2 mi (0.3 km), and turn left onto Mitchell St. At the stop sign, turn left onto Montgomery St. After 0.2 mi (0.3 km), turn onto Maple Ave., continuing for 0.5 mi (0.8 km). At the stop sign, Maple Ave. becomes Carlisle Rd. Follow Carlisle Rd. for 0.8 mi (1.3 km). As the road veers to the left, drive straight onto Old Sharon Rd. and proceed for 0.2 mi (0.3 km). The entrance to Wintergreen Park is on the right. Park in the upper lot.

COUNTY: Montgomery

TOWNSHIP: Canajoharie

PLACE: Canajoharie

WATERWAY: Canajoharie Creek

TYPE: ribbon falls

HEIGHT: 45 ft (13.7 m)

TRAIL: gravel; easy

WALKING TIME: 15 min

PEAK ACTIVITY: April-Sept.

LATITUDE: 42.8927

LONGITUDE: –74.5658

Considered a hidden gem, Canajoharie Falls is located in Wintergreen Park, a large park that encompasses the dramatic Canajoharie Gorge.

The gravel trail starts from the parking area, and during the walk in, you'll hear the sounds of rustling leaves and rushing water as you pass a number of lovely smaller waterfalls. Keep walking until you see a large wooden platform that overlooks the crest of Canajoharie Falls. This overlook is the waterfall's only vantage point — the lower section of the falls is on private property, with strictly enforced access. Still, the views from here are impressive, and the walk in is a real pleasure. There are picnic and day-use areas in the park, but they are not open year-round.

Canajoharie Creek runs through the gorge all the way to Canajoharie Falls, where the walls of the gorge soar nearly 100 feet (30.5 m) above the water. Then the walls gradually decrease in height until the creek reaches the Mohawk River, just past the old Beech-Nut factory.

From the lower portion of the park, you can wade so far into the creek that you are almost looking over the edge of the main falls, but the slippery creek bottom is treacherous, so be extremely cautious.

If you venture farther downstream, into the village of Canajoharie, you'll find two access points to the creek where you can see the other waterfalls in the lower portion of the Canajoharie Gorge. You can also swim in the Canajoharie Boiling Pot, a naturally occurring pothole that gets its name from the translation of the Iroquois word *canajoharie*, meaning "the pot that washes itself."

Walk upstream from this area, and you'll encounter a damlike structure posted with signs that caution against proceeding any farther upstream. No longer in service, this structure functions as a barrier between safe and unsafe portions of the gorge.

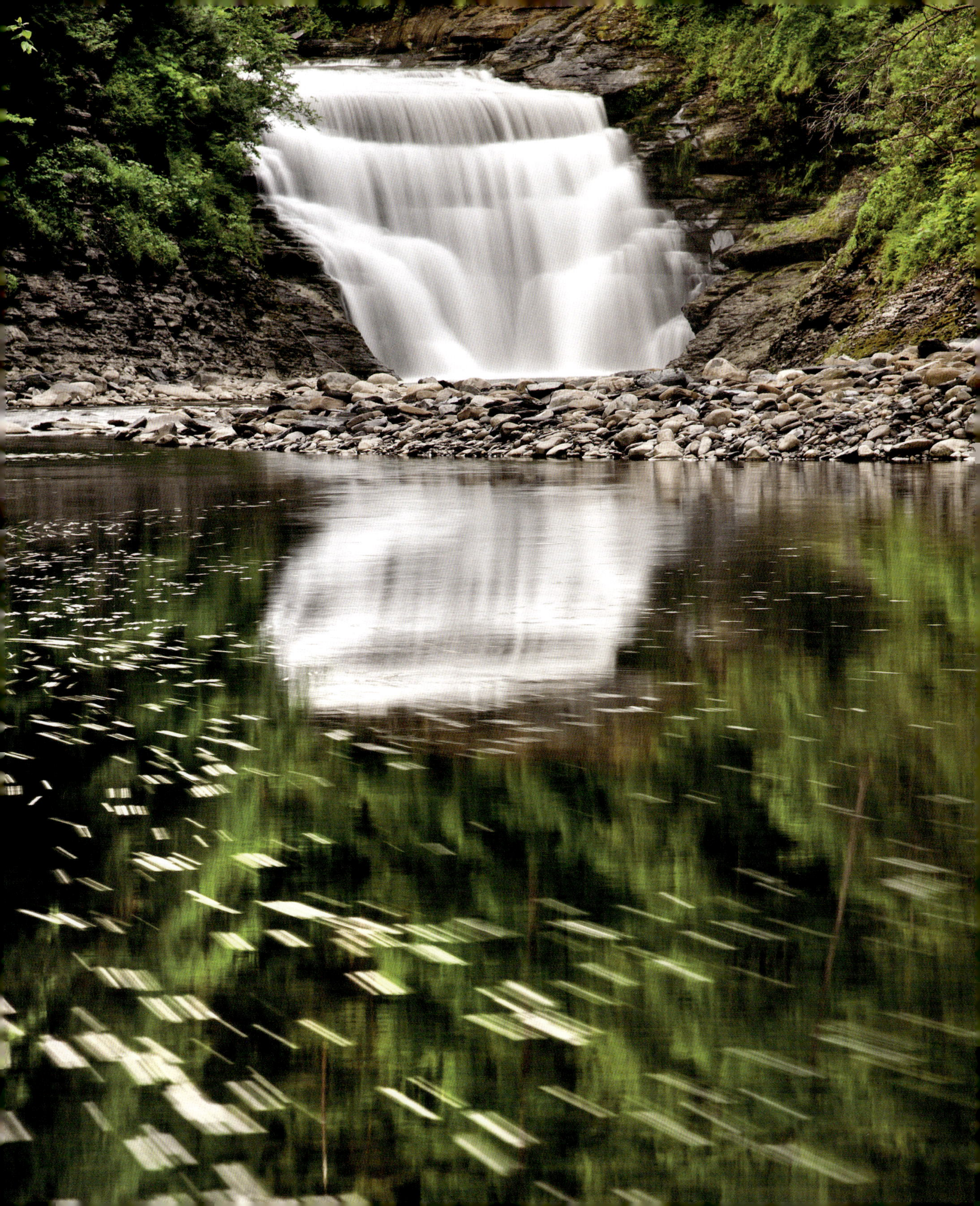

Yatesville Falls

From I-90, take exit 29, and turn left onto NY 5 south. Drive for 2.5 mi (4 km), and merge right onto NY 162, traveling uphill. After 4.8 mi (7.7 km), turn left onto Rankan Grove Rd. (Rural Grove Rd.). After 0.3 mi (0.5 km), turn left again onto Logtown Rd. Proceed for 1.8 mi (2.9 km), and turn left onto Anderson Rd. After 0.8 mi (1.3 km), the entrance to Yatesville Falls State Forest is on the left. Follow the main dirt road to the end.

COUNTY: Montgomery	
TOWNSHIP: Root	
PLACE: Rural Grove	
WATERWAY: Yatesville Creek	
TYPE: classical falls	
HEIGHT: 45 ft (13.7 m)	
TRAIL: dirt; easy to difficult	
WALKING TIME: 1-2 min	
PEAK ACTIVITY: May-Nov.	
LATITUDE: 42.8680	
LONGITUDE: –74.4503	

Yatesville Falls State Forest, one of two forests totaling more than 2,000 acres (809 ha) that were purchased by New York State in the 1930s, is managed by the Department of Environmental Conservation to promote timber production, provide recreational opportunities and protect wildlife habitat. It is also home to Yatesville Falls, a major attraction and a must-see for visitors to the area.

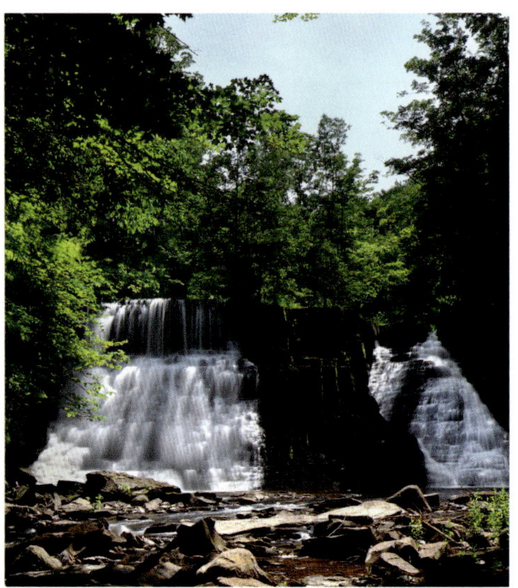

The small one-lane dirt road that leads to the waterfall can be rough at points, but it is generally well maintained and easily traveled. A seasonal road, it may be inaccessible by vehicles during the winter. The parking area is located near the crest of the waterfall, so it takes just a minute to walk to a great vantage point. To see the bottom of the falls, however, you'll have to take one of several worn paths to the creek below. It's a steep scramble and not recommended in wet weather.

Also known as Buttermilk Falls and Vrooman's Falls, this is not the only waterfall on Yatesville Creek. As you venture farther downstream from the main falls, you'll find several small waterfalls that are not listed in other references. The area is largely untouched and has only occasional visitors, which makes this a very appealing hike. Since the falls are safely buffered from traffic — they're over 2.5 miles (4 km) from any of the surrounding main roads — feel free to bring along the family dog.

There are many Amish communities in this part of the state, so on your way to the area, you'll likely encounter horse-drawn wagons and carts and farmers working their land.

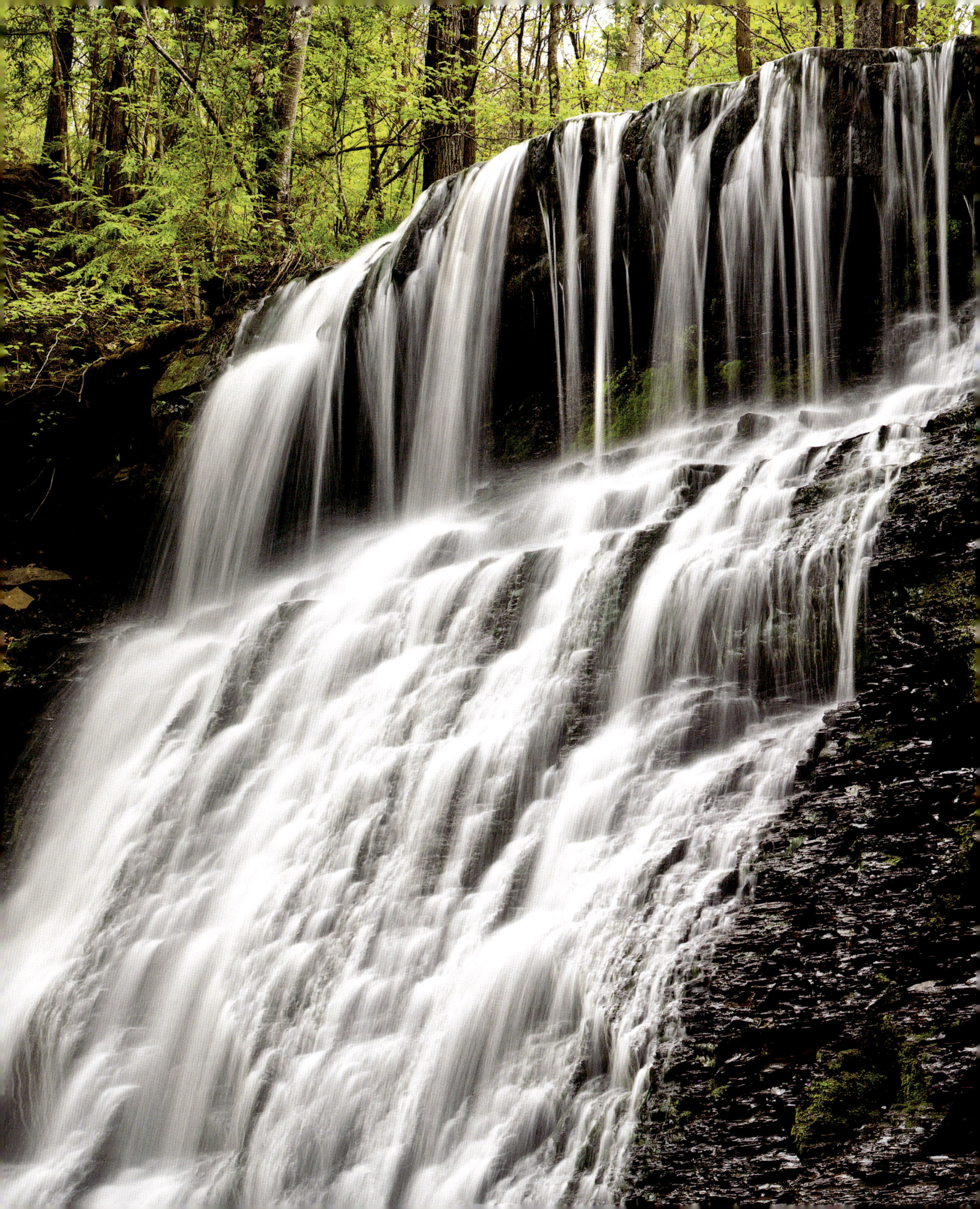

Plotter Kill Nature Preserve

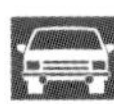

From I-90, take exit 25A and merge onto I-88. Then take exit 25 to NY 7 (Rotterdam/Schenectady). At Becker Rd., turn left at the stop sign, and turn left again onto NY 7 (Duanesburg Rd.). Drive 0.9 mi (1.4 km), and turn left onto NY 337 north (Burdeck St.). Continue for another 0.5 mi (0.8 km), and turn left onto NY 159 (Mariaville Rd.). Proceed for 3.8 mi (6.1 km), until you reach the preserve parking area on the right. You'll see a state sign at the entrance.

COUNTY: Schenectady

TOWNSHIP: Rotterdam

PLACE: Mariaville

WATERWAY: Plotter Kill

TYPE: ribbon falls

HEIGHT:
Upper: 60 ft (18.3 m)
Lower: 40 ft (12.2 m)

TRAIL:
dirt and stone; easy to difficult

WALKING TIME:
10 min to first waterfall

PEAK ACTIVITY: May-Sept.

LATITUDE: 42.8283

LONGITUDE: –74.0506

Named after a community outdoorsman and conservation activist, the Almy D. Coggeshall Plotter Kill Nature Preserve is a rugged 644-acre (261 ha) piece of protected wilderness. As it moves through an ancient gorge carved by ice and characterized by flat ledges, the Plotter Kill, a tributary of the Mohawk River, drops roughly 900 feet (274 m) over 3.5 miles (5.6 km). In addition to the upper and lower set of falls, known as Plotter Kill Falls, and a third waterfall, 40-foot (12.2 m) Rynex Creek Falls (which occurs on a small tributary of the Plotter Kill), there are about a dozen smaller waterfalls, mixed forests and more than 600 species of indigenous plants to enjoy.

If you follow the clearly marked red trail outlined on the map posted at the trailhead, it's possible to visit the three larger waterfalls in under an hour. Keep in mind, however, that parts of the hike involve steep climbing, so you may want to factor in a few breaks.

The top of the 60-foot (18.3 m) upper waterfall is about a five-minute walk down the trail from the parking area. Hiking the steep path to the creekbed at the bottom of the upper falls is a little more challenging, but it has its rewards. Roughly 200 yards (183 m) from the base of the upper falls, you'll see the crest of the 40-foot (12.2 m) lower waterfall. These two look-alike waterfalls are easily mistaken for each other in photographs.

The creek's radical change in elevation has created the preserve's other unnamed waterfalls, cliff faces and several wading pools. You'll find many places to swim, but be mindful of the sharp drops in the creek. Dogs are welcome in the preserve, provided they are leashed at all times.

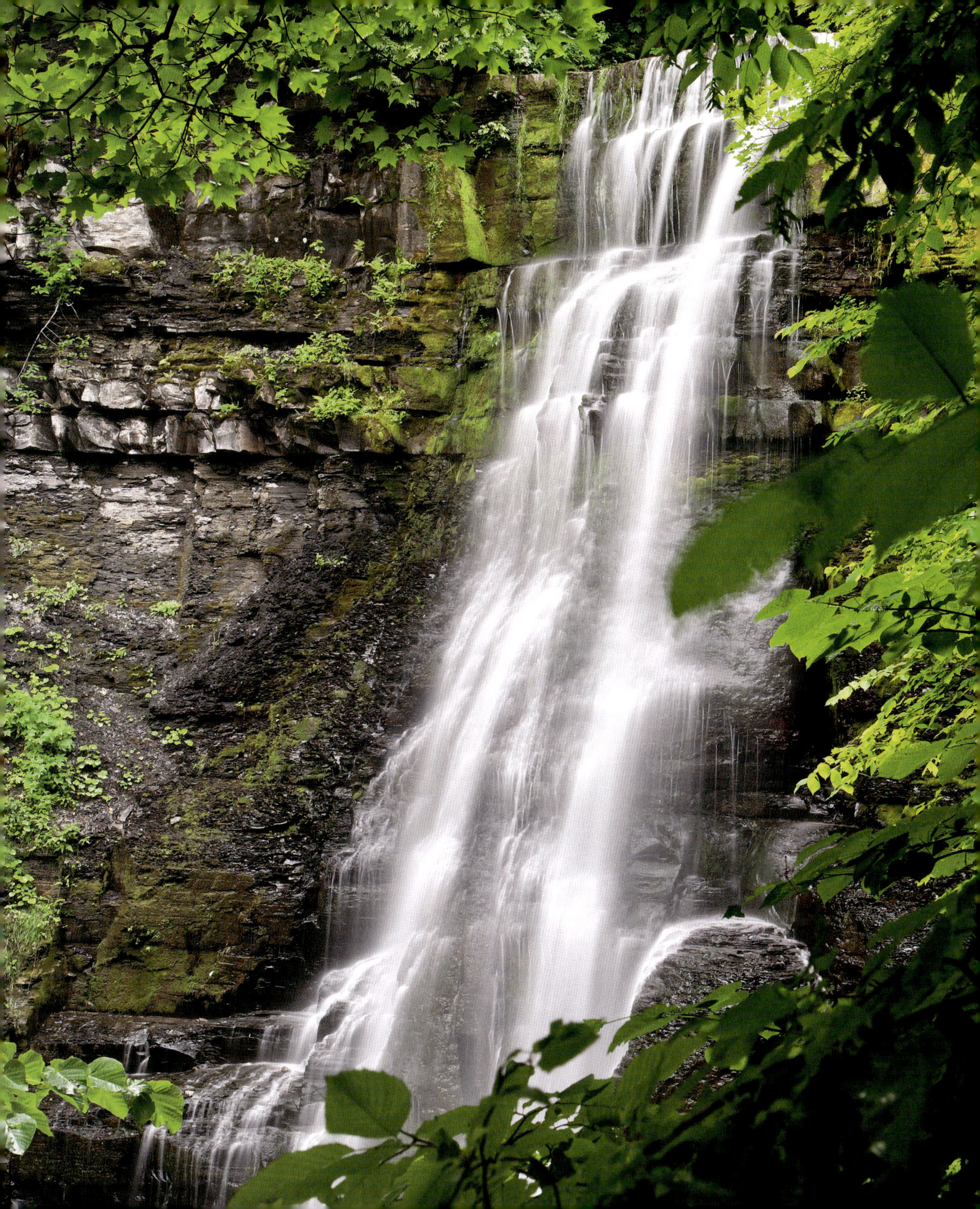

CAPITAL REGION

Christman Sanctuary

From 1-88, take exit 24 and the road toward NY 7. When you reach NY 7 (Schenectady Duanesburg Rd.), turn left and continue for 1.8 mi (2.9 km). Turn left onto CR 125 (Weaver Rd.). After 1 mi (1.6 km), turn left onto CR 74 (Schoharie Turnpike/CR 20). Continue for about 0.7 mi (1.1 km), until you see a small parking area on the right. This marks the trailhead.

COUNTY: Albany

TOWNSHIP: Delanson

PLACE: Duanesburg

WATERWAY: Bozen Kill

TYPE: classical falls

HEIGHT: 20 ft (6.1 m)

TRAIL: dirt and gravel; easy to moderate

WALKING TIME: 15 min

PEAK ACTIVITY: June-Sept.

LATITUDE: 42.7393

LONGITUDE: –74.1284

Bozen Kill Falls is located in the Christman Sanctuary, originally a 97-acre (39.3 ha) parcel of land that formed part of the homestead of farmer, poet and devoted naturalist William W. Christman. About 20 minutes outside of Albany, the preserve was formally established in 1931 by Christman and his wife. In 1970, it was purchased from their son by the Eastern New York Chapter of The Nature Conservancy.

The trail systems leading from the small parking area are well organized and lovingly maintained by area volunteers. Many of the trails have historical markers that commemorate important individuals or previous landowners. One that was dedicated to Christman and his wife in 1931 by the Mohawk Valley Hiking Club reads: "I give, bequeath, devote, devise, shelter to every bird that flies."

As you hike along the creekside trail, you'll see a handful of lovely unnamed waterfalls and cascades. Bozen Kill Falls, the preserve's showcase waterfall, is nestled in a basin created by sandstone and shale and surrounded by a curtain of mature mixed forest. As you approach, you'll hear the waterfall before you see it. From a lean-to, you can clearly view the falls. A small nearby fire pit suggests that some hikers have ignored the sanctuary-wide prohibition of fires. Don't be one of them. Remember, too, that domestic animals are not welcome here.

A classical waterfall, Bozen Kill Falls plunges straight down and is not much higher than it is wide. The pool at its base is shallow but deep enough to wade in. During rainy weather, the stream feeding the falls rises dramatically, so take care when you are beside the waterway.

While the sanctuary is open from dawn to dusk every day of the year, the falls are at their best during the wet seasons. From late autumn to late spring is the optimum time to view the falls at medium to high flow. During the hot summer months, the stream tends to dry up. Thanks to an elaborate trail system through this beautiful preserve, however, there are always other sights to see.

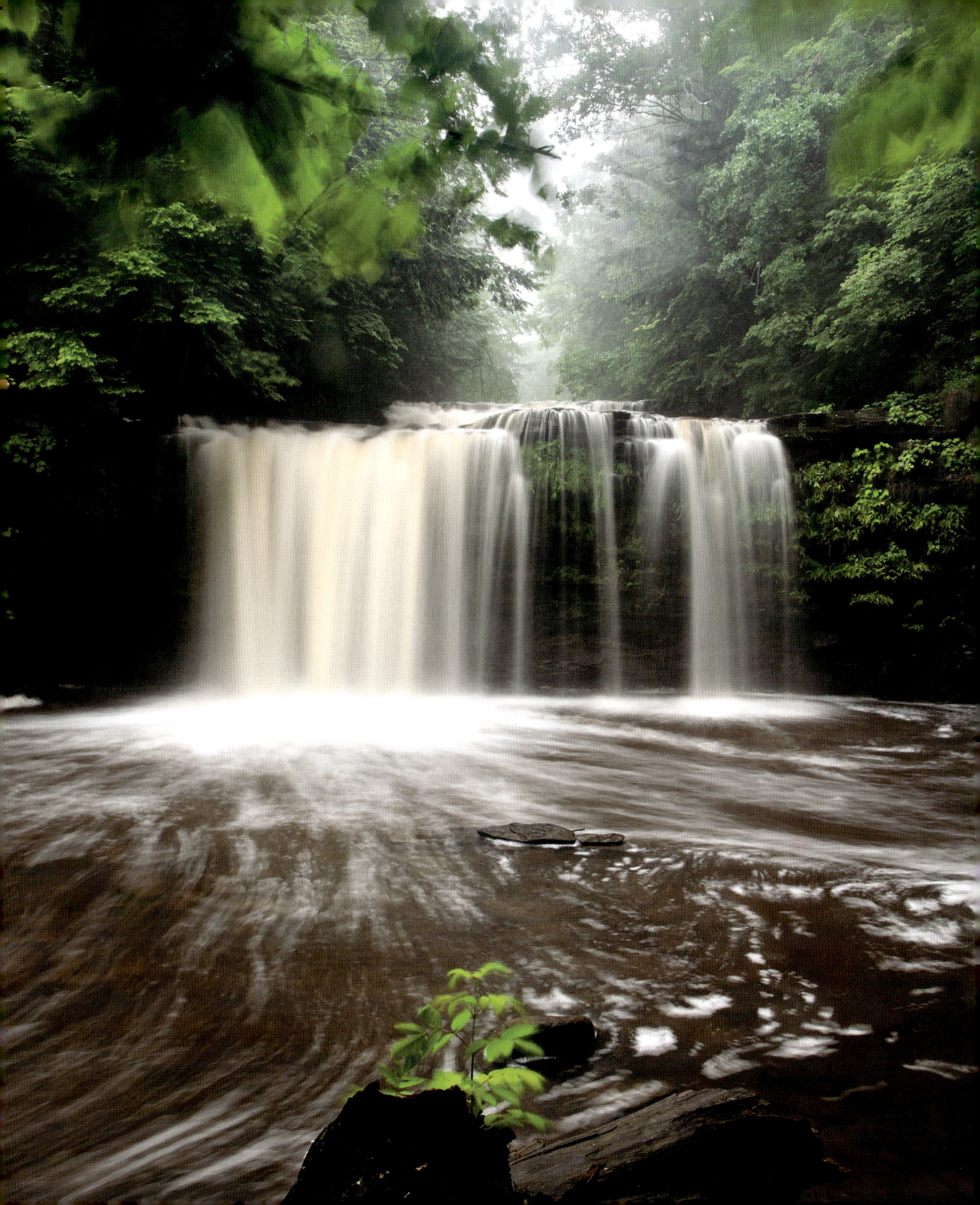

CAPITAL REGION

Cohoes Falls

Traveling north on I-787 from Albany, follow the highway to its end, at the intersection of NY 32 and North Mohawk St. Drive straight across onto North Mohawk, and follow it to the parking area for the Cohoes Falls Overlook Park on the left, at 0.8 mi (1.3 km). The park is directly across the street from the parking area.

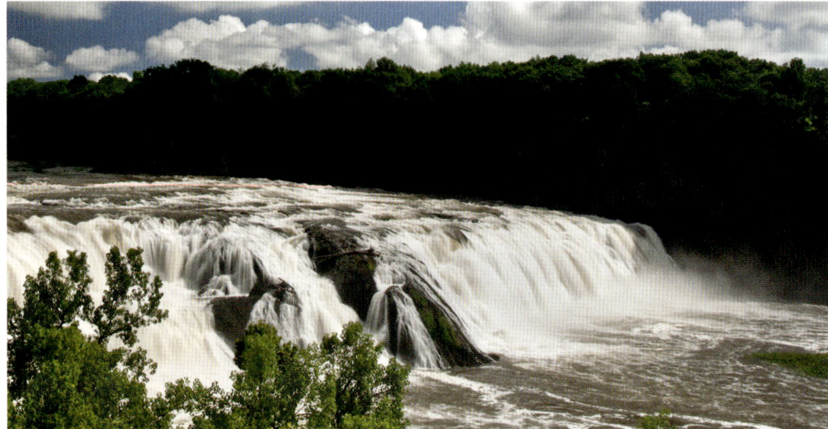

Cohoes Falls is just upstream from the point where the Mohawk and Hudson rivers converge and wrap around Peebles Island State Park. At 65 feet (19.8 m) high and over 600 feet (183 m) wide, this massive waterfall once competed with Niagara Falls for bragging rights as the greatest natural attraction in New York State. It's easy to see why.

Thanks to a small park system updated to include lower catwalk and trail systems, you can gain access at the top of the falls as well as the bottom. During the summer and the warm fall months, Falls View Park is open right to the river's edge, but the lower catwalk is closed in inclement weather due to the rise in water levels that even a short rain shower can cause.

During the spring thaw, this dynamic waterfall often appears as one large, turbulent rapid. In the summer months, nearly all the river's water is diverted to the hydroelectric plant located 200 yards (183 m) from the base of the falls. At those times, hundreds of long, skinny streams of water trickle over the edge of the falls across its entire width.

Cohoes Falls can be seen from the roadside and from a park located downstream from the hydroelectric plant. You can also enjoy more panoramic views much farther downstream, though they are partially obscured by a railroad bridge.

COUNTY: Albany
TOWNSHIP: Cohoes
PLACE: Cohoes
WATERWAY: Mohawk River
TYPE: curtain falls
HEIGHT: 65 ft (19.8 m)
TRAIL: grass and dirt; easy
WALKING TIME: under 5 min
PEAK ACTIVITY: April-Nov.
LATITUDE: 42.7874
LONGITUDE: –73.7091

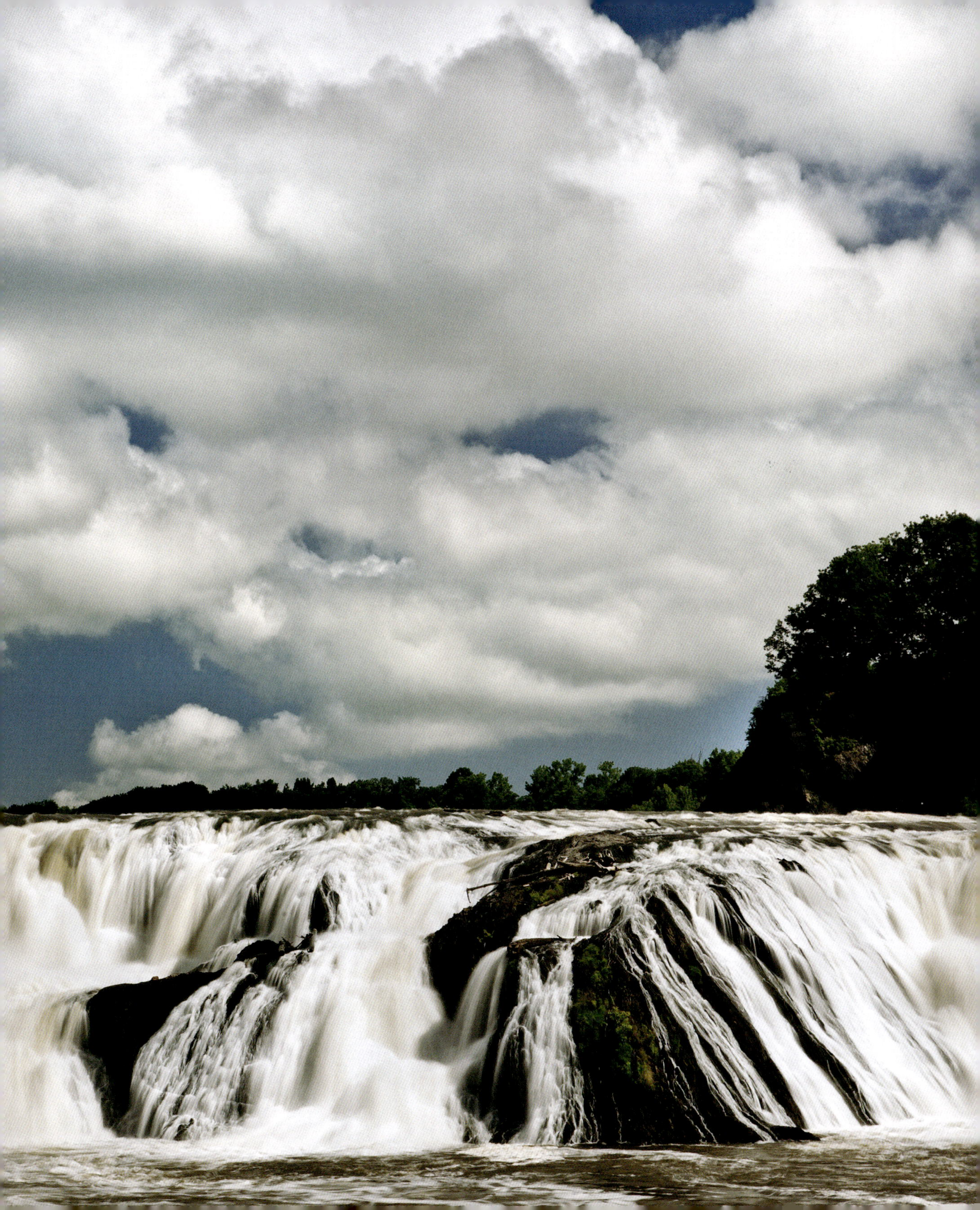

Mount Ida Falls

From Albany on I-787 north, take exit 7E and merge onto NY 378 east toward South Troy. After 1.1 mi (1.8 km), proceed straight onto Burden Ave. Continue for 0.3 mi (0.5 km), then take a slight right onto 4th St., and proceed for 0.9 mi (1.4 km). Turn right onto Canal Ave., and after 0.4 mi (0.6 km), turn onto Spring Ave. Take the first left onto Linden Ave. Parking for the waterfall is 0.2 mi (0.3 km) uphill on the left.

COUNTY: Rensselaer

TOWNSHIP: Brunswick

PLACE: Troy

WATERWAY: Poesten Kill

TYPE: ribbon cascade

HEIGHT: 175 ft (53 m)

TRAIL: grass and dirt; easy

WALKING TIME: under 5 min

PEAK ACTIVITY: April-Nov.

LATITUDE: 42.7213

LONGITUDE: –73.6781

Mount Ida Falls is a multitiered waterfall on Poesten Kill, which runs through the city of Troy, once the second largest producer of iron in the United States. Several hundred yards downstream from the base of the waterfall, the creek terminates at the Hudson River, just north of Albany.

From the parking area, you'll have no problem viewing the bottom portion of this waterfall, also known as Wire Mill Falls and Poesten Kill High Falls. The upper portion is largely obstructed by private properties and the angle at which the waterfall is situated inside the small gorge of crumbling black shale. Since industry stopped using the water to power the mills that lined the creek decades ago, the falls are largely undeveloped. But there are still remnants of the old channels and tubes that once directed the water to these mills. With a keen eye, you'll spot one of these toward the bottom area of the lower falls.

To reach the bottom tier of the falls, you have to walk down a steep path that leads to a grassy field and a smaller path. This second path takes you to an old burned-out platform; only charred posts and beams remain. Make your way carefully past this area to get to the streambed, where you can see the medium-sized pool at the bottom of the lower falls.

There are no signs posted to prohibit swimming or wading, but authorities are regularly called in to rescue students from the neighboring Rensselaer Polytechnic Institute who, while attempting to climb the gorge walls, become stranded on the cliffs. The area doesn't seem all that formidable at first glance, but as you walk a bit closer, the dangers of the sharp rocks become apparent.

Downstream from the main waterfall, smaller cascades offer further examples of the old factory water tubes drilled into the creek's bedrock. Some are large enough for an adult to walk through, were it not for the years of debris built up in the pipes.

Although a busy city surrounds this waterfall, you'll be surprised at the spacious natural beauty of Mount Ida Falls. Don't miss it if you are in the area.

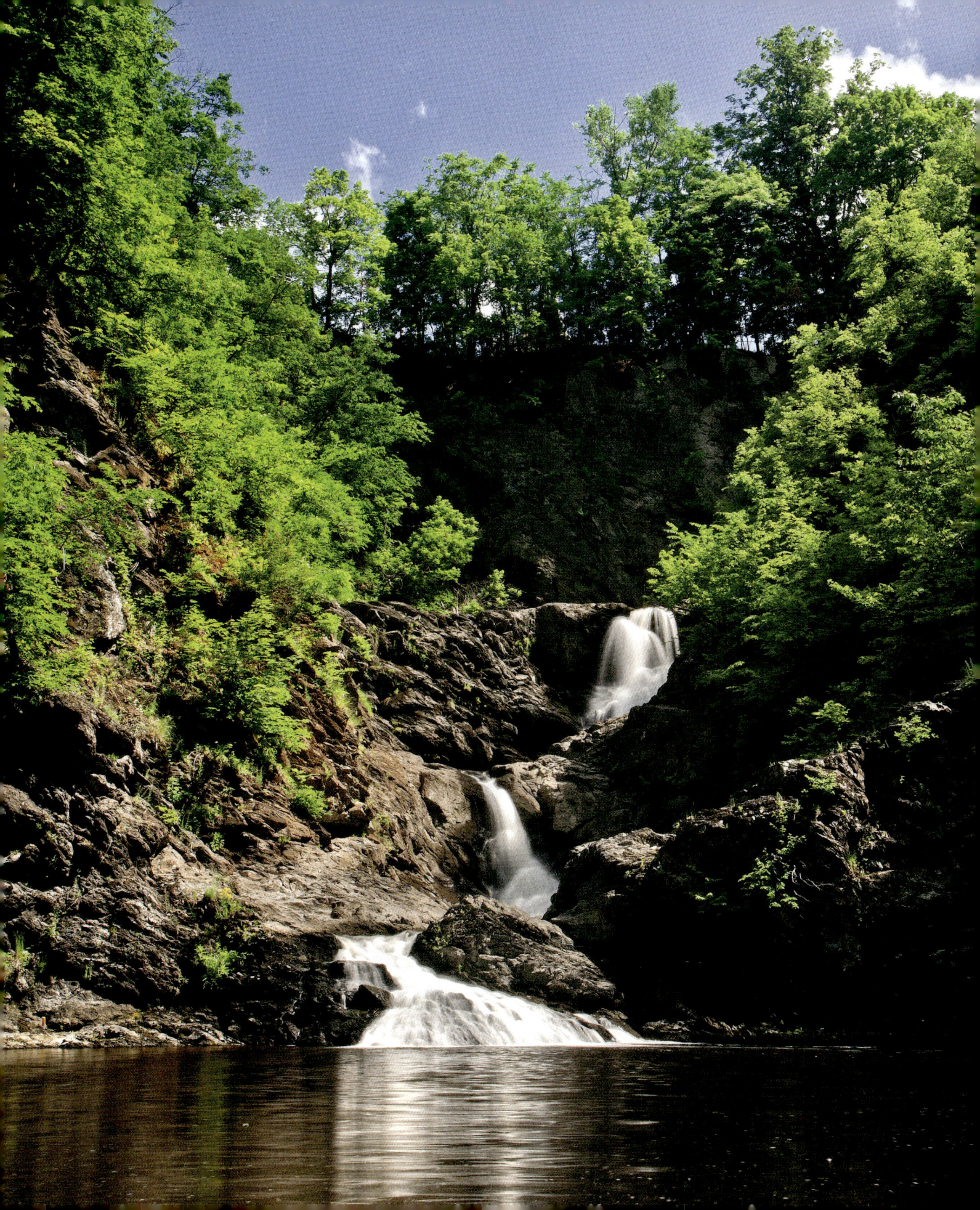

CAPITAL REGION

Barberville Falls

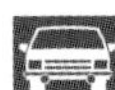

From Albany, take I-90 to exit 7. Follow Washington Ave. east to Defreestville. At the light at NY 4, continue to drive straight. Take NY 43 to West Sand Lake. Roughly 0.7 mi (1.1 km) after the light in West Sand Lake, turn left onto NY 351. Continue straight at the light at the intersection of NY 351 and NY 66 to Poestenkill. At Poestenkill, turn right at the blinking light onto CR 40 (Plank Rd.). Drive for 1.4 mi (2.3 km) to a parking area on the left, across from Broadside Cemetery.

COUNTY: Rensselaer

TOWNSHIP: Poestenkill

PLACE: Poestenkill

WATERWAY: Poesten Kill

TYPE: classical cascade

HEIGHT: 92 ft (28 m)

TRAIL: dirt and rock; easy to moderate

WALKING TIME: 15 min

PEAK ACTIVITY: June-Aug.

LATITUDE: 42.6847

LONGITUDE: –73.5401

By the time Poesten Kill reaches the hamlet of Barberville, it has gathered water drawn from roughly 35 square miles (90.6 sq km) of the Rensselaer Plateau. Descending over a bed of slate and limestone, the stream cascades a spectacular 92 feet (28 m) over a series of sandstone ledges as Barberville Falls.

Located in The Nature Conservancy's Barberville Falls Nature Preserve, the roughly 55-foot-wide (16.8 m) waterfall is well known for its robust flow and beauty. Although it is off the beaten track, Barberville Falls is easy to find. The Falls Trail is about 525 yards (480 m) south of the parking lot. Take the first road on the left. This narrow two-lane country road leads to the trailhead, and the trail leads to the top of the falls. Nearby is the former site of a mill that was once powered by the waterfall's tremendous force.

You'll also find a fairly steep path of dirt, and possibly mud, to the base of the waterfall. Bring appropriate footwear to avoid slipping. As you look up, the waterfall fans out over a vertical drop and looks as wide at the base as it is tall. The fairly deep plunge pool is used by local kids as a swimming hole, despite the sign posted at the parking area that forbids swimming.

Watch out for the broken glass left behind by inconsiderate visitors. One side of the stream running over the falls is bordered by private property, which is heavily posted by the landowners, perhaps in response to the vandalism and litter in the area around this otherwise pristine waterfall. It's an eloquent reminder that we are all responsible for maintaining these idyllic natural spaces.

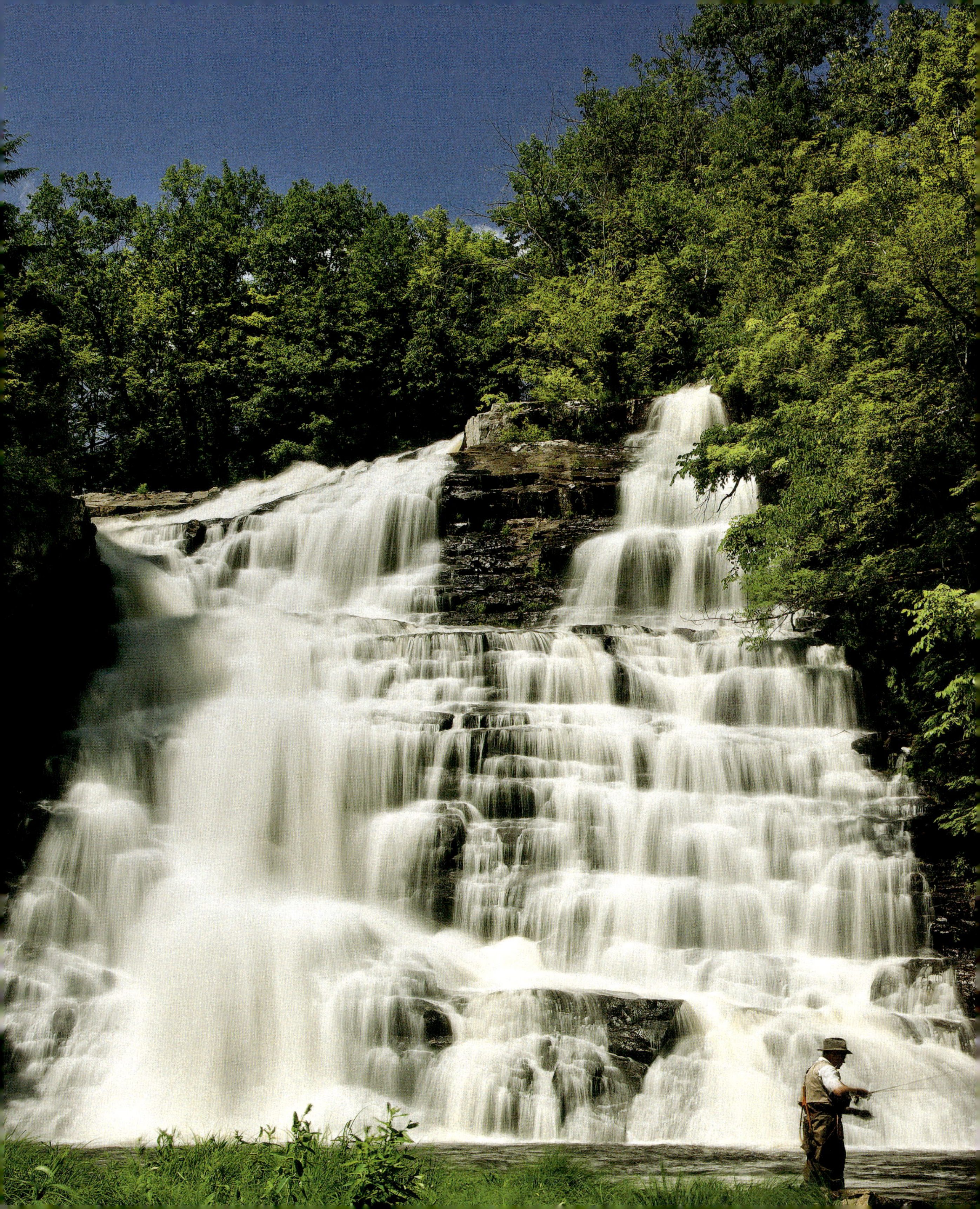

CAPITAL REGION

John Boyd Thacher State Park

From exit 1S off I-87/ I-90, follow the off ramp for 0.5 mi (0.8 km) to US 20. Turn right onto US 20 (Western Ave.), and drive for 2.4 mi (3.9 km) to NY 155 west. Turn left onto NY 155 west (State Farm Rd.). Continue west for 3.9 mi (6.3 km). At the traffic circle, take the first exit for NY 85A west (Maple Rd.), and drive for another 3.8 mi (6.1 km). Turn right onto NY 85 west (New Scotland Ave.), and after 0.9 mi (1.4 km), turn right onto NY 157 west (Thacher Park Rd.). Drive 3.5 mi (5.6 km) to the parking area on the right.

COUNTY: Albany

TOWNSHIP: Voorheesville

PLACE: Voorheesville

WATERWAY: Mine Lot Creek

TYPE: ribbon falls

HEIGHT: 116 ft (35.4 m)

TRAIL: gravel and dirt with metal stairs; difficult

WALKING TIME: under 20 min

PEAK ACTIVITY: May-Oct.

LATITUDE: 42.6527

LONGITUDE: –74.0138

Located on the Helderberg Escarpment, one of the richest fossil-bearing formations in the United States, John Boyd Thacher State Park overlooks the Hudson-Mohawk valleys and the Adirondack and Green mountains. Home to open meadows and woodlands, the park features several waterfalls that range in height from under 15 feet (4.6 m) to more than 100 feet (30.5 m). With its 116-foot (35.4 m) drop, Mine Lot Falls — also known as Big Falls and Indian Ladder Falls — is one of the most dramatic.

From the parking lot, the Indian Ladder Trail leads down to a trail along the base of the towering escarpment via a 60-foot (18.3 m) metal staircase. As you walk along the limestone cliff to the waterfall, be sure to look at the embedded fossils. The trail leads behind the falls, into a sculpted amphitheater created by years of erosion. Through the slender ribbon of falling water, you'll have a misty view of the towns stretched out below. On a blazing summer day, it's always a popular place to take a cooling break.

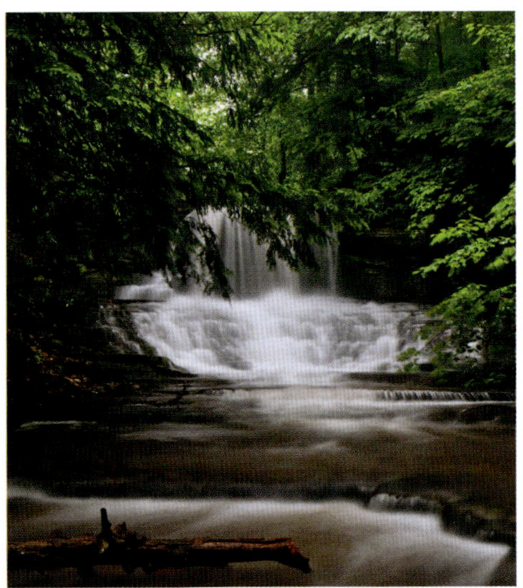

From a trail above, you can stand at the very top of the waterfall. Because there are no ropes or fences at this point and the slate and shale are extremely slippery, this area can be dangerous. Along other stretches of the escarpment, wooden fences follow the length of the cliff-edge trail system. These serve as a good trail marker, and the trails are well kept and well traveled.

Directly upstream from Mine Lot Falls are two waterfalls, each about 15 feet (4.6 m) tall. Several other falls can be accessed easily from the park's extensive trail system.

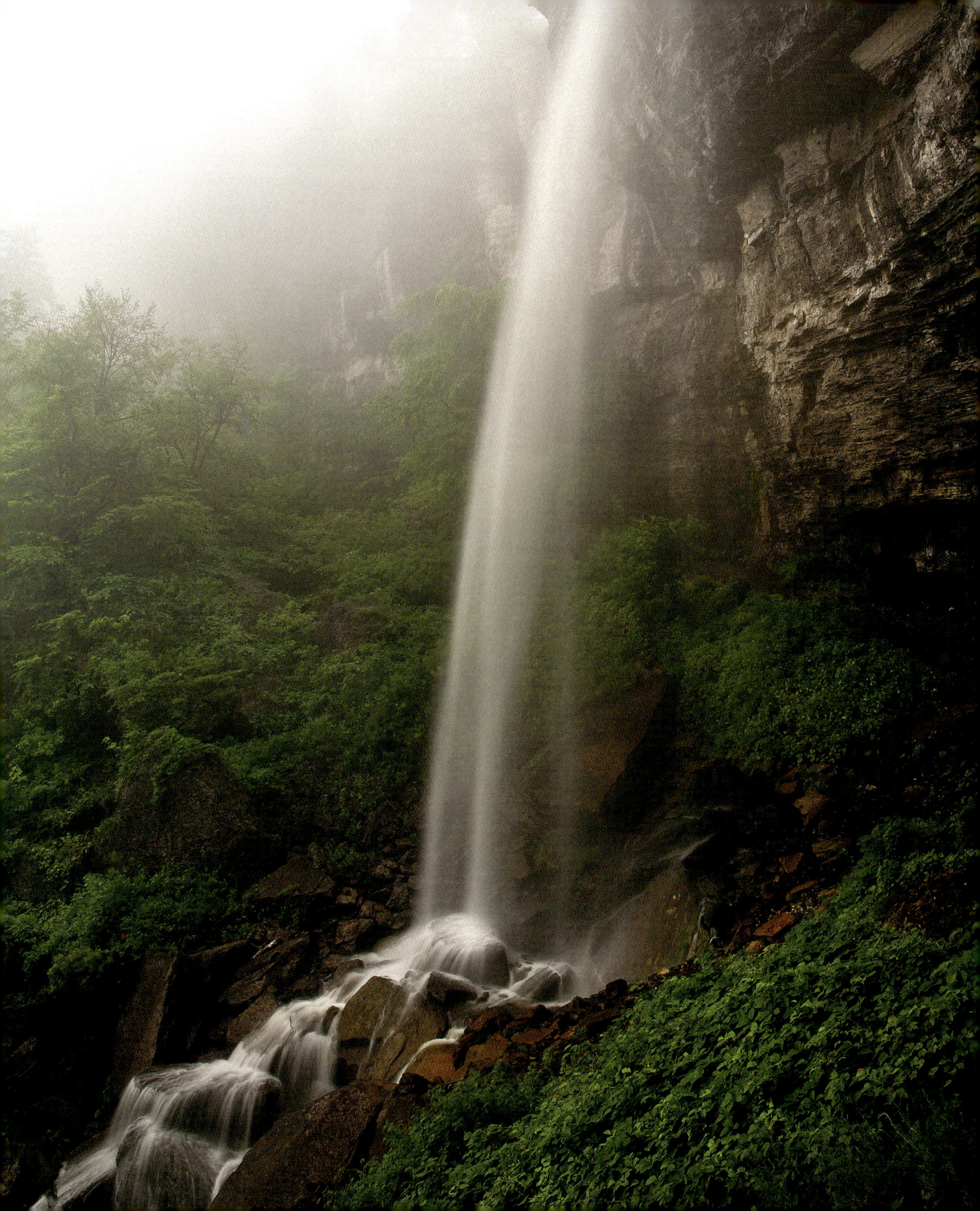

Cascade at Hannacroix Creek Preserve

From I-87, take exit 21B and turn right onto US 9W north toward Ravena. After 3.0 mi (4.8 km), turn right onto NY 144 north, and continue for 3.3 mi (5.3 km). The parking area is on the right.

Originally called Ravena Falls and now also known as Hannacroix Ravine Falls, the Cascade at Hannacroix Creek Preserve is located in a 120-acre (48.6 ha) tract of protected land owned by the Town of New Baltimore and New York's Open Space Institute.

From the parking area to the waterfall is about a 0.7-mile (1.1 km) hike. Consult the trail map posted at the trailhead kiosk. The Irving Trail, an old jeep trail that is partially overgrown in some sections, goes up the hill to the base of the falls. On the left, you'll see a loop trail that leads past some interesting rock formations to a scenic view.

The water in Hannacroix Creek once powered a paper mill, and remnants of the mill buildings can be seen at the side of the trail. Foundations and canals are easily distinguished from the surrounding stone, trees and brush. A small plaque identifies one as the former location of the Croswell-Parsons Paper Mill.

At the waterfall, a large section of the canal system that was used to funnel water from the creek to the mill is visible. From here, you can easily hike to the top of the waterfall, which is relatively wide and offers a great viewing area. Here, there are small wading pools, while at the base, there is a much larger pool suitable for swimming.

At first glance, the creekbed under the waterfall looks like a jumble of giant boulders. When the water is high, these rocks are completely covered. In truly high water, the creek floods over into the old channel system on its southern bank.

COUNTY: Greene and Albany

TOWNSHIP: Coeymans

PLACE: Coeymans

WATERWAY: Hannacroix Creek

TYPE: curtain cascade

HEIGHT: 25 ft (7.6 m)

TRAIL: dirt; moderate

WALKING TIME: 25 min

PEAK ACTIVITY: April-Nov.

LATITUDE: 42.4604

LONGITUDE: –73.8001

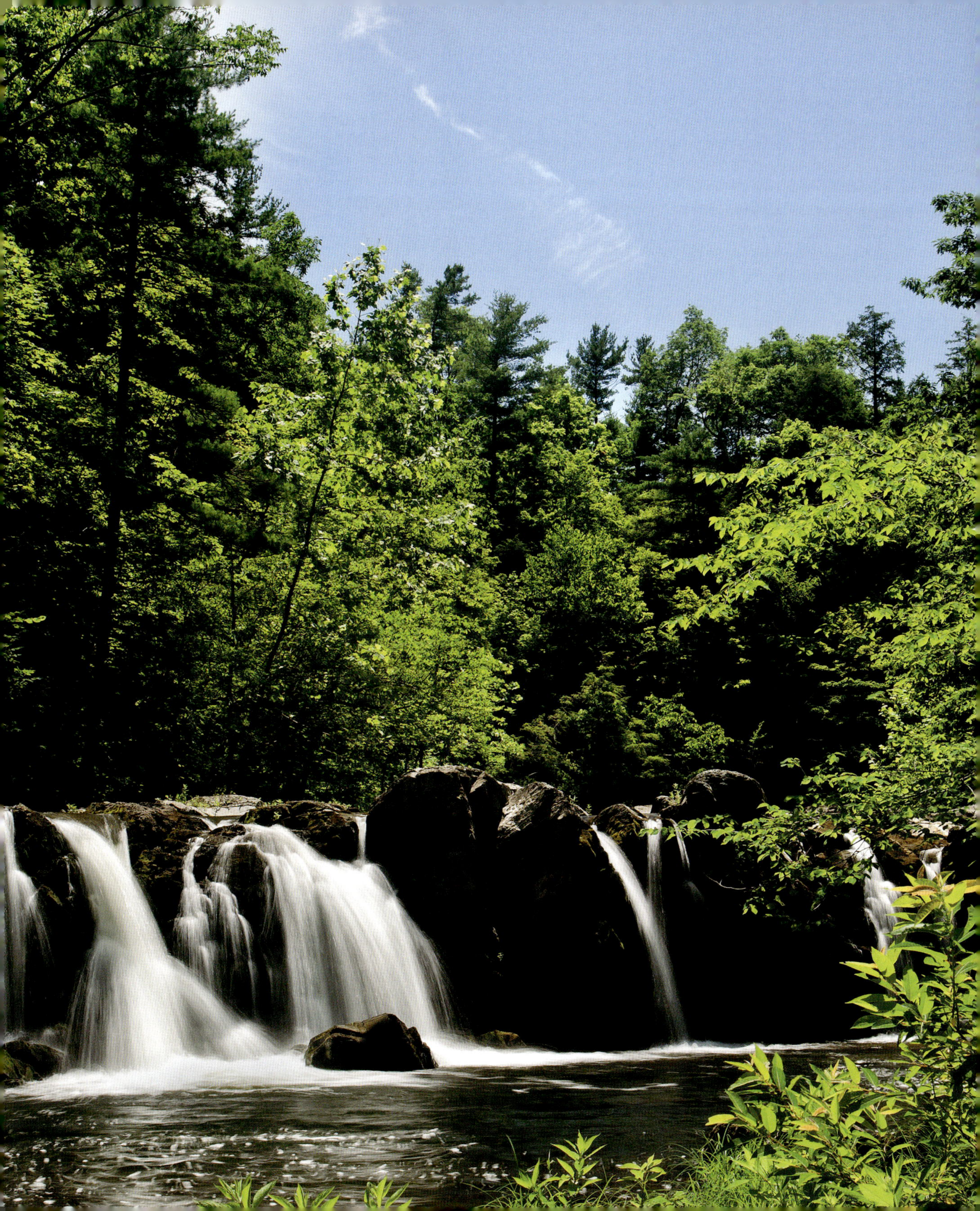

Rensselaerville Falls

From I-88, take exit 23 and turn onto NY 30 south toward Schoharie/Middleburgh. Drive 8.5 mi (13.7 km) to the traffic lights in Middleburgh. Turn left onto NY 145, follow it for 9.5 mi (15.3 km), and turn left onto CR 9A (Hauverville Rd.). After 3.4 mi (5.5 km), continue straight onto CR 353 (Delaware Turnpike/Livingston Ave.). In 4.7 mi (7.6 km), immediately after you cross the bridge, you'll see the entrance to the preserve on your left.

COUNTY: Albany

TOWNSHIP: Rensselaerville

PLACE: Rensselaerville

WATERWAY: Tenmile Creek

TYPE: ribbon cascade

HEIGHT: more than 100 ft (30.5 m)

TRAIL: gravel and dirt; easy to moderate

WALKING TIME: 5 min

PEAK ACTIVITY: year-round

LATITUDE: 42.5148

LONGITUDE: –74.1438

Rensselaerville Falls is an extended cascade on Tenmile Creek, part of the Hudson River watershed. Over roughly half a mile (1 km), the creek drops some 200 feet (60 m) through a deep ravine as it rushes toward the historical town of Rensselaerville.

Tenmile Creek runs through a 2,000-acre (809 ha) tract of land known as the Edmund Niles Huyck Preserve and Biological Research Station. Established in 1931, the preserve protects natural treasures, such as old-growth forest and a diverse collection of flora and fauna. It's also one of the oldest biological research stations in the United States. A short walk from the preserve's parking area, a wooden bridge spans Tenmile Creek and affords views of the lower cascades. On the preserve itself, there are several miles of hiking trails. Some create loops that offer great views of Lake Myosotis and Lincoln Pond; others showcase the remnants of mills that once lined the creek. Plaques and markers describe the area's history.

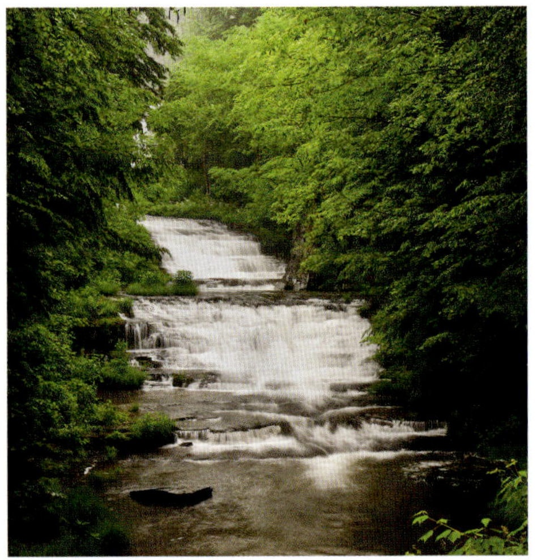

For a different perspective, walk from the waterfall trail up to the middle stretch of the waterfall. If you wish to take advantage of this short trail, however, visit during dry weather. Precipitation and spring runoff profoundly affect creekside trail conditions, making this trail unsafe for foot traffic.

The Huyck Preserve is open year-round, and cross-country skiing and snowshoeing are permitted, as are dogs on leash. All trails are very well maintained, though some are closed during certain times of the year. Steeped in history and adjacent to this unique piece of protected nature, the town of Rensselaerville is a perfect destination for the whole family.

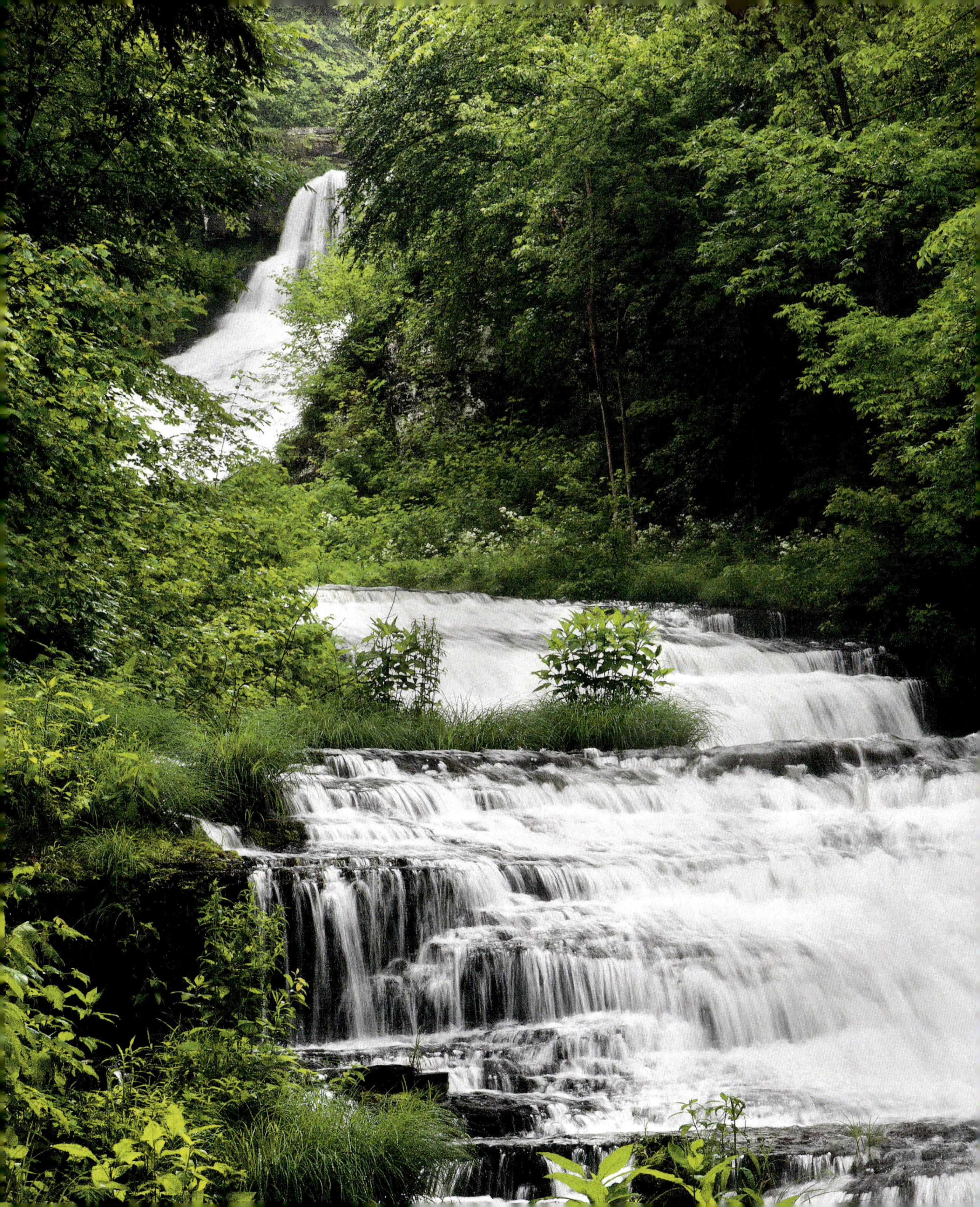

Mine Kill Falls

From I-88, take exit 23 and turn left onto NY 30A south (Zicha Rd.). After 0.9 mi (1.4 km), continue south on NY 30 for 7.6 mi (12.2 km) to the intersection of NY 30 and NY 145. Turn right. Continue on NY 30 for another 16.6 mi (26.7 km), and cross over the bridge. Mine Kill Falls is in Mine Kill State Park, but parking for the falls is just down the road from the main park entrance, on the right.

COUNTY: Schoharie

TOWNSHIP: Gilboa

PLACE: Gilboa

WATERWAY: Mine Kill

TYPE: ribbon falls

HEIGHT:
upper: 20 ft (6.1 m)
middle: 30 ft (9 m)
lower: 20 ft (6.1 m)

TRAIL: gravel and decking; easy to moderate

WALKING TIME:
5 min to upper
15 min to lower

PEAK ACTIVITY: April-Sept.

LATITUDE: 42.4291

LONGITUDE: –74.4721

Mine Kill Falls is found in Mine Kill State Park, which encompasses Schoharie Creek and over 500 acres (202.4 ha) of the area's fields and woodlands. A portion of the waterfall can be seen from the bridge crossing over Mine Kill, but that view doesn't come close to showing the stunning nature of the three separate drops of this waterfall.

With the green, lush foliage of the summer months, this is a beautiful spot to stop during a road trip. The dirt-and-grass path from the trailhead becomes decking from which you can observe the upper and middle falls. The upper portion is located almost directly under the bridge. The waterfall is fairly wide at this point but is quickly narrowed by the cliff walls that enclose the middle waterfall.

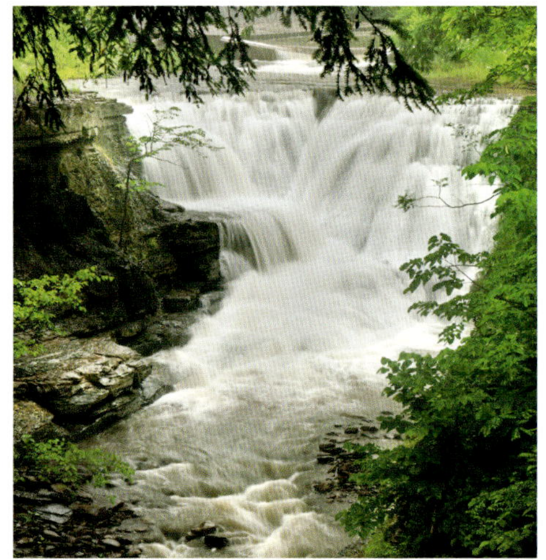

From the lower viewing platform, the middle falls can be seen almost entirely.

As you hike to the top viewing area, there is a path on the right. If you want to make the more difficult hike to the lower waterfall viewing area, return to this path. It leads down a steep roadway that can be muddy in parts. Once you reach the bottom viewing area, the lower falls explodes out of a slender crack in the cliff face and fans out until it hits the pool below. At certain times of the year, this fan effect creates the optical illusion that more water is cascading into the pool than is traveling downstream. To the right of the lower falls, you may notice another waterfall that extends straight down the entire height of the cliff face before hitting the creek below. It is even more impressive when it freezes during the winter. One friend described it as a frozen cathedral-like structure.

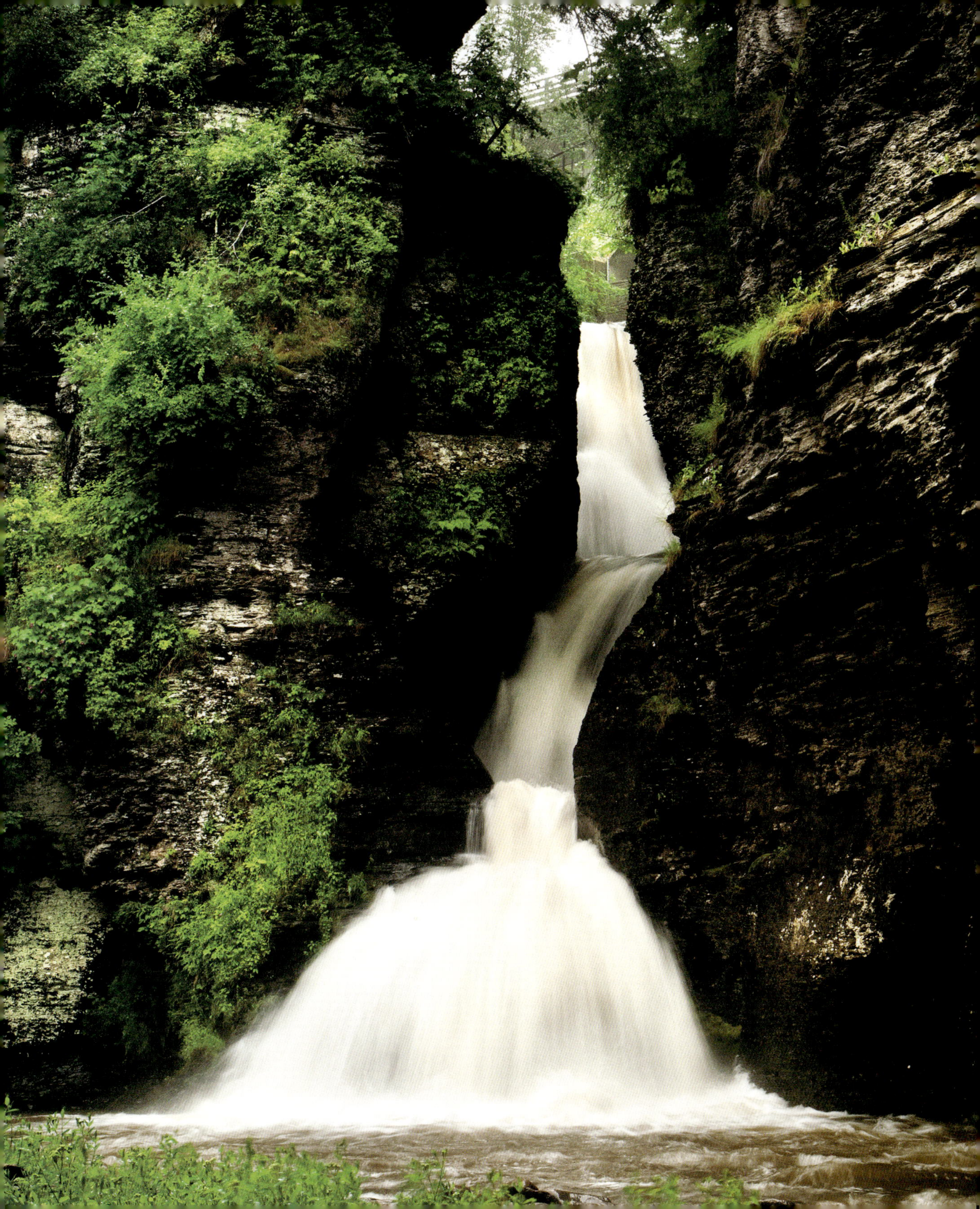

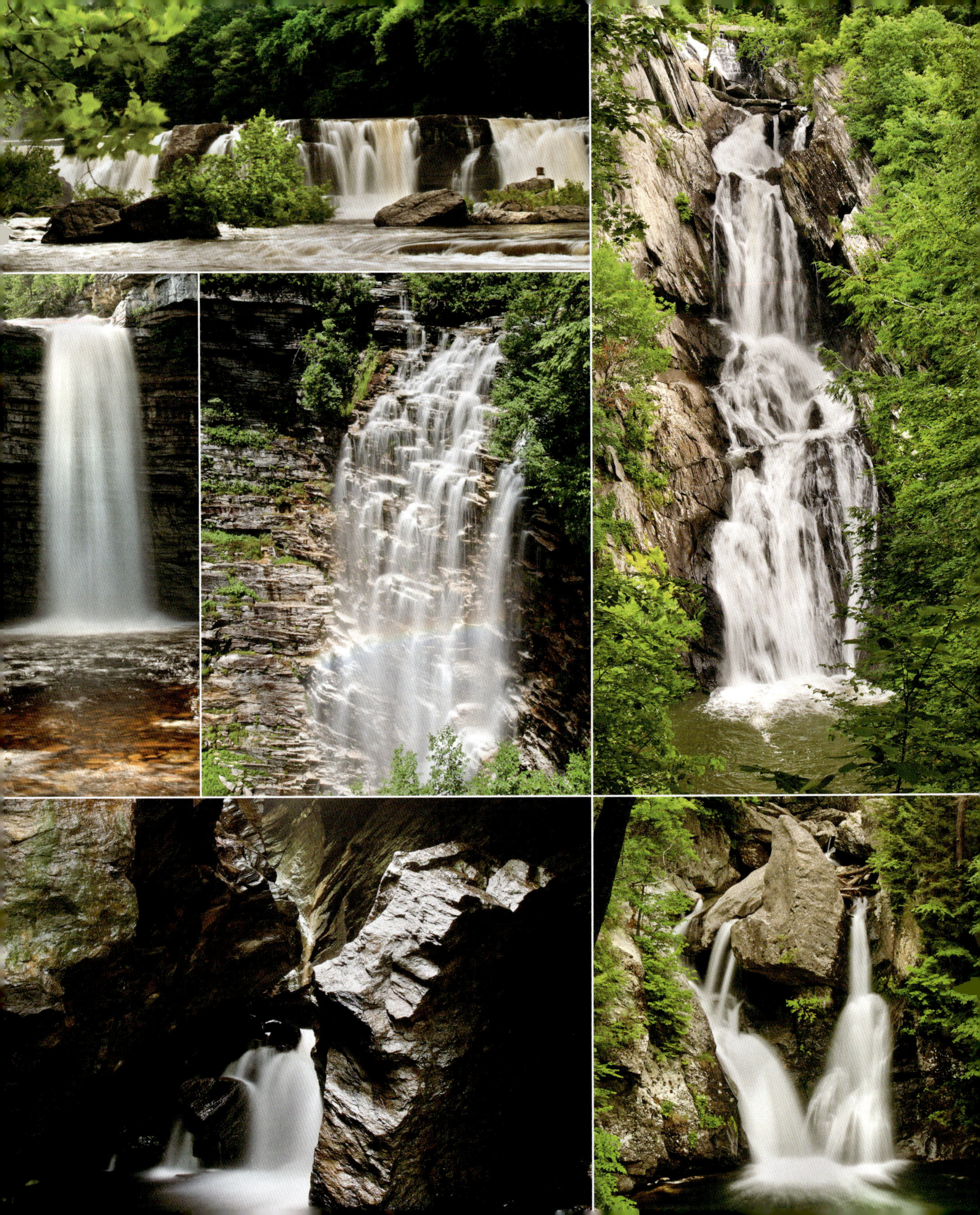

Hudson Valley

The Hudson Valley is well known for its diverse landscapes, from the Hudson River sweeping south to New York City and the Atlantic Ocean to the mountains and escarpments that make this one of the state's most challenging regions for outdoor enthusiasts — and one of the most rewarding. Shawangunk Ridge, designated "one of Earth's last great places" by The Nature Conservancy, is famous for not only its rock climbing but also its biodiversity. The steep valleys and plunging waterways of the storied Catskill Mountains characterize the southeastern part of the state, while on the northeastern border lie the Taconic Range and Taconic State Park, with hundreds of miles of trails, including sections of the Appalachian National Scenic Trail.

Parks, peaks and natural preserves dot the area, as well as an abundance of waterfalls of all types and sizes in all kinds of spectacular settings. It's easy to create an exciting trip itinerary to the Hudson Valley Region in any season, but for waterfall aficionados, the months between spring and fall offer some of the most inspiring views. Even in the warmest months, almost every waterfall described here flows with enough water to make any hike a rewarding experience.

If you plan carefully, you can easily visit several waterfalls in as few as two to three days, or maybe you'd prefer to spend a week at one of the state parks, exploring the many miles of trails and visiting all its waterfalls and cascades.

If time is at a premium, a good bet is a trip to Minnewaska State Park Preserve. The park is home to several stunning waterfalls, and hiking, biking and boating are also on offer.

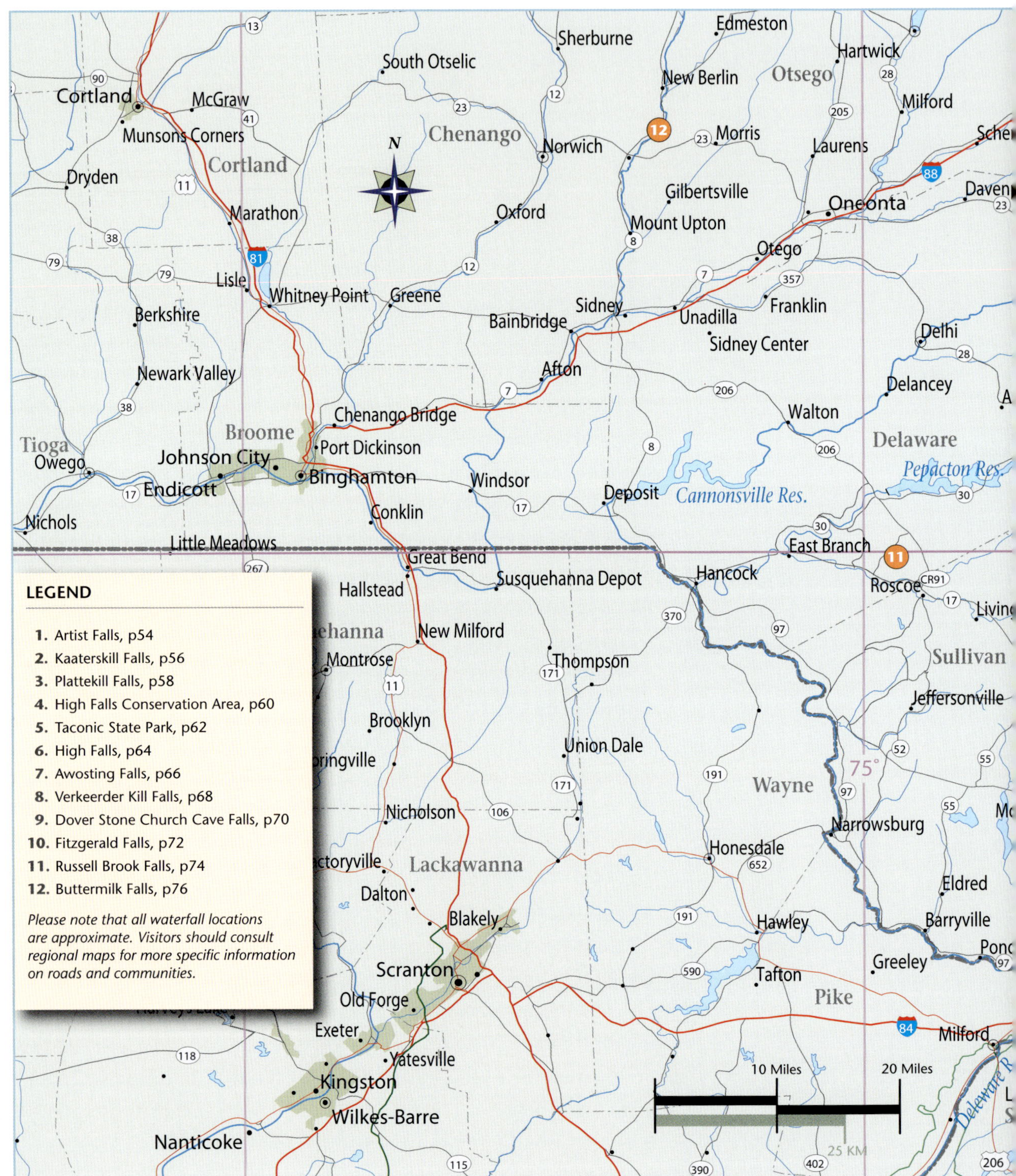

LEGEND
1. Artist Falls, p54
2. Kaaterskill Falls, p56
3. Plattekill Falls, p58
4. High Falls Conservation Area, p60
5. Taconic State Park, p62
6. High Falls, p64
7. Awosting Falls, p66
8. Verkeerder Kill Falls, p68
9. Dover Stone Church Cave Falls, p70
10. Fitzgerald Falls, p72
11. Russell Brook Falls, p74
12. Buttermilk Falls, p76
Please note that all waterfall locations are approximate. Visitors should consult regional maps for more specific information on roads and communities.
N
Cortland
McGraw
Munsons Corners
Dryden
Marathon
Lisle
Whitney Point
Greene
Berkshire
Newark Valley
South Otselic
Chenango
Norwich
Oxford
Sherburne
Edmeston
New Berlin
Otsego
Morris
Gilbertsville
Mount Upton
Hartwick
Milford
Laurens
Oneonta
Otego
Franklin
Unadilla
Sidney
Sidney Center
Bainbridge
Afton
Delhi
Delancey
Walton
Delaware
Pepacton Res.
Cannonsville Res.
Deposit
Windsor
Chenango Bridge
Port Dickinson
Broome
Tioga
Owego
Johnson City
Endicott
Binghamton
Conklin
Nichols
Little Meadows
Great Bend
Hallstead
Susquehanna Depot
Hancock
East Branch
Roscoe
Sullivan
Jeffersonville
New Milford
Montrose
Thompson
Brooklyn
Union Dale
Wayne
Nicholson
Honesdale
Narrowsburg
Lackawanna
Dalton
Blakely
Scranton
Old Forge
Exeter
Yatesville
Kingston
Wilkes-Barre
Nanticoke
Hawley
Tafton
Pike
Eldred
Barryville
Greeley
Milford
10 Miles
20 Miles
25 KM
75°

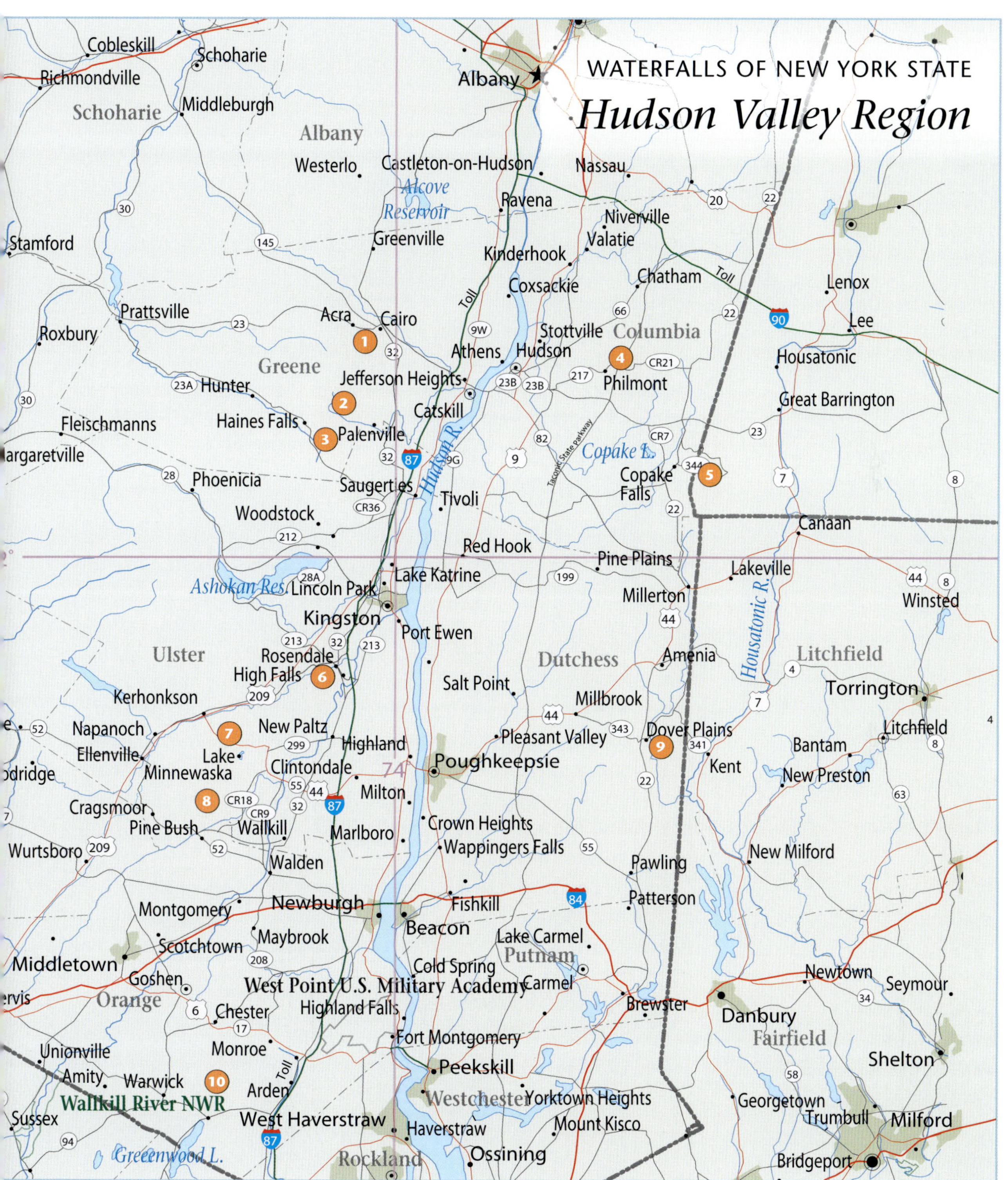
WATERFALLS OF NEW YORK STATE
Hudson Valley Region
Albany
Schoharie
Greene
Columbia
Ulster
Dutchess
Litchfield
Orange
Putnam
Westchester
Rockland
Fairfield
Hudson R.
Housatonic R.
Alcove Reservoir
Ashokan Res.
Copake L.
Greenwood L.
Wallkill River NWR
West Point U.S. Military Academy
Cobleskill
Richmondville
Middleburgh
Westerlo
Castleton-on-Hudson
Nassau
Ravena
Niverville
Valatie
Kinderhook
Greenville
Stamford
Coxsackie
Chatham
Lenox
Lee
Prattsville
Roxbury
Acra
Cairo
Athens
Hudson
Stottville
Housatonic
Hunter
Jefferson Heights
Philmont
Great Barrington
Catskill
Haines Falls
Fleischmanns
Palenville
Margaretville
Phoenicia
Saugerties
Tivoli
Copake Falls
Woodstock
Canaan
Red Hook
Pine Plains
Lakeville
Lake Katrine
Lincoln Park
Millerton
Winsted
Kingston
Port Ewen
Amenia
Rosendale
High Falls
Salt Point
Torrington
Kerhonkson
Millbrook
Napanoch
New Paltz
Highland
Pleasant Valley
Dover Plains
Litchfield
Ellenville
Lake Minnewaska
Bantam
Clintondale
Poughkeepsie
Kent
New Preston
Milton
Cragsmoor
Pine Bush
Wallkill
Crown Heights
Marlboro
Wappingers Falls
Wurtsboro
Walden
Pawling
New Milford
Montgomery
Newburgh
Fishkill
Patterson
Beacon
Maybrook
Scotchtown
Lake Carmel
Middletown
Cold Spring
Goshen
Carmel
Newtown
Seymour
Chester
Highland Falls
Brewster
Danbury
Unionville
Monroe
Fort Montgomery
Peekskill
Shelton
Amity
Warwick
Arden
Yorktown Heights
Georgetown
Sussex
West Haverstraw
Haverstraw
Mount Kisco
Trumbull
Milford
Ossining
Bridgeport
Toll
1
2
3
4
5
6
7
8
9
10

HUDSON VALLEY REGION

Artist Falls

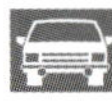

From I-87, take exit 21 and turn left onto Main St. Proceed for 0.3 mi (0.5 km) to the on ramp for NY 23 on the right. Continue on NY 23 for 3 mi (4.8 km), then turn left onto Cairo Junction Rd. In 3 mi (4.8 km), turn left onto NY 32. After 2.2 mi (3.5 km), turn right onto Heart's Content Rd. In 3 mi (4.8 km), turn left onto Winter Clove Rd. and follow it to the end. Parking areas are available near the trailhead.

COUNTY: Greene

TOWNSHIP: Cairo

PLACE: Round Top

WATERWAY: Kiskatom Brook

TYPE: classical falls

HEIGHT: 15 ft (4.6 m)

TRAIL: dirt path; easy

WALKING TIME: 5 min

PEAK ACTIVITY: year-round

LATITUDE: 42.2411

LONGITUDE: –74.0332

Although it is close to an appealing selection of hiking trails and several other waterfalls, Artist Falls is lovely enough to justify a visit on its own. As it flows beneath a handcrafted covered bridge specially built for local hikers and the clientele of nearby Winter Clove Inn, this waterfall is truly one of nature's great works of art.

Located off a small parking area just across from the inn, the trail is well maintained, and the short hike can be easily managed by the entire family. Don't let the modest stream that runs alongside the trail fool you. Upon entering the small amphitheater below the covered bridge, you'll see that the stream size doesn't even hint at the grand nature of this waterfall.

At a mere 15 feet (4.6 m) high, Artist Falls rivals the beauty of many of New York's tallest waterfalls. You'll be hard-pressed to find many in the state that share the specific attributes which make this one so memorable.

Artist Falls is set in a wooded area, so the scenery changes dramatically with each season. The spring thaw swells the waterfall substantially, while the summer months reduce the flow almost to a trickle. Autumn creates the most colorful backdrop, and the winter months offer up a large, glorious frozen mass of ice, arrested in time.

In 1897, a guest at the Winter Clove Inn, which has been in operation since 1863, engraved a portrait of the historic inn on the cliff's rock wall to the left of the waterfall. If you have a sharp eye, you may be able to find the carving.

Family pets are allowed to visit this area, but dogs must be leashed at all times. This is a private retreat, so please be mindful of other visitors. Check in with the friendly staff at the inn's front desk before starting your hike, and when you're finished, as a courtesy, let them know you've returned safely.

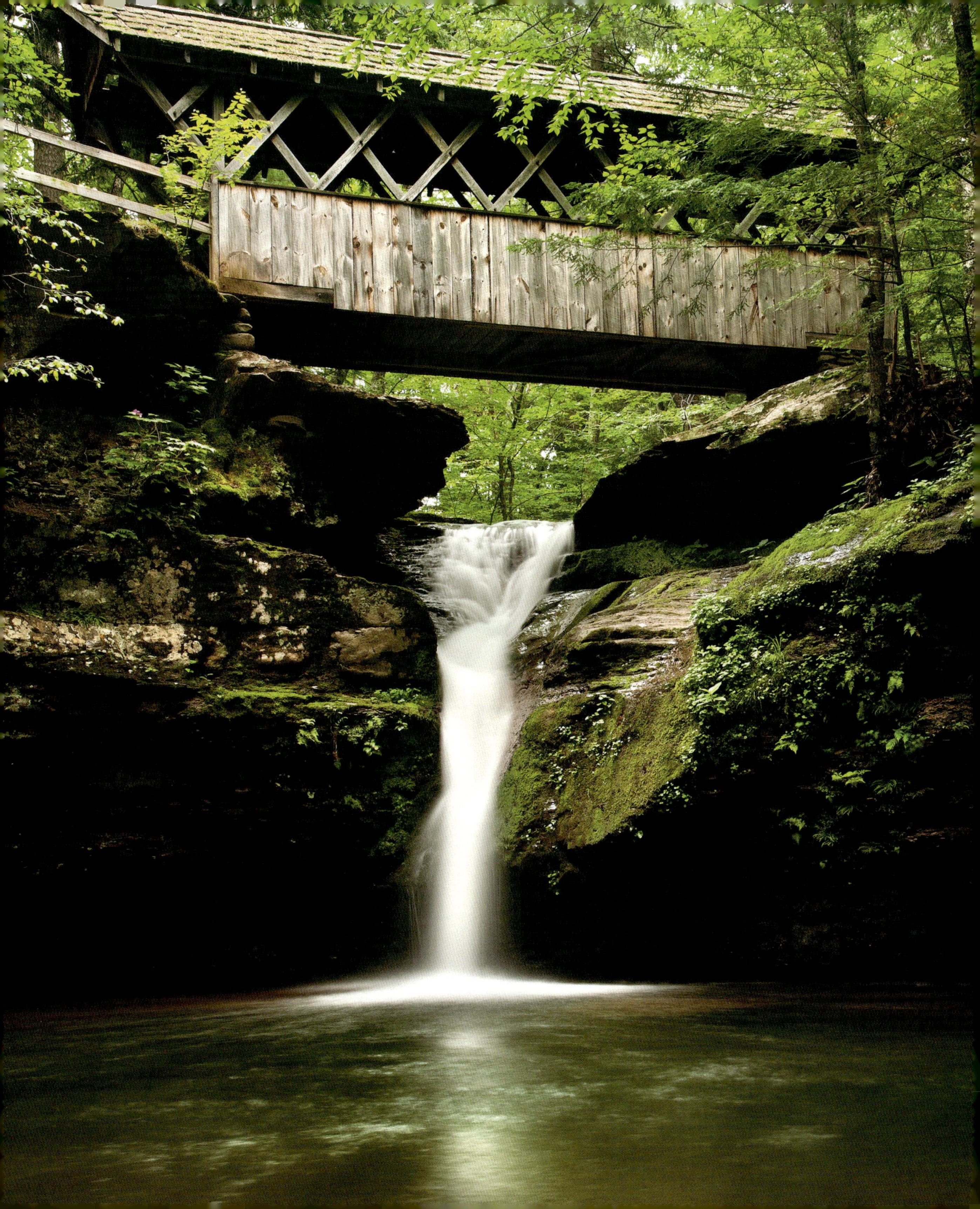

HUDSON VALLEY REGION

Kaaterskill Falls

From I-87, take exit 21 and turn left onto CR 23B (Main St.). Drive for 1.7 mi (2.7 km), and take the ramp to Maple Ave. Bear slightly to the right, and drive 0.8 mi (1.3 km) to West Bridge St. Stay straight and continue for another 0.6 mi (1 km). Proceed onto NY 23A west, and drive 11.9 mi (19.2 km) to the parking area on the left.

COUNTY: Greene

TOWNSHIP: Hunter

PLACE: Haines Falls

WATERWAY: Kaaterskill Creek

TYPE: ribbon falls

HEIGHT: 64 ft (19.5 m) and 165 ft (50.3 m)

TRAIL: dirt and rock; easy to moderate

WALKING TIME: 40 min

PEAK ACTIVITY: May-Oct.

LATITUDE: 42.1933

LONGITUDE: –74.0633

One of the most beautiful waterfalls in the eastern Catskill Mountains and commonly considered the highest two-tiered waterfall in New York State, popular Kaaterskill Falls is, quite simply, an amazing sight. In two phenomenal sections, this waterfall plummets roughly 230 feet (70 m).

From the roadside parking area, it is a short walk downhill along NY 23 to the trailhead. Stay inside the guardrails, as this is a busy road that links many communities to the Adirondack Northway.

Kaaterskill Creek and its tributary feed roughly a dozen or more waterfalls, among them Bastion Falls, which can be viewed from the trailhead. Take a little time to see this impressive waterfall before your hike to Kaaterskill Falls.

The trail system, which is maintained by volunteers and is generally easy to navigate, is basically a single track (though some portions are a little wider) that runs along the hillside bordering the creek. The main trail ends at the base of the Kaaterskill Falls' second drop. Please respect the posted rules, and do not try to scale the gorge walls to the bottom of the first section of the main waterfall. Doing so will cause further degradation of the erosion-prone cliff face.

There is another vantage point from which to see Kaaterskill Falls in its entirety. Drive uphill from the parking area, and take the first major road on your right (CR 18/North Lake Road). Proceed for approximately 1.8 miles (2.9 km) to Laurel House Road. In the parking area at the end of the road is the trail to the top of Kaaterskill Falls. From here, you can observe both drops and enjoy a spectacular view of the Catskill Mountains as well.

Most of the area's runoff and precipitation funnels into the Kaaterskill Clove, an ancient gorge formed by Kaaterskill Creek, and several massive floods in the past have washed away entire roads. The last major flood closed NY 23 for almost a year, as crews worked to rebuild it. The culvert underneath the road is 15 feet (4.6 m) high, and in the dry season, it's hard to imagine the creek swelling to such dangerous proportions.

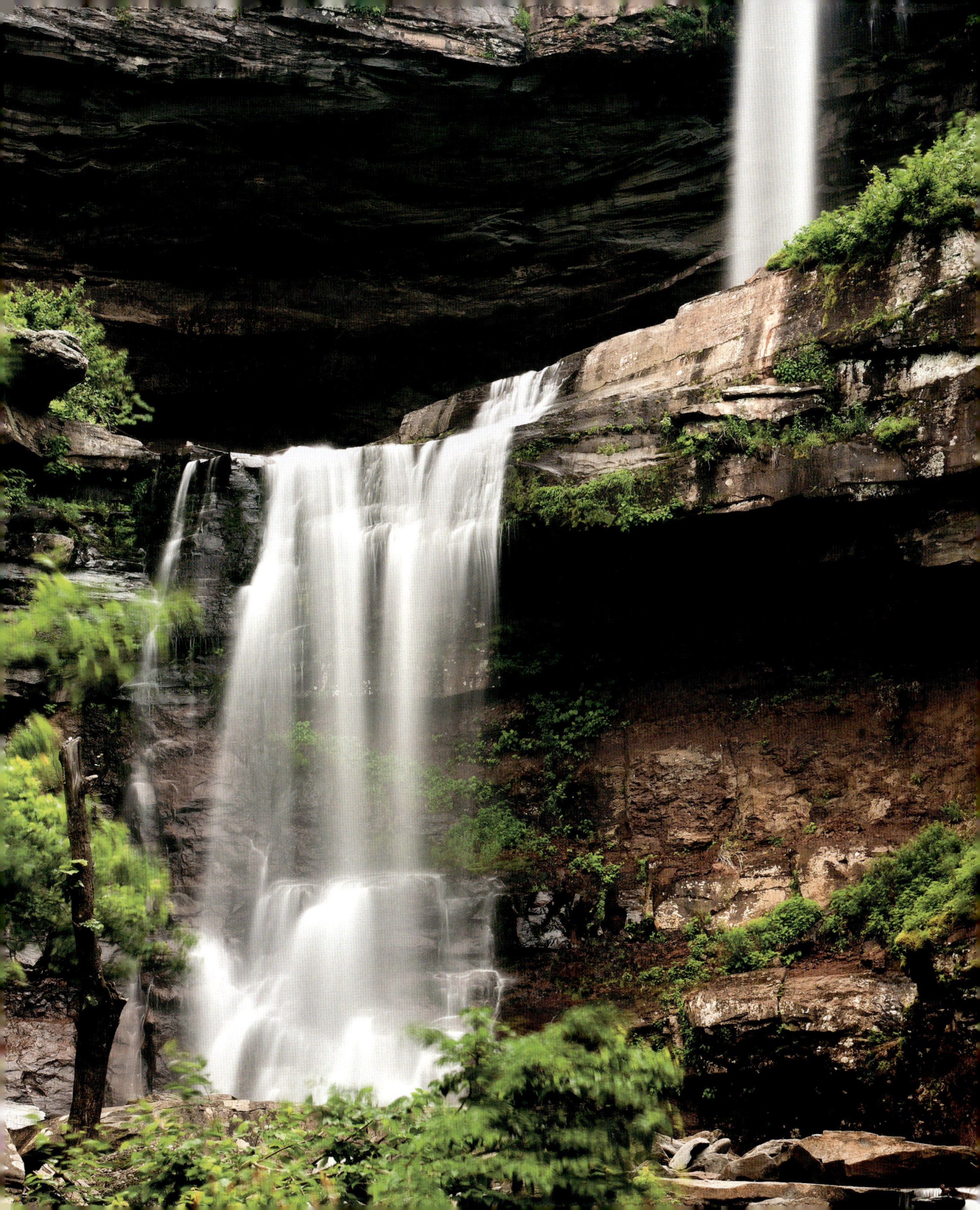

Plattekill Falls

From I-87, take exit 20 and turn right onto NY 32 north. After 3.1 mi (5 km), turn left onto Blue Mountain Quarryville Rd. (CR 36/Harry Wells Rd.). Proceed for 2 mi (3.2 km) to CR 36 (West Saugerties Rd.), and turn right. After 3 mi (4.8 km), continue straight onto Platte Clove Rd. In about 1.3 mi (2.1 km), there is a parking area on the right with a state sign posted at the entrance.

COUNTY: Greene

TOWNSHIP: Hunter

PLACE: Platte Clove

WATERWAY: Plattekill Creek

TYPE: ribbon falls

HEIGHT: less than 70 ft (21.3 m)

TRAIL: dirt and stone; moderate

WALKING TIME: 25 min

PEAK ACTIVITY: May-Sept.

LATITUDE: 42.1313

LONGITUDE: –74.0841

Like Kaaterskill Clove, Plattekill Clove is a deep valley that dramatically cuts through the Catskill Escarpment in the northeastern Catskill Mountains. The region's rugged beauty was famously depicted by the Hudson River School artists in the mid-19th century.

Plattekill Creek runs east through the clove on its way to the Hudson River, and Plattekill Falls (also known as Plattekill Clove Falls) is one of several impressive waterfalls located on or near the creek. The Catskills are renowned for their colorful autumn foliage, so plan your trip for the fall.

Platte Clove Road is a narrow, steep road that runs the length of the clove, climbing some 1,200 feet (366 m) in under 2 miles (3.2 km). Although it is the only road in the area, it is not plowed during the winter. A small red house, set slightly back from the road, marks the trailhead. The parking area is about 200 yards (183 m) from here, on the opposite side of the road. With the red house on your right, follow a path that varies between very steep and relatively level. The trail that hugs the right side of the ravine leads to the streambed, where you'll enjoy an almost straight-on view of the entire waterfall. The trail down to the waterfall is punctuated by several smaller paths that offer more views of the creek and surrounding waterfalls.

Plattekill Falls is set in a smaller nook within the clove and seems to flow directly from the woods at the top of its 75-foot (23 m) cliff face. The water shoots out and down in a fan-shaped motion into the small pool at the bottom. When the flow is low, the waterfall breaks into two smaller sets of falls, created by a rock ledge that juts out about halfway down the cliff face.

It cannot be said too often that the clove banks are steep and sometimes slippery with pine needles, so wear appropriate footwear, and stay on the well-established trails and roadways. Traveling the length of Platte Clove Road, you're likely to spot at least one car among the brush and boulders that never made it to the bottom of the mountain. It's a grim reminder that all this beauty can be treacherous as well.

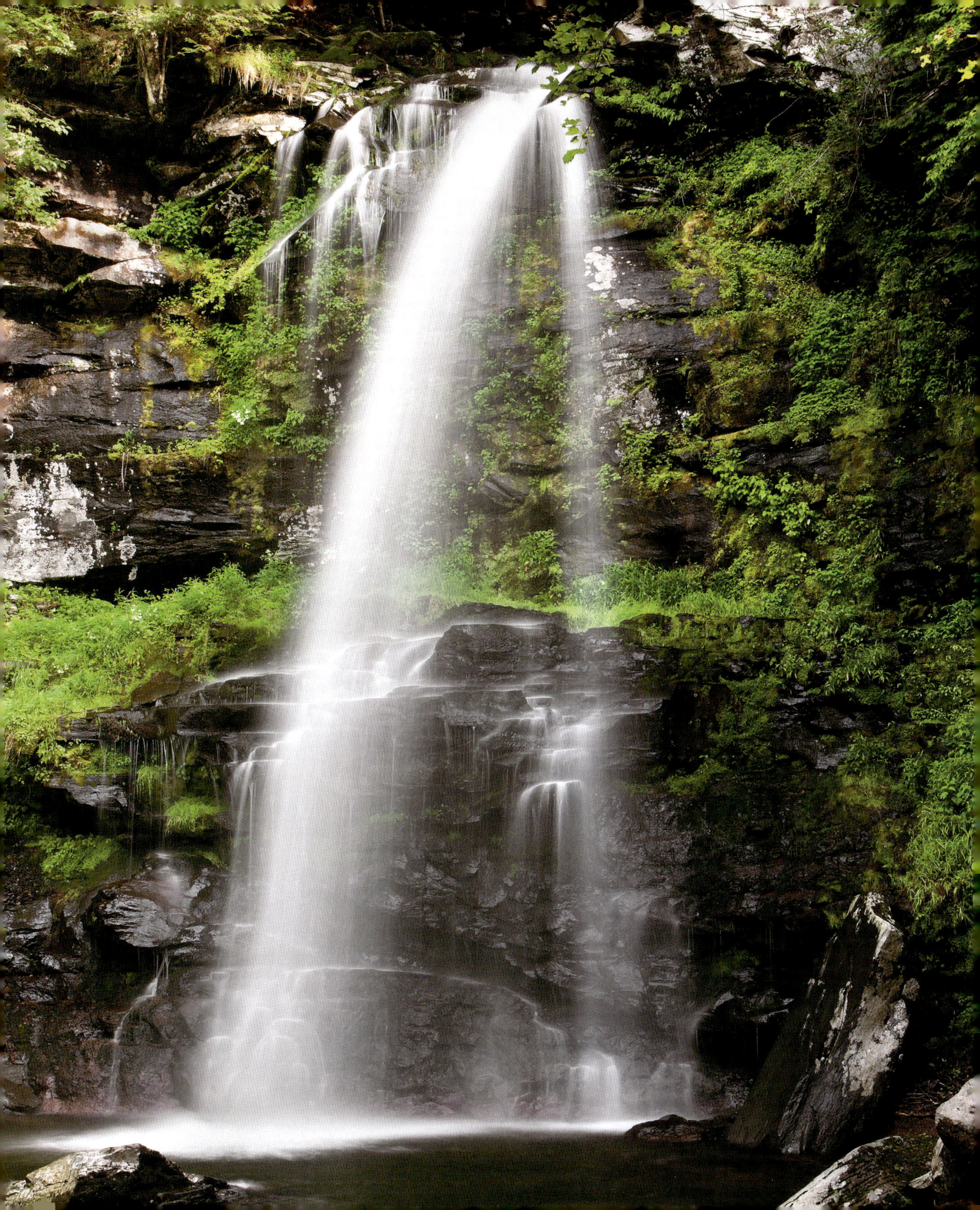

High Falls Conservation Area

From the Taconic State Parkway, take the exit for NY 217 west. Continue for 2.5 mi (4 km), then turn left onto Roxbury Rd. The conservation-area parking lot and entrance are on the left.

COUNTY: Columbia

TOWNSHIP: Claverack

PLACE: Philmont

WATERWAY: Agawamuck Creek

TYPE: ribbon falls

HEIGHT: 150 ft (46 m)

TRAIL: gravel; easy to moderate

WALKING TIME: 15 min

PEAK ACTIVITY: April-Oct.

LATITUDE: 42.2459

LONGITUDE: –73.6500

High Falls is located on Agawamuck Creek in the High Falls Conservation Area, a 47-acre (19 ha) nature preserve that is managed by volunteers of the Columbia Land Conservancy. The preserve's trail systems are well maintained and marked for easy hiking, and you can pick up a map at the trailhead before starting your hike to the waterfall.

A short distance from the parking area, a wooden bridge spans a very small brook that is a tributary of Agawamuck Creek. You can hike to the spot where these two waterways converge, but High Falls offers a much greater visual reward.

Apart from the hard work required to develop and maintain the trail systems, the park remains relatively untouched. For your own safety and comfort, remember that poisonous plants grow wild in the forest. Stinging nettle is fairly common in the state and has been identified in the conservation area. Absentmindedly grabbing a plant by the stem may result in an extremely unpleasant sensation that can linger for a surprisingly long time. Wear long pants, and don't pick any of the vegetation.

The hike to the falls over a couple of hills is short, and when you reach the viewing area at the top of the trail, sections of the falls are visible. In the summer, tree foliage frames the waterfall; once the leaves have fallen in autumn, the view is unobstructed. To see the waterfall in its entirety, you have to descend a relatively steep hill.

High Falls plummets over several drops for an estimated 150 feet (46 m). A small drop at the very top of the falls is barely visible from the available vantage points. The base of the falls is off-limits, although there is a small trail that locals take to observe the waterfall from the bottom.

Swimming and wading are prohibited in the park, and dogs must be leashed at all times. Safety regulations are posted at the trailhead.

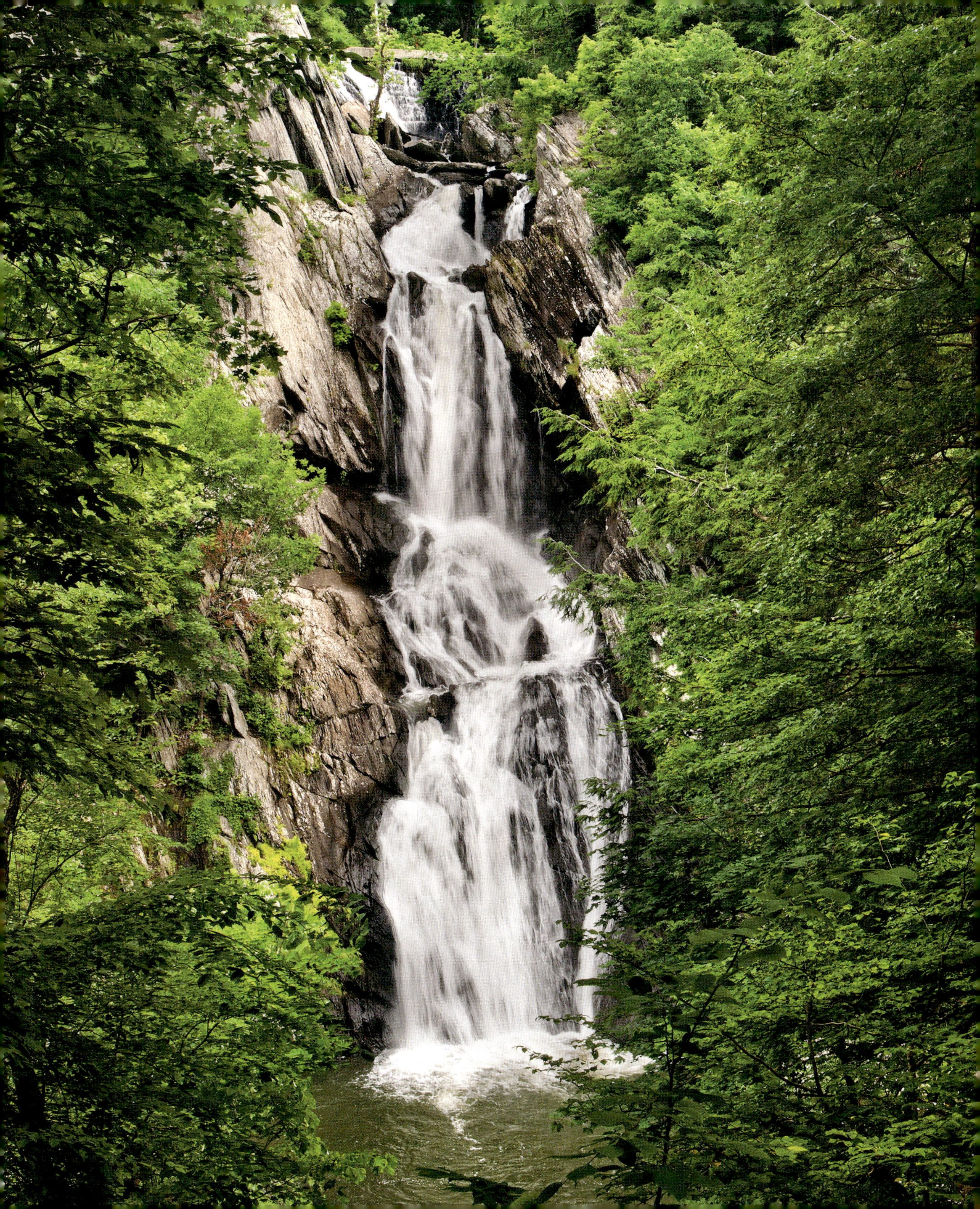

Taconic State Park

From I-90, take exit B2 and follow the Taconic State Parkway for 16.2 mi (26.1 km). Take the exit for NY 23, and turn left onto NY 23 east. Drive for 7.2 mi (11.6 km), and at the intersection of NY 23 and NY 22, turn right onto NY 22. Continue for 4.6 mi (7.4 km), then turn left onto NY 344 (Old New York 22). After 0.5 mi (0.8 km), you'll see the parking area for the trailhead on the right.

COUNTY: Columbia
TOWNSHIP: Copake
PLACE: Copake Falls
WATERWAY: Bash Bish Brook
TYPE: classical falls
HEIGHT: 60 ft (18.3 m)
TRAIL: crushed stone; easy
WALKING TIME: 25 min
PEAK ACTIVITY: May-Oct.
LATITUDE: 42.1154
LONGITUDE: –73.4935

Taconic State Park sprawls across New York's Columbia and Dutchess counties and crosses into Massachusetts and Connecticut via the Taconic Range. Designated one of America's "Last Great Places" by The Nature Conservancy, the park encompasses 14,400 acres (5,828 ha) of protected forest and is a magnet for nature lovers.

One of the park's most popular destinations is Bash Bish Falls. Although technically in Massachusetts, the waterfall is included here because it would be a shame to miss it when you're in this part of the state.

There is no admission fee to the park, and dogs are permitted, provided they are leashed at all times. The park also has a campground area, along with a historic ironworks that was once powered by Bash Bish Falls.

A small parking area is located downstream from Bash Bish Falls, and there is another one near the top of the waterfall. From the bottom parking area, it is only about 0.8 mile (1.3 km) to Bash Bish Falls. The trail runs along Bash Bish Brook, and on the way, you'll see several smaller unnamed cascades and waterfalls. Bash Bish Falls is easily recognized by the distinctive boulder at the top that divides the waterfall into two. From the platform, a set of stairs leads to the base of the falls. Wading and swimming are prohibited in the very inviting pool at the bottom of the falls, though many visitors blatantly disregard the posted rules.

Additional trails at the base of the waterfall lead past the falls and into other appealing parts of the park. A segment of the Appalachian National Scenic Trail also runs through Taconic State Park.

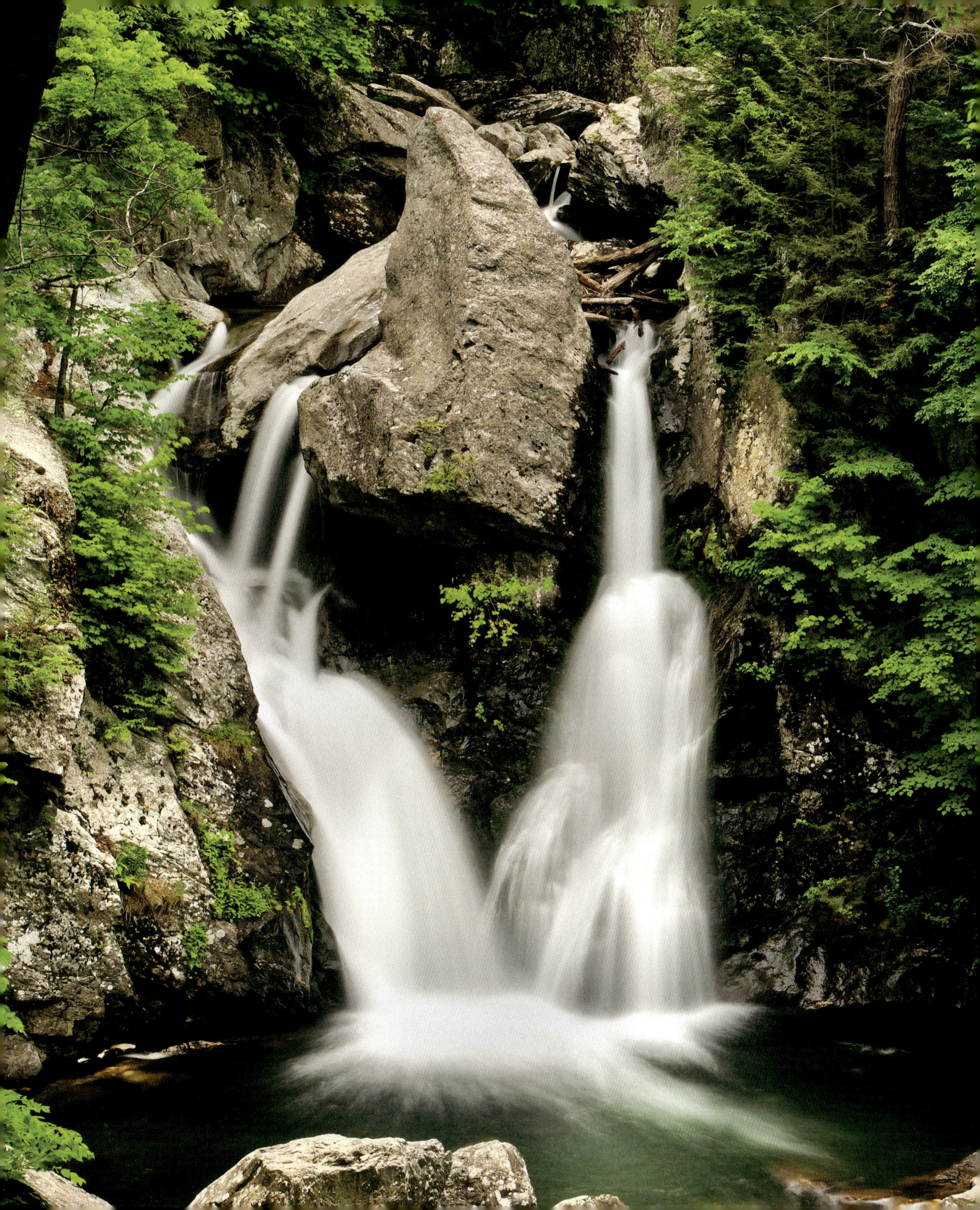

High Falls

From I-87, take exit 18 and turn left onto NY 299 (Main St.). Drive for 1.7 mi (2.7 km), then turn right onto Springtown Rd. Continue for 0.5 mi (0.8 km) to CR 6 (Mountain Rest Rd.). Follow CR 6 for 5.1 mi (8.2 km), then proceed on CR 6A (Mohonk Rd.) for another 3.1 mi (5 km). Turn left onto NY 213, and drive for 0.3 mi (0.5 km). On the right side of the road, just before you reach the bridge, is the parking area for the waterfall.

COUNTY: Ulster
TOWNSHIP: Marbletown
PLACE: High Falls
WATERWAY: Rondout Creek
TYPE: curtain falls
HEIGHT: 25 ft (7.6 m)
TRAIL: paved; easy
WALKING TIME: 5 min
PEAK ACTIVITY: June-Aug.
LATITUDE: 41.8298
LONGITUDE: –74.1327

Over the past 200 years, the dynamic flow of High Falls has powered a host of factories and mills. Today, it fuels a hydroelectric plant located about 100 yards (91.4 m) from Rondout Creek's south bank.

The land surrounding the waterfall is owned by the Central Hudson Gas & Electric Corporation, but the company has generously arranged for public access by means of an unrestricted paved road and a turnstile. While it's possible to view the falls from a very busy bridge over the river, we recommend using the trails instead, which provide access to almost the entire riverbank.

Along the paved road, you'll notice the fenced-in remains of an old mill on the left. The structure has no roof, but its outer walls are still standing. Follow the fence around to the right, and you'll find a trail that leads to the river's edge, where there's a beautiful view of High Falls.

Spanning more than 550 feet (167.6 m), High Falls is a massive waterfall when the water is running high, but even at lower flows, it is impressive. A short, unobtrusive cement cap has been placed at the top of the falls to regulate the water flow for the hydro plant. This cap is not evident during high flow, when the water covers the entire width of the falls.

If you walk farther downstream, you can enjoy a smaller waterfall. At 10 feet (3 m) high, it is not as dramatic as High Falls, but the setting provides a great view of the river and a lovely place to sit and relax.

During your visit, you may see people swimming and wading in the river. It is not clear whether this activity is sanctioned, and we recommend against it. As always, use caution: rivers near hydro plants are known to rise unexpectedly.

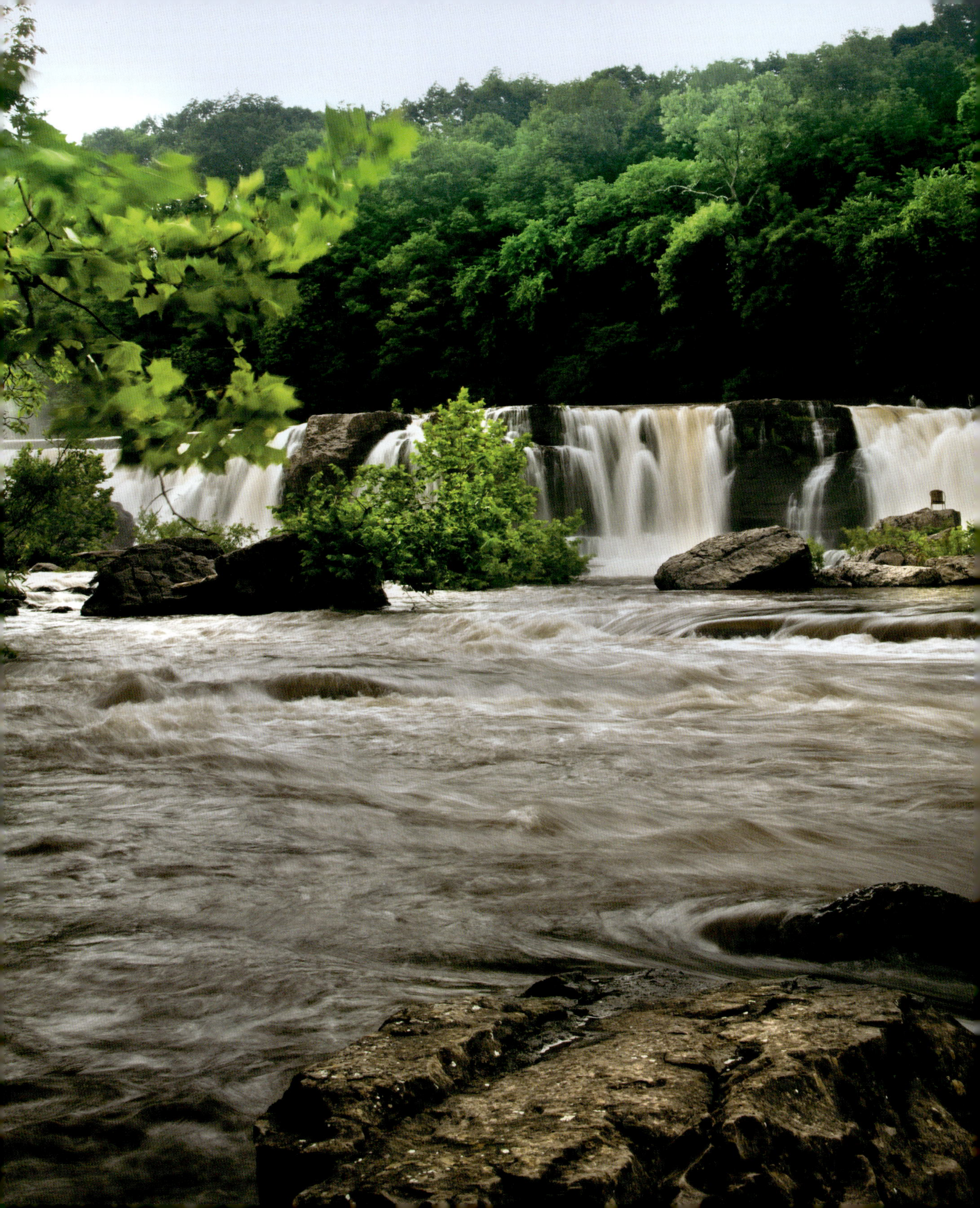

HUDSON VALLEY REGION

Awosting Falls

From I-87, take exit 19 and turn right onto NY 28. Continue for 0.6 mi (1 km) until you see the sign for US 209 south. Merge onto US 209 south, and follow for 20.7 mi (33.3 km). Turn left onto NY 55 (US 44), and proceed for 5.8 mi (9.3 km). The Minnewaska State Park Preserve entrance is on the right. Park in the upper lot for access to the Hamilton Point Trail/Carriageway that leads directly to the waterfall.

COUNTY: Ulster

TOWNSHIP: Rochester

PLACE: Lake Minnewaska

WATERWAY: Peters Kill

TYPE: ribbon falls

HEIGHT: 60 ft (18.3 m)

TRAIL: crushed stone; easy to moderate

WALKING TIME: 15 min

PEAK ACTIVITY: May-Sept.

LATITUDE: 41.7344

LONGITUDE: –74.2372

In a single drop, Awosting Falls plunges over a 60-foot (18.3 m) cliff into a large pool of crystal-clear, tan-colored water on Peters Kill in Minnewaska State Park Preserve. Situated on Shawangunk Ridge, which tops out at roughly 2,000 feet (610 m) above sea level, the park features a number of waterfalls. Awosting Falls is considered the most appealing among them.

The falls are quickly reached via a well-maintained trail that starts from the upper parking area near the park's entrance. After a short, easy hike to the crest, take time to enjoy the mountain views, and see whether you can spot one of the peregrine falcons that have been reintroduced to the area.

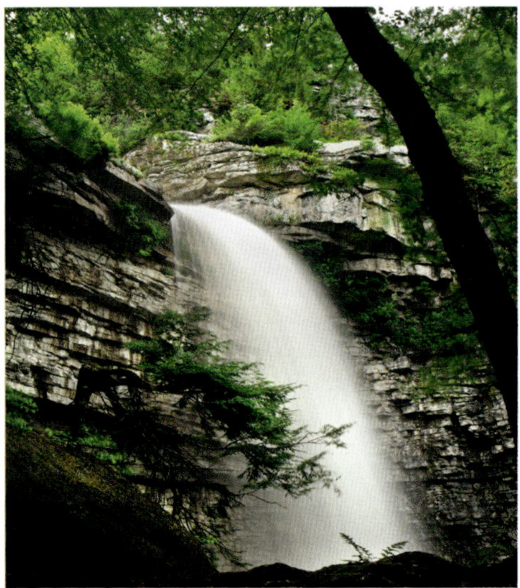

As you head down the trail toward the base of Awosting Falls, the sounds and smells of the fresh water rushing over the crest of the falls will entice you to pick up your pace. The trail leads down and away from the waterfall briefly, then turns almost 180 degrees back toward it. In a few more steps, you'll catch glimpses of the falling water through the evergreens around the basin. Walk about 100 yards (91.4 m) farther down the trail to the viewing area, where the path levels off. There are no signs warning against wading, but if the water is high after a heavy rain, be cautious. Dogs are allowed in the park, so if you've brought along a canine friend, your pet may also enjoy the refreshing water.

You'll find something for everyone to do during your visit, from rock climbing, biking and hiking to scuba diving and horseback riding. Take advantage of the park's 50-mile (80.5 km) trail system to explore this slice of nature.

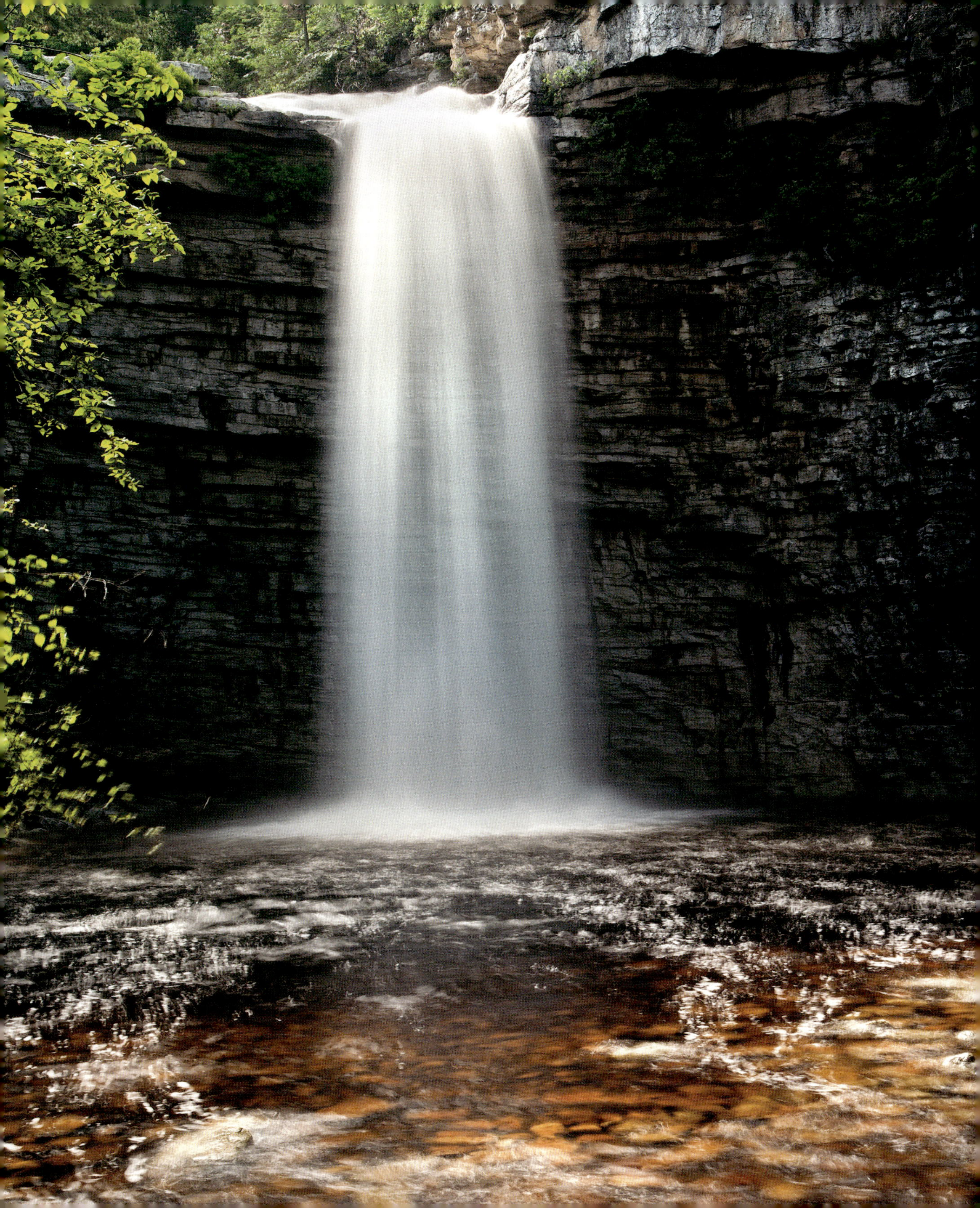

Verkeerder Kill Falls

From I-87, take exit 18 and turn left onto NY 299. Drive for 0.9 mi (1.4 km), and turn left onto NY 208. Continue on NY 208 (note that the road name changes several times). At about 12.1 mi (19.5 km), turn left onto Bruyn Turnpike (CR 18), and proceed for 1.3 mi (2.1 km). Turn left onto Albany Post Rd. (CR 9), and follow it for 2.1 mi (3.4 km). Turn right onto NY 52 west. After 12 mi (19.3 km), turn right onto Cragsmoor Rd., and drive 1.4 mi (2.3 km). Turn right onto South Gully Rd. Take the first right onto Sam's Point Rd., and continue to the visitor's center parking area.

COUNTY: Ulster

TOWNSHIP: Gardiner

PLACE: Cragsmoor

WATERWAY: Verkeerder Kill

TYPE: ribbon falls

HEIGHT: more than 70 ft (21.3 m)

TRAIL: gravel and rock; difficult

WALKING TIME: less than 3 hr

PEAK ACTIVITY: May-Sept.

LATITUDE: 41.6851

LONGITUDE: –74.3279

Verkeerder Kill Falls is located in Sam's Point Preserve, a 5,400-acre (2,185 ha) tract of land on the rugged Shawangunk Ridge, in the Catskill Mountains. Managed by The Nature Conservancy, the preserve contains one of the few remaining dwarf pine ridges in the state. It is also home to the country's largest-known open fault and the Ellenville Fault Ice Caves. The cool micro-climate created by the caves stabilizes the local environment, promoting the growth and survival of the hardy indigenous plant life.

The walk in to the falls may appear to be straightforward, but that is deceiving. Be prepared for a tough hike. About 3.5 miles (5.6 km) long, the route is over extremely uneven terrain on a single-track trail. From time to time, you'll be obliged to step into the bushes to allow fellow hikers to pass. To avoid scrapes and scratches from trailside twigs and branches, wear long pants or protective gaiters.

As you hike, enjoy the gorgeous view of dwarf pines that mark the surrounding mountains and valleys. The route allows you to explore the ice caves as well, and if you visit on a sweltering summer day, there are several small cooling streams along the way.

Once you reach the waterfall, gaze over its crest and take the time to appreciate the miles of mountain range and river valley that stretch before you. For a view of the entire falls from top to bottom, cross the creek and walk another 100 yards (91.4 m) to the open-face cliff. At certain times of the day, the sun is at just the right angle to create a rainbow in the mist of falling water.

Parts of the preserve are open only seasonally, so plan your visit accordingly. Guided hikes are offered for groups, and plenty of workers and volunteers are available to answer questions. The preserve is dog-friendly, but be sure your four-footed companion is leashed at all times.

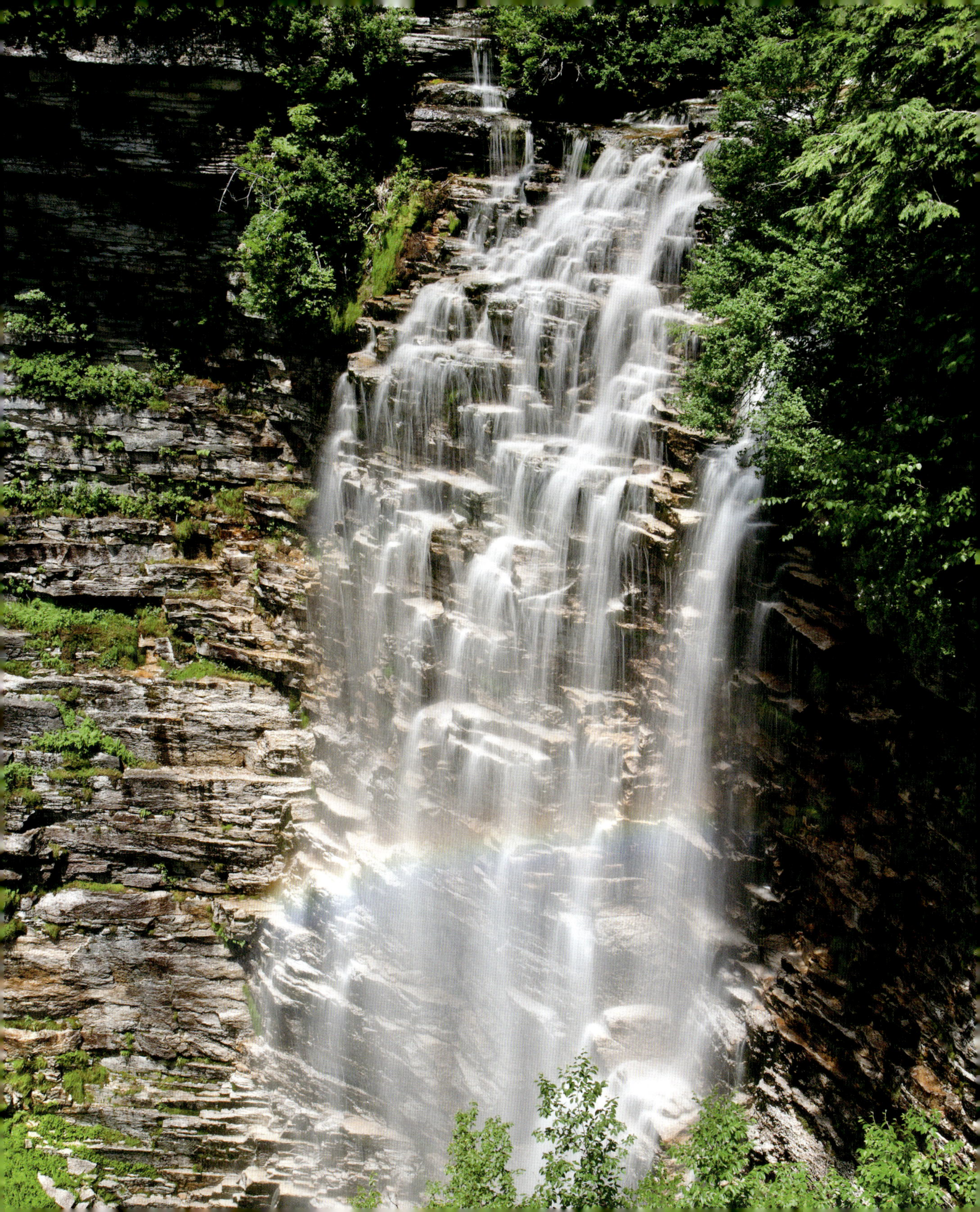

HUDSON VALLEY REGION

Dover Stone Church Cave Falls

From the Taconic State Parkway, take the exit for Tinkertown and merge onto US 44 east toward Dover Plains. At about 1 mi (1.6 km), continue straight on NY 82 south. After 1.9 mi (3.1 km), proceed straight onto NY 343 east for 7.1 mi (11.4 km). Merge onto Tinkertown Rd., and continue downhill for 0.7 mi (1.1 km), then turn right onto NY 22 south. After about 0.4 mi (0.6 km), you'll see the trailhead for the waterfall on the right. Find parking nearby.

COUNTY: Dutchess

TOWNSHIP: Dover

PLACE: Dover Plains

WATERWAY: Stone Church Brook

TYPE: classical falls

HEIGHT: est. 20 ft (6.1 m)

TRAIL: well maintained but variable; easy

WALKING TIME: 20 min

PEAK ACTIVITY: April-Oct.

LATITUDE: 41.7383

LONGITUDE: –73.5882

Unlike several "cave waterfalls" that have been deemed unsafe in New York State, Dover Stone Church Cave Falls is open to visitors almost year-round.

The Gothic cathedral-like cave entrance inspired its name, which is reinforced by the nickname given to the large boulder inside: the Pulpit Rock. To the left of this rock is the first of two waterfalls.

This is not, according to the technical definition of the word, a cave, which is generally characterized as a naturally occurring underground area. Here, the cave has been created by a stream that has worn a channel through the rock where the waterfall is located. The slender opening through which the water sculpted this unique attraction is visible along the top of the cave. The light that enters here varies depending on the time of day and the cloud cover. On a bright day, you can see without extra lighting, but bring a flashlight just in case.

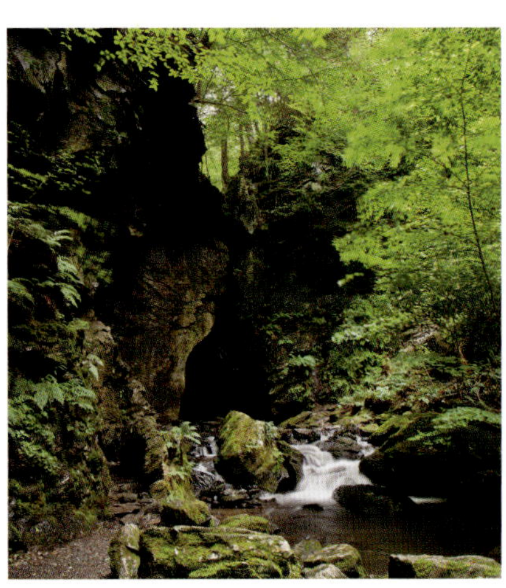

The trailhead lies between two private residences. Park in one of the strip malls across the street. As you walk up the drive between the two houses, you'll spot the very picturesque trail leading to the waterfall: a crushed stone path with a straight row of trees on either side. At the end of the open path, you'll enter a wooded area and the trail turns to grass. Continue on the trail to the left until you reach a small bridge. Cross it, and follow the stream to the mouth of the cave.

Several small sets of plunges in the stream make for a pretty hike. When you reach the cave, be sure that the water is not too high to visit the inner waterfall. The park is closed during inclement weather for good reason. The stream may be small, but it collects the local runoff when it rains.

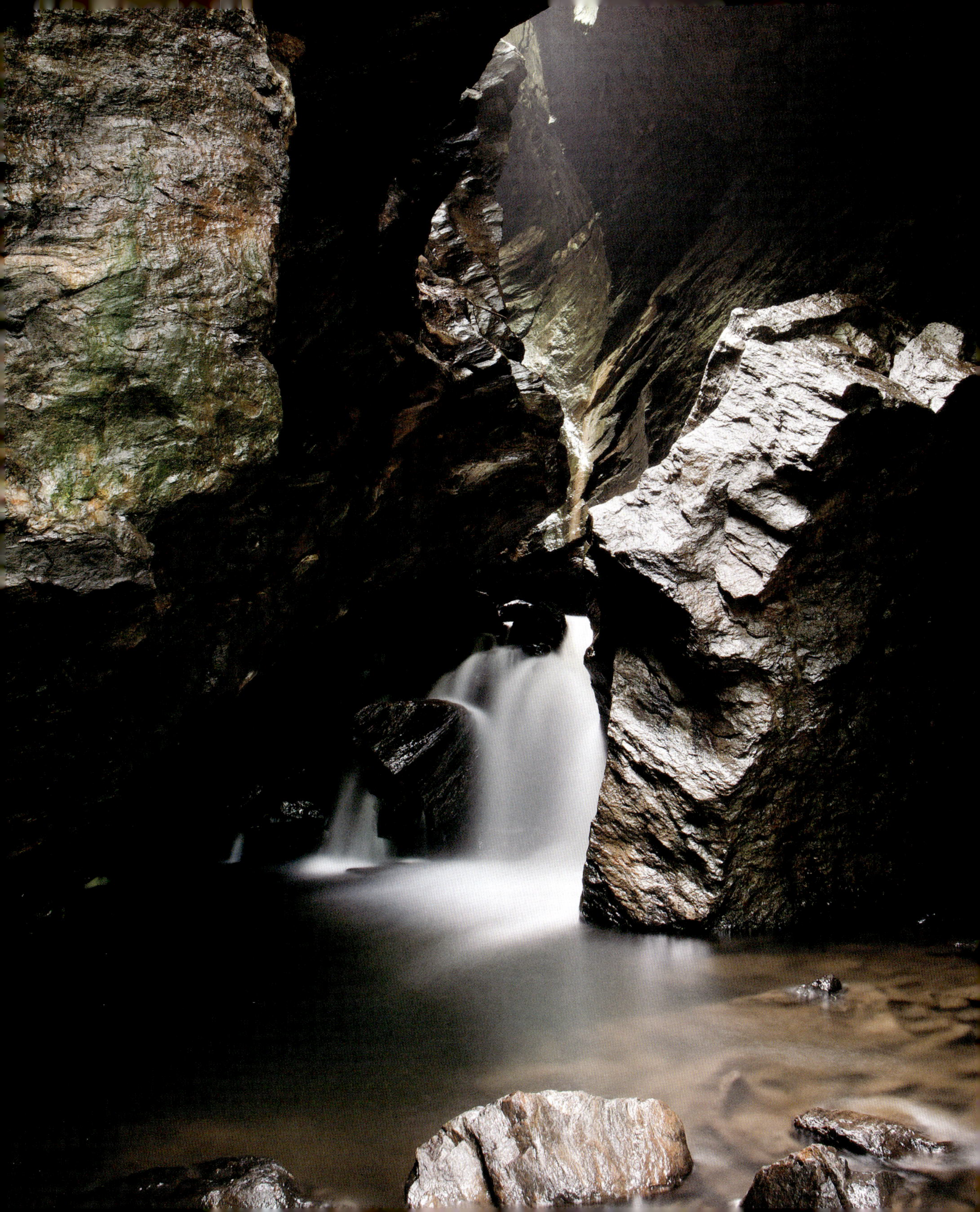

HUDSON VALLEY REGION

Fitzgerald Falls

From I-87, take exit 16 and merge onto NY 17 west toward US 6 (Harriman Rd.). Drive about 4 mi (6.4 km) to exit 130 for NY 208. Turn left onto NY 208 south, and continue for 0.7 mi (1.1 km). Turn right onto Schunemunk Rd. After 0.3 mi (0.5 km), turn left onto NY 17M east and proceed for 0.5 mi (0.8 km). Turn right onto CR 5 (Lakes Rd.), and drive for about 5.3 mi (8.5 km). There is roadside parking for the Appalachian Trail system just past a utility-line clearing on the left.

COUNTY: Greene

TOWNSHIP: Catskill

PLACE: Hensonville

WATERWAY: tributary to East Kill

TYPE: ribbon cascade

HEIGHT: 35 ft (10.7 m)

TRAIL: dirt and single track; easy

WALKING TIME: 35 min

PEAK ACTIVITY: May-Aug.

LATITUDE: 41.2709

LONGITUDE: –74.2514

Fitzgerald Falls is a medium-sized waterfall located on the New York segment of the roughly 2,180-mile-long (3,508 km) Appalachian National Scenic Trail. The trail to the base of the falls is well traveled and easy to follow. But, as on any hike, wear good hiking shoes or boots for the rugged and occasionally slippery terrain. Waders are recommended during wet weather.

From the parking area, the trailhead is easily found. The trail runs parallel to the road for about 200 yards (183 m), and before you enter the woods, you'll notice utility lines overhead. After crossing a small wooden bridge, follow the trail straight, then to the right. There's a rock wall a short distance from the trail on the right. A small section of the wall has crumbled, and some hikers use this break to cross the bordering stream.

Alongside the path are the remnants of old fires, broken glass and other litter left by local people who use the area as a hangout. Although this debris doesn't mar too much of the trail, please keep it in mind if you have a dog with you.

Once you pass the rock wall, you are at the edge of the stream. If you follow the stream or stay on the trail directly across the stream, you'll reach the base of the waterfall about 440 yards (402.3 m) upstream. Fitzgerald Falls rises from the flat creek bottom and is the first major rise in elevation you'll encounter.

Although the ground cover around the waterfall is sparse, the foliage on the tall trees obscures big swaths of the sky. There are unimpeded views of the falls from about 180 degrees around its base.

The Appalachian Trail system passes the foot of the waterfall and continues well past the top. From the top, you are afforded an excellent view of this beautiful spot.

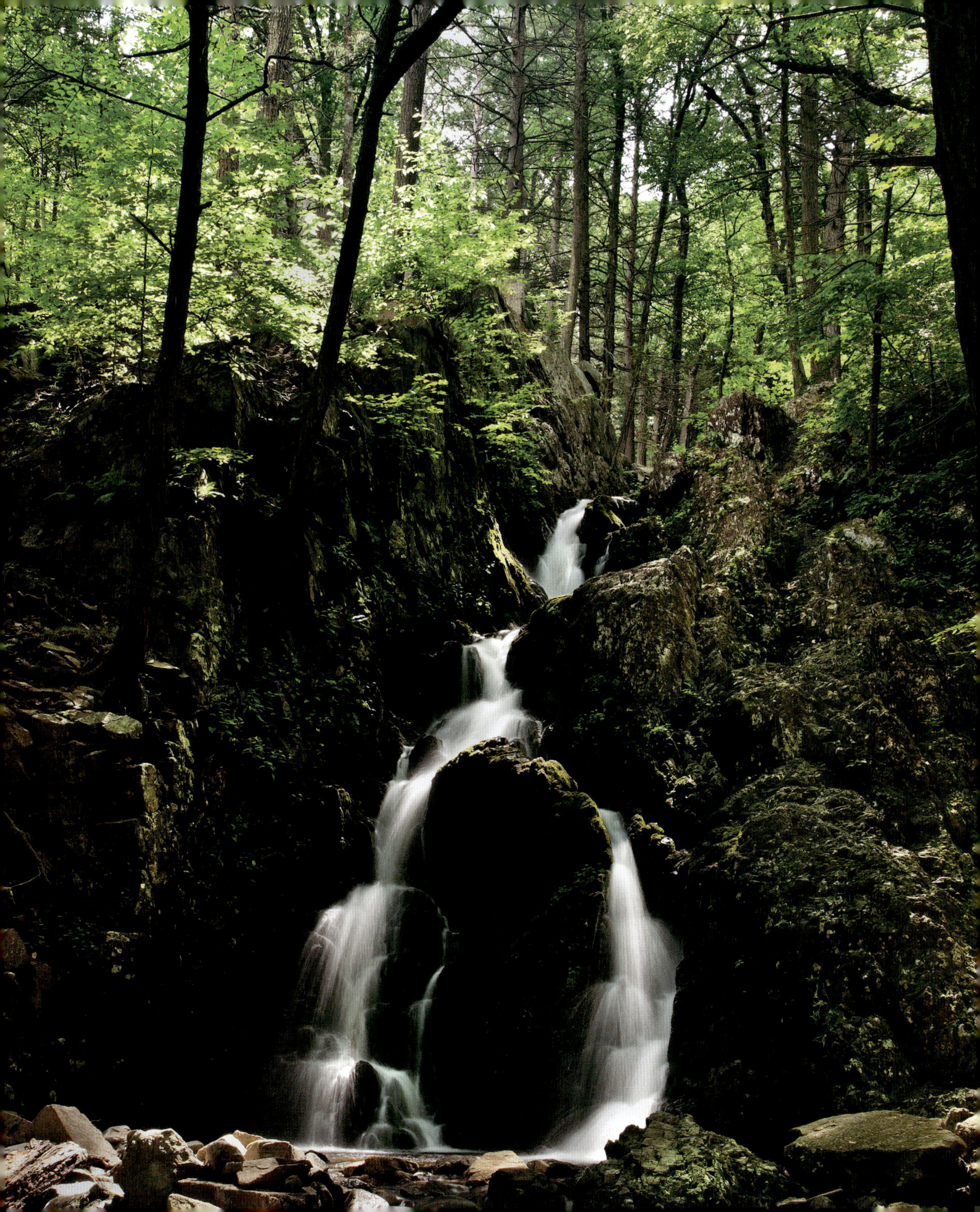

Russell Brook Falls

From NY 17 (I-86), take exit 94 and turn left onto CR 179 (Old Route 17). Follow CR 179 for 0.9 mi (1.4 km). Proceed on NY 206 (CR 91/ Rockland Rd.) for another 1.7 mi (2.7 km), then turn left onto Morton Hill Rd. Drive 3.1 mi (5 km) to Russell Brook Rd. (note that this road is closed during the winter months). After about 0.2 mi (0.3 km), you'll see the parking area for the waterfall's trail on the left.

COUNTY: Delaware
TOWNSHIP: Catskill
PLACE: Mountain Lake
WATERWAY: Russell Brook
TYPE: classical falls
HEIGHT: 20-30 ft (6.1-9 m)
TRAIL: roadside and dirt; easy
WALKING TIME: 15 min
PEAK ACTIVITY: June-Sept.
LATITUDE: 41.9968
LONGITUDE: –74.9394

Russell Brook Falls is found high in the western Catskill Mountains in the 18,000-acre (7,285 ha) Cherry Ridge Wild Forest, an area that is often included in the Southern Tier region. This waterfall has two distinct sections. When you walk uphill from the parking area, you'll get a great view of the upper falls, although the view of the lower falls is partially obstructed. For a good vantage point for the lower falls, hike down the closed road in front of the parking area for about five minutes. After you cross a small bridge, there is an overgrown trail to the right that leads to the best views of the falls.

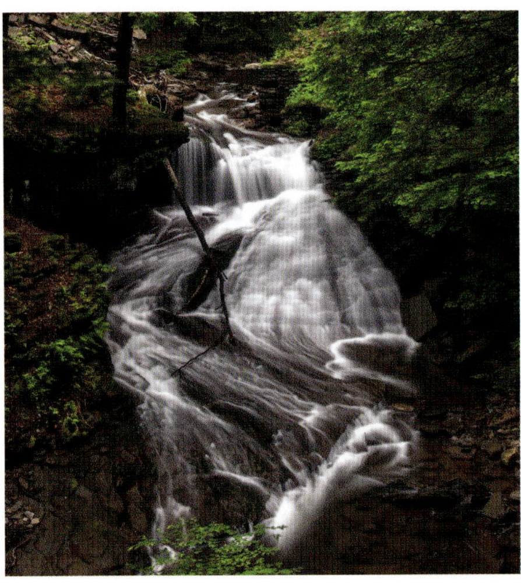

Walk about 20 yards (18.3 m) up the small path and a short way into the woods to gain access to the streambed and the base of the lower falls.

Although you can't see the upper waterfall from the base, you will notice remnants of a stone structure at the top right. Two rock-and-mortar dams once spanned the top of each segment. The year "1895" has been chiseled on the lower wall. Look carefully, and you'll see some old abutments that were part of the road that now serves as the path to the bridge you crossed earlier. To get to the top of the falls, proceed in a straight line, just inside the tree line, where you'll find a less-traveled path that will take you there.

While Russell Brook Falls is an easy hike and has accessible vantage points, keep in mind that this region is a fair distance from any moderately populated area and a substantial drive. It's located on a seasonally limited highway that is closed during the winter. And even when the road is open, you'll find it's a very rough ride.

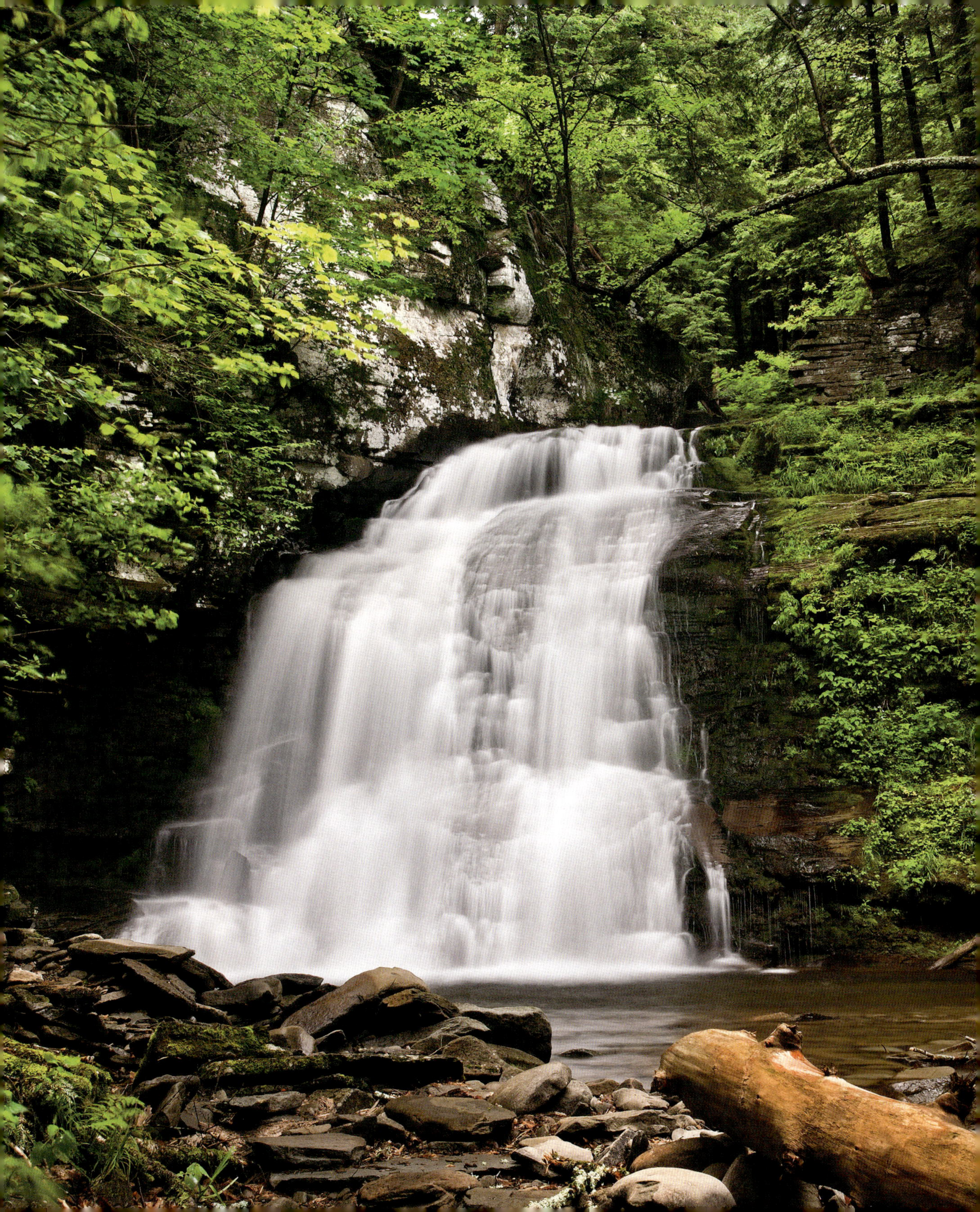

Buttermilk Falls

From I-90, take exit 31 and follow the signs for Genesee St. south (NY 5 south/ Downtown Utica). At the stop sign, turn left and follow Genesee St. for 1 mi (1.6 km), then turn right onto Liberty St. (Oriskany St. W). Continue for about 0.6 mi (1 km), and merge onto NY 12 south (NY 5 west/ NY 8 south). After 3.6 mi (5.8 km), take the exit for NY 8 south toward New Hartford. At about 39.3 mi (63.2 km), turn right onto Buttermilk Falls Rd. Halfway up the hill, the waterfall is on the right side of the road.

This relatively unknown waterfall is located on Buttermilk Falls Road, a minor stone-and-tar road that runs through the middle of a beautiful portion of central New York. An oddity among all the falls that share the same name, this 25-foot (7.6 m) waterfall has few visitors, apart from appreciative area residents who hear about it through word of mouth. Even so, with simple directions, it's not hard to find, and its appealing setting easily justifies a day trip.

We've been unable to turn up much historical detail about this particular waterfall, although the surrounding region has a rich past. The small towns and communities in the area have been settled for well over a hundred years, and their populations have stayed relatively modest, despite the exponential growth of large cities to the north and south.

From your roadside parking spot, you'll catch sight of the falls almost immediately. Buttermilk Falls is the final and biggest waterfall on a tributary that collects runoff from three smaller creeks, which converge above a series of waterfalls. The creek then gradually levels out and enters the Unadilla River.

Upstream are three unnamed waterfalls, each about 10 to 15 feet (3-4.6 m) high. During good weather, it is possible to scramble down to the base of these waterfalls, but even so, the paths are steep and somewhat hazardous. The rocky trails are in almost constant shade and are covered with moss and broken by the occasional crevice. When planning your visit, check the weather forecast for rain; there is no easy path out of the creekbed, and the trails are even more slippery when wet.

A short distance from the last of these three waterfalls, the land is posted, and your hike is officially at an end.

COUNTY: Chenango

TOWNSHIP: New Berlin

PLACE: New Berlin

WATERWAY: tributary to Unadilla River

TYPE: classical cascade

HEIGHT: 25 ft (7.6 m)

TRAIL: roadside; easy

WALKING TIME: n/a

PEAK ACTIVITY: n/a

LATITUDE: 42.5673

LONGITUDE: –75.3588

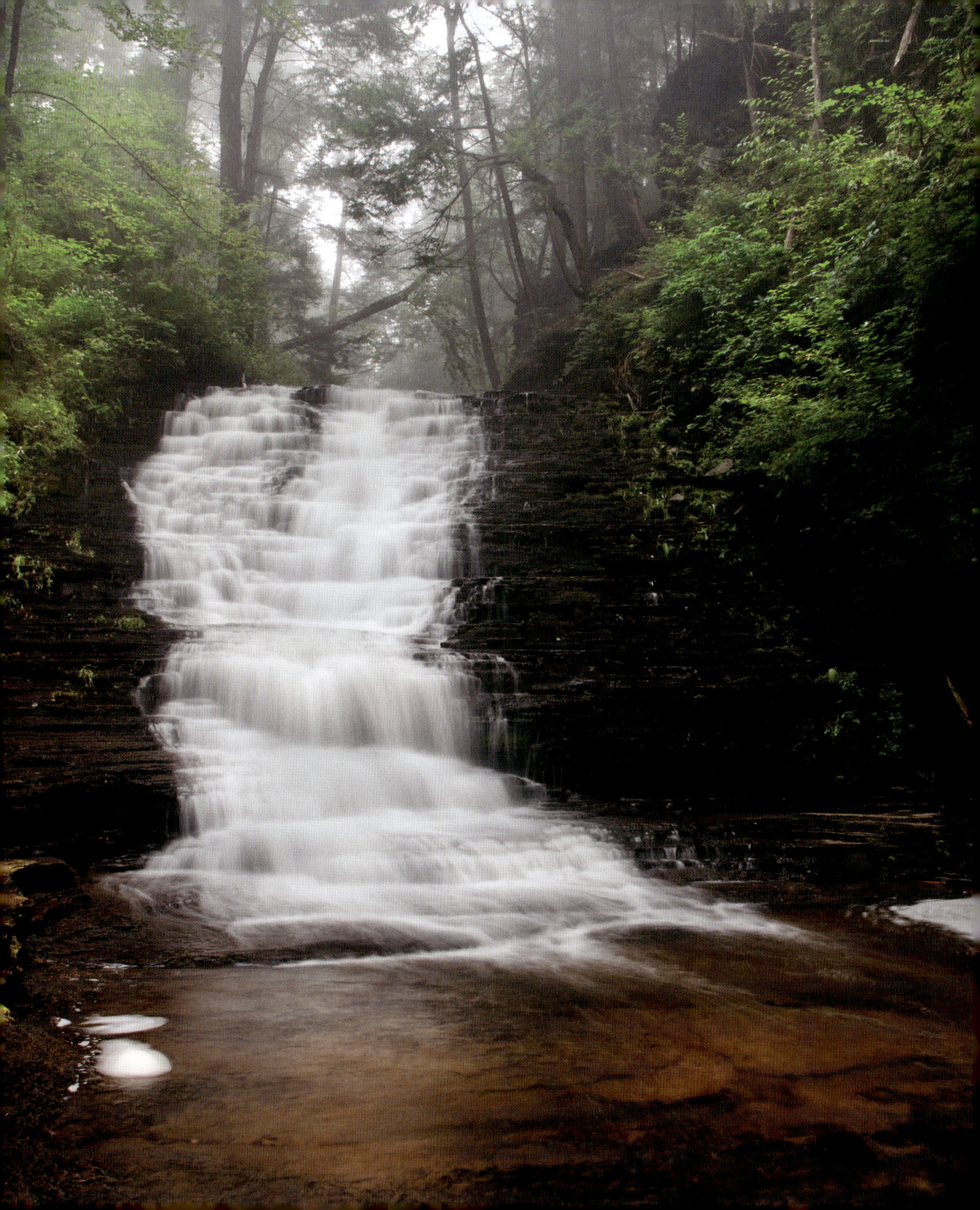

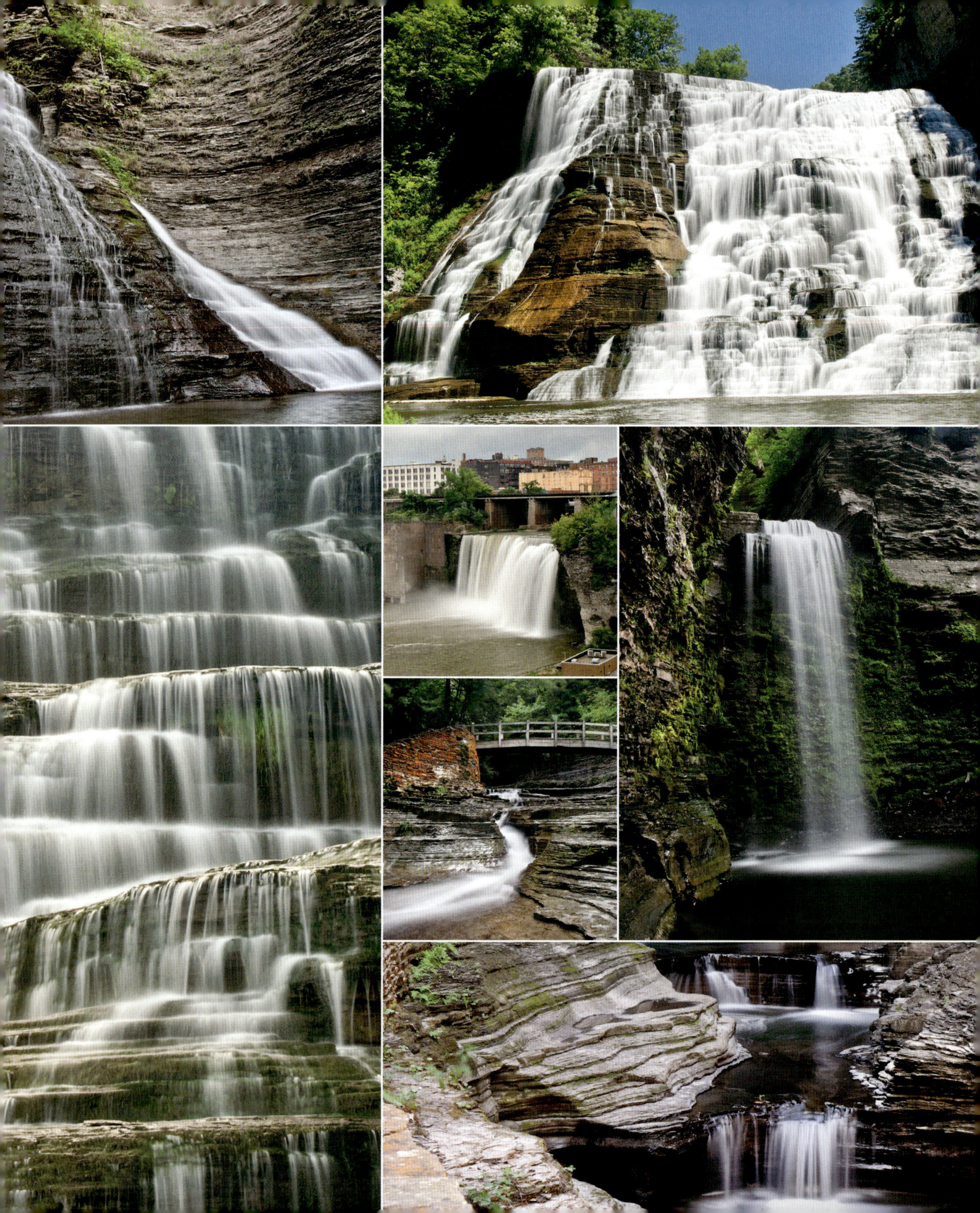

Finger Lakes

Like the imprint of a giant's hands, the Finger Lakes span the center of the state. It is for these distinctively deep, long, narrow lakes that the region is named. The north/south-oriented lakes were formed over two million years by the advance and retreat of glaciers during the last Ice Age. Two of these lakes, Cayuga Lake and Seneca Lake, are among the deepest lakes in the United States.

The fertile Finger Lakes Region is increasingly renowned for its vineyards, but its spectacular scenery remains its core strength. Its lakes and rivers provide incredible recreational opportunities; its landscape is dotted with state parks and national forests. And it is home to some of New York's most impressive waterfalls and deepest chasms, many of which are clustered together in one easy-to-visit location. The 19 waterfalls in unforgettable Watkins Glen State Park are magically tucked along a stream flowing through cliffs that soar 200 feet (60 m) overhead. The Enfield Glen that defines Robert H. Treman State Park itself lays claim to 12 waterfalls.

It's an embarrassment of riches, and the hikes to these waterfalls vary as much as the settings themselves. While a waterfall enthusiast can see several falls in a single day, a focused trip to the Watkins Glen or Ithaca area offers up great waterfall experiences, hiking opportunities and breathtaking views with minimal driving between any of the locations.

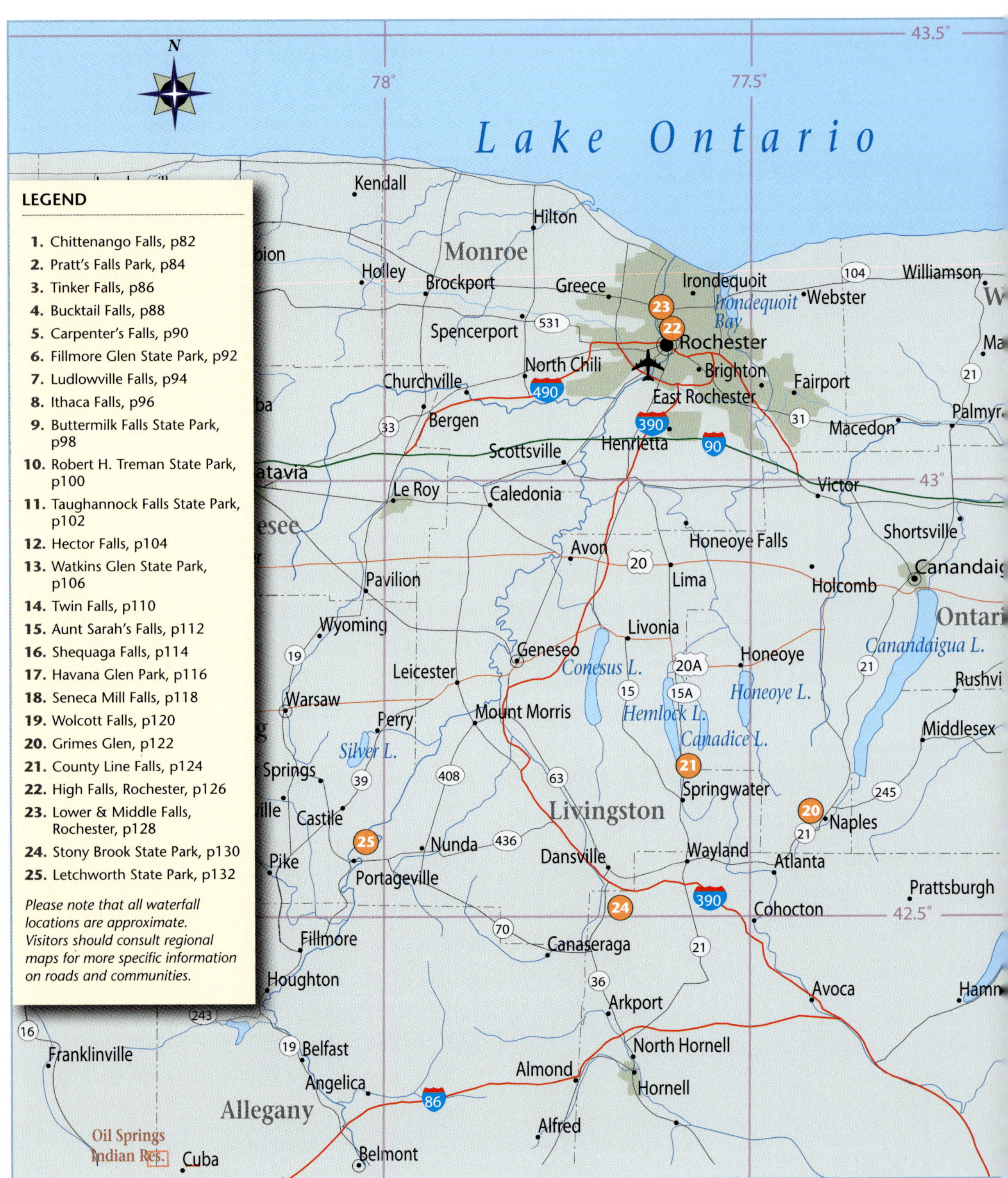

N
Lake Ontario
78°
77.5°
43.5°
43°
42.5°
LEGEND
1. Chittenango Falls, p82
2. Pratt's Falls Park, p84
3. Tinker Falls, p86
4. Bucktail Falls, p88
5. Carpenter's Falls, p90
6. Fillmore Glen State Park, p92
7. Ludlowville Falls, p94
8. Ithaca Falls, p96
9. Buttermilk Falls State Park, p98
10. Robert H. Treman State Park, p100
11. Taughannock Falls State Park, p102
12. Hector Falls, p104
13. Watkins Glen State Park, p106
14. Twin Falls, p110
15. Aunt Sarah's Falls, p112
16. Shequaga Falls, p114
17. Havana Glen Park, p116
18. Seneca Mill Falls, p118
19. Wolcott Falls, p120
20. Grimes Glen, p122
21. County Line Falls, p124
22. High Falls, Rochester, p126
23. Lower & Middle Falls, Rochester, p128
24. Stony Brook State Park, p130
25. Letchworth State Park, p132
Please note that all waterfall locations are approximate. Visitors should consult regional maps for more specific information on roads and communities.
Kendall
Hilton
Monroe
Holley
Brockport
Greece
Irondequoit
Irondequoit Bay
Webster
Williamson
Spencerport
Rochester
North Chili
Churchville
Brighton
Fairport
East Rochester
Bergen
Henrietta
Macedon
Palmyra
Scottsville
Le Roy
Caledonia
Victor
Shortsville
Honeoye Falls
Avon
Lima
Holcomb
Canandaigua L.
Pavilion
Wyoming
Livonia
Geneseo
Conesus L.
Honeoye
Leicester
Warsaw
Hemlock L.
Honeoye L.
Rushville
Perry
Mount Morris
Canadice L.
Middlesex
Silver L.
Springwater
Castile
Livingston
Naples
Nunda
Dansville
Wayland
Atlanta
Pike
Portageville
Cohocton
Prattsburgh
Fillmore
Canaseraga
Houghton
Arkport
Avoca
Franklinville
Belfast
North Hornell
Almond
Hornell
Angelica
Allegany
Alfred
Oil Springs Indian Res.
Cuba
Belmont

Finger Lakes Region

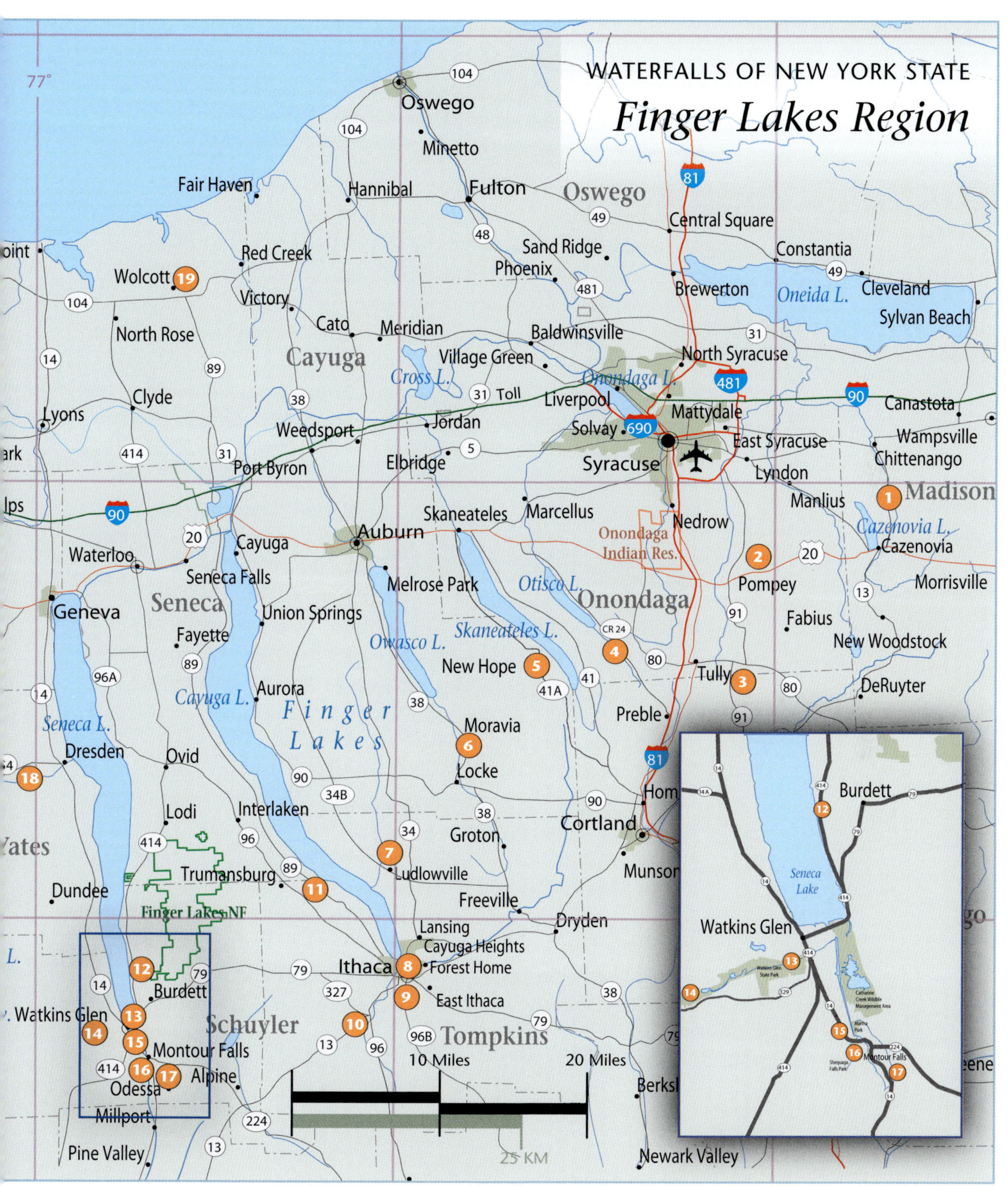

Chittenango Falls

From I-90, take exit 34 and turn left onto NY 13 south (N Peterboro St.). In 1.3 mi (2.1 km), turn right onto NY 13 south/NY 5 west (Seneca Turnpike), and continue for 5.9 mi (9.5 km). At Genesee St., turn left. After 0.7 mi (1.1 km), turn left again onto NY 13 south (Falls Blvd.). Proceed for roughly 5 mi (8 km), and you'll cross a bridge. Take the first road on the right after the bridge into the Chittenango Falls State Park parking area.

COUNTY: Madison

TOWNSHIP: Cazenovia

PLACE: Chittenango Falls

WATERWAY: Chittenango Creek

TYPE: classical falls

HEIGHT: 167 ft (51 m)

TRAIL: dirt and gravel; easy

WALKING TIME: under 5 min

PEAK ACTIVITY: April-Oct.

LATITUDE: 42.9787

LONGITUDE: –75.8415

The sparkling centerpiece of Chittenango Falls State Park, multitiered Chittenango Falls is an irresistible excuse to visit the park, which is located south of Oneida Lake (sometimes referred to as the thumb of the Finger Lakes) and east of Cazenovia Lake. The 167-foot (51 m) waterfall flows over bedrock estimated to be some 400 million years old. Although the waterfall puts on a great show all year, the most scenic views are, without a doubt, on offer in the early summer and fall.

The entire waterfall can be viewed from a large platform at the upper parking area, which is open year-round. From here, follow the railing to the left to reach the lower trail system, downstream from the falls. Be sure to wear good hiking shoes. Although the trails are well maintained, there are portions that are steep and slippery.

Roughly 100 yards (91.4 m) from the base of the falls, a footbridge spanning the creek provides one of the best vantage points in the park. Like the lower trail system, the footbridge is closed during the icy winter months for safety reasons. The lower trail loop is a little over 1 mile (1.6 km) long and snakes in and out of the 200-foot-high (60 m) gorge, affording a number of great views. Other perspectives of the top of the falls and the gorge below can be enjoyed by walking out toward the road.

The 194-acre (78.5 ha) park is home to a variety of plants and wildlife. As you enjoy the falls, look carefully at the cliff sides and moist areas. You may catch a glimpse of the endangered Chittenango ovate amber snail (*Novisuccinea chittenangoensis*). About the size of a dime, the snail sports a camouflaged color that allows it to hide in plain sight in its habitat, which is entirely restricted to this lone waterfall.

Hiking, fishing and picnicking are permitted in the park, whose upper portions are wheelchair-accessible. Family pets are allowed on the trails as long as they are leashed. From April to September, an admission fee is charged for both cars and individual hikers.

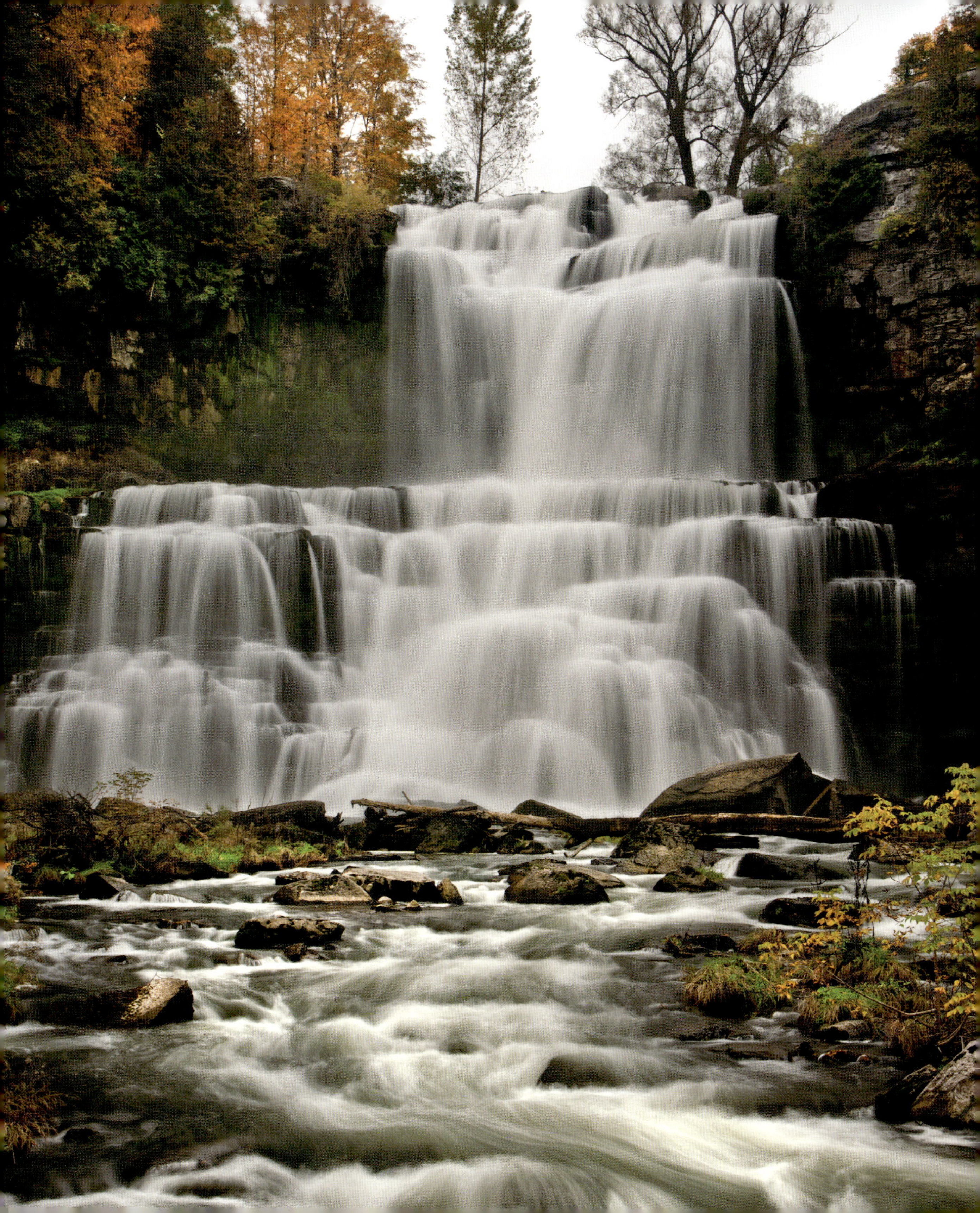

Pratt's Falls Park

From the intersection of NY 20 and NY 91, just south of Pompey, follow NY 20 east for 1 mi (1.6 km) to Gardner Rd., and turn left. Continue for 1.4 mi (2.3 km) to Pratt's Falls Rd., and turn right. After 0.3 mi (0.5 km), turn left into Pratt's Falls Park. The park is open from 8:30 a.m. to 5:30 p.m., April through October. A modest admission fee per car is charged.

COUNTY: Onondaga
TOWNSHIP: Pompey
PLACE: Pompey
WATERWAY: Limestone Creek, West Branch
TYPE: ribbon falls
HEIGHT: 137 ft (41.8 m)
TRAIL: dirt and stairs; moderate
WALKING TIME: 20 min
PEAK ACTIVITY: May-Oct.
LATITUDE: 42.9313
LONGITUDE: –75.9941

Pratt's Falls Park encompasses a little more than 300 acres (121 ha) on the watershed of the West Branch of Limestone Creek. An extremely scenic member of the Onondaga County park system, the park features an archery range, ball fields and picnic areas, as well as an extensive system of trails. Its centerpiece is spectacular Pratt's Falls.

To view this waterfall, park in the northwest corner of the main parking lot and follow the blue markings for the Falls Trail down several flights of stairs into the gorge. At the T-junction, turn left and follow the trail as it curves to the south. The trail ends at a viewing area near the base of the falls. This very steep 137-foot (41.8 m) waterfall faces to the northwest and has an 8-foot-wide (2.4 m) crest. It is developed in the Skaneateles Formation, which consists of a medium to dark gray shale with beds of mudrock and limestone. The formation dates from the Middle Devonian Period, so the rock is roughly 394 million years old.

To view the falls near the crest, return to the top of the gorge and follow the trail west. A viewing area is located on the eastern side of the falls, just before the trail crosses the creek. In 1796, Manoah Pratt, Sr. and Abraham Smith built the county's first sawmill near this site.

Pratt's Falls is not the only waterfall attraction here — there are at least seven unnamed waterfalls in the park. To view the highest one, follow the yellow markings for the North Rim Trail west along the top of the gorge. Roughly 1,000 feet (305 m) west of the park office, the trail crosses the West Branch of Limestone Creek and curves north. A short distance after crossing the creek, turn around and look south for a view of an unnamed waterfall that is roughly 30 feet (9 m) high.

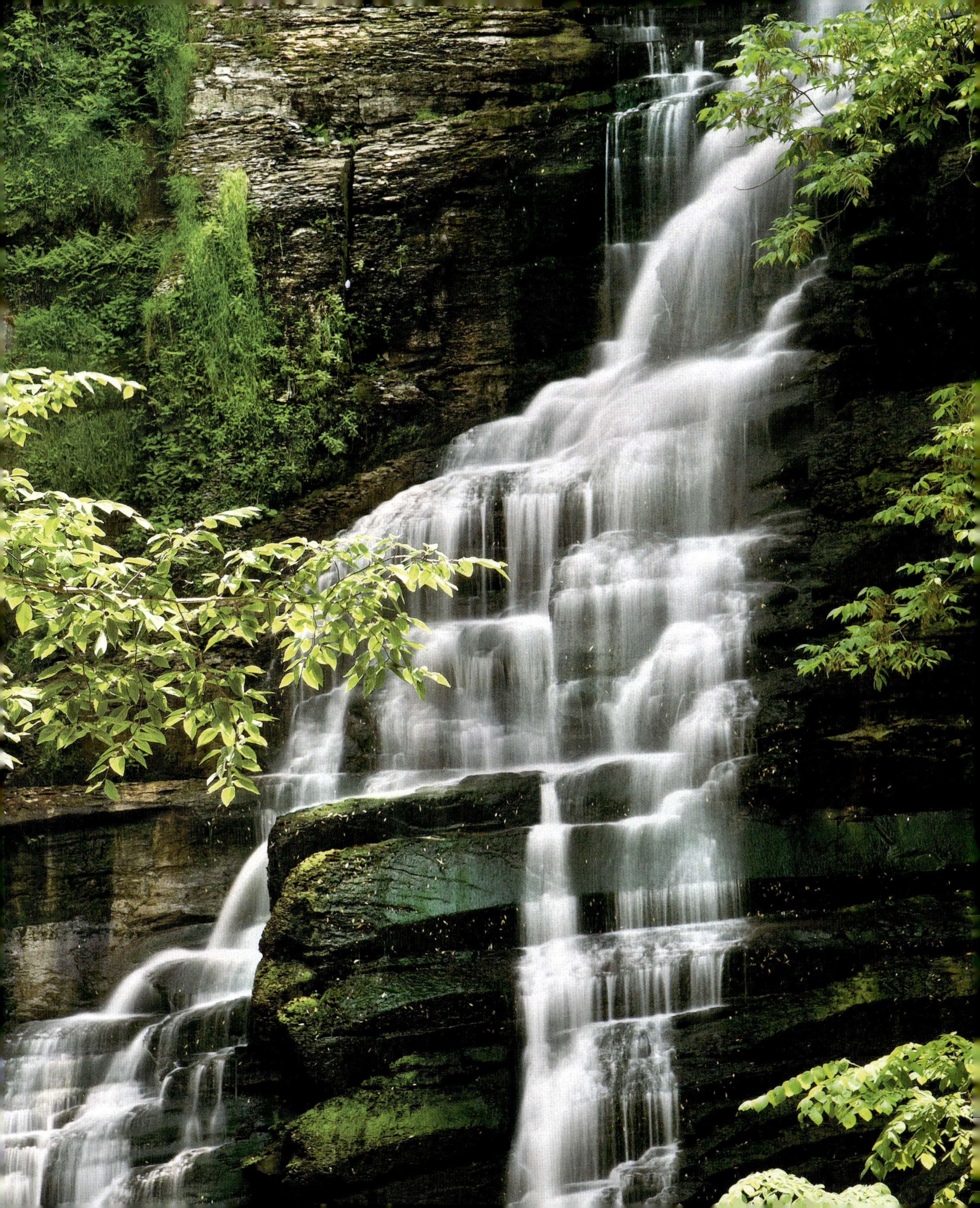

Tinker Falls

From Apulia Station on NY 80, go east for 1 mi (1.6 km) to the intersection with NY 91. Turn right. Roughly 3 mi (4.8 km) south of NY 80, there are three parking areas for Tinker Falls that are easy to miss. Two are located on the west side of NY 91, and one designated as handicapped parking only is on the east side. From either of the western parking areas, cross NY 91, and look for a sign on the northern edge of the eastern parking lot that marks the Universal Access Trail to Tinker Falls.

COUNTY: Cortland
TOWNSHIP: Truxton
PLACE: Apulia Station
WATERWAY: Tinker Falls Creek
TYPE: classical falls
HEIGHT: 45 ft (13.7 m)
TRAIL: stone dust; easy
WALKING TIME: 25 min
PEAK ACTIVITY: May-Oct.
LATITUDE: 42.7831
LONGITUDE: –76.0327

As it passes over a 24-foot-wide (7.3) crest, Tinker Falls Creek drops freely through space for 30 feet (9 m), strikes a ledge and steeply cascades for another 15 feet (4.6 m).

What makes this waterfall truly distinctive is the large overhang at the crest. Roughly 100 feet (30.5 m) wide, 30 feet (9 m) high and 30 feet (9 m) deep, the overhang creates a rare opportunity for visitors to actually walk behind the waterfall. In addition, the waterfall is located in a natural rock amphitheater. The rock is Tully Limestone, a hard, light gray to ashen-colored stone that averages 17 feet (5.2 m) in thickness. It dates from the Middle Devonian Period, making it roughly 391 million years old. The rock below the limestone is known as the Moscow Formation, a mixture of gray to black shales with thin limestone beds.

According to the town historian, there are no facts to explain the waterfall's name. But it is commonly believed that nomadic gypsies, also known as tinkers, moved through the region in the mid-1800s. Skilled tinsmiths who made and mended pots, pans and other household items, the tinkers may have camped at the falls.

The roughly 1,000-foot-long (305 m) Universal Access Trail to the falls is packed stone dust and is wheelchair-accessible. It ends at a viewing area about 200 feet (60 m) before you reach the falls. Unfortunately, trails created by visitors to the waterfall have caused severe erosion and degradation to the area. Construction of a designated trail to the falls, around the falls amphitheater and up to the top of the falls began in late August of 2011 and was scheduled for completion in the fall of 2012.

Tinker Falls is located in the DEC-managed Labrador Hollow Unique Area, a steep-sided glacial valley that features a 120-acre (48.6 ha) glacial lake called Labrador Pond. On the north shore of the pond, there is a wetland boardwalk that can be reached from the Tinker Falls parking areas by driving north on NY 91 for 1.1 miles (1.8 km) and turning left onto Labrador Crossing Road. The access road to the boardwalk is to your left. The wheelchair-accessible boardwalk allows visitors to easily experience the many distinctive wetland plants and animals.

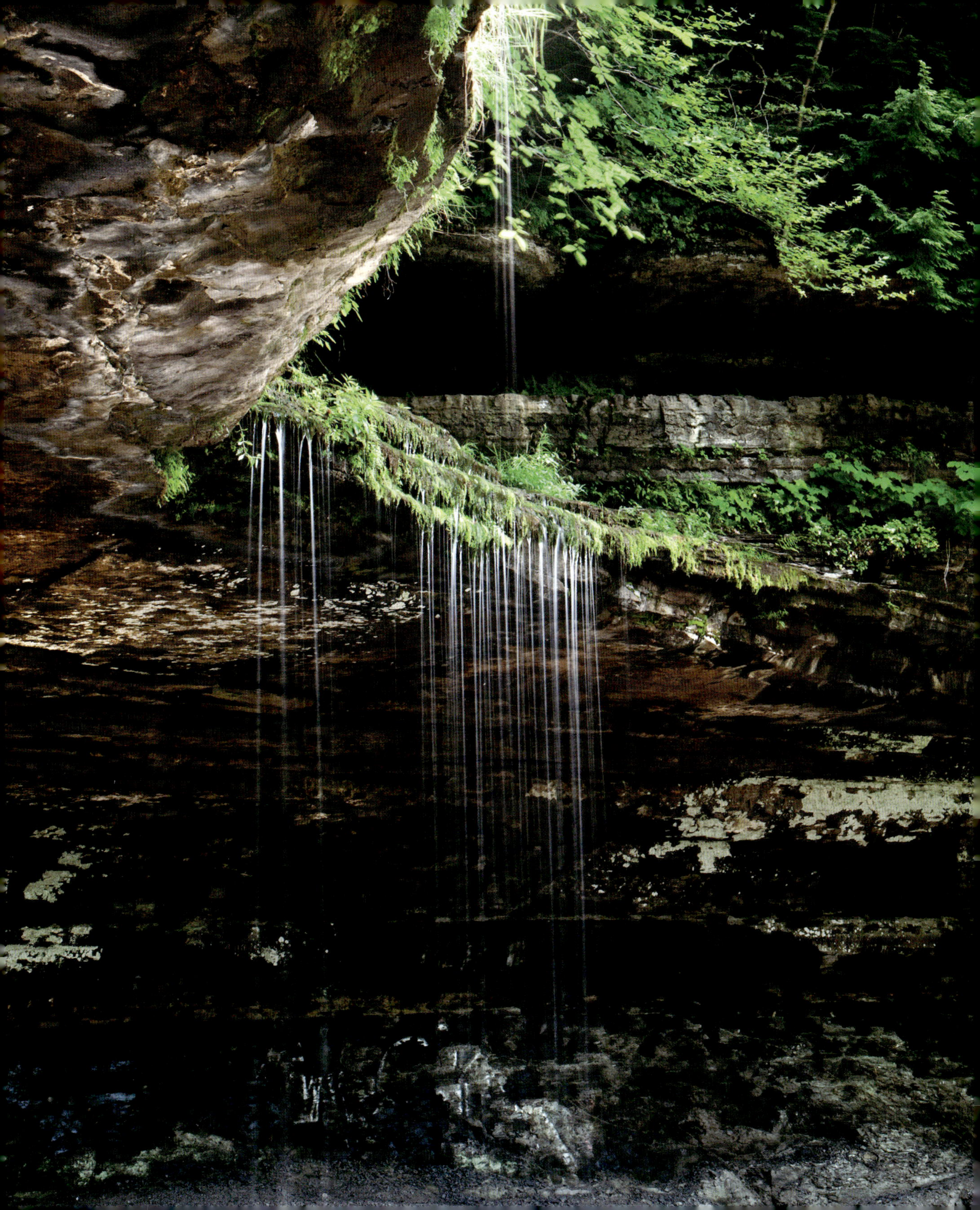

FINGER LAKES REGION

Bucktail Falls

From Amber, on the east side of Otisco Lake, follow Otisco Valley Rd. (CR 124) south for 5.4 mi (8.7 km) to Sawmill Rd. Turn right, and drive 0.6 mi (1 km). Just past West Valley Rd. is a T-junction at Moon Hill Rd. and Masters Rd. Turn right onto Moon Hill Rd., and drive uphill. In less than 100 feet (30.5 m), you'll cross Bucktail Creek. Turn left into a very small parking area. Alternative parking is available on the shoulders of Masters Rd. or Sawmill Rd.

COUNTY: Onondaga
TOWNSHIP: Spafford
PLACE: Amber
WATERWAY: Bucktail Creek
TYPE: ribbon falls
HEIGHT: 28 ft (8.5 m)
TRAIL: dirt; easy
WALKING TIME: 5 min
PEAK ACTIVITY: June-Sept.
LATITUDE: 42.8222
LONGITUDE: –76.2412

Bucktail Falls is located on private property, but in 2011, the owner graciously granted the public permission to view the waterfall. As a result, the property and access trail are currently unposted, but visitors must work together to ensure that the falls remain open to the public. Please keep your time here short, respect the land, and pick up any trash left by others.

From the parking area, follow an unmarked dirt trail southwest. The base of Bucktail Falls is roughly 150 feet (46 m) from Moon Hill Road. The waterfall, which faces northeast, is developed in the Ludlowville Formation of the Middle Devonian Period and comprises black shale with layers of limestone and sandstone. Note the lush green mosses, lichens, liverworts and ferns to the right of the falls. When the leaves are on the trees, the waterfall is in shadow even on the sunniest days.

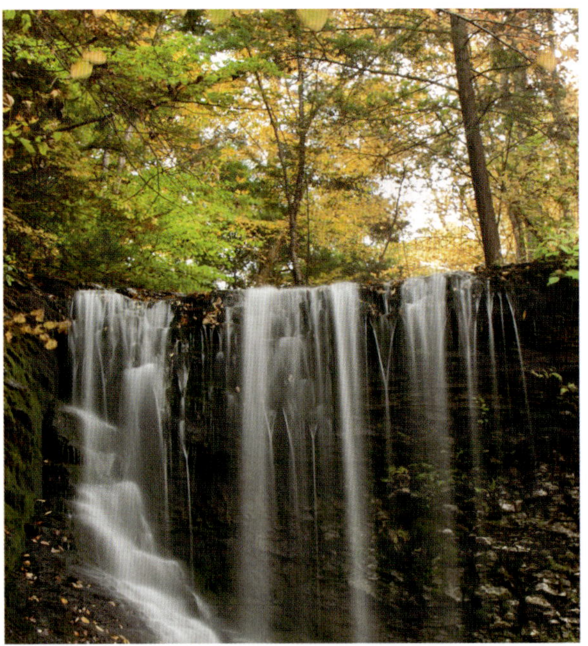

As Bucktail Creek flows over an 11-foot-wide (3.4 m) crest, it falls freely. The veil of falling water then strikes a ledge, turns slightly northward and cascades into a small pool below. On the southern flank of the falls, the vertical drop is about 8 feet (2.4 m), while on the northern flank, the drop is roughly 17 feet (5.2 m). Because of this angled descent, the appearance of Bucktail Falls changes dramatically as you move around the base.

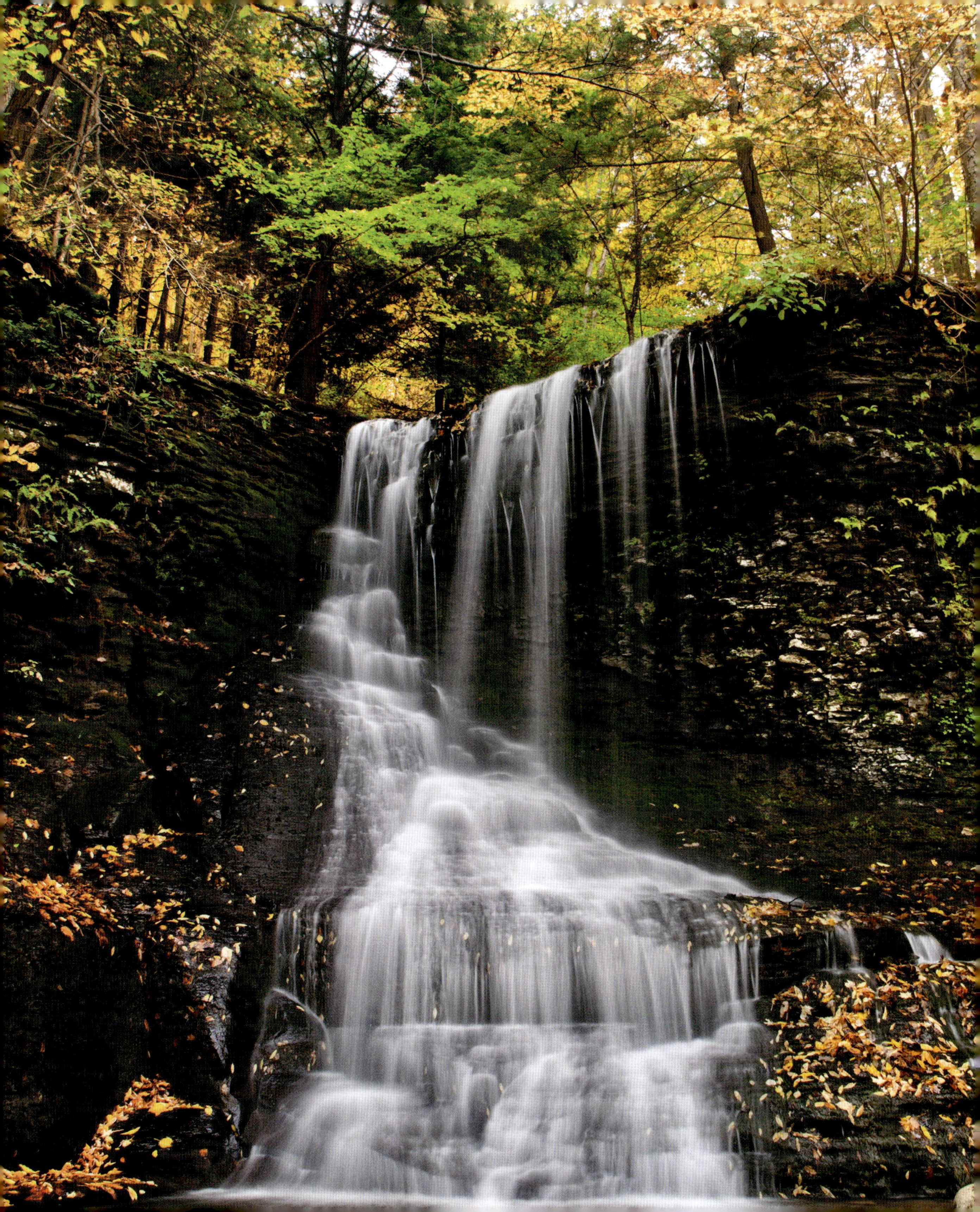

Carpenter's Falls

From New Hope, 7.2 mi (11.6 km) northeast of Moravia, drive north on NY 41A for 0.8 mi (1.3 km) to Appletree Point Rd. Turn right. Follow the winding road for roughly 0.5 mi (0.8 km). Just before a T-junction with Carver Rd. on the right, there is a small parking area for the Carpenter's Falls State Unique Area on the left.

COUNTY: Cayuga

TOWNSHIP: Niles

PLACE: New Hope

WATERWAY: Bear Swamp Creek

TYPE: ribbon falls

HEIGHT: 86 ft (26.2 m)

TRAIL: dirt; moderate

WALKING TIME: 15 min

PEAK ACTIVITY: May-Oct.

LATITUDE: 42.8118

LONGITUDE: –76.3431

In 2008, the Finger Lakes Land Trust transferred 36 acres (14.5 ha) of land around the falls and upper ravine to the Department of Environmental Conservation (DEC), creating the Carpenter's Falls State Unique Area. The Trust owns the lower ravine, which is known as the Bahar Nature Preserve, named for Hu and Dawn Bahar, who owned the original 25-acre (10 ha) preserve. The adjacent land is privately owned. Please respect the landowners' rights, and don't trespass on posted land.

A short distance from the parking area, near the rusting hulk of an old truck, there is an information kiosk posted with a large map. From the kiosk, follow the trail to the left. In just over 500 feet (153 m), you'll find a steep, rugged trail that leads to the base of Carpenter's Falls. Another trail leads behind the falls.

From the Appletree Point Road Bridge, Bear Swamp Creek descends the erosion-resistant Tully Limestone in a series of small drops totaling 10 feet (3 m). The creek is channeled into a narrow notch in the overhanging caprock, then drops vertically 14 feet (4.3 m) down the caprock and free-falls 62 feet (18.9 m) into the plunge pool below. A short distance downstream is a small cascade waterfall. Farther downstream, Bear Swamp Creek flows into Skaneateles Lake.

In 1834, John H. Carpenter and Kenyon Wicks bought the property at the falls, which featured a whiskey distillery that had originally been built by a man named Townsend. Around 1845, Carpenter bought out Wicks and built a gristmill, which was later converted to a sawmill. In 1855, the distillery is said to have produced 550 barrels of whiskey. When Carpenter died in 1865, the business was carried on by his son James.

In the 1870s, the government began imposing heavy taxes on whiskey producers. To evade these taxes, as one story tells it, James Carpenter showed a tax revenue agent some trout in a watering trough near the creek while an employee opened a trapdoor in the distillery and sent the whiskey barrels over the falls.

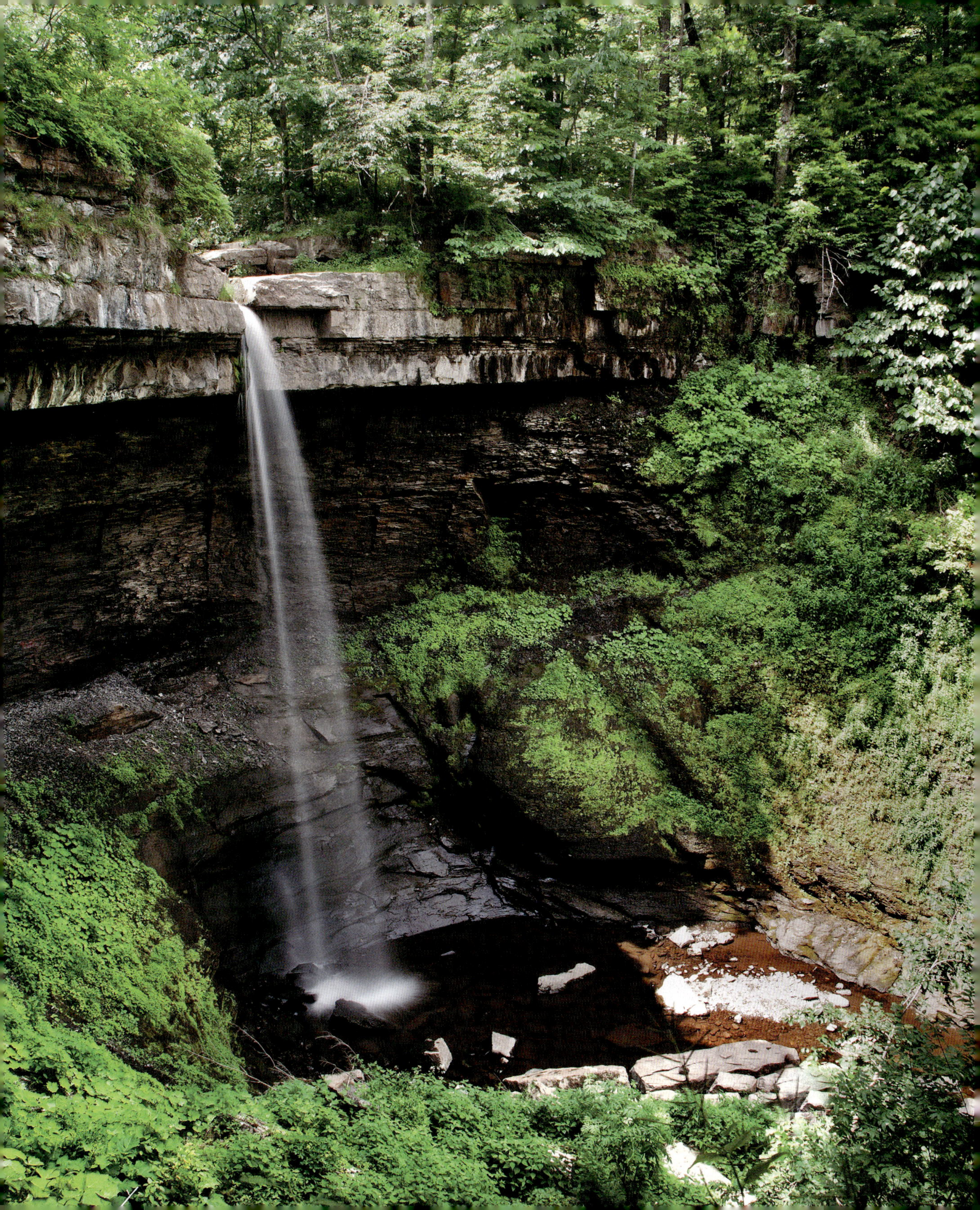

Fillmore Glen State Park

Fillmore Glen State Park is located in south-central Cayuga County. From Moravia, drive south on NY 38 for 1 mi (1.6 km). The entrance to the park is on the left side of the road. (Facing page: Photo © Scott A. Ensminger)

A long, narrow gorge with waterfalls, shady woodlands and a variety of unique rock formations, Fillmore Glen possesses such a diversity of plant life that it inspired amateur botanist Dr. Charles Atwood to lobby for the creation of a public park here in 1921. Ownership was transferred to the state in 1925, and the park was named for the 13th president of the United States, Millard Fillmore, who was born in a log cabin just east of the park in 1800.

At the western end of the park, there is a campground with a stream-fed swimming hole. A short side trail on the northern bank of Dry Creek (sometimes called Fillmore Creek) leads to a large recess created by a ledge of Tully Limestone. It is known as "The Cowsheds," because grazing cows once sheltered there to escape the summer heat.

Next to The Cowsheds is Lower Falls, also called Cowsheds Falls and Dry Falls. The waterfall is 37 feet (11.3 m) high and has a curving crest 42 feet (12.8 m) wide. Its rock face is a mixture of gray to black shale and thin limestone beds known as the Moscow Formation. At the base is a jumble of large limestone boulders.

To view the park's other waterfalls, head back toward the swimming area and cross the stone bridge over the creek. Follow the Gorge Trail eastward as it ascends a steep hill and enters the gorge above Lower Falls. Continue on the trail as it crisscrosses the creek, and after roughly 0.75 mile (1.2 km), you'll see 85-foot-high (26 m) Dalibarda Falls across the gorge. Located on a tributary of Dry Creek, the waterfall has an 8-foot-wide (2.4 m) crest. The upper section is a very steep cascade, while the lower section is nearly vertical.

Shortly after crossing the creek again, you'll come to Lower Pinnacle Falls. It faces northwest and has a 14-foot (4.3 m) drop and a 22-foot-wide (6.7 m) crest. Across the creek and just upstream is the Pinnacle, a large stone spire that has been separated from the gorge wall by erosion. A short distance past the Pinnacle is 14-foot-high (4.3 m) Upper Pinnacle Falls. This north-facing waterfall has a 29-foot-wide (8.8 m) crest. Return the way you came, or continue on to junctions with the North and South Rim trails. You can follow either of these trails downstream to get back to the parking area.

COUNTY: Cayuga

TOWNSHIP: Moravia

PLACE: Moravia

WATERWAY: Dry Creek, or Fillmore Creek

TYPE: classical falls

HEIGHT: 37 ft (11.3 m)

TRAIL: crushed stone and dirt; easy

WALKING TIME: 10 min to Lower Falls

PEAK ACTIVITY: May-Sept.

LATITUDE: 42.6980

LONGITUDE: –76.4128

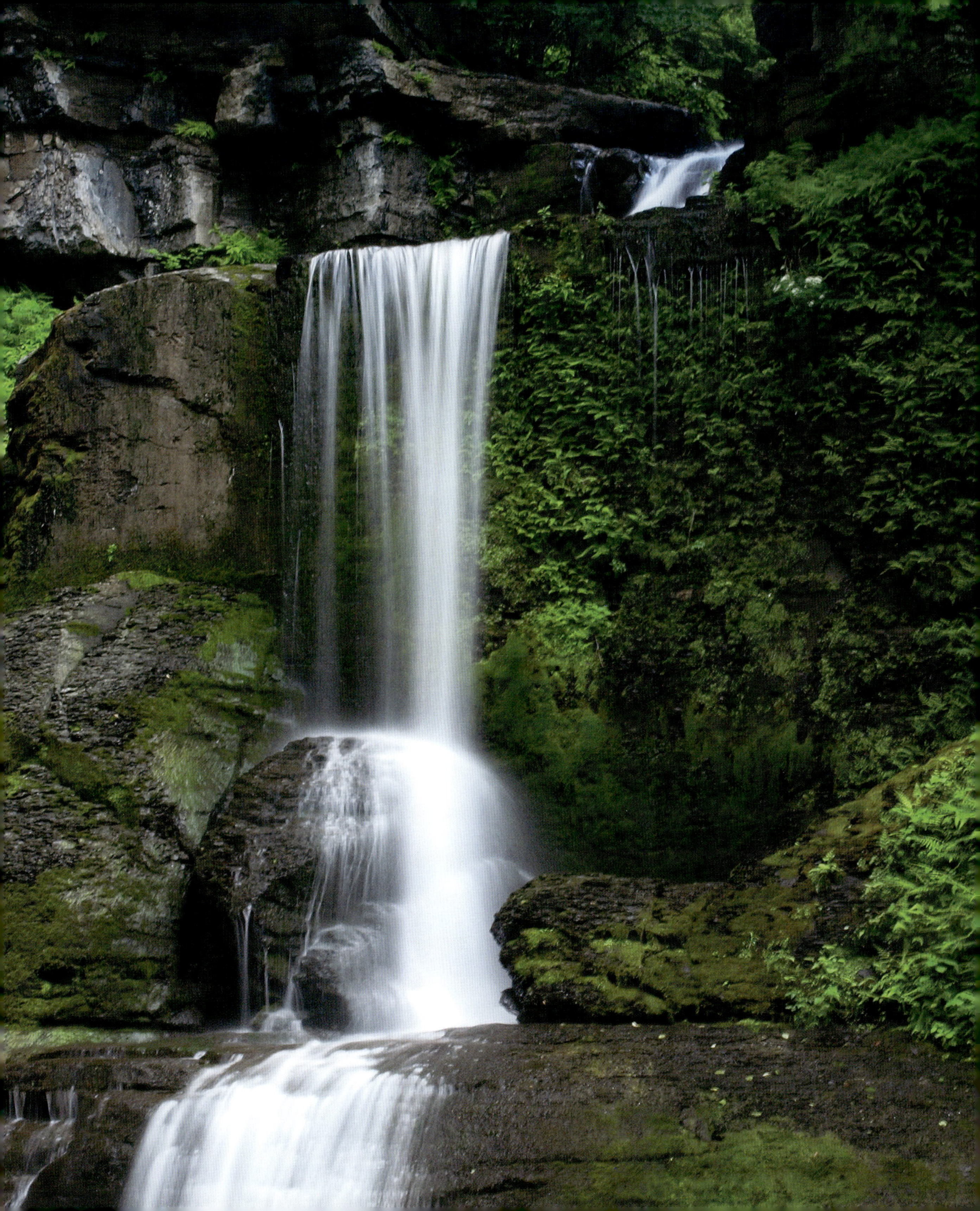

FINGER LAKES REGION

Ludlowville Falls

From the intersection of NY 34 and NY 34B, 5 mi (8 km) north of Ithaca, follow NY 34B north for roughly 2.7 mi (4.3 km) to Ludlowville Rd. Turn right, and continue for 1 mi (1.6 km) until you reach the T-junction at Mill St. The entrance to Ludlowville Park, which is maintained by the Town of Lansing, is across Mill St. and a short jog to the right.

COUNTY: Tompkins
TOWNSHIP: Lansing
PLACE: Ludlowville
WATERWAY: Salmon Creek
TYPE: curtain falls
HEIGHT: 45 ft (13.7 m)
TRAIL: grass; easy
WALKING TIME: 5 min
PEAK ACTIVITY: May-Oct.
LATITUDE: 42.5546
LONGITUDE: –76.5373

From the parking area, walk north past the playground to a chain-link fence. From here, there is an excellent view of Ludlowville Falls, also known as Salmon Creek Falls. The 45-foot-high (13.7 m) waterfall faces to the east-southeast and has a 117-foot-wide (35.7 m) crest. But perhaps the waterfall's most impressive feature is the huge overhang on its southern flank. Made of light gray Tully Limestone, it is 30 feet (9 m) high, 60 feet (18.3 m) wide and 40 feet (12.2 m) deep. Below the limestone is the Moscow Formation, which consists of black shale and thin layers of sandstone and limestone dating from the Middle Devonian Period.

A flume near the northern flank of Salmon Creek typically creates an impressive rooster tail. When the creek runs high, the overhang amplifies the sound of the falling water to an impressive roar and the rooster tail shoots out several feet before plunging to a large Tully Limestone boulder at the base of the falls.

A short distance to the east of the village park, you'll find another waterfall. Exit the park, turn left onto Mill Street, and follow it downhill. At the end of the street, there is a DEC parking area that provides fishing access to Salmon Creek. Walk a short way upstream along the bank — across the creek is Little Ludlowville Falls. The 12-foot-high (3.7 m) waterfall faces west and has a 24-foot-wide (7.3 m) crest.

The village of Ludlowville is named after brothers Henry and Silas Ludlow, who arrived in the area along with Henry's son Thomas in March 1791. In 1795, they built a gristmill near the falls. The small community that grew up around the mill was known as Ludlow's Mill, and a post office was established there in 1806.

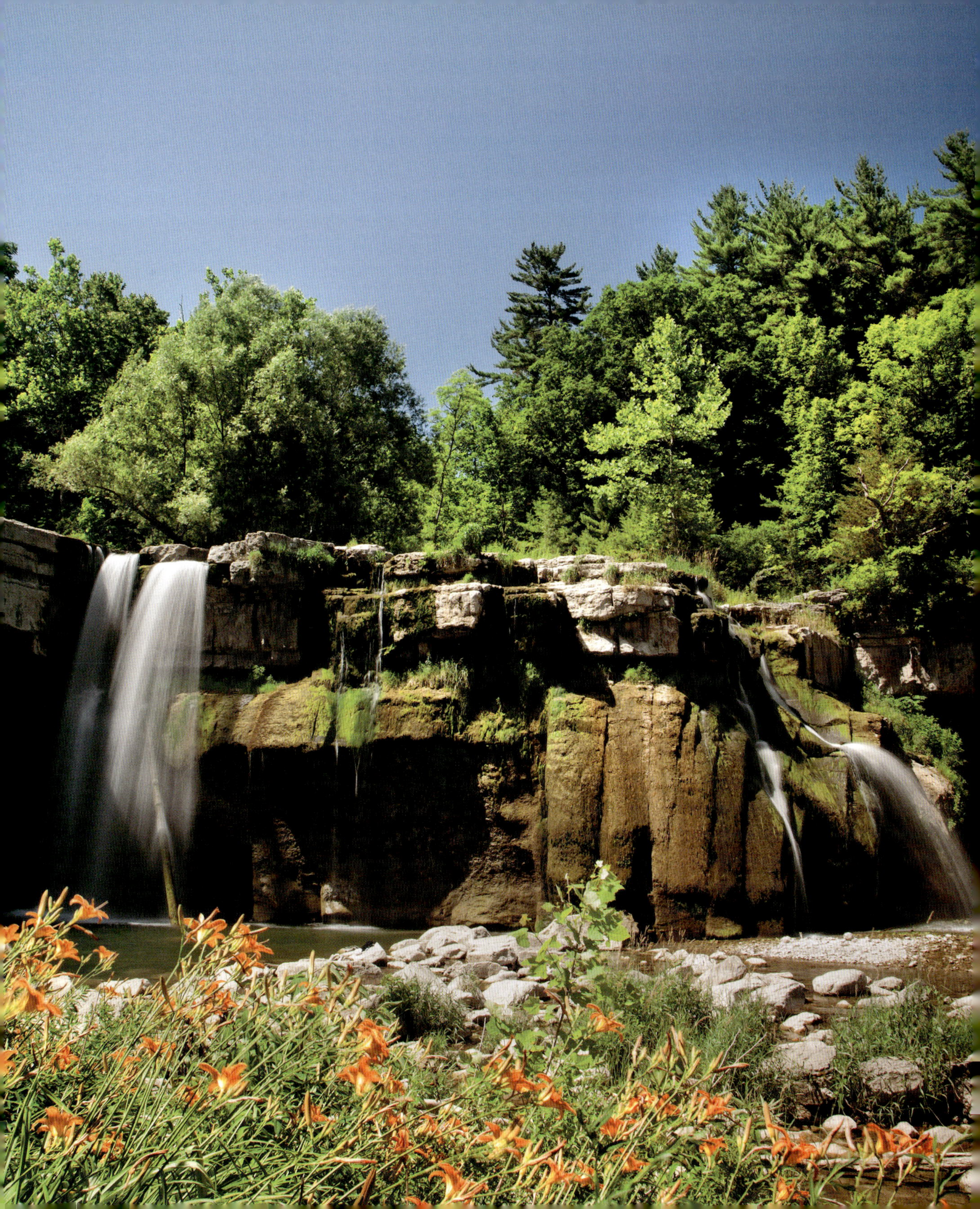

Ithaca Falls

In Ithaca, the falls can be reached from NY 13 and NY 34 by taking the Dey St. exit. Once on Dey St., turn left at the first intersection onto West Lincoln St., which changes to East Lincoln St. three blocks after you cross North Cayuga St. Continue on East Lincoln St. for five blocks until it meets Lake St. Turn left onto Lake St., and make an immediate right into a small parking area for Ithaca Falls. If the lot is full, street parking may be available nearby.

COUNTY: Tompkins

TOWNSHIP: Ithaca

PLACE: Ithaca

WATERWAY: Fall Creek

TYPE: classical cascade

HEIGHT: 150 ft (46 m)

TRAIL: stone; easy

WALKING TIME: 15 min

PEAK ACTIVITY: May-Oct.

LATITUDE: 42.4529

LONGITUDE: –76.4923

From the intersection of East Falls Street and Lake Street, cross Lake Street and walk north over the Lake Street Bridge. On the right is an excellent view of Ithaca Falls.

To reach the base of this impressive cataract, follow a trail along the southern bank of Fall Creek. The trail starts in a small grassy area at the southeast corner of the bridge. After descending a few steps, continue east on the trail. Watch for a small ribbon waterfall on your right, located on a tributary of Fall Creek. Follow the trail for about 1,000 feet (305 m) to the base of Ithaca Falls.

This immense waterfall is 150 feet (46 m) high, with a 175-foot-wide (53 m) crest. It faces north-northwest and has a multitude of closely spaced vertical leaps and extremely steep cascades. The sedimentary rock layers that make up the face of the falls are known as the Ithaca Formation, a mixture of shale, sandstone and limestone from the Late Devonian Period. Since the glaciers receded from the area some 10,000 years ago, Ithaca Falls has retreated upstream roughly 800 feet (244 m).

When the volume of Fall Creek is high, the thundering waters can be somewhat intimidating, but if conditions are right, a breathtaking rainbow spans the creek in front of the waterfall. During low water, the waterfall is broken up into numerous sparkling cascades.

The deep plunge pool at the base of the falls is a popular fishing spot for lake trout and salmon, but swimming in the pool or climbing the falls or adjacent cliffs is strictly prohibited. There have been a few fatalities at this site.

Around 1815, settlers began to build mills near the falls, eventually to be replaced by factories that exploited the creek's abundant water power. The most infamous factory, however, was the Ithaca Gun Company, which opened in 1883 and operated here until 1987. Gun testing left millions of tiny lead shotgun pellets embedded in the gorge next to the falls. In 1998, DEC tested soil adjacent to the falls and found lead levels as high as 215,000 parts per million, more than 500 times the recommended safe level. Environmental cleanup efforts in this beautiful area are ongoing.

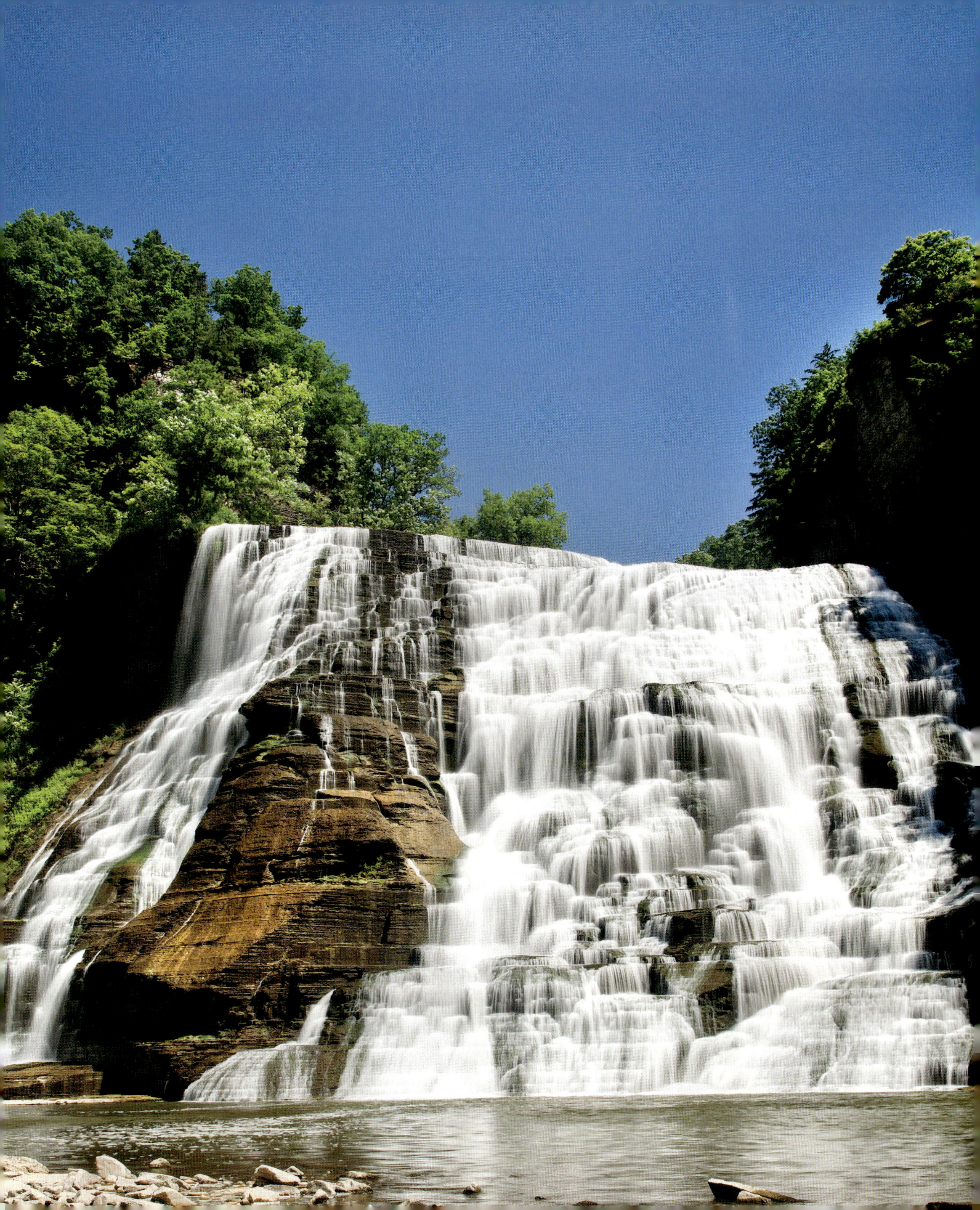

FINGER LAKES REGION

Buttermilk Falls State Park

The lower entrance to Buttermilk Falls State Park is 2 mi (3.2 km) south of Ithaca, on the southeast side of NY 13 (Elmira Rd.), just before you cross Buttermilk Creek.

The upper entrance is on West King Rd., 3.6 mi (5.8 km) from the lower entrance. Starting at the lower entrance, exit the park and turn left onto NY 13. After about 500 ft (153 m), turn left onto Sand Bank Rd and follow it for 2.3 mi (3.7 km), until it forms a T-junction with West King Rd. Turn left. Drive for 1.3 mi (2.1 km), and turn right into the upper entrance for the park.

COUNTY: Tompkins

TOWNSHIP: Ithaca

PLACE: Ithaca

WATERWAY: Buttermilk Creek

TYPE: ribbon cascade

HEIGHT: 90 ft (27 m)

TRAIL: stone with many steps; moderate

WALKING TIME: 10 min to Buttermilk Falls; 1.5 hr to view all the waterfalls in the park

PEAK ACTIVITY: May-Sept.

LATITUDE: 42.4158

LONGITUDE: –76.5200

As you drive into the lower entrance of Buttermilk Falls State Park, you'll catch a glimpse of this park's namesake. From the parking area, walk to the southwest, past the small concession stand, to the downstream end of the swimming area, which is the starting point for the Gorge Trail. As you cross the creek, stop in the middle of the bridge for a grand view of Buttermilk Falls.

This cascade faces north-northwest and has a total natural drop of 90 feet (27 m). When the dam for the swimming area is in place, the drop is shortened by roughly 5 feet (1.5 m). The waters of Buttermilk Creek pour over the 45-foot-wide (13.7 m) crest and descend a series of small, evenly spaced steps. Tumbling over step after step causes the creek to churn and bubble, creating a dazzling white plume of foam all the way to the plunge pool. When the creek volume is low, the waters hiss and sizzle. At high volume, the waters rumble and roar.

The sedimentary rock layers in the lower part of Buttermilk Falls Glen are known as the Ithaca Formation, a mixture of shale and limestone. In the upper reaches of the glen, the rocks are from the Sonyea Group, a mixture of shale, mudstone, sandstone and siltstone. Both the Ithaca Formation and Sonyea Group date from the Late Devonian Period.

Look above the crest of Buttermilk Falls, and you'll see the lower half of 80-foot-high (24.4 m) Upper Buttermilk Falls, sometimes called the Second Falls. It is steeper than the falls below it, faces north and has a 75-foot-wide crest (23 m). As at Buttermilk Falls, the creek descends Upper Buttermilk Falls in a dazzling white plume of foam.

Buttermilk Creek drops more than 550 feet (167.6 m) as it flows through Buttermilk Falls State Park. Along the creek's course, there are a number of waterfalls and several sets of rapids. Once you've enjoyed Buttermilk Falls, continue your hike along the park's trail system and discover the many natural treasures in this state park.

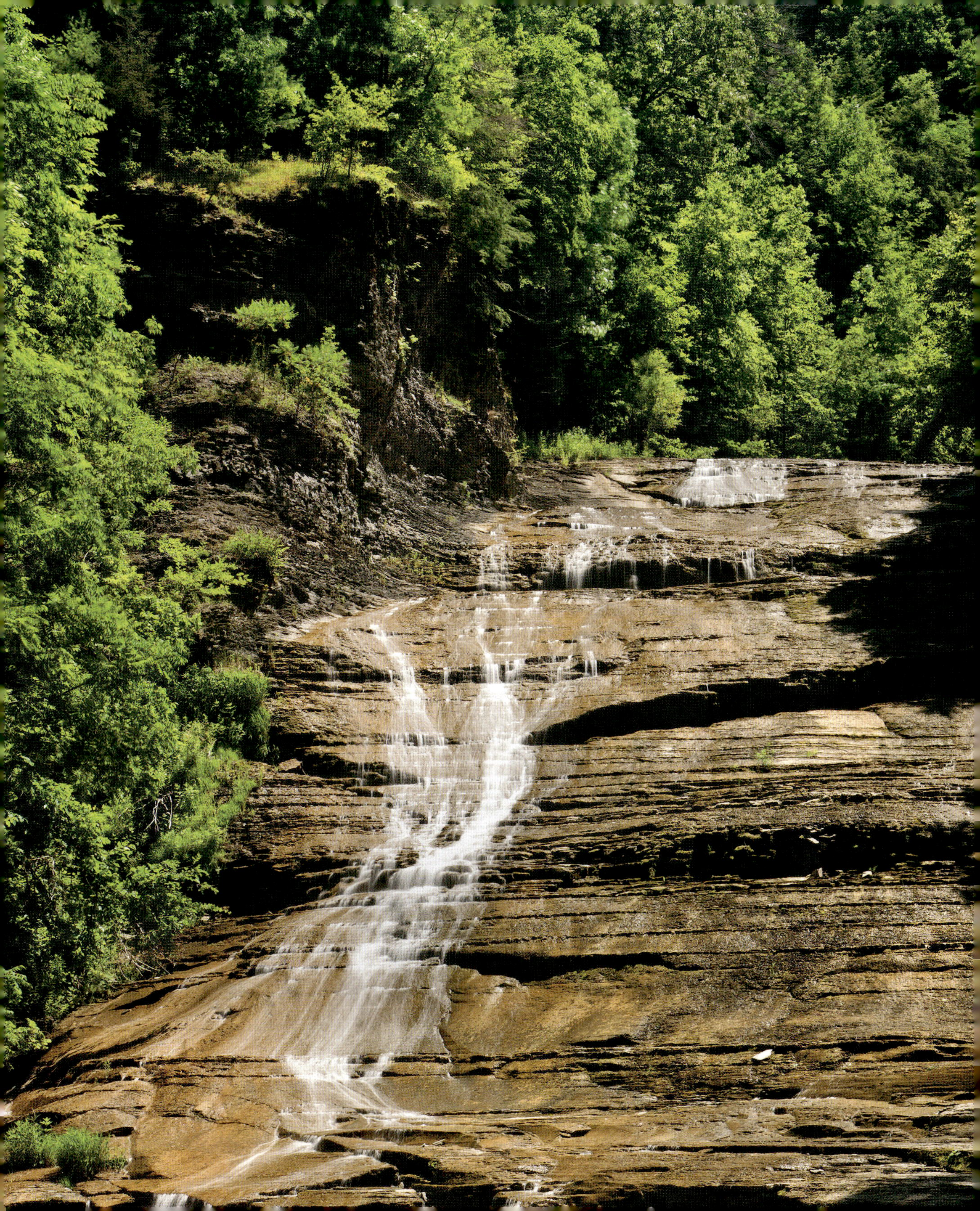

Robert H. Treman State Park

From the intersection of NY 13 and NY 327, 2 mi (3.2 km) south of Ithaca, follow NY 327 west for 0.3 mi (0.5 km) to the lower entrance to Robert H. Treman State Park. It is another 2.2 mi (3.5 km) to the upper entrance, where you'll find parking in the lot closest to the Old Mill.

COUNTY: Tompkins

TOWNSHIP: Enfield and Ithaca

PLACE: Ithaca

WATERWAY: Enfield Creek

TYPE:
Falls by the Old Mill: complex falls
Lucifer: ribbon falls
Lower: classical cascade

HEIGHT:
Falls by the Old Mill: 15 ft (4.6 m)
Lucifer: 115 ft (35 m)
Lower: 32 ft (9.8 m)

TRAIL:
stone with steps; moderate

WALKING TIME:
10 min to first falls;
1.5 hr to view all the falls

PEAK ACTIVITY: May-Oct.

LATITUDE:
Falls by the Old Mill: 42.4018
Lucifer: 42.4006
Lower: 42.3974

LONGITUDE:
Falls by the Old Mill: –76.5896
Lucifer: –76.5843
Lower: –76.5612

A rugged shale and limestone gorge known as Enfield Glen and a waterfall-studded waterway named Enfield Creek are the centerpiece of Robert H. Treman State Park. The hike along the creek to visit these falls is demanding but rewarding. Maps posted at the trailheads provide more detailed directions.

The Old Mill is located in an area once known as Enfield Falls, a community that grew up around the mill in the early 1800s. Behind the mill on a creek called Fish Kill is the Falls by the Old Mill, a terraced waterfall with two nearly equal leaps that total 15 feet (4.6 m). A small set of rapids just downstream adds to the charm. Keep walking downstream for roughly 400 feet (122 m), turn right and cross Fish Kill. A large wooden sign indicates the park trails. Follow the Gorge Trail into the glen, past several chutes, flumes and small waterfalls. Across a bridge, you'll find 15-foot-high (4.6 m) Devil's Kitchen Falls.

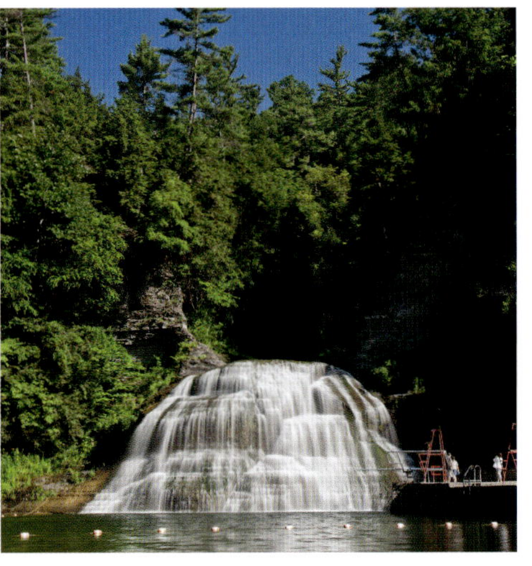

Just beyond that is Lucifer Falls, which plunges 115 feet (35 m) between towering gorge walls. The trail quickly descends deeper into the gorge. Continue along the trail and cross a bridge on your right. The Rim Trail climbs the side of the gorge in a series of switchbacks. When you reach the top, you'll be rewarded with a stunning view of Lucifer Falls.

Enter the park from the lower entrance to view the picturesque 32-foot-high (9.8 m) Lower Falls, which faces south and falls directly into the swimming area. Enfield Creek is about 20 feet (6.1 m) wide as it flows from the shadowy glen above the falls. After passing over the convex crest, the sparkling waters fan out quickly and descend the steeply sloped face of the falls.

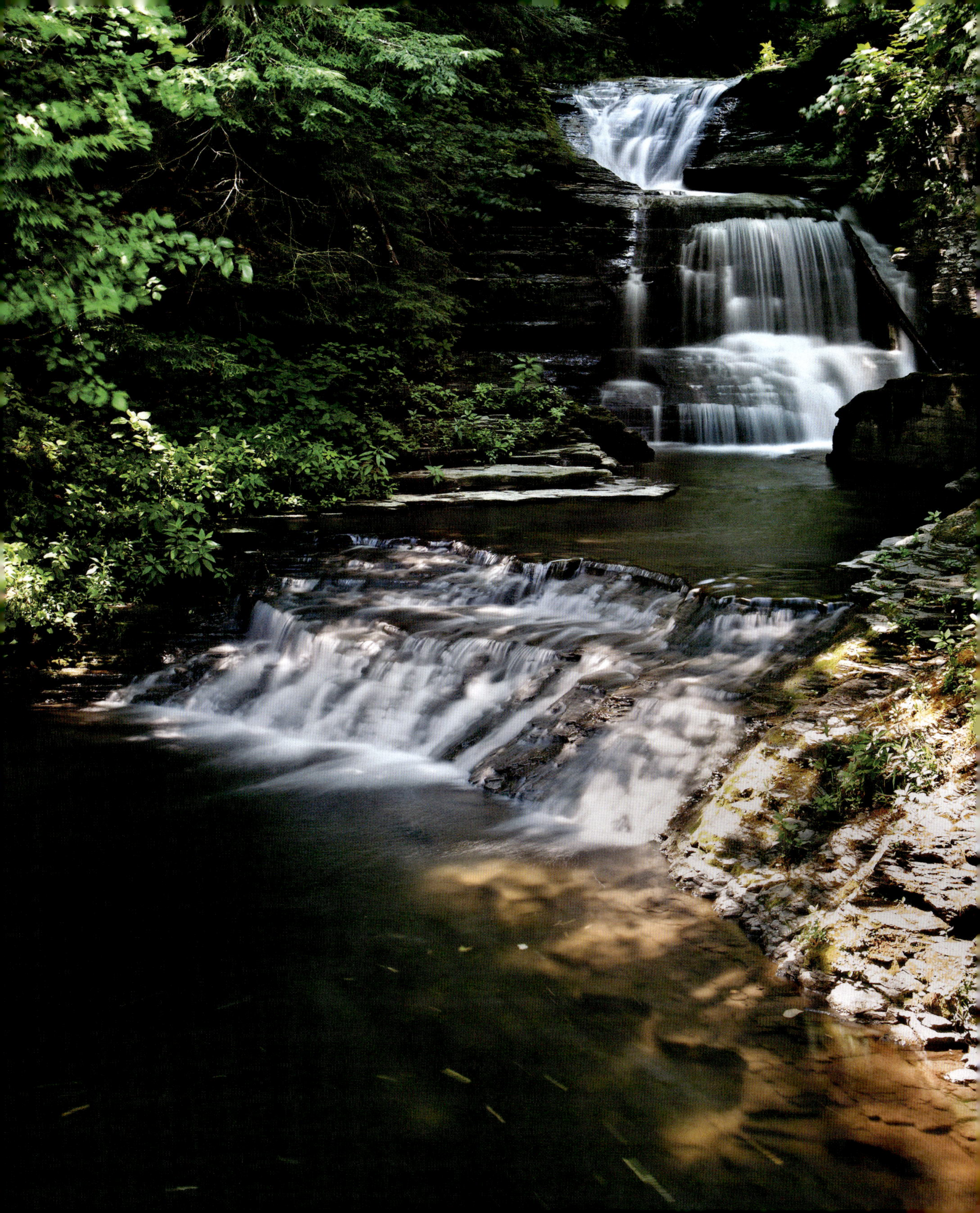

Taughannock Falls State Park

Taughannock Falls State Park is located 8 mi (12.9 km) north of Ithaca on NY 89. The gorge parking area is located on the left side of NY 89, just past Gorge Rd.

COUNTY: Tompkins

TOWNSHIP: Ulysses

PLACE: Trumansburg

WATERWAY: Taughannock Creek

TYPE: ribbon falls

HEIGHT: Taughannock: 215 ft (65.5 m) Upper Taughannock: 80 ft (24.4 m)

TRAIL: stone; easy

WALKING TIME: 5 min to first waterfall; 1 hr. 15 min to view all the waterfalls in the park

PEAK ACTIVITY: May-Oct.

LATITUDE: Taughannock: 42.5366 Upper Taughannock: 42.5324

LONGITUDE: Taughannock: –76.6101 Upper Taughannock: –76.6159

Following the Gorge Trail west from the gorge parking area along the bank of Taughannock Creek in Taughannock Falls State Park, you'll soon encounter 20-foot-high (6.1 m) Lower Taughannock Falls. With a crest roughly 70 feet wide (21.3 m), the waterfall is capped by Tully Limestone of the Middle Devonian Period.

Continue hiking upstream along the easy and very scenic Gorge Trail. In less than 1 mile (1.6 km), you'll reach a bridge over the creek. From there, you'll get your first view of Taughannock Falls. Once you cross the creek, it is a short distance to a lookout near the base of the falls.

Taughannock Creek takes a dramatic plunge in one glorious leap. At 215 feet (65.5 m), it is the highest single vertical-drop waterfall in the northeastern United States. The view of the falls is stunning, with the encircling cliffs soaring to a height of roughly 400 feet (122 m). Look closely at the cliff face, and you'll notice three major rock formations. About 25 feet (7.6 m) above the 35-foot-wide (10.7 m) crest, the rock layer is known as Ithaca Shale, dating from the Late Devonian Period. Below are the tan layers of the Sherburne Formation, a mixture of sandstone and siltstone layers about 150 feet (46 m) thick. The natural joint and bedding plane structure of the rock causes it to break off in rectangular blocks. Beneath that is a 90-foot (27 m) layer of black Geneseo Shale. The creekbed downstream from the plunge pool is lined with Tully Limestone.

For another outstanding view of Taughannock Falls, turn left onto NY 89 from the gorge parking area, then left onto Taughannock Park Road. In just under 1 mile (1.6 km), you'll come to the Falls Overlook parking area, on the left. On the southeastern edge of the parking area, a stairway leads down to the overlook, which offers a spectacular view of the falls and its amphitheater.

You can also enjoy 80-foot-high (24.4 m) Upper Taughannock Falls by following the park road from the Falls Overlook lot for 0.5 mile (0.8 km) and turning left onto Jacksonville Road. Cross Taughannock Creek and turn left into a small parking area. Follow the Rim Trail to the top of an abandoned railroad embankment. From the bridge, you'll have a great view of the falls once known as First Fall.

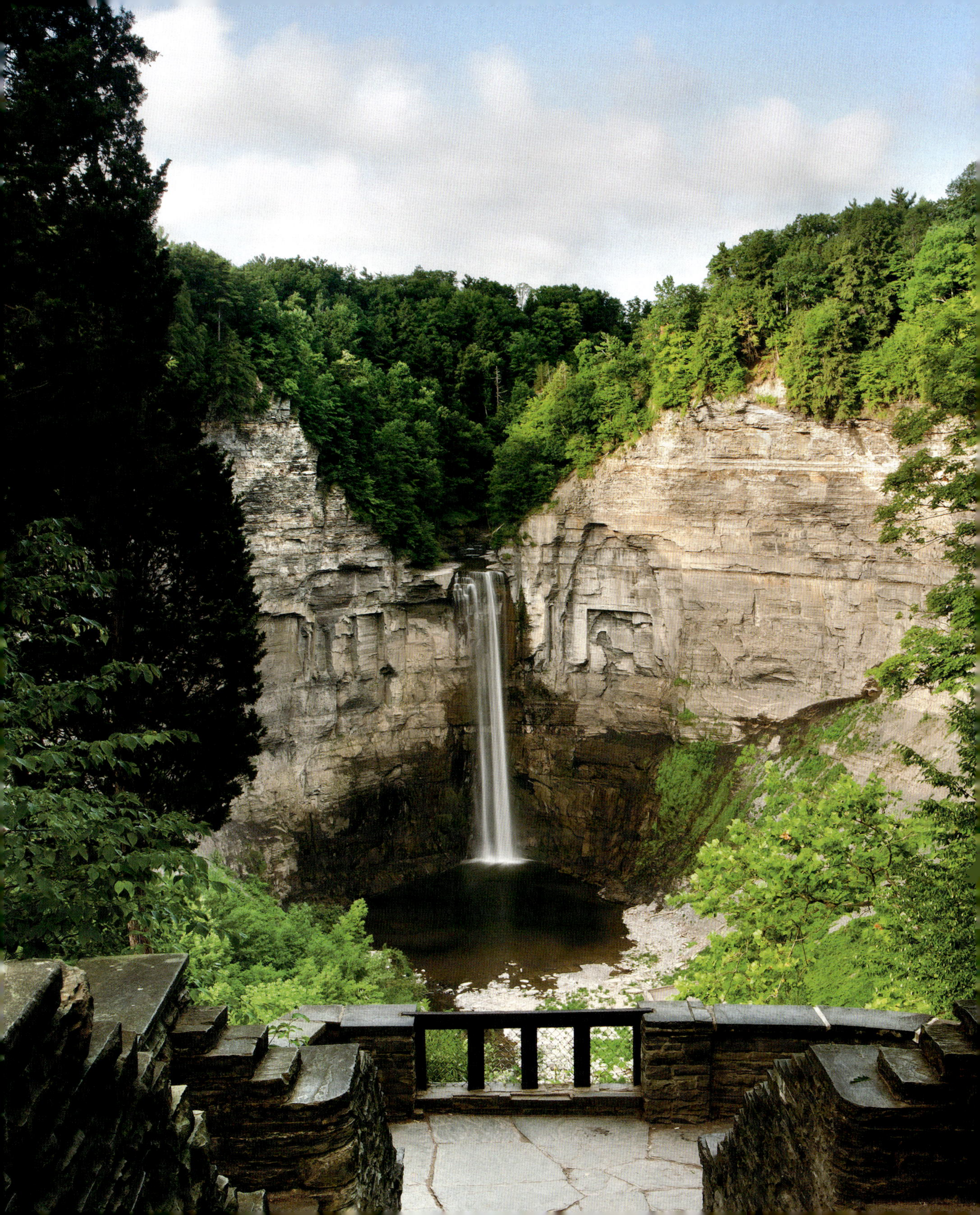

Hector Falls

From Watkins Glen, follow NY 414 (East 4th St.) east. After rounding the tip of Seneca Lake, keep to the left. Hector Falls is located about 1.5 mi (2.4 km) past NY 79. Parking is available along each side of NY 414, immediately north and south of the bridge that crosses Hector Falls Creek. After parking your car, walk to the center of the bridge for an up-close view of the first section of this three-tiered waterfall.

The first section of Hector Falls, which faces to the west, is roughly 50 feet high (15.3 m) and has a crest about 25 feet (7.6 m) wide. This section consists of innumerable vertical plunges and near-vertical cascades. During its descent of the cliff, the waterfall widens considerably and the view of the sparkling waters splashing and tumbling down the cliff is dazzling. The more adventurous falls viewers may want to hop over the guardrail near the northeastern parking area and scramble down to the creekbed for another magnificent perspective.

From the other side of the bridge, you can look down on the crests of the second and third sections of this waterfall, which are on private land. On the western horizon, there is a grand view of Seneca Lake and its western shore in the distance, roughly 150 feet (46 m) below you. The total height of Hector Falls is reported as 165 feet (50.3 m). The hillside that Hector Falls Creek descends is composed of West River Shale, Genundewa Limestone, Penn Yan Shale and Geneseo Shale, all of the Late Devonian Period.

The Town of Hector was established in 1802, and the township is the largest in Schuyler County. In 1801, Samuel Seely (Seeley) erected a woolen mill at the falls, the first in the county, and added a gristmill and log mill in 1805. The county's first store was built near the falls and run by John Seely (Seeley).

In the fall of 1823, a schooner named the *Mary and Hannah*, owned by John Osborne and Samuel Seely (Seeley), was loaded with 800 bushels of wheat, three tons of butter and four barrels of beans. Captained by a man named Jackson, the boat departed Hector Falls Point and plied the Seneca and Erie canals and the Hudson River, delivering the cargo to New York City on November 17. It is believed to be the first produce shipped from the western part of the state via the canal system.

COUNTY: Schuyler

TOWNSHIP: Hector

PLACE: Burdett

WATERWAY: Hector Falls Creek

TYPE: ribbon falls

HEIGHT: 50 ft (15.3 m)

TRAIL: roadway; easy

WALKING TIME: 5 min

PEAK ACTIVITY: May-Oct.

LATITUDE: 42.4180

LONGITUDE: –76.8664

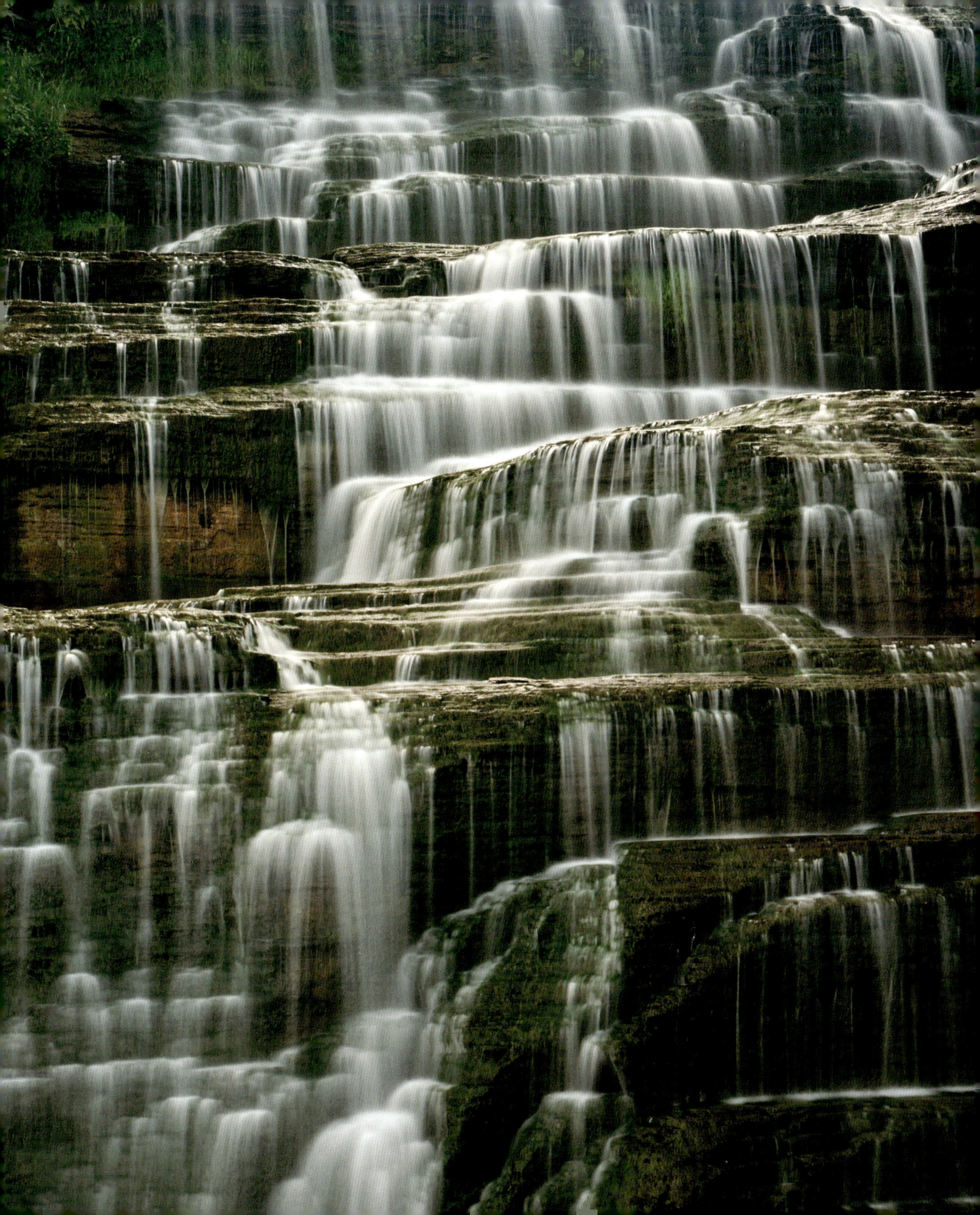

FINGER LAKES REGION

Watkins Glen State Park

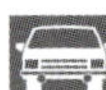

Starting from the junction of NY 414 and NY 14, in the village of Watkins Glen, drive south on NY 14 (N Franklin St.) for 0.4 mi (0.6 km), and turn right into the main, or lower, entrance of Watkins Glen State Park.

COUNTY: Schuyler

TOWNSHIP: Dix

PLACE: Watkins Glen

WATERWAY: Glen Creek

TYPE: several

HEIGHT: 19 waterfalls, ranging from 5 ft (1.5 m) to 95 ft (29 m)

TRAIL: stone and many steps; moderate

WALKING TIME: 10 min to first falls from parking area; 3 hr to view all the waterfalls

PEAK ACTIVITY: May-Oct.

LATITUDE: 42.3747

LONGITUDE: –76.8742

Cutting through sedimentary layers of West River Shale, Genundewa Limestone, Penn Yan Shale and Geneseo Shale, all of the Late Devonian Period, the waters of Glen Creek have sculpted a famously scenic gorge that features high cliffs, fantastically carved potholes, sparkling pools and marvelous waterfalls. The village was named for Dr. Samuel Watkins, who settled in the area in 1828. The glen was opened to the public in 1863, after British businessman and journalist Morvalden Ells installed trails, stairways and bridges. In 1906, the glen was purchased by the state.

The best way to view the glen's waterfalls is to hike uphill from the main entrance (sometimes called the lower entrance), along the 1.5-mile (2.4 km) Gorge Trail, to the upper entrance. The trail has more than 830 steps and ascends roughly 500 feet (153 m). Sections are often very wet, either from the spray of the waterfalls or from springs, and hiking boots are recommended. To return to the main entrance, hike back along the Gorge Trail. The Indian Trail on the north side of the glen leads to the upper entrance. There is also a park shuttle bus. Before starting out, pick up a map of the park and ask about the bus schedule, as well as information about guided hikes.

There are 19 waterfalls in the glen, ranging from vertical drops to twisting cascades confined to narrow chutes, all of which can be viewed in half a day. Here are some of the highlights.

Starting from the main entrance parking lot, walk west to the entrance tunnel. When you exit the tunnel, you'll be standing on Sentry Bridge, 52 feet (15.8 m) above Glen Creek. To your right is Entrance Cascade, a 41-foot-high (12.5 m) twisting cascade with a 6-foot-wide (1.8 m) crest. A short distance on, a side trail to the right descends to a viewing area for 21-foot-high (6.4 m) Minnehaha Falls. Continue along the Gorge Trail to a viewing area above the waterfall's 24-foot-wide (7.3 m) crest. Cavern Cascade lies just ahead, falling vertically 38 feet (11.6 m) before striking a ledge and cascading into the pool below. The trail passes behind the falling waters of this overhung waterfall and enters the Spiral Tunnel.

Pass under Suspension Bridge, which connects the rim trails a

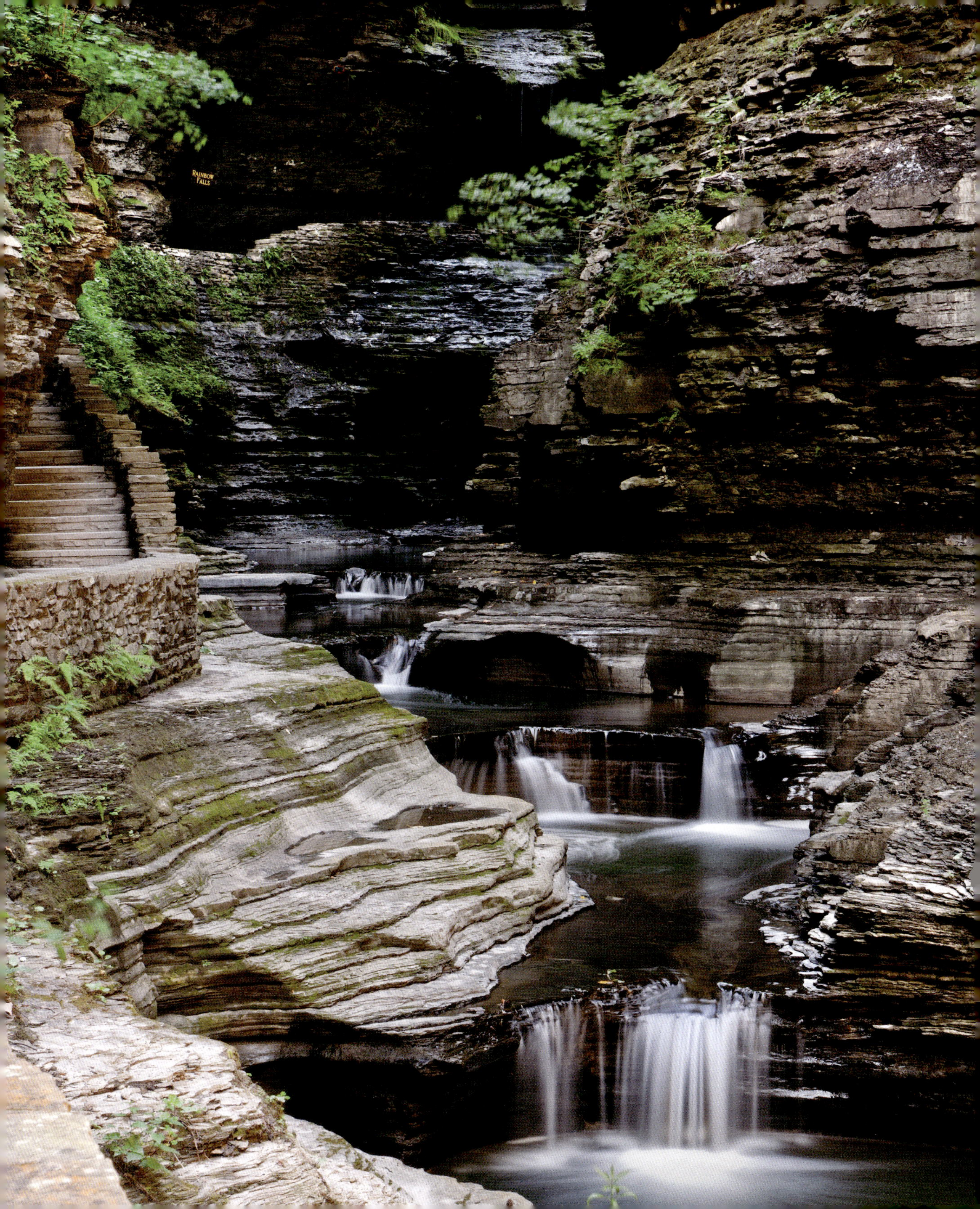
RAINBOW
FALLS

dizzying 85 feet (26 m) above the creekbed. On the other side is a glen fittingly known as The Vista, for its splendid views. This glen widens into the 600-foot-long (183 m) Cathedral, with 200-foot (60 m) cliff walls that soar up on both sides. About halfway through the Cathedral, just before a long flight of steps, there is a viewing area for Central Cascade. Extremely steep, the cascade has a vertical drop of 42 feet (12.8 m) and a 4-foot-wide (1.2 m) crest. Climb the steps to enter Cathedral Tunnel. Across Glen Greek, you'll find the Glen of Pools, a series of beautifully sculptured pools and potholes, and 95-foot-high (29 m) Rainbow Falls. As at Cavern Cascade, the trail passes behind this splendid waterfall. At certain hours of the day, a dazzling rainbow forms as sunlight filters into the glen and strikes the falling water.

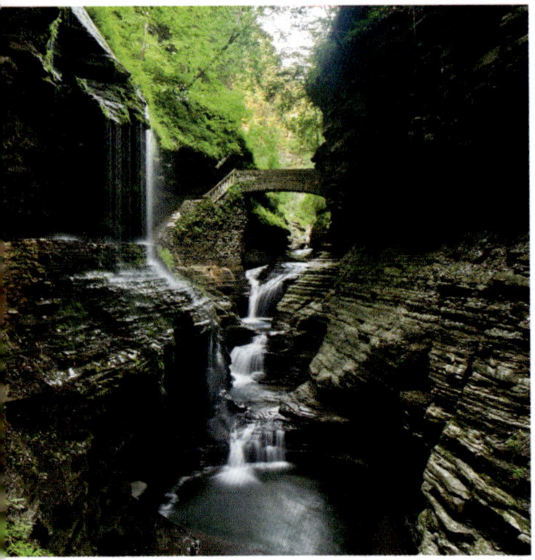

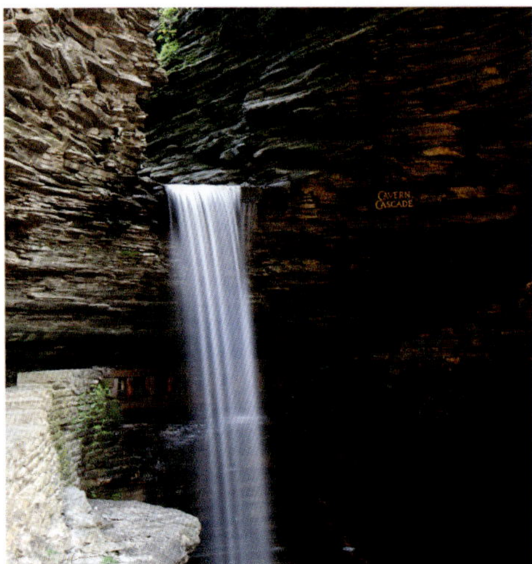

Just past Rainbow Falls, under a bridge, is a waterfall known as the Cascade at Rainbow Falls. Here, Glen Creek drops 12 feet (3.7 m) as it flows over the 15-foot-wide (4.6 m) crest. Downstream are two smaller falls, both under 10 feet (3 m).

Beyond the bridge at Rainbow Falls is the very narrow Spiral Gorge, which has a number of sculpted pools and springs that drip from the overhanging cliffs. Near the western end is Pluto Falls, where the very narrow gorge and overhanging cliffs ensure that the area is always in gloomy shadow.

Ahead is Mile Point Bridge, where the park's three main trails intersect. You have several choices about how to continue (or finish) your hike. The Gorge Trail carries on west through the Elfin Gorge and eventually ends in the upper entrance parking lot.

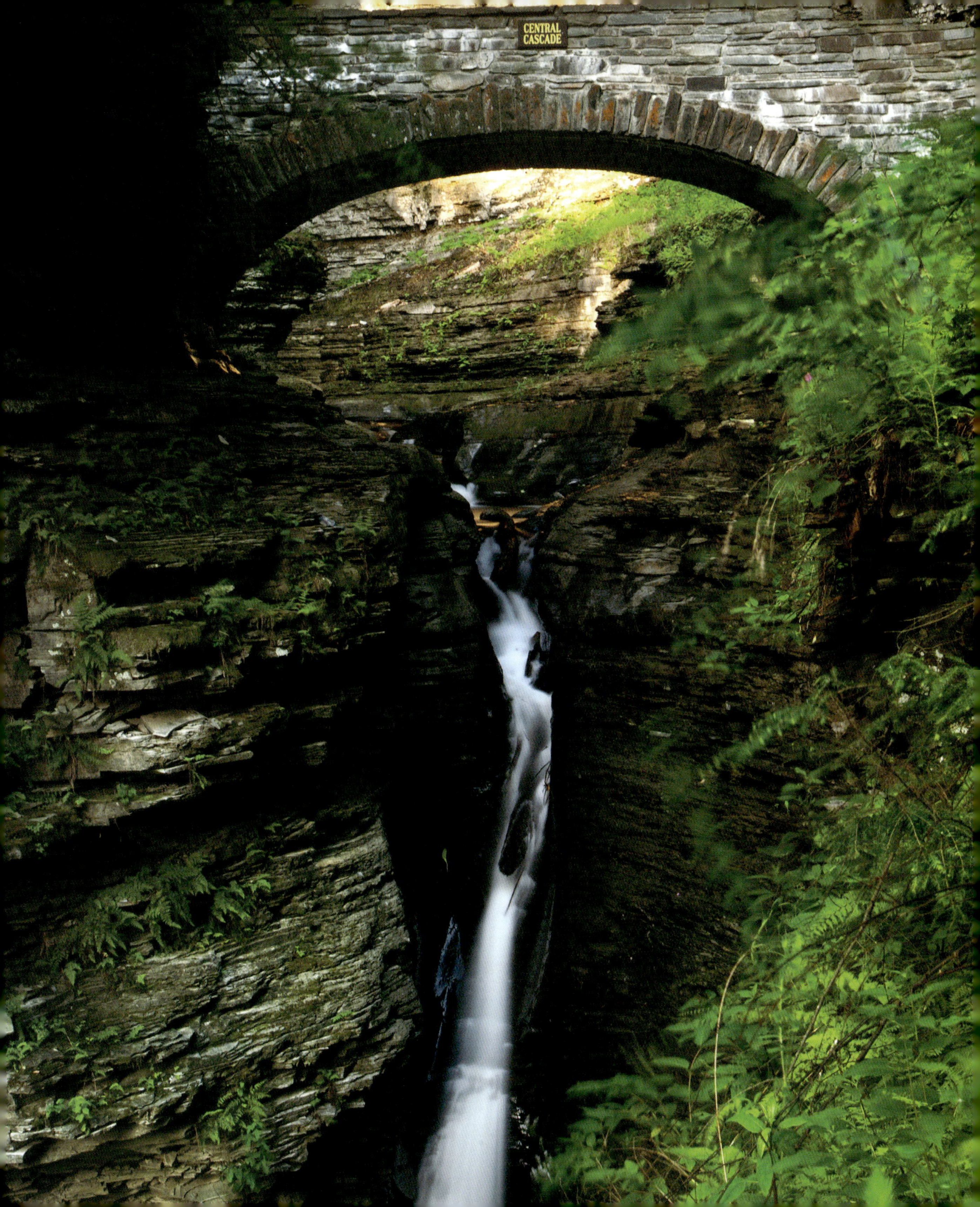
CENTRAL
CASCADE

Twin Falls

From the main entrance to Watkins Glen State Park, turn right onto NY 14. Drive for 500 ft (153 m), then turn right onto NY 329 (Corning St.); in 2.3 mi (3.7 km), it becomes Townsend Rd. After 2.4 mi (3.9 km), make a sharp right onto Vanzandt Hollow Rd. In 1.2 mi (1.9 km), Vanzandt Hollow Rd. turns right. Don't turn; continue going straight on Templar Rd. In roughly 500 ft (153 m), you can pull off and park on the right side of the road. The parking area provides access to the Finger Lakes Trail and Sugar Hill State Forest.

COUNTY: Schuyler

TOWNSHIP: Dix

PLACE: Watkins Glen

WATERWAY: Glen Creek

TYPE: classical falls

HEIGHT:
Upper: 12 ft (3.7 m)
Lower: 8 ft (2.4 m)

TRAIL:
dirt and creekbed; moderate

WALKING TIME: 15 min

PEAK ACTIVITY: May-Sept.

LATITUDE:
Upper: 42.3687
Lower: 42.3687

LONGITUDE:
Upper: –76.9587
Lower: –76.9585

From your parking spot, follow the Finger Lakes Trail east toward Glen Creek until you reach a flat, usually shallow part of the creek. You must ford the creek, so wear water shoes or other appropriate footwear and bring along a hiking stick to help steady yourself. Take your time and be careful as you cross the creek — the rocks may be loose or slippery. If the creek is very high and flowing swiftly, do not attempt to cross.

On the other side of the creek, turn right and follow the waterway for a short distance to the crest of Upper Twin Falls.

As the name implies, Twin Falls is actually two waterfalls separated by a short level section of the creek. A classical falls, Upper Twin Falls is 12 feet (3.7 m) high, with a 10-foot-wide (3 m) crest that is 1,260 feet (384 m) above sea level. From here, Lower Twin Falls is just barely visible.

Lower Twin Falls is 8 feet (2.4 m) high, with a 10-foot-wide (3 m) crest. Both waterfalls face northeast. If you want a good full-on view of each, you have to climb down into the mini ravine. But be careful, as the wet sandstone and shale are covered with algae and can be very slippery.

Twin Falls is also known as The Falls at Ebenezer's Crossing. The creek crossing is named for Ebenezer and Jane Buck, early area settlers. The falls are developed in the Wiscoy Formation, a mixture of sandstone and black to gray shale dating from the Late Devonian Period.

The Six Nations Recreation Trail System is located in nearby Sugar Hill State Forest, with a portion of the trail in Goundry Hill State Forest. Together, these lands comprise over 11,000 acres (4,452 ha) in Schuyler County. The trail system is nearly 40 miles (64.4 km) long and is designed for hiking, horseback riding and snowmobiling.

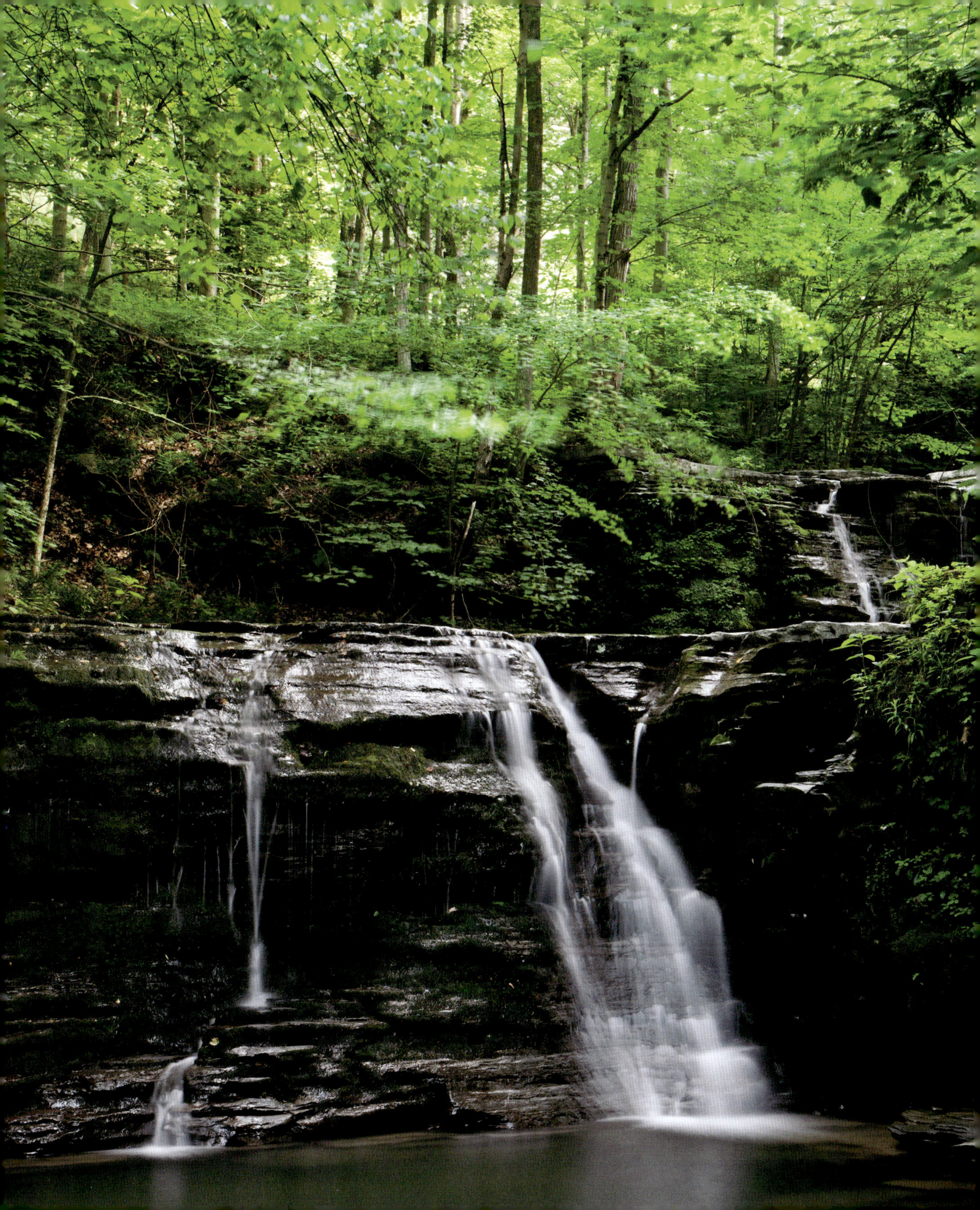

Aunt Sarah's Falls

Aunt Sarah's Falls can be seen from the parking area for the Catharine Creek Wildlife Management Area, located on the east side of NY 14, immediately north of the village of Montour Falls, 600 ft (183 m) northwest of the intersection with North Genesee St.

If you're coming from the north, the parking area is about 1.5 mi (2.4 km) south of Watkins Glen. After spring runoff or a heavy rain, several waterfalls cascade down the cliffs between Watkins Glen and Montour Falls.

COUNTY: Schuyler

TOWNSHIP: Montour

PLACE: Montour Falls

WATERWAY: Aunt Sarah's Creek

TYPE: ribbon falls

HEIGHT: 90 ft (27 m)

TRAIL: grass; easy

WALKING TIME: 5 min

PEAK ACTIVITY: May-Oct.

LATITUDE: 42.3517

LONGITUDE: –76.8563

From the parking area on the east side of NY 14, this spectacular 90-foot-high (27 m) waterfall is plainly visible about 200 feet (60 m) to the west. For a more intimate view, you can cross NY 14 to a small grassy area.

The creek plunges over the 15-foot-wide (4.6 m) crest, free-falls about 35 feet (10.7 m) and strikes a ledge. It then descends the cliff as a steep cascade, fanning out across 35 feet (10.7 m) of the cliff face. Finally, the creek makes a 20-foot (6.1 m) free-fall into a pool at the base of the falls. The cliff comprises West River Shale, Genundewa Limestone, Penn Yan Shale and Geneseo Shale of the Late Devonian Period.

But who was Aunt Sarah? One of the several legends regarding the name suggests that Aunt Sarah was a middle-aged Native American who was befriended by the early settlers of the area. Unable to pronounce her Native name, the settlers affectionately called her Aunt Sarah. Reportedly, Aunt Sarah had an understanding of the medicinal properties of the indigenous plants, and when any of the settlers' infants suffered from fever or shivering, Aunt Sarah's skillful treatment eased their symptoms. As she had often expressed a wish to live at the waterfall, the settlers built a cabin for her. She lived there until her death at an extremely old age, when she was deeply mourned by her community.

According to another less happy legend, Aunt Sarah was a Native American who married a local settler and ultimately jumped to her death from the falls. It is well documented that at one time, there was a rock carving of a Native woman's face at the falls, which was destroyed by men who believed there was gold hidden behind it.

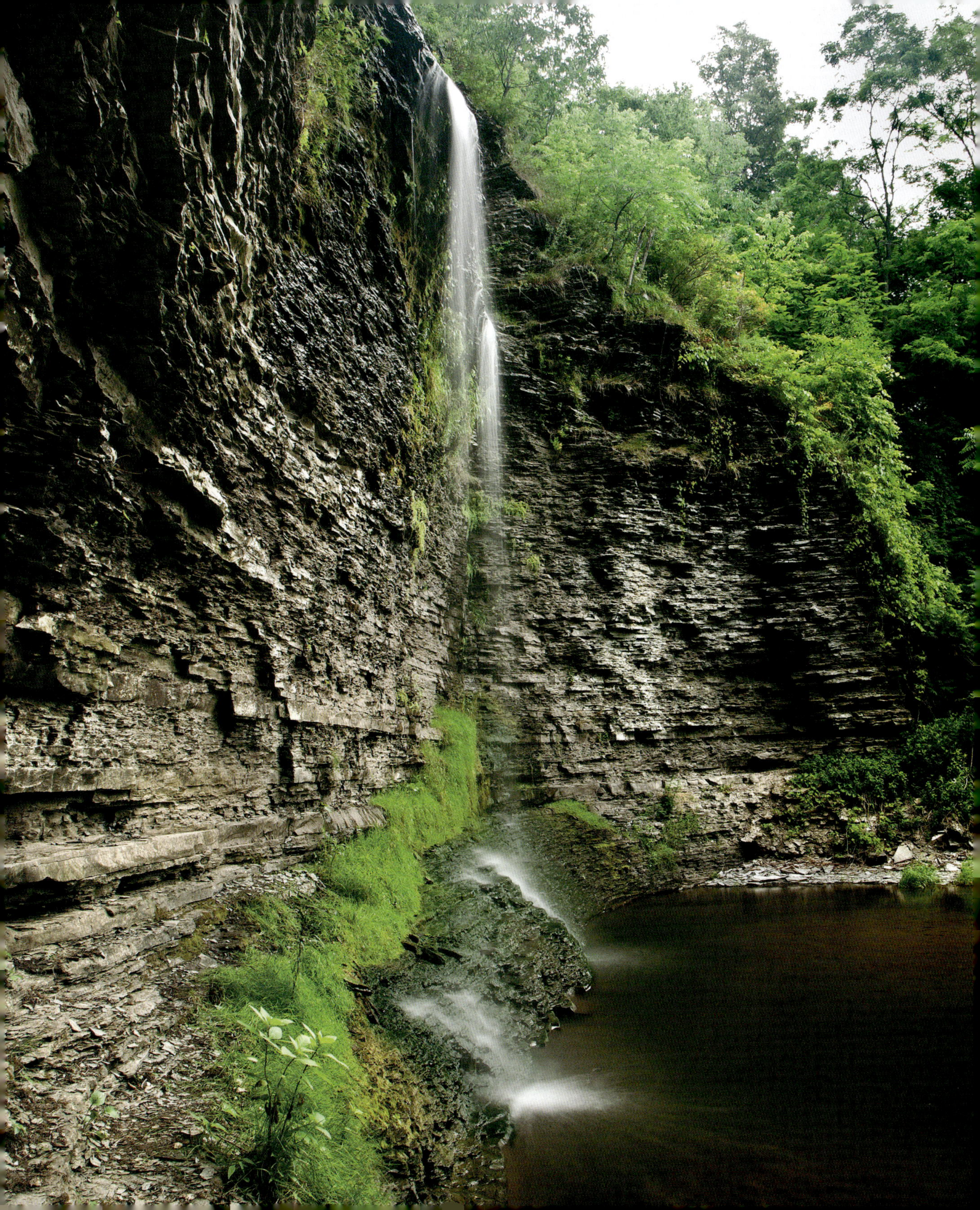

Shequaga Falls

From the intersection of NY 14 and NY 224 in the village of Montour Falls, proceed south on NY 14 for one block to Main St., and turn right. After 0.3 mi (0.5 km), turn left onto Genesee St. Park along the west side of the street, near the entrance to a small park, where you'll find a wheelchair-accessible viewing area.

This magnificent waterfall is 156 feet (47.5 m) high and has a 36-foot-wide (11 m) crest. Shequaga Creek tumbles down the cliff in an attractive mixture of vertical falls and extremely steep cascades. The width of the falls gradually increases as the water makes its descent. It is a fantastic sight any time of the year but is outstanding during the spring thaw. You'll notice that the bottom of the falls is surrounded by a concrete basin, installed as part of a 1953 flood-control project.

A Seneca settlement near the falls was called Catharinestown by early settlers to the area, after Catharine Montour, a prominent local Native leader. Angered at the Native tribes that had sided with the British during the Revolutionary War, George Washington ordered the total destruction and devastation of their settlements. Catharinestown was destroyed in 1779 by an expedition led by Major General John Sullivan, as were at least 40 other Native villages throughout the Finger Lakes region.

Later settlers to the area built a village near the same location around 1790 and called it Havana, so named because of its proximity to a steamy marshland with lots of mosquitoes. (For that reason, Shequaga Falls was also once known as Havana Falls.) The village was renamed Montour Falls in 1895 in honor of Catharine Montour.

According to local legend, Seneca Chief Red Jacket (Sagoyewatha), a diplomat and skilled public speaker, came to the waterfall not only to enjoy its beauty but also to train his voice against the sound of the falling water. He named the creek "the place of the roaring waters." Others have interpreted the name as "tumbling waters." Shequaga is variously presented as She-Qua-Ga, She-Qua-Gah and Che-Qua-Ga. The area around the village of Montour Falls is sometimes called the "Valley of Tumbling Waters" because of its numerous waterfalls.

The hillside that Shequaga Creek descends is composed of West River Shale, Genundewa Limestone, Penn Yan Shale and Geneseo Shale of the Late Devonian Period, which makes the rock about 380 million years old.

COUNTY: Schuyler
TOWNSHIP: Montour
PLACE: Montour Falls
WATERWAY: Shequaga Creek
TYPE: ribbon falls
HEIGHT: 156 ft (47.5 m)
TRAIL: concrete sidewalk; easy
WALKING TIME: 5 min
PEAK ACTIVITY: May-Oct.
LATITUDE: 42.3444
LONGITUDE: –76.8516

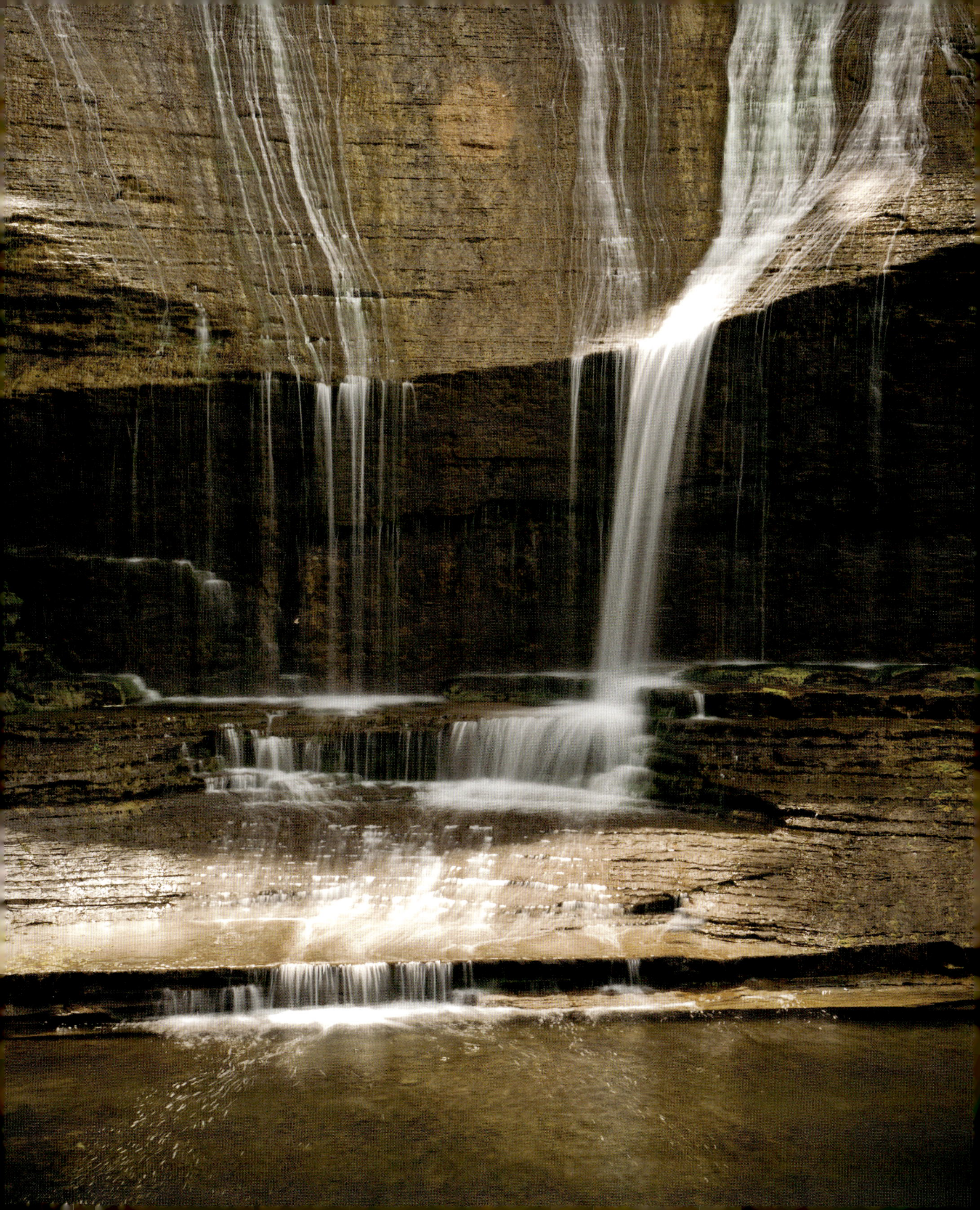

Havana Glen Park

From the village of Montour Falls, follow NY 14 south for 1 mi (1.6 km) to Havana Glen Rd., and turn left. Drive for a short distance, then turn right into Havana Glen Park.

The waters of McClure Creek in Schuyler County have cut a magnificent glen through layers of West River Shale, Genundewa Limestone, Penn Yan Shale and Geneseo Shale of the Late Devonian Period. This refreshingly cool glen features a variety of ferns, lichens, liverworts and mosses. Open from mid-May to mid-October, Havana Glen Park has picnic facilities, a playground, a ball field, a camping area — and the sensational Eagle Cliff Falls.

A quarter-mile-long (0.4 km) trail to the glen starts at a parking area on the east side of the park. As you walk the trail along the north bank of McClure Creek, you'll pass several small waterfalls. The first view at the mouth of the ravine is an intriguing one, with the sound of the constantly falling waters inviting you to enter the glen. Once you do, you are standing above 12-foot-high (3.7 m) Portal Cascade. A chain of miniature staircaselike waterfalls parallels the trail, which ends in the amphitheater of Eagle Cliff Falls, where the cliffs tower above the crest of the waterfall.

Eagle Cliff Falls, which faces northwest, is 41 feet (12.5 m) high, with a 15-foot-wide (4.6 m) crest. The falls was originally named for a large eagle's nest that was once built on the rugged cliffs opposite the falls. As McClure Creek tumbles over the crest of the falls, it drops roughly 7 feet (2.1 m) to a small ledge. The creek then rebounds off the ledge and free-falls dramatically into the deep plunge pool below.

The glen above Eagle Cliff Falls contains several more waterfalls. In 1876, the local Masonic Lodge built wooden stairways in the upper glen, which was known for a time as Masonic Glen. A popular attraction in the late 1800s, with nearly 10,000 people paying admission to the park in 1881, Havana Glen was sidelined with the creation of an admissions-free policy at Watkins Glen in 1906. With the decline in revenue, the wooden stairways in the upper glen could no longer be maintained. Deemed unsafe, they were removed around 1915. The glen above Eagle Cliff Falls is now inaccessible.

COUNTY: Schuyler

TOWNSHIP: Montour

PLACE: Montour Falls

WATERWAY: McClure Creek

TYPE: ribbon falls

HEIGHT: 41 ft (12.5 m)

TRAIL: dirt, stone and stairs; easy

WALKING TIME: 25 min

PEAK ACTIVITY: May-Oct.

LATITUDE: 42.3351

LONGITUDE: –76.8274

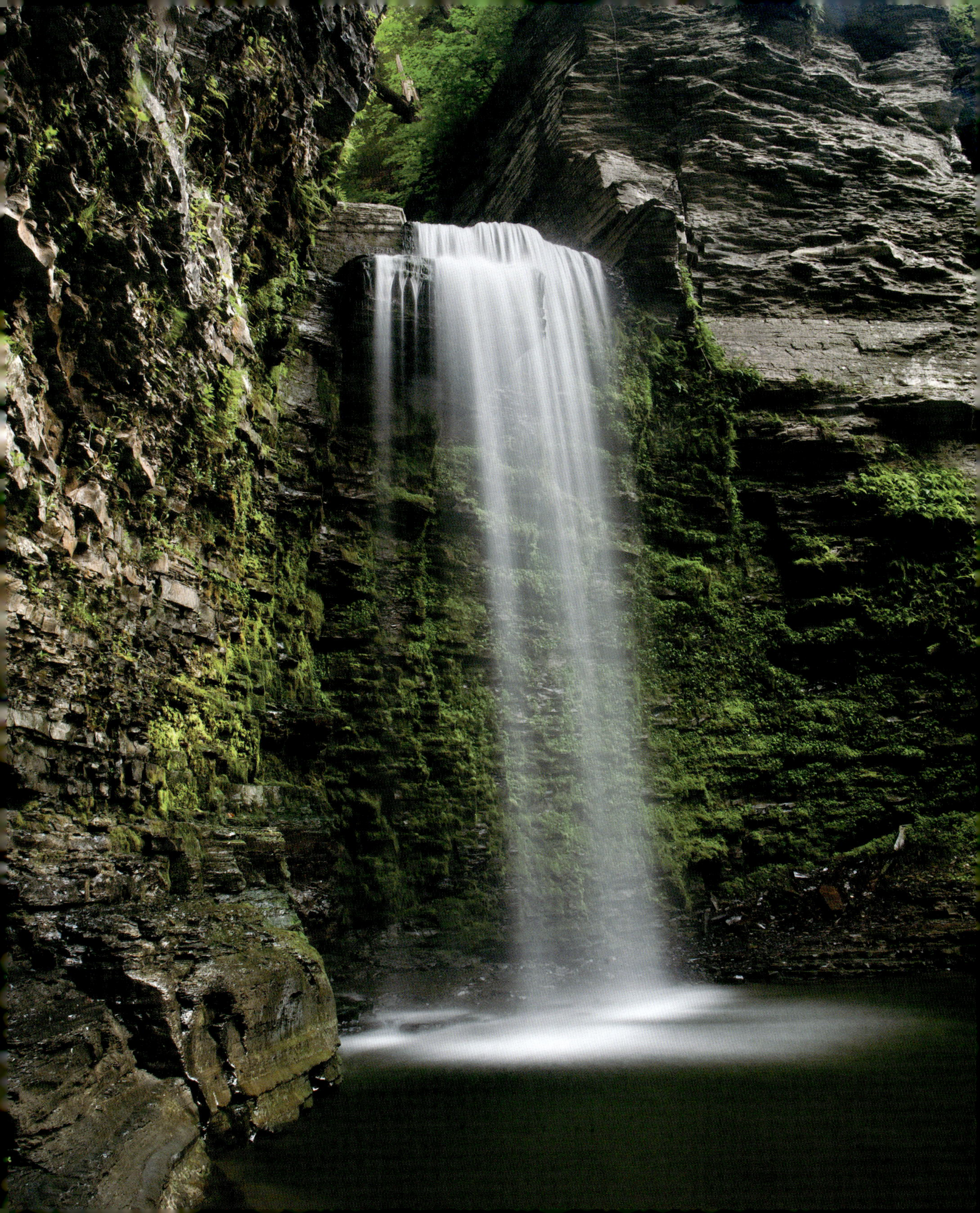

Seneca Mill Falls

From the intersection of NY 14 and NY 54 near Dresden, follow NY 54 west for 1.9 mi (3.1 km) to Ridge Rd. (Yates CR 9), and turn left. Follow Ridge Rd. for 1.2 mi (1.9 km) to the bottom of the hill, and turn right onto Outlet Rd, just before crossing the bridge over the Keuka Lake Outlet. At 0.5 mi (0.8 km) from Ridge Rd., you'll see the Seneca Mill parking area on the left side of Outlet Rd. This is an access point for the Keuka Outlet Trail.

COUNTY: Yates
TOWNSHIP: Milo
PLACE: Penn Yan
WATERWAY: Keuka Lake Outlet
TYPE: curtain falls
HEIGHT: 22 ft (6.7 m)
TRAIL: stone; easy
WALKING TIME: 25 min
PEAK ACTIVITY: May-Sept.
LATITUDE: 42.6608
LONGITUDE: –77.0041

Due to its unusual Y-shape, Keuka Lake is sometimes called Crooked Lake. Its waters flow into Seneca Lake via a natural stream called the Keuka Lake Outlet. In the early 1830s, the 7.5-mile-long (12.1 km) Crooked Lake Canal was built alongside the outlet, using 28 wooden locks to descend the nearly 300-foot (91.5 m) drop in elevation between the two lakes. New York State closed the canal in 1877, and in 1884, a railroad was built along the canal's old towpath. Almost a century later, in 1972, floodwaters from Hurricane Agnes damaged the tracks beyond repair, and two years later, the railroad was abandoned.

In the early 1980s, interest in developing a trail on the railroad bed gained momentum, and on July 4, 1984, the Keuka Outlet Trail officially opened. In the late 1990s, the Friends of the Outlet, a local not-for-profit group, took control of a 5.7-mile (9.2 km) section of the trail, which is open year-round from sunrise to sunset.

From the Seneca Mill parking area, follow the trail upstream for about 0.3 mile (0.5 km), until you reach the ruins of the Seneca Paper Mill. Originally built in 1884, the mill produced sugar bags, heavy wrapping paper and paper used to print books. Next to the ruins is Seneca Mill Falls.

The 70-foot-wide (21.3 m) waterfall consists of two distinct leaps separated by a horizontal break that varies from roughly 3 to 35 feet (1–10.7 m) in length. The first leap is largely a 10-foot (3 m) vertical drop. The southern end of the second leap is a very steep cascade, while the sections of the northern end are nearly vertical, almost merging with the first drop. The waterfall has a total height of 22 feet (6.7 m) and is developed in Tully Limestone of the Middle Devonian Period. A short distance above the falls is a pavilion for picnickers.

Also just upstream is a dam with a 7-foot-high (2.1 m) spillway built to supply water to the mill. In the late 1880s, electricity produced at the mill was used to light the streets of the village of Penn Yan, a couple of miles to the west. Northeast of the mill ruins, the Keuka Outlet Trail passes through lock number 17 of the Crooked Lake Canal.

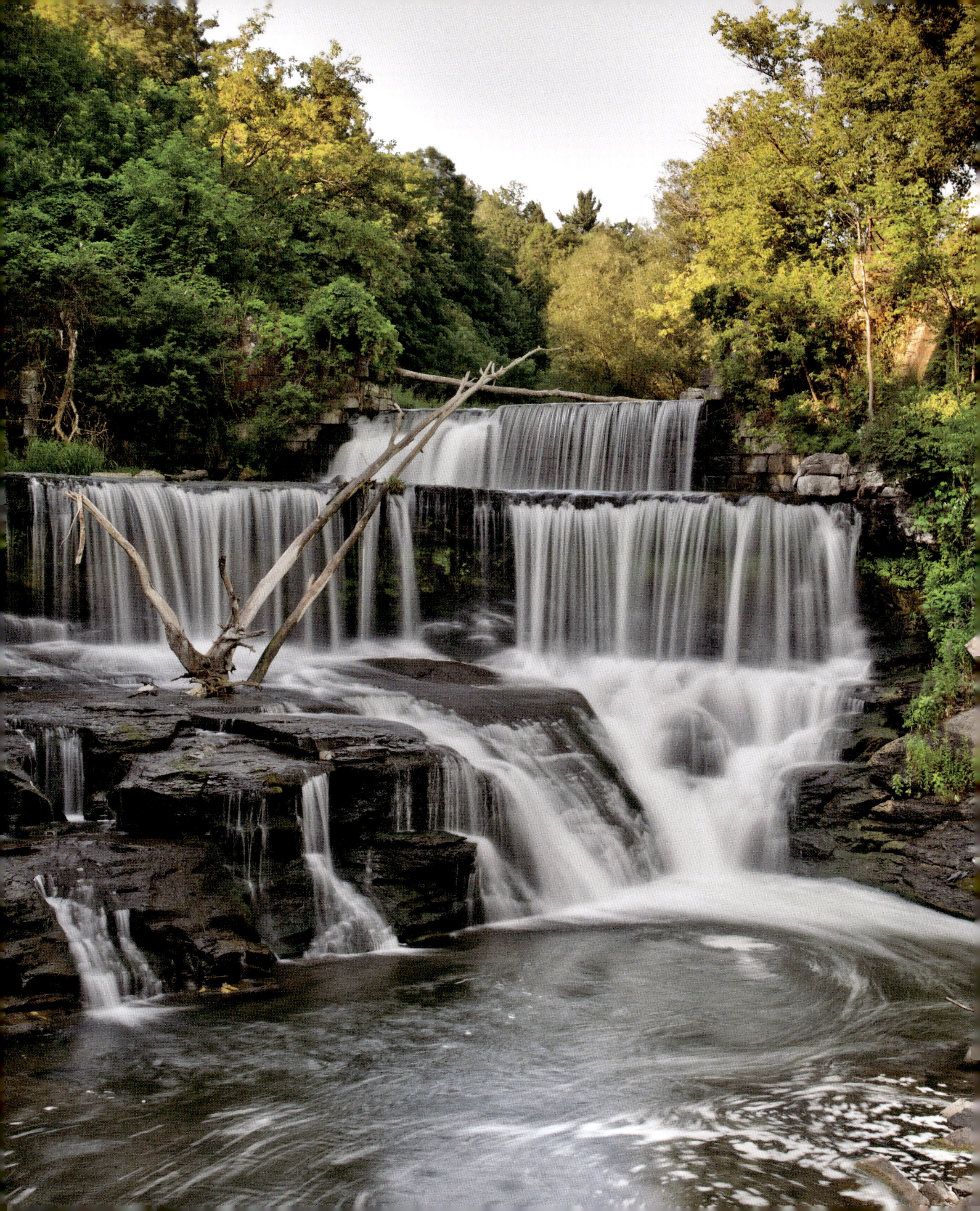

FINGER LAKES REGION

Wolcott Falls

From the intersection of NY 104 and NY 414, follow NY 104 east for 4.5 mi (7.2 km), and turn left onto Whiskey Hill Rd. (CR 258). As you near Wolcott, Whiskey Hill Rd. becomes New Hartford St. At 0.8 mi (1.3 km) from NY 104, turn right onto Main St. After 500 ft (153 m), turn left onto Mill St. In another 500 ft (153 m), turn left into the parking area for Wolcott Falls Park.

COUNTY: Wayne

TOWNSHIP: Wolcott

PLACE: Wolcott

WATERWAY: Wolcott Creek

TYPE: ribbon falls

HEIGHT: 33 ft (10 m)

TRAIL: grass and dirt; easy

WALKING TIME: 5 min to top of falls; 10 min to base

PEAK ACTIVITY: May-Sept.

LATITUDE: 43.2215

LONGITUDE: –76.8121

Native Americans originally knew Wolcott Falls as Ganadasgua, meaning "leaping waters above the lake." Located in Wolcott Falls Park, the waterfall can be viewed from the wheelchair-accessible overlook and information kiosk that is located near the parking area. The park is open year-round from sunrise to sunset — Wolcott Falls is illuminated at night — and there are picnic tables and a playground.

From the kiosk, walk to the northwest along the fence to a trail that leads southeast to the base of the waterfall. As Wolcott Creek flows over the 12-foot-wide (3.7 m) crest, it falls freely for roughly 17 feet (5.2 m), strikes a steep shale embankment and cascades into a pool. The caprock of this falls is DeCew Dolostone, a dark gray sandy rock that is 10 feet (3 m) thick. Below the dolostone is black to dark gray Rochester Shale. Both dolostone and shale date from the Early Silurian Period, making them around 432 million years old. At just 340 feet (103.6 m) above sea level, the crest of Wolcott Falls is a mere 95 feet (29 m) above the level of Lake Ontario, making it one of the lowest elevations for a waterfall in this region.

In 1805, Jonathan Melvin from the Phelps, New York, area, believed to be a soldier in the Revolutionary War and one of Wolcott's first settlers, purchased 500 acres (202.4 ha) of land at the falls. Around 1809, he built a gristmill and sawmill here. The mills were destroyed by a fire in the 1960s.

In the center of the village, at the intersection of Main and New Hartford streets, there is a cast-iron statue of "Venus Rising From the Sea," one of only eight such statues in the United States. Cast by J. L. Mott Iron Works, the statue was purchased in 1913 for about $875. The statue was once a public drinking fountain, and sister statues are found in Port Townsend, Washington, and Redlands, California.

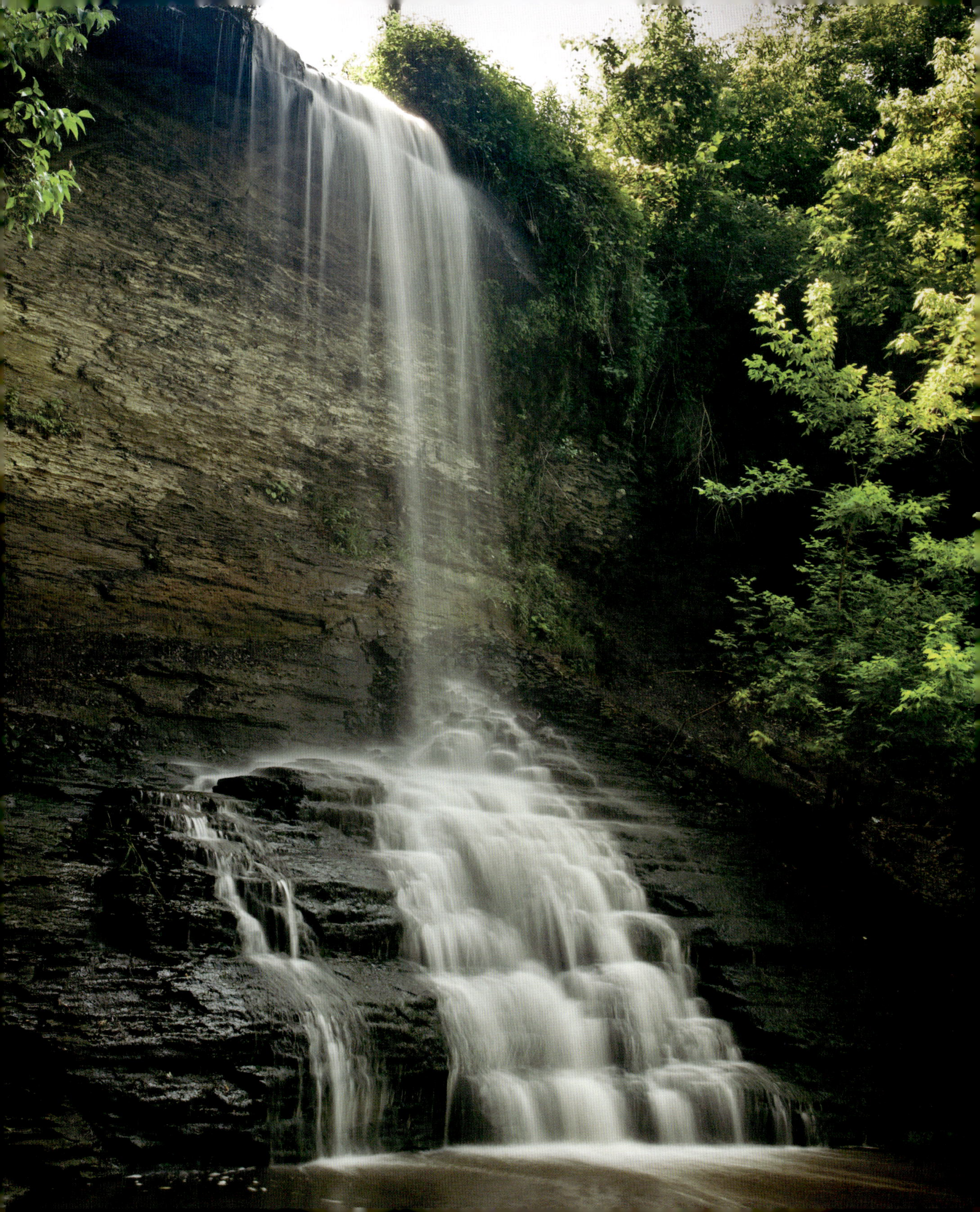

FINGER LAKES REGION

Grimes Glen

From the intersection of NY 21 and NY 245 north of Naples, proceed south on NY 21, entering Naples. At 1 mi (1.6 km) south of NY 245, turn right onto Vine St., passing the fire station. Continue for roughly 0.5 mi (0.8 km) until the street ends, and turn right. A small hill leads to a parking area for Grimes Glen.

COUNTY: Ontario

TOWNSHIP: Naples

PLACE: Naples

WATERWAY: Grimes Creek

TYPE:
First Falls: ribbon falls
Second Falls: classical falls

HEIGHT:
First Falls: 59 ft (18 m)
Second Falls: 62 ft (18.9 m)

TRAIL:
dirt and creekbed; moderate

WALKING TIME:
20 min to First Falls

PEAK ACTIVITY: June-Sept.

LATITUDE:
First Falls: 42.6160
Second Falls: 42.6190

LONGITUDE:
First Falls: –77.4193
Second Falls: –77.4184

By 2008, the Finger Lakes Land Trust and Ontario County had raised sufficient funds to purchase and transfer a beautiful 32-acre (13 ha) parcel of privately owned land to public parkland. Today, Grimes Glen — developed from shale that is roughly 383 million years old — is protected from development in perpetuity.

The trail in to the glen starts on the west side of the parking area, but to see the falls, you have to walk up Grimes Creek. Follow a short trail to the west and continue upstream in the creekbed, or cross the creek via a bridge to the southwest and follow the trail along the western bank of the creek. After roughly 600 feet (183 m), you'll encounter First Falls on a tributary called Springstead Creek. A nearly vertical waterfall, it has a 15-foot-wide (4.6 m) crest and tumbles down the glen's western wall.

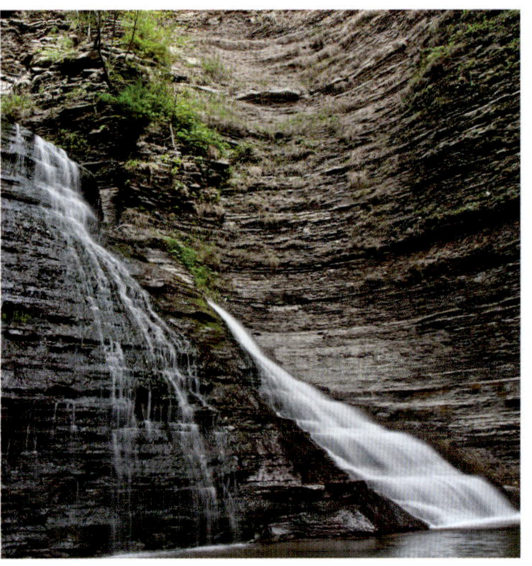

Continue upstream for 1,000 feet (305 m) to Second Falls, which consists of two leaps separated by a 20-foot (6.1 m) break. The first leap, which can't be seen from the base of the falls, is 16 feet (4.9 m) high and has a curving 48-foot-wide (14.6 m) crest. It is nearly vertical on the eastern flank and moderately steep on the western flank. The second leap is 46 feet (14 m) high and has a 32-foot-wide (9.8 m) crest. The western flank is nearly vertical, while the eastern flank is an extremely steep cascade. A small natural grotto found at the base of the second leap on the eastern side is known as the Devil's Bedroom.

The park officially ends at the crest of this falls. The land above the falls is privately owned, and the success of the park depends in large part on your respect for the area property owners.

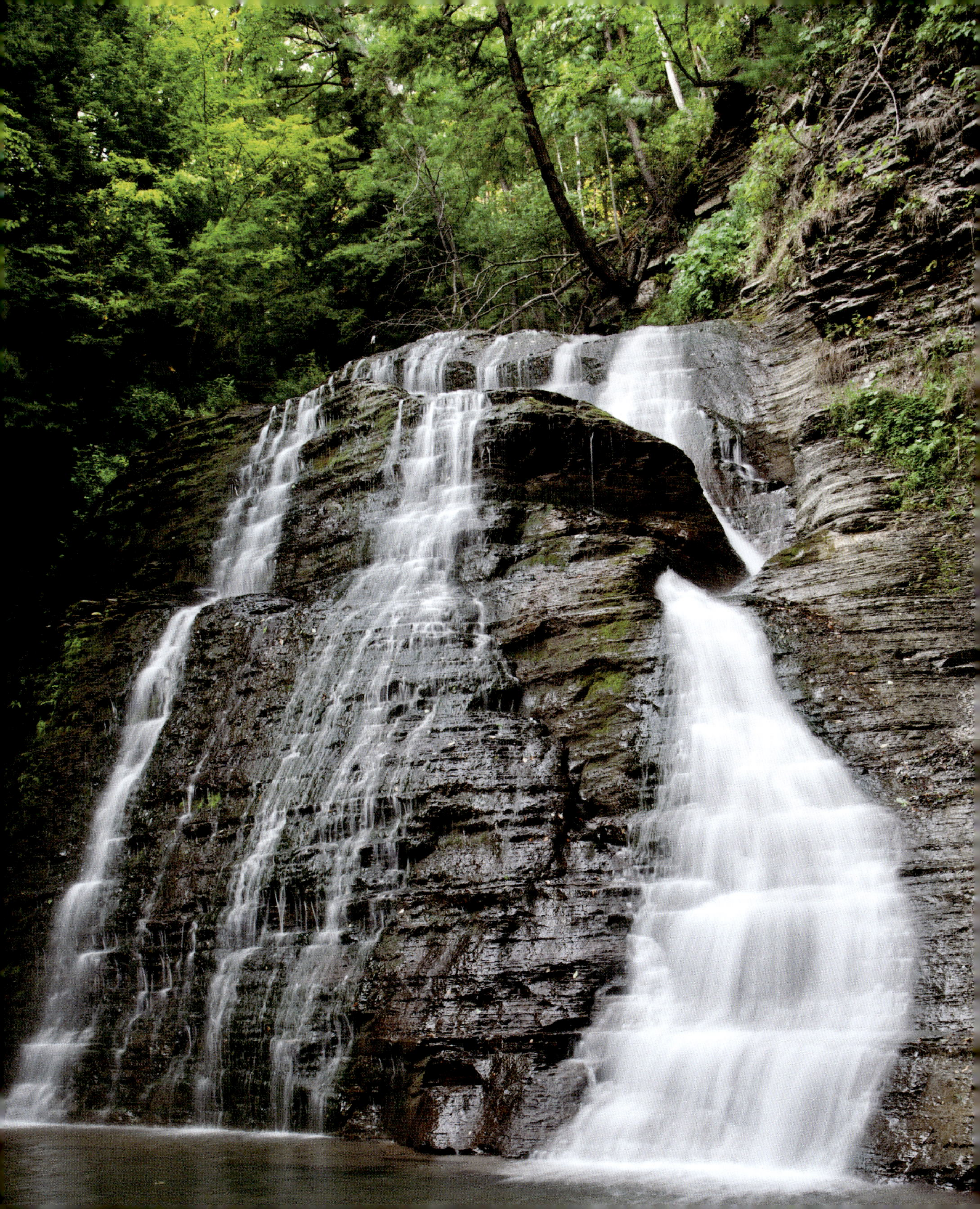

County Line Falls

Upper and Lower County Line Falls are located in the 6,684-acre (2,705 ha) Hemlock-Canadice State Forest. Two undeveloped Finger Lakes in the area, Hemlock and Candice, are the main sources of Rochester's drinking water.

From Springwater, follow NY 15A north for 2.7 mi (4.3 km), and turn right onto Old Bald Hill Rd. After about 500 ft (153 m), turn right onto Johnson Hill Rd. In 300 ft (91.5 m), turn right into a small grass parking area. (Photos © Scott A. Ensminger)

COUNTY: Livingston

TOWNSHIP: Springwater

PLACE: Springwater

WATERWAY: unnamed tributary of Hemlock Lake

TYPE: both ribbon falls

HEIGHT:
Upper: 59 ft (18 m)
Lower: 25 ft (7.6 m)

TRAIL:
Upper: grass and dirt; easy
Lower: creekbed; moderate

WALKING TIME:
Upper: 25 min
Lower: 45 min

PEAK ACTIVITY: June-Sept.

LATITUDE:
Upper: 42.6708
Lower: 42.6716

LONGITUDE:
Upper: –77.5852
Lower: –77.5896

The trailhead to both Upper and Lower County Line Falls starts on the south side of the parking area. Pass through a metal gate, and continue south on what was once a logging road; in summer, this trail is usually overgrown with grass. In under 0.5 mile (0.8 km), the trail curves east, and you can just catch a glimpse of the Upper County Line Falls through the trees.

The Upper County Line Falls has a 21-foot-wide (6.4 m) crest that faces north-northwest. This waterfall is developed in both West Hill Formation and Gardeau Formation, a mixture of shale and siltstone dating from the Late Devonian Period. As the creek, an unnamed tributary of Hemlock Lake, descends the 59-foot-high (18 m) cliff, it turns to the west.

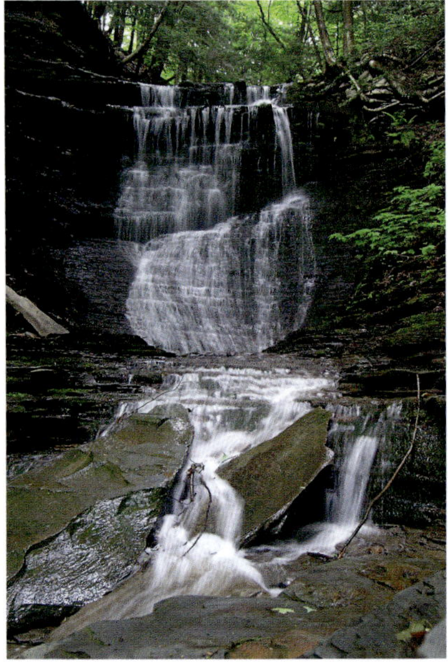

To view the Lower County Line Falls from the base, continue carefully along the edge of the extremely steep-sided gorge. Past the falls, cautiously descend into the gorge, then hike back to the falls. For stability and safety, tie a rope securely to a tree and hold on to it during both your descent and the difficult climb back up.

For an easier route to Lower County Line Falls, return to your vehicle after viewing the first waterfall. Drive to NY 15A, and turn left. About 0.5 mile (0.8 km) past Old Bald Hill Road, just after you cross Reynolds Creek, there is a dirt parking area on the left side of the road. Park next to the creek, and walk north (the direction you just came from) along NY 15A. In just over 0.2 mile (0.3 km), you'll come to a creek. Follow the creek east to reach Lower County Line Falls. The falls are 25 feet (7.6 m) high, have a 10-foot-wide crest (3 m) and face west.

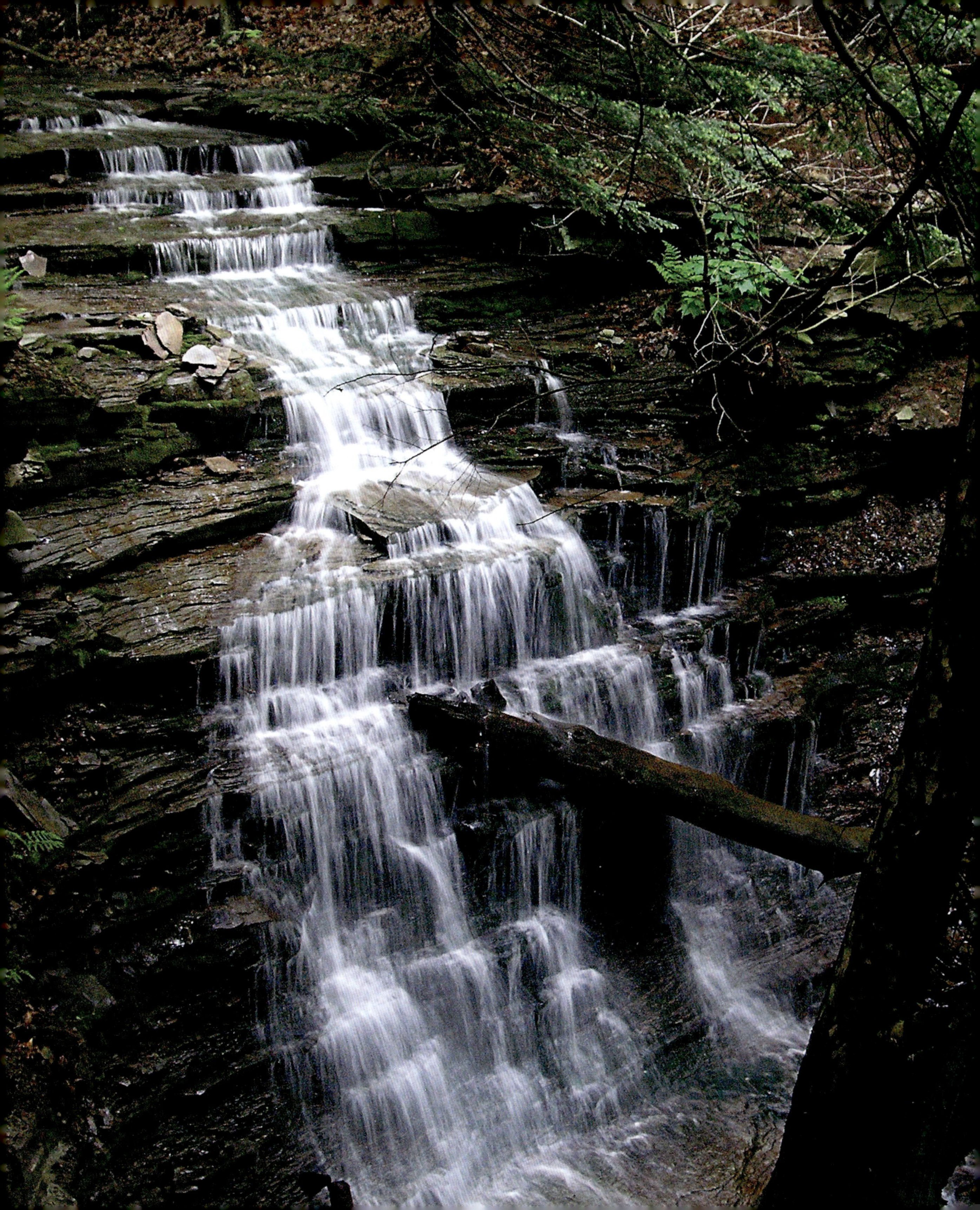

High Falls, Rochester

From the intersection of I-390 and I-490, follow I-490 east into Rochester. As you near the center of the city, leave I-490 at exit 12 (Brown St.). Cross Brown St., and proceed straight on Allen St. In 0.3 mi (0.5 km), after Allen St. crosses W Broad St. (NY 31), it makes a 45-degree turn to the left under I-490. Allen St. now becomes Morrie Silver Way. Continue on Morrie Silver Way northwest, passing Frontier Field on the right. After Morrie Silver Way crosses State St., it becomes Platt St. Continue on Platt St. for two blocks, and turn right (southeast) onto Browns Race. The High Falls Visitor Center at 60 Browns Race is about half a block from Platt St. There is limited street parking, but parking is available at the High Falls Garage.

COUNTY: Monroe

TOWNSHIP: Rochester

PLACE: Rochester

WATERWAY: Genesee River

TYPE: curtain falls

HEIGHT: 96 ft (29.3 m)

TRAIL: concrete and cobblestone sidewalks; easy

WALKING TIME: 20 min

PEAK ACTIVITY: May-Oct.

LATITUDE: 43.1613

LONGITUDE: –77.6136

When the Genesee River rushes over the Niagara Escarpment in Rochester, High Falls is the impressive result. Also known as Upper Falls, Genesee Falls and the Great Falls of the Genesee, High Falls faces northwest, and its entire 200-foot (60 m) crest is overhung, resulting in a fantastic curtain of falling water. The 96-foot (29.3 m) waterfall is at its best in the spring, when the flow of the river is torrential. In the summer, the river volume can be rather low.

The crest of the falls is DeCew Dolostone, the lowest member of the Lockport Formation. Below the DeCew is gray Rochester Shale, which is about 61 feet (18.6 m) thick. Both rocks date from the Early Silurian Period, making them roughly 421 million years old.

Once you've parked, go to the High Falls Visitor Center to pick up information about the area; be sure to check online before your visit to confirm the operating hours. Walk across the High Falls Bridge, which starts at the intersection of Browns Race and Platt Street, to enjoy some interesting views of the falls. Continue to the other side of the bridge, and turn right onto the Genesee Riverway Trail for other appealing views.

Sam Patch, the infamous daredevil who, in the late 1820s, had earned a reputation for making death-defying leaps from great heights, put on his last show at High Falls. Patch had already twice leapt 100 feet (30.5 m) into the swirling waters of the Niagara River from a tower built beside the American Falls. On November 6, 1829, Patch and his pet bear, Papa Bruin, made a 96-foot (29.3 m) leap from High Falls. Disappointed by the money collected from the crowd, he planned an even higher jump several days later and had a 120-foot (36.6 m) platform built near the crest of the falls. The stunt was scheduled for Friday the 13th, and an estimated crowd of 7,000 gathered for the event. At 2 p.m., Patch made his leap. He disappeared after hitting the water. His body was found the following spring and buried in Charlotte Cemetery, near the mouth of the Genesee River.

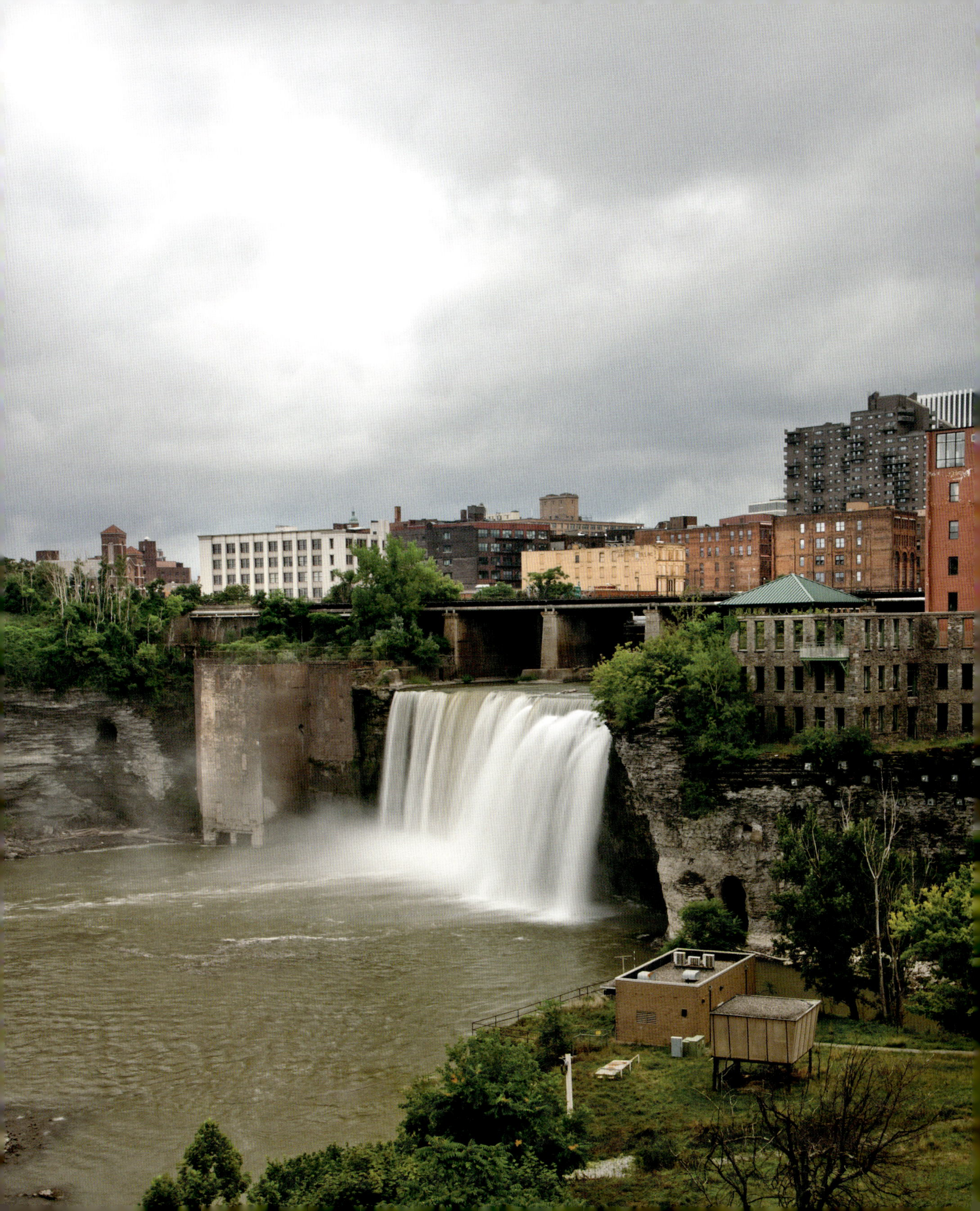

Lower & Middle Falls, Rochester

From the High Falls Visitor Center at 60 Browns Race, turn southwest onto Furnace St. Drive 1 block, and turn right onto Mill St. A block later, turn left onto Platt St. Drive 1 block, and turn right onto State St. Continue north, and in 0.4 mi (0.6 km), as you cross Smith St., State St. becomes Lake Ave. Continue north for 1.2 mi (1.9 km), and turn right onto Driving Park Ave. In roughly 400 feet (122 m), turn left into a parking area for the Maplewood Park and Rose Garden, at the corner of Lake Ave. and Driving Park Ave.

COUNTY: Monroe

TOWNSHIP: Rochester

PLACE: Rochester

WATERWAY: Genesee River

TYPE: curtain falls

HEIGHT:
Middle: 20 ft (6.1 m)
Lower: 110 ft (33.5 m)

TRAIL: concrete sidewalk; easy

WALKING TIME: 35 min

PEAK ACTIVITY: May-Oct.

LATITUDE:
Middle: 43.1766
Lower: 43.1794

LONGITUDE:
Middle: – 77.6280
Lower: –77.6278

On the eastern side of the parking lot at Rochester's Maplewood Park and Rose Garden, a stairway leads down to a trail. Follow this trail south, under the Driving Park Avenue Bridge. The trail merges with the road in Lower Falls Park, which leads to a viewing area above the crest of Lower Falls.

Farther along the road, near the end of the park, is a viewing area for Middle Falls, a 20-foot-high (6.1 m) natural waterfall with a dam on its crest to divert water downstream to the power plant on the eastern flank of Lower Falls.

From here, turn north and follow the road uphill to Driving Park Avenue. Turn right and walk along the sidewalk to the middle of the bridge. You are standing about 200 feet (60 m) above the Genesee River, known to the Seneca as Casconchiagon, "river of falls" or "river of many falls." This is the best view of the dramatic Lower Falls, about 600 feet (183 m) to the south. The 110-foot-high (33.5 m) waterfall faces northwest, has a 276-foot-wide (84 m) crest and can be classified as a complex curtain, with the eastern half being overhung and the western half a steeply terraced cascade. The slightly curving crest of the falls is capped by a concrete dam that helps divert water to the power plant on its eastern flank. A little to the west of the waterfall's center is a 45-foot-tall (13.7 m) fin of rock that distinctively divides the lower section of the falls in two. The fin is most noticeable during times of low water.

The Genesee River flows over Reynales Limestone of the 424-million-year-old Early Silurian Period. The natural rock crest of Lower Falls is Kodak Sandstone, which is medium gray to white and about 8 feet (2.4 m) thick. In the Niagara River Gorge, 105 miles (169 km) to the west, it is known as Thorold Sandstone. Below the Kodak Sandstone is Grimsby Sandstone, which consists of reddish sandstone and shale about 55 feet (16.8 m) thick. The upper layers are mottled with pale green and white. Both Kodak and Grimsby sandstone date from the Early Silurian Period. Below the Grimsby Sandstone are the reddish to purplish layers of Queenston Shale that date from the Late Ordovician Period.

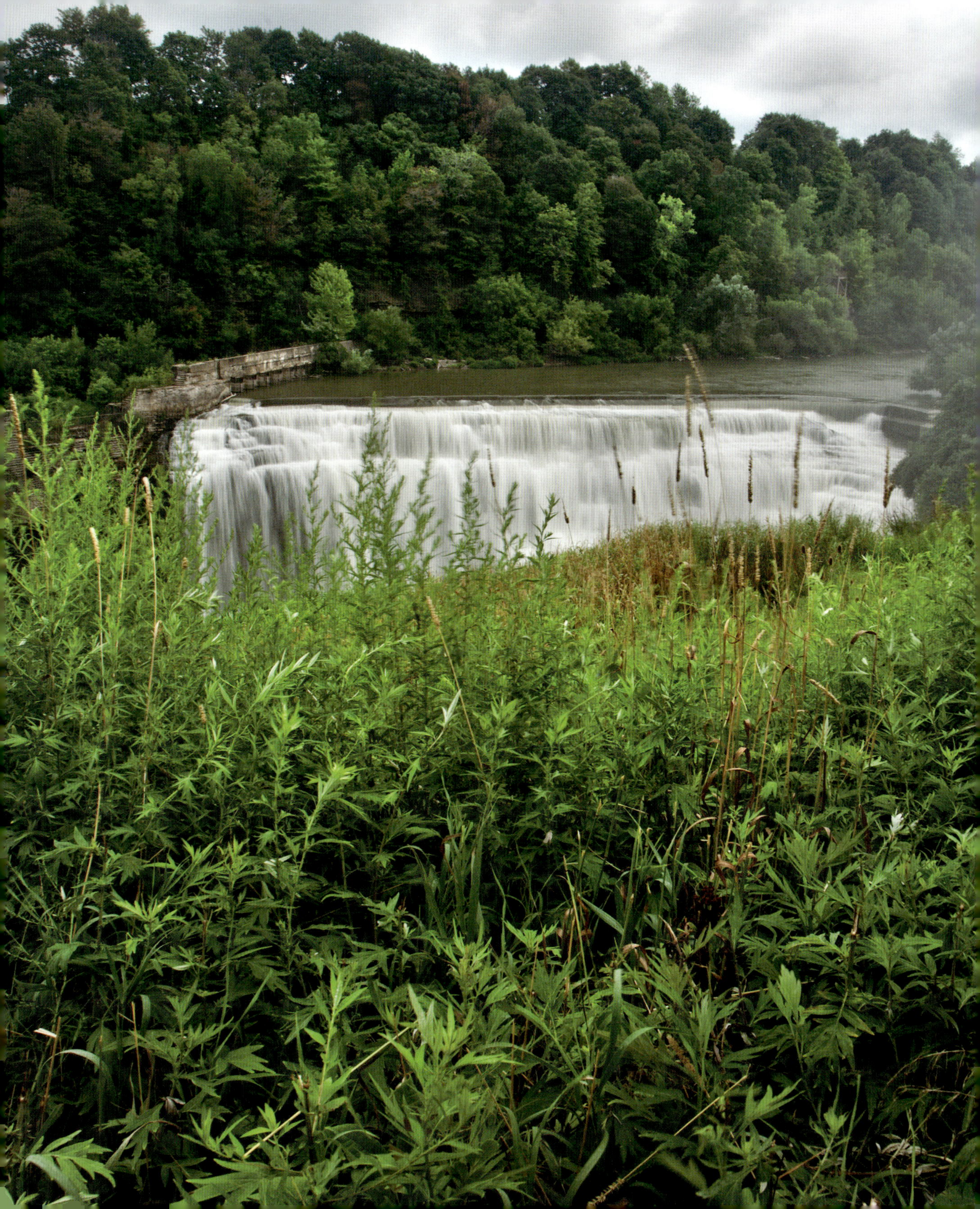

Stony Brook State Park

The lower entrance to Stony Brook State Park is located 3 mi (4.8 km) south of Dansville on NY 36. The upper (or campground) entrance is located 1.1 mi (1.8 km) to the south of the lower entrance, near the junction with Stony Brook Road (CR 47).

COUNTY: Steuben

TOWNSHIP: Dansville

PLACE: Dansville

WATERWAY: Stony Brook

TYPE:
Lower: classical falls
Middle: curtain falls

HEIGHT:
Lower : 36 ft (11 m)
Middle: 25 ft (7.6 m)

TRAIL: stone; easy

WALKING TIME:
15 min to the first waterfall
1.5 hr to view park

PEAK ACTIVITY: May-Oct.

LATITUDE:
Lower: 42.5166
Middle: 42.5158

LONGITUDE:
Lower: –77.6925
Middle: –77.6931

Three major waterfalls occur along the twisting gorge carved by the waters of Stony Brook as it flows through Stony Brook State Park. The gorge is developed in layers of shale and sandstone of the Late Devonian Period's Nunda Formation.

Follow the path from the lower parking lot to the snack bar, and pick up a brochure on the Gorge and West Rim trails. Then head southeast along the trail to the lower swimming area, where Stony Brook emerges from the gorge and flows into an enticing cliffside pool. This is the trailhead for the Gorge Trail, which is about 0.8 mile (1.3 km) long and ascends roughly 230 feet (70 m). As you continue south along the trail, the lovely scenery only improves.

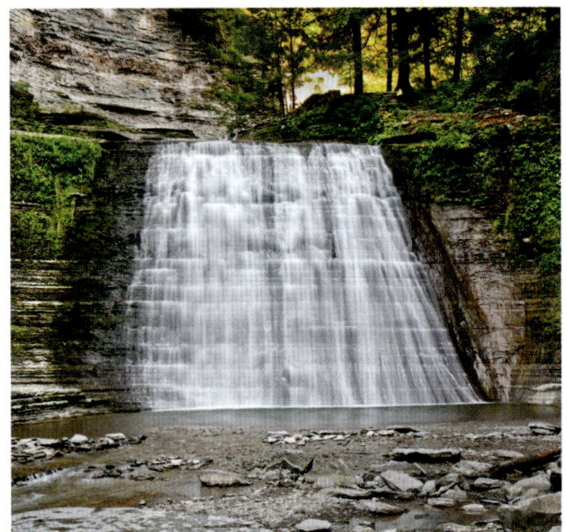

After passing several charming small waterfalls and rapids, you'll cross the brook for the second time. Continue along the trail, and in the distance is 36-foot-high (11 m) Lower Falls, with its 40-foot-wide (12.2 m) crest. During the low-water summer months, the brook flows only over the falls' western flank, but no matter what the water volume, this extremely steep waterfall is always pleasing.

The trails ascends beside Lower Falls, and just past its crest, you'll enter a small wooded area. Ahead is Middle Falls, a multiterraced waterfall that is 25 feet (7.6 m) high, with a 50-foot-wide (15.3 m) crest. Roughly 800 feet (244 m) beyond Middle Falls, the trail begins its ascent to the top of the gorge and the upper parking area. Along the way, you may catch a glimpse of 42-foot-high (12.8 m) Upper Falls between the trees to your left. At the top of the gorge, the West Rim Trail is on your right. Follow this trail north for 0.8 mile (1.3 km) to reach the lower parking area, where you started.

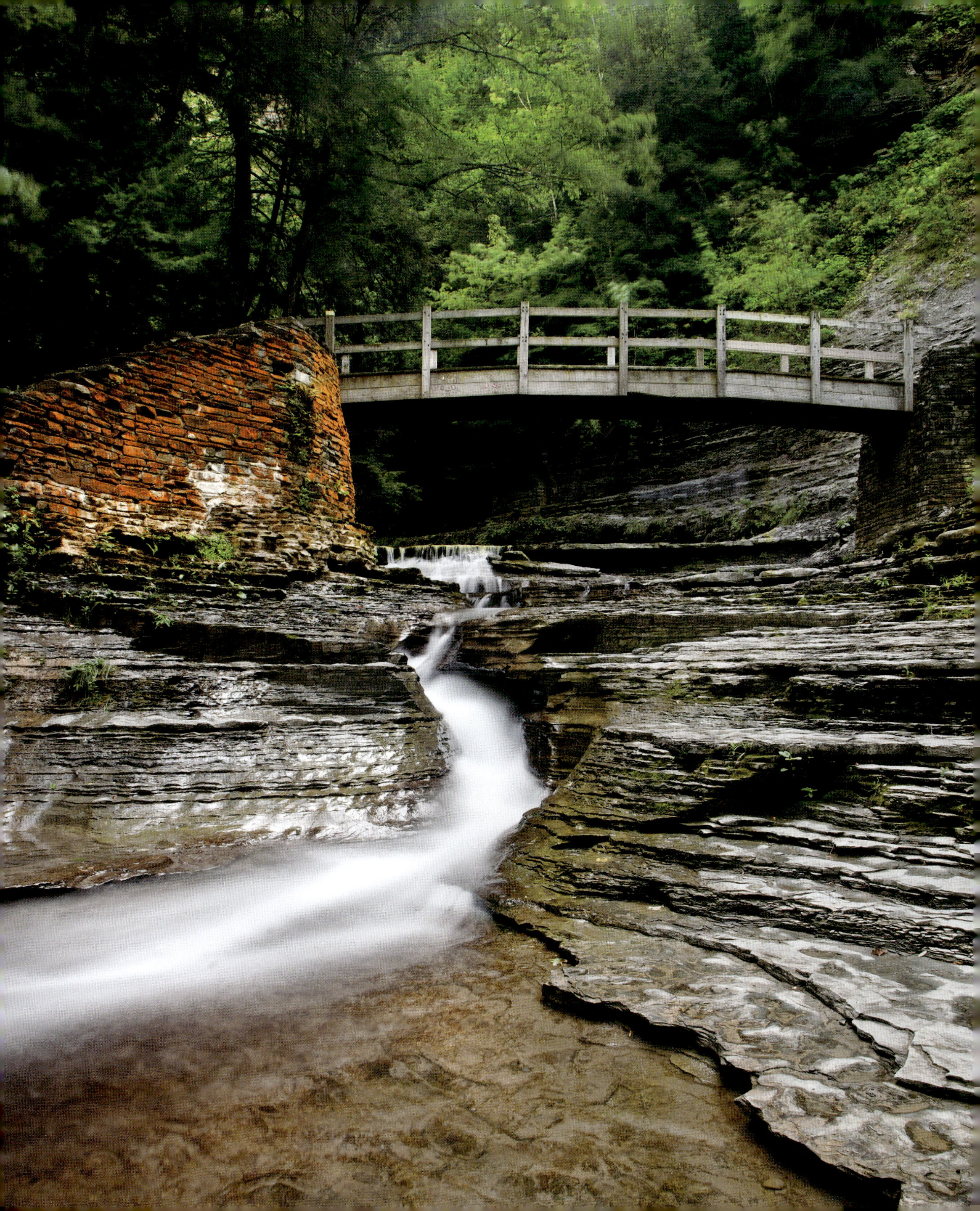

Letchworth State Park

Letchworth State Park is 35 mi (56.3 km) southwest of Rochester, between Mount Morris in the north and Portageville in the south. The park has six entrances: Mount Morris (NY 36), Perry (NY 39), Castile (NY 19A), Portageville (NY 19A), Parade Grounds (NY 436) and Mount Morris Dam (NY 408). Some entrances are closed during the winter. For detailed directions to the falls, pick up a map at the entrance.

COUNTY: Livingston and Wyoming

TOWNSHIP: Portage and Genesee Falls

PLACE: Mount Morris, Castile and Portageville

WATERWAY: Genesee River

TYPE: curtain falls

HEIGHT:
Upper: 70 ft (21.3 m)
Middle: 107 ft (32.6 m)
Lower: 70 ft (21.3 m)

TRAIL: stone, dirt, stairs and blacktop; easy to moderate

WALKING TIME:
Upper: 10 min
Middle: 10 min
Lower: 30 min

PEAK ACTIVITY: May-Oct.

LATITUDE:
Upper: 42.5786
Middle: 42.5831
Lower: 42.5856

LONGITUDE:
Upper: –78.0489
Middle: –78.0426
Lower: –78.0209

Massive Letchworth State Park encompasses 14,000 acres (5,666 ha) along the Genesee River. Given the park's scenic gorges, trails, roadways and recreational opportunities, visitors are never at a loss for something to do. But for some, the park's main attraction is its waterfalls. Its showcase waterfalls are the Upper, Middle and Lower falls, but more than 20 other waterfalls can be found on tributary streams that flow into the Genesee River. When you enter the park, be sure to ask for a map so that you can explore more of this incredibly beautiful park.

With a curving horseshoe-shaped crest about 300 feet (91.5 m) wide, Upper Falls is 70 feet (21.3 m) high. A substantial portion of the crest is overhung or nearly vertical. The caprock is Nunda Sandstone and is roughly 25 feet (7.6 m) thick. Below this layer are shale, siltstone and sandstone of the Gardeau Formation that date from the Late Devonian Period.

The Seneca believed that the sun stopped at midday to gaze in awe at the great beauty of Ska-ga-dee, Middle Falls. At 107 feet (32.6 m), this waterfall is generally considered the most remarkable of the three cataracts found in the park. Every evening from April through October, Middle Falls is illuminated by 5,000-watt white lights. The northwest end of the 285-foot-wide (86.8 m) crest is overhung, while the remainder is nearly vertical or very steeply terraced. Middle Falls is capped by a thick, erosion-resistant layer of sandstone from the Gardeau Formation.

Since the early 1950s, the lower section of Lower Falls has gradually eroded into two smaller falls. These are located about 250 feet (76 m) downstream from the upper section and have a total drop of roughly 15 feet (4.6 m). The riverbed between the two sections has been deepened considerably by the powerful Genesee River. The upper section now has a 55-foot (16.8 m) drop and faces north-northeast. The waterfall is capped by a thick layer of sandstone, and the crest is overhung for much of its width. As the two lower sections continue to retreat upstream, they will eventually unite with the upper section, forming a single waterfall with a 70-foot (21.3 m) drop and a 300-foot-wide (91.5 m) crest.

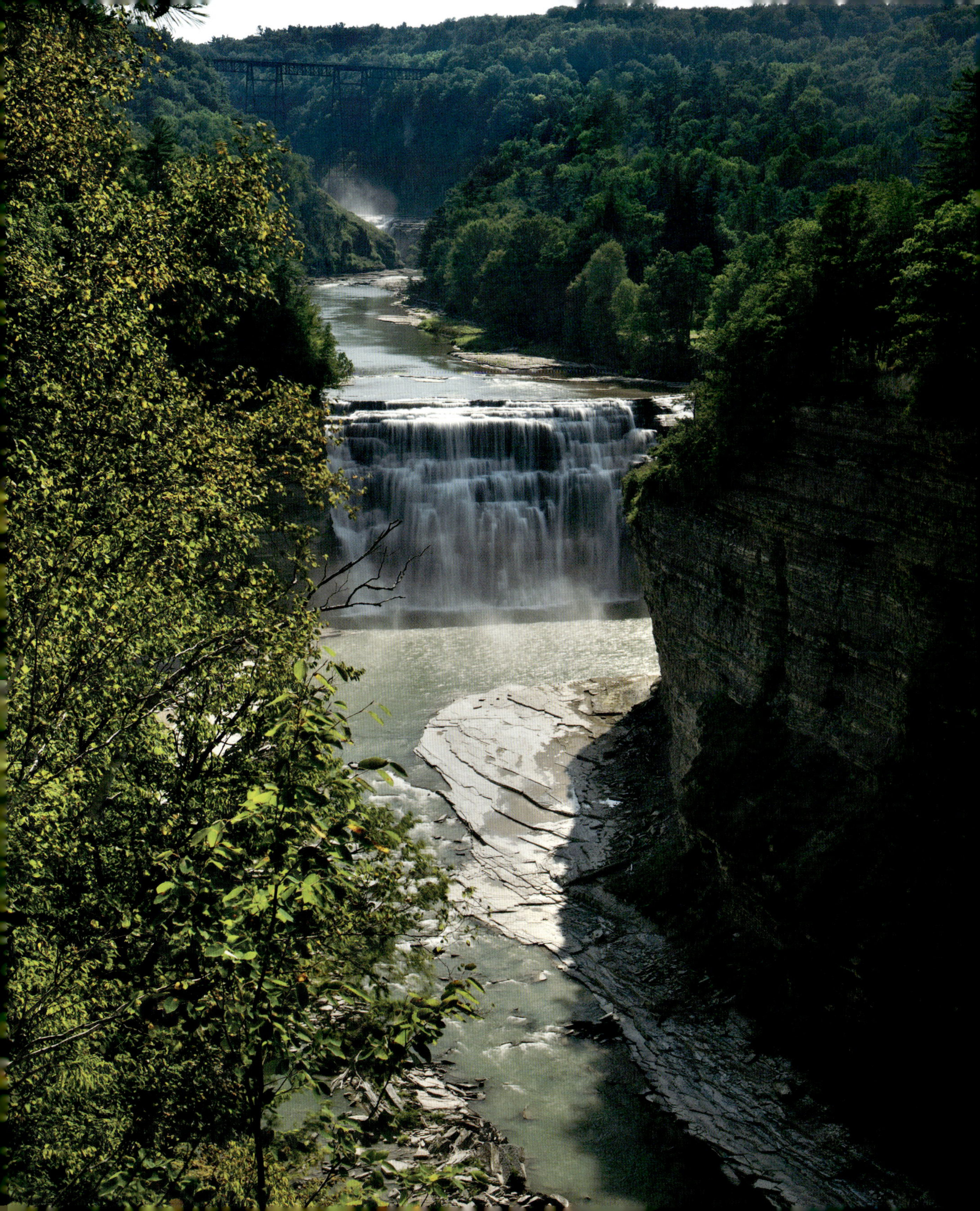

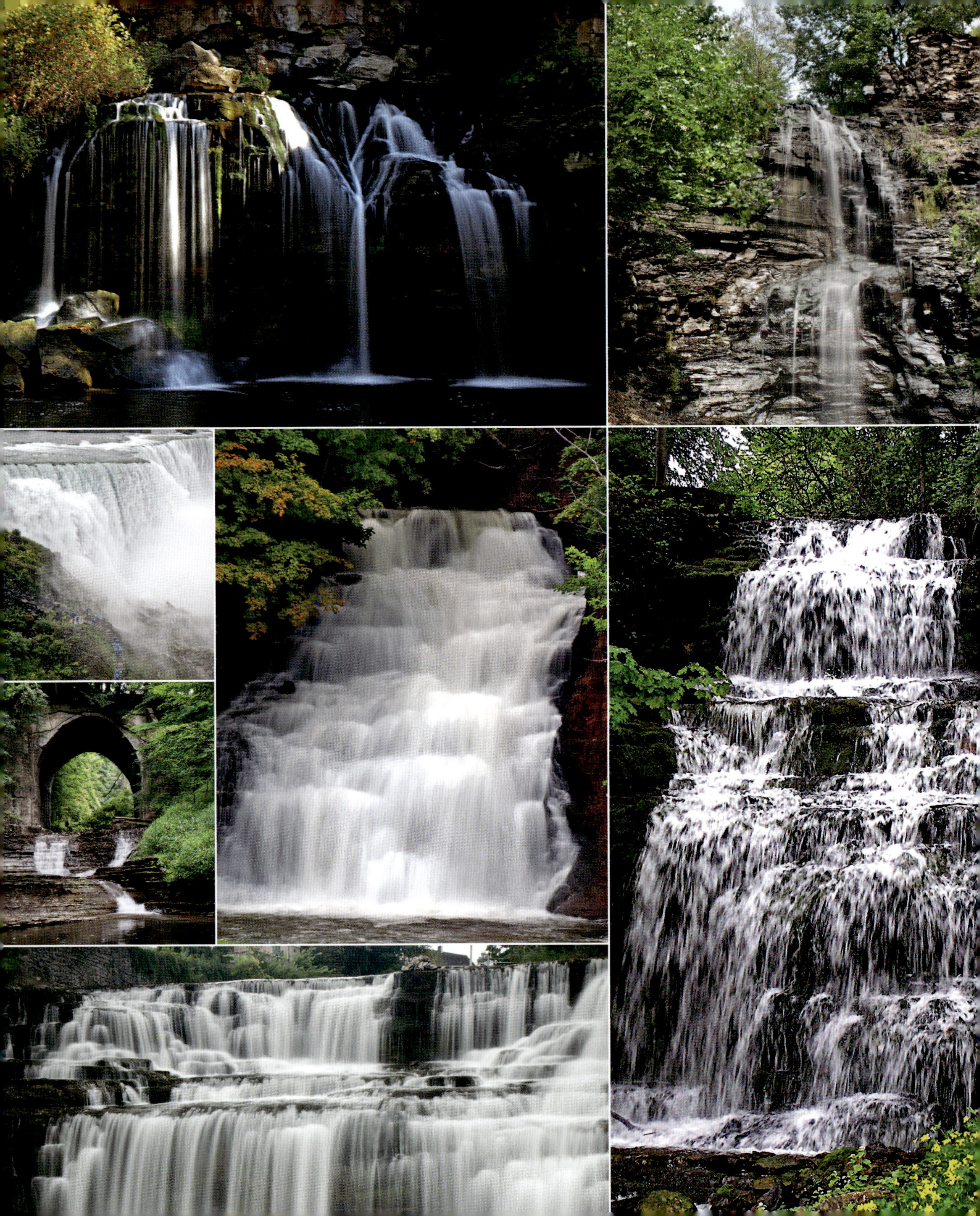

WATERFALLS OF NEW YORK STATE

Greater Niagara

Obvious bragging rights to the most popular and well-known waterfall in the state go to the Greater Niagara Region. Thundering over the Niagara Escarpment, Niagara Falls easily steals the world's attention, and it's not hard to understand how this natural wonder came to fuel a thriving tourist economy.

But if we follow the southern shores of Lake Erie and Lake Ontario and explore a little farther inland, we discover waterfalls that offer up their own unique charms. Eternal Flame Falls, for example, is one of several "burning springs" in this part of the state, as natural gas is released through cracks in the shale grotto at its base. Each waterfall is part of the intriguing story of the continent's geological history, and all impart details about the country's human history. Long ago, Native Americans made their homes around the waterfalls, and when European settlers arrived, most of the falls were used to power mills along the region's waterways. Even today, the waterfalls offer clues about the life of these early communities.

For waterfall lovers who have a thirst for an enchanting journey off the beaten path, the Greater Niagara Region has much to offer. Diverse and beautiful, this area's waterfalls will satisfy the most discriminating waterfall enthusiast, while offering a memorable setting for a family vacation.

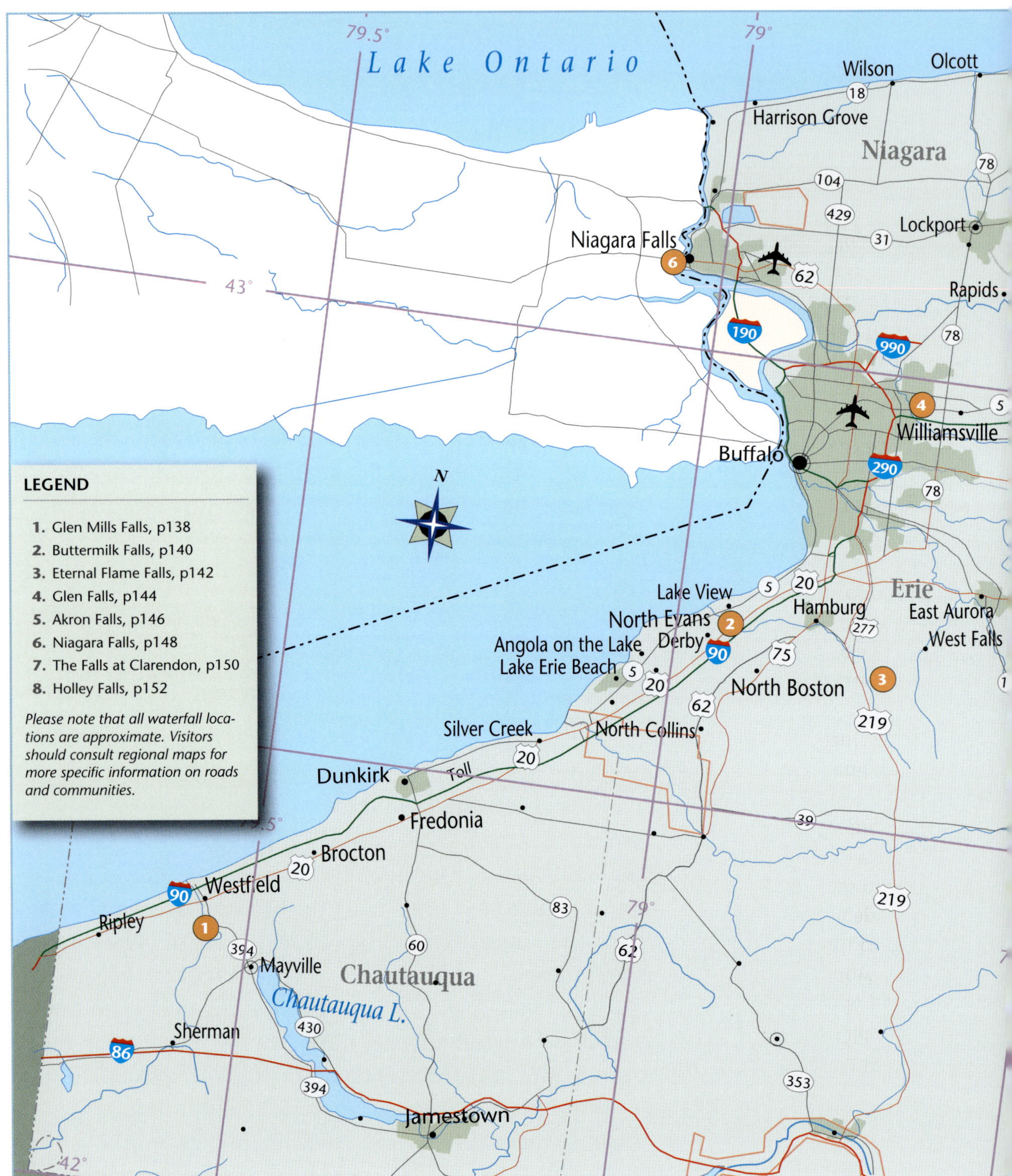
Lake Ontario
79.5°
79°
43°
42°
Wilson
Olcott
Harrison Grove
Niagara
Lockport
Rapids
Niagara Falls
Buffalo
Williamsville
Lake View
North Evans
Derby
Angola on the Lake
Lake Erie Beach
Hamburg
Erie
East Aurora
West Falls
North Boston
Silver Creek
North Collins
Dunkirk
Toll
Fredonia
Brocton
Westfield
Ripley
Mayville
Chautauqua
Chautauqua L.
Sherman
Jamestown
N
LEGEND
1. Glen Mills Falls, p138
2. Buttermilk Falls, p140
3. Eternal Flame Falls, p142
4. Glen Falls, p144
5. Akron Falls, p146
6. Niagara Falls, p148
7. The Falls at Clarendon, p150
8. Holley Falls, p152
Please note that all waterfall locations are approximate. Visitors should consult regional maps for more specific information on roads and communities.

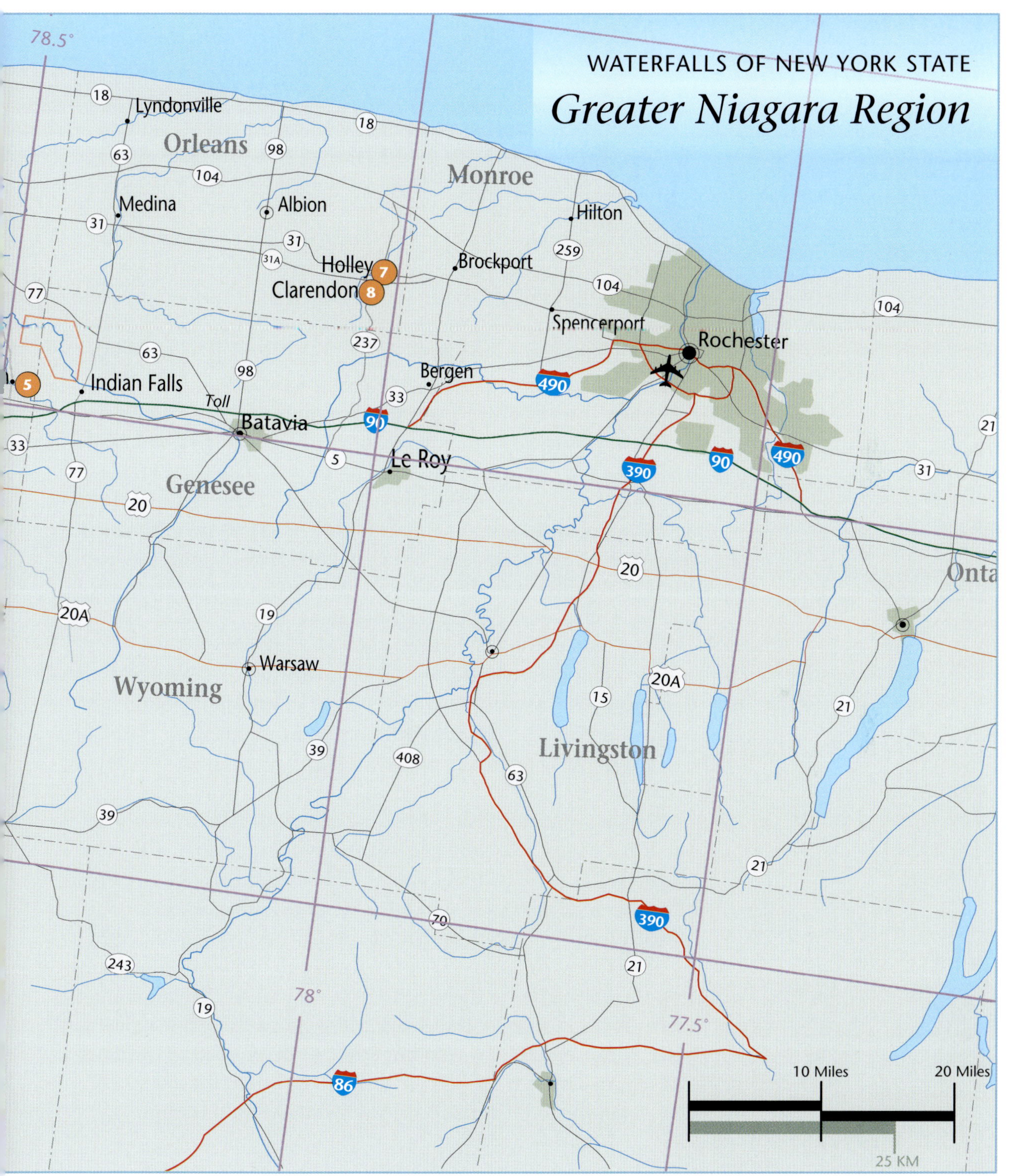

WATERFALLS OF NEW YORK STATE
Greater Niagara Region
78.5°
Lyndonville
Orleans
Medina
Albion
Holley
Clarendon
Monroe
Hilton
Brockport
Spencerport
Rochester
Bergen
Indian Falls
Toll
Batavia
Le Roy
Genesee
Wyoming
Warsaw
Livingston
Onta
78°
77.5°
10 Miles
20 Miles
25 KM

Glen Mills Falls

From exit 60 on I-90, follow NY 394 (North Portage St.) south into Westfield. Cross US 20, and continue south on NY 394 (now South Portage St.) for less than 1 mi (1.6 km), then turn right onto Old Portage Rd., which makes a 90-degree turn to the left. Find a place to park along the shoulder.

For alternative parking, take Old Portage Rd. east and turn right onto South Portage St. (NY 394). After 0.25 mi (0.4 km), make a sharp right-hand turn onto South Gale St. In less than 0.3 mi (0.5 km), there is a small parking area on the right and a viewing site for the falls to the east.

COUNTY: Chautauqua
TOWNSHIP: Westfield
PLACE: Westfield
WATERWAY: Little Chautauqua Creek
TYPE: curtain falls
HEIGHT: 12 ft (3.7 m)
TRAIL: old roadbed and dirt; moderate
WALKING TIME: 10 min
PEAK ACTIVITY: May-Oct.
LATITUDE: 42.3056
LONGITUDE: –79.5727

Walk south down the abandoned section of Old Portage Road from the parking area. Just before the Old Portage Road Bridge over the Little Chautauqua Creek, you'll see an unmarked trail to the right. Follow this rugged trail down into the gorge. The trail is very steep in spots, so proceed with care.

During the descent into the gorge, you'll notice what appears to be an overlook for the falls. It's actually the remains of an old iron bridge that once spanned Little Chautauqua Creek in the early part of the 20th century. While it offers a nice view of the ravine and falls, there is no railing, so again, use caution.

When you reach Little Chautauqua Creek, turn left and follow the creek upstream a short distance to the waterfall. Glen Mills Falls has two sections with a total vertical drop of 12 feet (3.7 m). The north-facing upper section has a 39-foot-wide (11.9 m) crest and a steep 8-foot (2.4 m) cascade. The creek then rushes along a 33-foot (10 m) flat segment to the 15-foot-wide (4.6 m) crest of the lower section. The creek is usually confined in a narrow flume on the southern side that has a vertical 4-foot (1.2 m) drop.

The waterfall is developed in the Northeast Shale Member of the Canadaway Formation. Northeast Shale consists mainly of beds of medium gray shale with a few beds of light gray siltstone; the shale dates from the Late Devonian Period, making it around 372 million years old.

The first mill at this site, a carding and cloth mill, was built by Timothy Pope in 1820 and later owned by Hiram Couch and Lester Stone. In 1850, the building was purchased and converted to a gristmill. A later owner of the mill, Charles Rhinehard, named it Glen Mills. The mill was destroyed by fire on Christmas night in 1895.

In October 1860, 11-year-old Grace Bedell of Westfield, a nearby town, wrote a letter to then presidential candidate Abraham Lincoln suggesting that if he let his whiskers grow, he would look a great deal better because his face was so thin. Lincoln responded to the letter, and within a month, he had grown a full beard. In February 1861, he met young Grace in person at the Westfield train station.

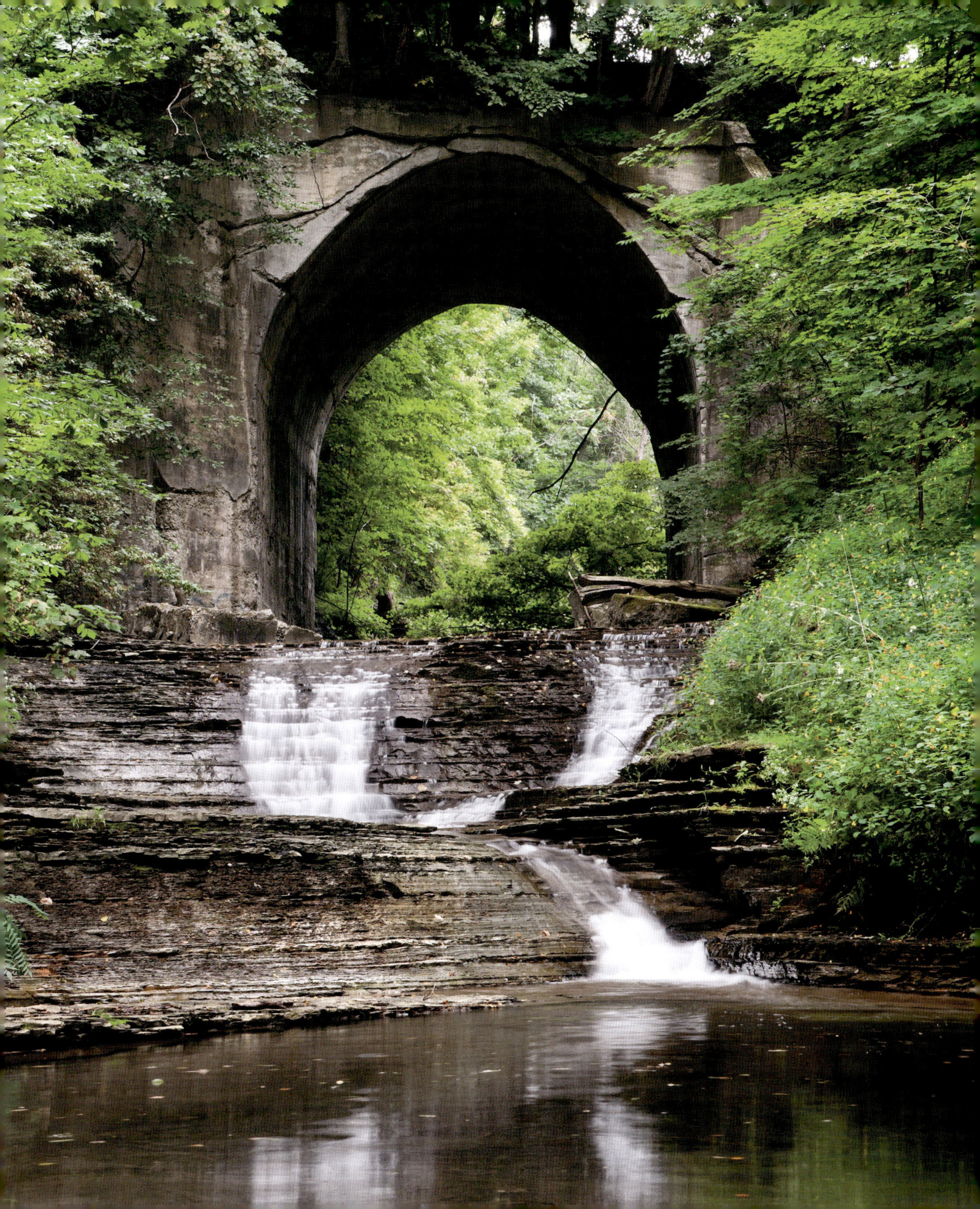

Buttermilk Falls

From the intersection of US 20 and NY 75, northwest of Hamburg, proceed south on US 20 for 5.5 mi (8.9 km) to the South Creek Rd. intersection. Turn right. After 0.3 mi (0.5 km), turn right onto Versailles Plank Rd. Drive slowly, as the road curves to the right and then makes a very sharp left down a hill. At the bottom of the hill, there is a small parking area for the Hobuck Flats Fishing Access Site that is mainly for access to Eighteen Mile Creek.

From the parking area, cross the pedestrian bridge that spans Eighteen Mile Creek, and continue along the trail with the creek to your right. Soon, you'll reach an old roadbed that leads up the hill. Turn right, walk down a small hill and along the creek until you come to a tributary. Be careful as you cross the slippery makeshift bridge over this part of the creek. Turn left and follow the tributary creek, which takes you to the base of Buttermilk Falls.

A tiered ribbon waterfall with two major drops, southwest-facing Buttermilk Falls has a crest elevation of 700 feet (213 m), a width of 11 feet (3.4 m) and a total drop of 15 feet (4.6 m). The upper drop is a very steep cascade and can be seen from the trail as you approach. The second drop of 54 feet (16.5 m) is nearly vertical. The cliffs are made of a soft, olive-gray-colored shale. Known as Cashaqua Shale, it dates from the Late Devonian Period and is roughly 370 million years old.

During a long, hot summer, the creek may dry up, so this waterfall is best seen in midspring. Please remember that access to Eighteen Mile Creek is a courtesy, thanks to the landowners. Respecting the property will ensure that this courtesy is extended, so please keep your visit to the falls short.

The nearby hamlet of North Evans was originally known as Johnson's Settlement. A tannery, sawmill and gristmill were once located on Eighteen Mile Creek, which is also the site of a popular fishing spot named Hobuck Flats. There are two slightly different stories about the origin of the name Hobuck Flats. The first is that an ox named Buck was used to pull wagons to and from the mills and tannery. To command him, the driver would call out, "Ho, Buck." In the other, the name of this ox was Hobuck. Upon its death, the animal was buried next to a tree in a nearby field. The North Evans Volunteer Fire Company, founded in 1927, has the image of an ox on its fire engines and rescue truck.

COUNTY: Erie

TOWNSHIP: Hamburg

PLACE: North Evans

WATERWAY: unnamed tributary of Eighteen Mile Creek

TYPE: ribbon falls

HEIGHT: 69 ft (21 m)

TRAIL: dirt; easy

WALKING TIME: 15 min

PEAK ACTIVITY: May-Oct.

LATITUDE: 42.7009

LONGITUDE: –78.9369

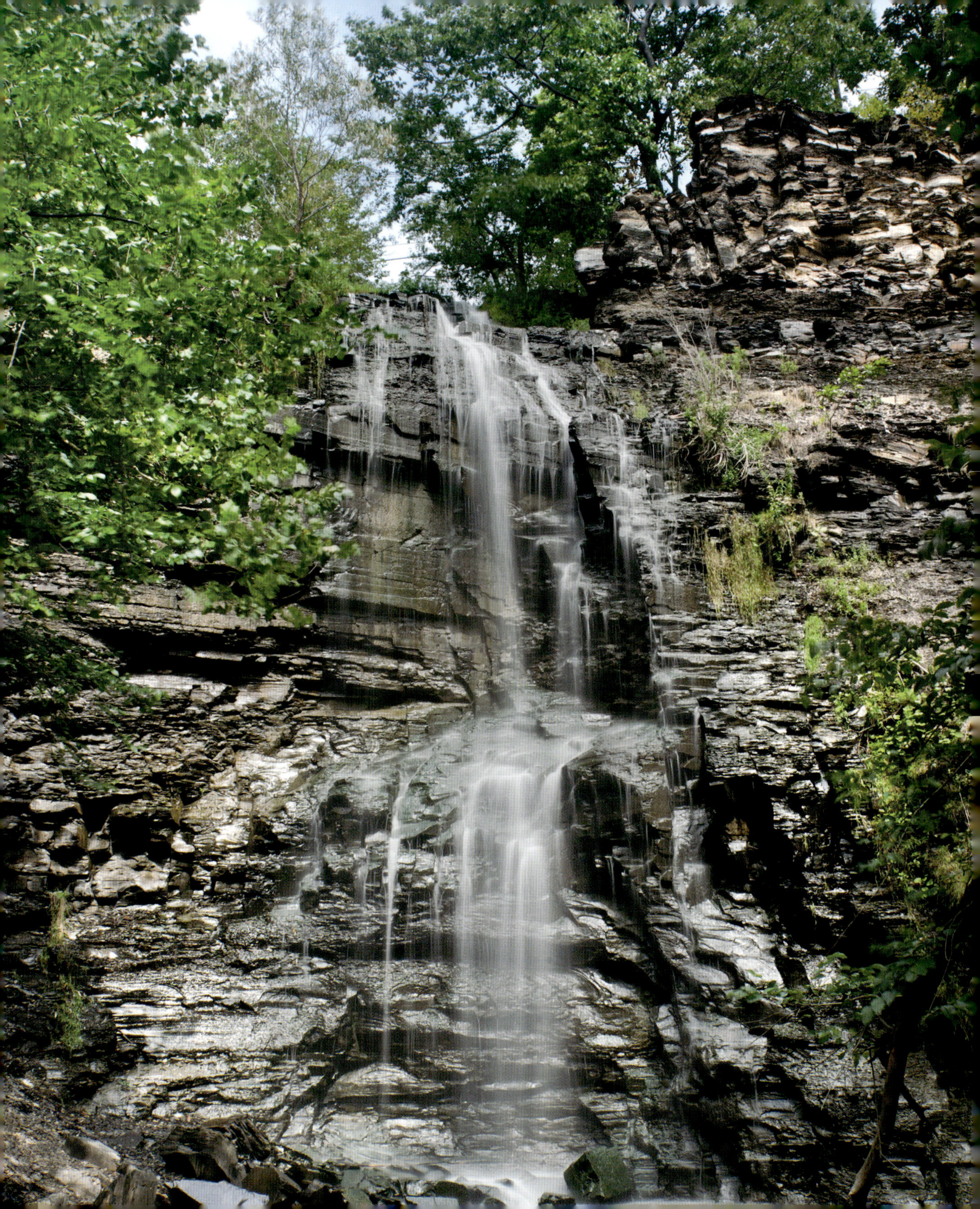

Eternal Flame Falls

Eternal Flame Falls is located in Chestnut Ridge Park, 3.5 mi (5.6 km) south of Orchard Park. From the main entrance to Chestnut Ridge Park on NY 277, drive south for 1.3 mi (2.1 km) to Seufert Rd. and turn right. In roughly 250 ft (76 m), there is a gravel parking area along the shoulder of the road, where parking is available from 7 a.m. to 7 p.m.

COUNTY: Erie

TOWNSHIP: Orchard Park

PLACE: North Boston

WATERWAY: Shale Creek

TYPE: ribbon falls

HEIGHT: 30 ft (9 m)

TRAIL: stone and dirt; moderate

WALKING TIME: 45 min

PEAK ACTIVITY: May-Oct.

LATITUDE: 42.7016

LONGITUDE: –78.7508

Shale Creek carved a deep glen in the southern end of Chestnut Ridge Park, eventually creating the 30-foot (9 m) waterfall known as Eternal Flame Falls. With its 10-foot (3 m) crest, the waterfall is developed in Hanover Shale of the Late Devonian Period. The greenish gray shale is 85 to 95 feet (26–29 m) thick and features black bands.

The trailhead to the falls is marked by two white brick pillars and an orange gate. Follow the trail north for about 500 feet (153 m) to a kiosk, where a map of the area trails is posted. (You'll see a large redwood log nearby.) From the kiosk, follow the blue diamond blazes nailed to trees. After less than 1 mile (1.6 km), you'll come to Shale Creek. Cross the creek and continue following the markers northwest, keeping to the left along the top of the ravine. Soon, the trail descends into the ravine to the creek. When you reach the creek, turn left and head upstream for about 0.4 mile (0.6 km) to the falls. Take note of your route, as you'll be returning the same way.

In a small grotto on the right side of the falls, you'll discover the reason for this waterfall's name. When lit, natural gas emissions from cracks in the shale produce a flame from 3 to 8 inches (7.6–20 cm) high, depending on the pressure of the gas. (At times, there have been as many as three flames in the back of the grotto.) Flooding, pressure fluctuations and ice may occasionally extinguish the flame, but it is easily reignited with a lighter.

These natural emissions are sometimes called "burning springs," and there are at least six other such springs in the western half of the state. The first commercial attraction at Niagara Falls was a burning spring. In the late 1700s, a forceful gas emission was discovered on the Canadian side of the Niagara River, less than 1 mile (1.6 km) upriver from Horseshoe Falls. A barrel with a pipe was positioned over the vent and a cork placed in the pipe to allow the buildup of gas. After an audience had gathered, the cork was removed and the gas lit. Guidebooks of the day cited this as a place one must visit. The attraction continued to operate until the late 1880s, when the area was turned into a park.

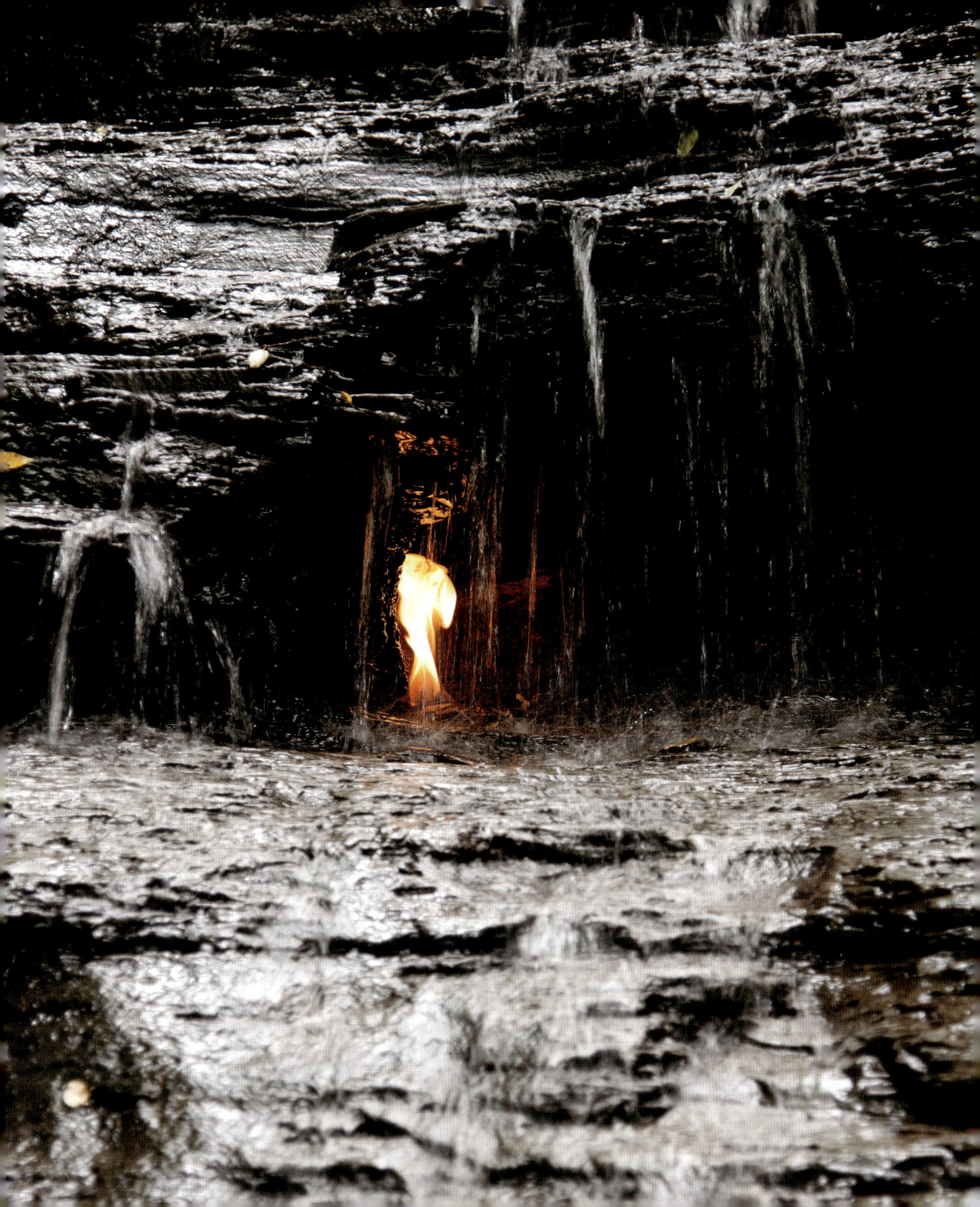

Glen Falls

From the intersection of I-290 and NY 5, follow NY 5 east for about 1.5 mi (2.4 km) to Mill St. in Williamsville. Turn left onto Mill St. After 0.2 mi (0.3 km), turn left onto Glen Ave. Cross Ellicott Creek, and turn right into the Glen Park parking lot. (The cross street is Rock St.) Cross Glen Ave. to enter the park. The waterfall is about 400 ft (122 m) south of Glen Ave.

A wheelchair-accessible parking lot and viewing area are located on the south side of Glen Ave., just before you cross Ellicott Creek.

COUNTY: Erie

TOWNSHIP: Amherst

PLACE: Williamsville

WATERWAY: Ellicott Creek

TYPE: curtain falls

HEIGHT: 27 ft (8.2 m)

TRAIL: blacktop; easy

WALKING TIME: 10 min

PEAK ACTIVITY: May-Oct.

LATITUDE: 42.9638

LONGITUDE: –78.7441

As Ellicott Creek descends the Onondaga Escarpment, Glen Falls plunges 9 feet (2.7 m), then 8 feet (2.4 m) over a steep cascading section and, finally, another 10 feet (3 m) to the base of the falls. The bedrock at the waterfall's 76-foot-wide (23 m) crest is Onondaga Limestone, from the Early Devonian Period, while the bedrock at the base of the falls is Akron Dolostone, from the Late Silurian. The limestone contains significant outcrops of black chert (similar to flint), which the Seneca — who called this area Ga-sko-sa-da-ne-o, meaning "many falls" — used to make spear points, arrowheads and hide scrapers.

In 1799, John Thomson and Joseph Ellicott, for whom Ellicott Creek is named, purchased land near the falls. Ellicott built a sawmill on the east bank of the creek. Initially unsuccessful, the mill was repaired around 1804 by Jonas Williams, who later built another sawmill, two gristmills, a tannery and a distillery. To power all the mills, Williams developed a system of dams and raceways. The settlement that grew up around the mills was first known as Williams Mills but was soon renamed Williamsville.

In 1911, Louis M. Conshafter bought the land surrounding the falls and opened Conshafter's Picnic Grounds. During the 1920s, the grounds were sold to Harry Altman, who built the Harry Altman Glen Park Casino complex.

Glen Falls was not always beautiful. Some time after the amusement park was developed on the west side of the falls, a small zoo and a night club were added. In 1968, the amusement park and the night club, known as the Inferno — a famous performance hall for the era's musicians — were destroyed by fire. The village board favored commercial development with a small overlook for the falls. In a 1973 referendum, however, the majority of villagers voted that the entire area be used as a park. Four years later, Glen Park opened to the public.

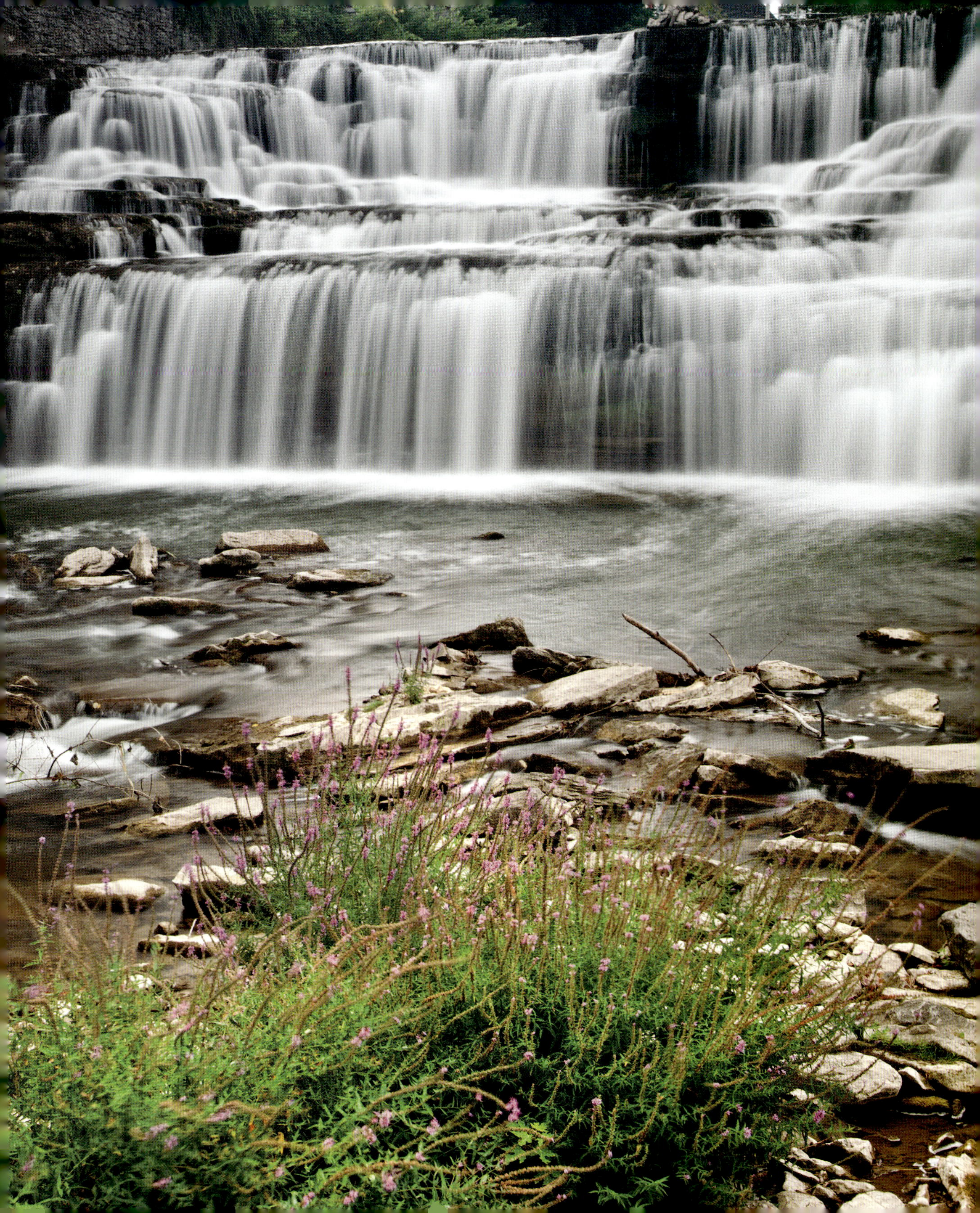

Akron Falls

Owned and maintained by Erie County, Akron Falls Park is located on the southeast side of Akron. From the intersection of NY 5 and NY 93, go east on NY 5 for 1.3 mi (2.1 km). At Crittenden Rd., turn left. In 0.9 mi (1.4 km), turn left onto Skyline Dr. and continue for a little more than 0.2 mi (0.3 km). Keep right, and you'll enter Akron Falls Park. After about 500 ft (153 m), turn right into the parking area for comfort station number 4. (Facing page: Photo © Scott A. Ensminger)

COUNTY: Erie

TOWNSHIP: Newsted

PLACE: Akron

WATERWAY: Murder Creek

TYPE: classical falls

HEIGHT: 44 ft (13.4 m)

TRAIL: blacktop and stone stairs; easy

WALKING TIME: 10 min

PEAK ACTIVITY: May-Oct.

LATITUDE: 43.0152

LONGITUDE: –78.4837

By definition, 44-foot (13.4 m) Akron Falls is a classical waterfall. But for most of the year, the waterfall, which is developed in Akron Dolostone of the Late Silurian Period, resembles a ribbon. Only in times of high water does Murder Creek flow over the entire 40-foot-wide (12.2 m) crest.

Typically, the creek plunges from a 5-foot (1.5 m) channel on the southwest side of the crest, free-falls 20 feet (6.1 m) and strikes a ledge. It then fans out across about 20 feet (6.1 m) and drops into a plunge pool.

When the water is very low, the stream disappears into cracks in the dolostone creekbed before it reaches the crest of the falls, then reappears from horizontal cracks about 15 feet (4.6 m) below the crest as a series of springs on the northeast side of the falls.

To view the falls, follow the blacktop trail that starts at the entrance end of the parking lot. The trail descends into the ravine and turns to the east, heading upstream. Roughly 400 feet (122 m) after entering the ravine, you'll reach the viewing area. Please stay on the established trail.

The Seneca knew Akron Falls as Wun-ne-pac-tuc, meaning "beautiful waterfall." In the late 1820s, early settlers called it Falkirk Falls. In 1831, at a meeting held to name the settlement just west of the falls, Sylvester Goff submitted the name Akron, reportedly inspired by the Greek word *akros*, meaning "extreme" or "highest," for the hills in the area.

According to local legend, Murder Creek derives its name from the slaying of Chief Great Fire by a settler named Sanders. Shortly after, Sanders and Gray Wolf, a Seneca, fought over the affections of Wild Rose, the chief's daughter. After a terrible battle with hunting knives, Sanders fell dead and Gray Wolf was severely wounded. He took a few steps toward Wild Rose but succumbed to his wounds. Some time later, Wild Rose was found cold and lifeless on the grave of her beloved Gray Wolf, dead of a broken heart. As the legend goes, if you walk along Murder Creek on a moonlit night, you may hear the voices and footsteps of the two lovers as they wander the ancient trails.

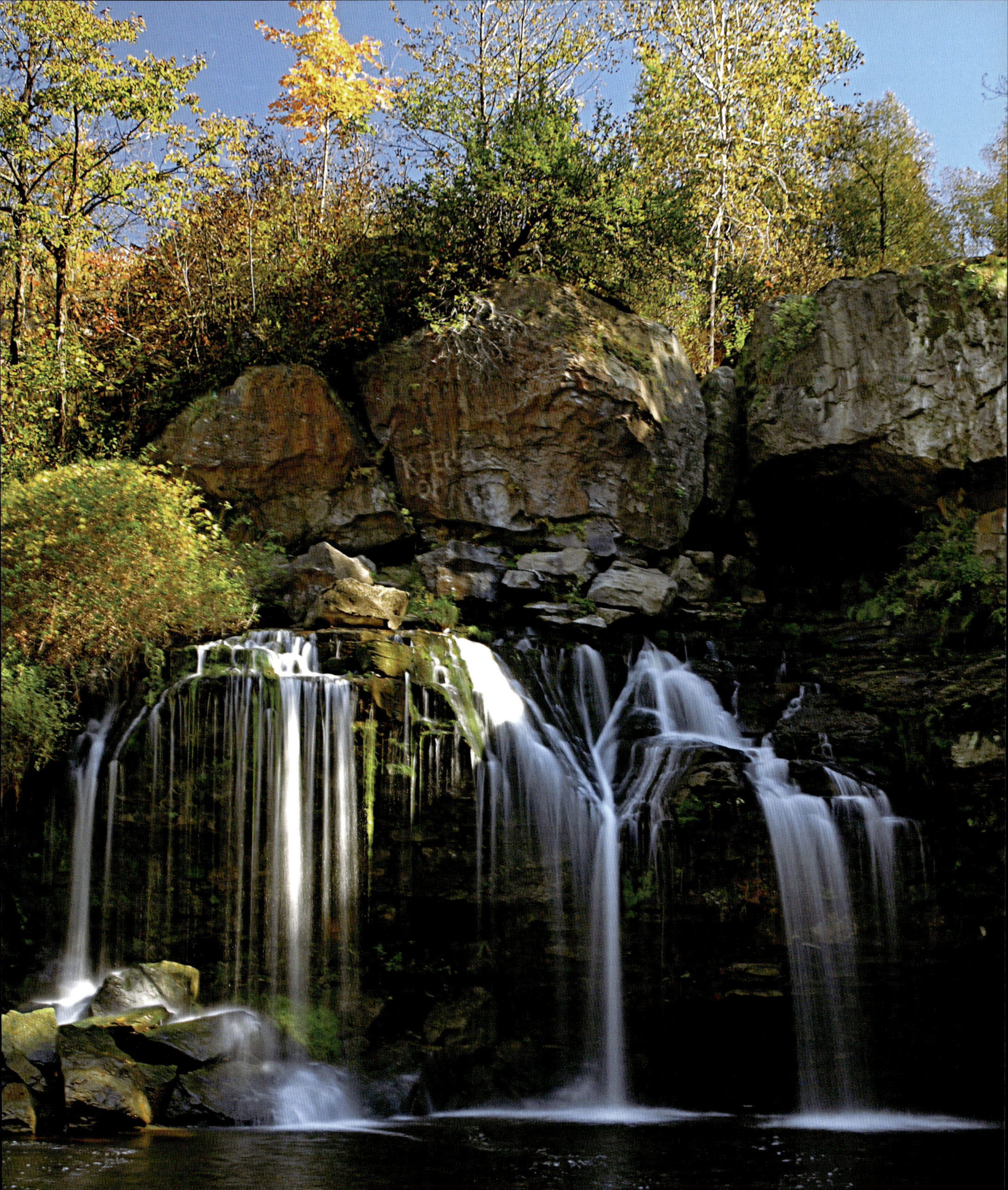

GREATER NIAGARA REGION

Niagara Falls

From the intersection of NY 62 and I-290 on the north side of Buffalo, follow I-290 west for 5 mi (8 km) and merge with I-190. Follow I-190 north for 7.9 mi (12.7 km). RIght after the North Grand Island Bridge, take exit 21, pass under the bridge, and merge onto the Robert Moses State Parkway. Drive west along the Niagara River for 3.2 mi (5.1 km) to the city of Niagara Falls. Keep left, and in 0.4 mile (0.6 km), just past Old Falls St., you'll see the entrance to Niagara Falls State Park's main parking lot. Alternative parking can be found on Goat Island and in private lots.

COUNTY: Niagara

TOWNSHIP: Niagara Falls

PLACE: Niagara Falls

WATERWAY: Niagara River

TYPE: Horseshoe and American, curtain; Bridal Veil, ribbon

HEIGHT: Horseshoe: 173 ft (52.7); American: 183 ft (55.8 m); Bridal Veil: 181 ft (55.2 m)

TRAIL: concrete sidewalks; easy

WALKING TIME: varies

PEAK ACTIVITY: May-Sept.

LATITUDE:
Horseshoe: 43.0773
American: 43.0846
Bridal Veil: 43.0835

LONGITUDE:
Horseshoe: –79.0747
American: –79.0695
Bridal Veil: –79.0708

On the border of New York State and the Province of Ontario, the Niagara River thunders over the Niagara Escarpment as Niagara Falls. One of the world's greatest waterfalls and certainly one of its most famous is actually three separate waterfalls: two colossal cataracts, Horseshoe Falls and American Falls, and the narrower Bridal Veil Falls.

The average natural water flow over Niagara Falls is 202,000 cubic feet (5,720 m^3) per second. Since the mid-1950s, however, more than half of that volume has been diverted from April to October for hydroelectric power production. From November to March, three-quarters of the water is diverted. The smaller water volumes result in a lowering of the plunge pool below the falls and thus an increase in the height of the falls. The height measurements given here are for the April to October viewing time, when the total volume of water passing over Niagara Falls is 100,000 cubic feet (2,832 m^3) per second.

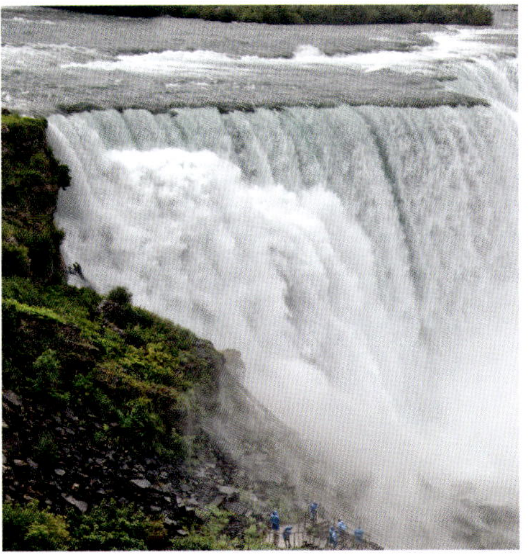

There's a lot to see at this major tourist attraction. Walk south from the main parking lot to the Visitors Center, which offers a wealth of information on the park. Don't miss the Niagara Falls Observation Tower, the boat tour below the falls, Luna Island, Cave of the Winds and the Niagara Gorge Discovery Center. An alternative to walking is to take the Niagara Falls Scenic Trolley. Aboard the trolley, you can enjoy a 3-mile (4.8 km) 30-minute guided tour of the park, and you can also disembark at various stops along the way to explore on your own.

On the Ontario side of the falls, the Journey Behind the Falls, located at the Table Rock Welcome Centre, is a must-see.

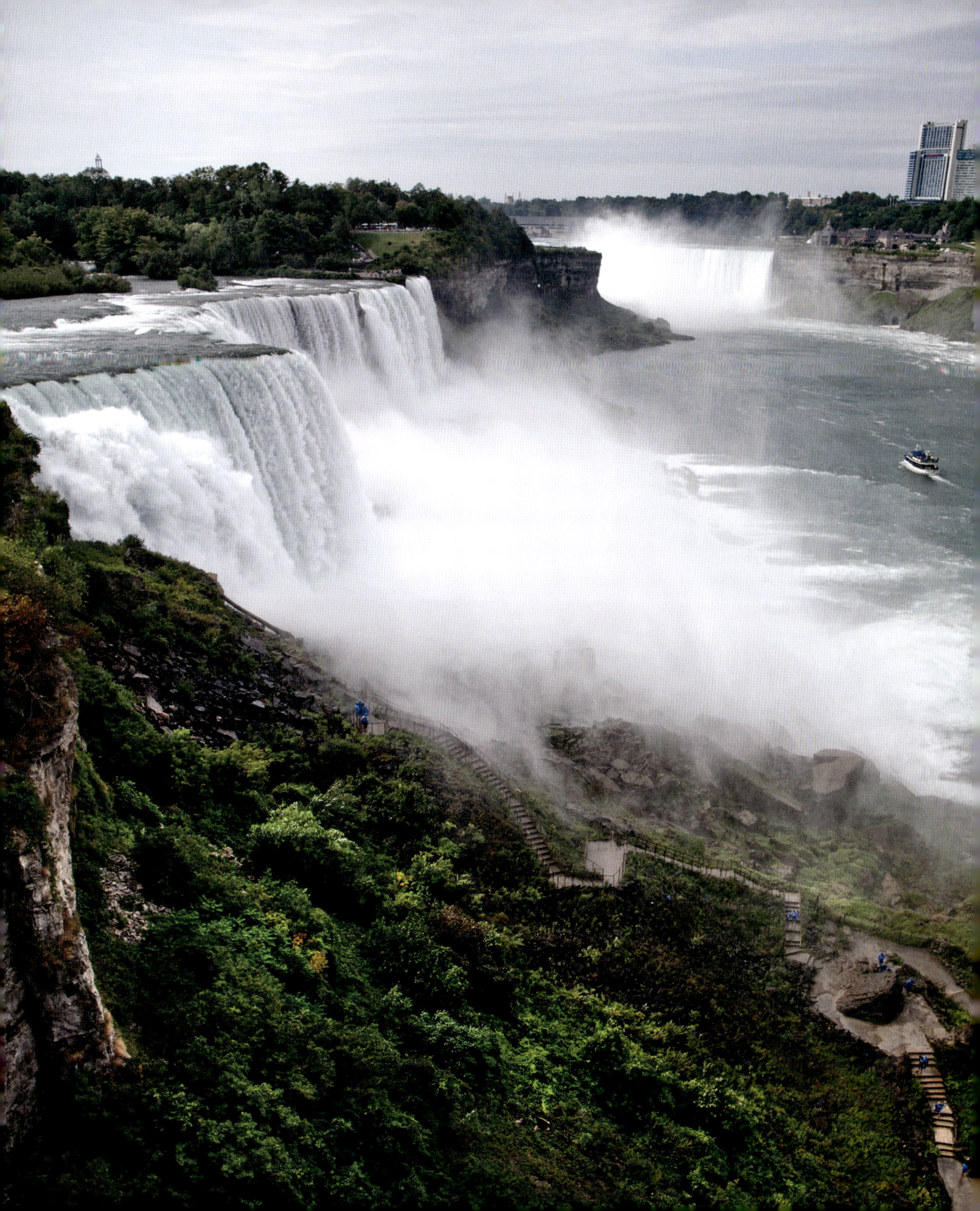

The Falls at Clarendon

From the intersection of NY 31A and NY 237 in Clarendon, turn south on NY 237. Drive for about 0.1 mi (0.2 km), and turn right into the parking lot of the town park. The Falls at Clarendon is located about 200 ft (60 m) west of the parking lot. Walk directly to the base of the falls, or follow the trail that crosses the creek near the picnic pavilion. (Facing page: Photo © Scott A. Ensminger)

COUNTY: Orleans
TOWNSHIP: Clarendon
PLACE: Clarendon
WATERWAY: unnamed
TYPE: ribbon falls
HEIGHT: 26 ft (7.9 m)
TRAIL: grass; easy
WALKING TIME: 5 min
PEAK ACTIVITY: May-Oct.
LATITUDE: 43.1918
LONGITUDE: –78.0660

The waterway, an unnamed tributary of Sandy Creek's East Branch, cascades before making a 7-foot (2.1 m) vertical leap. After the first plunge, there is a short break, and then the creek fans out to a width of about 20 feet (6.1 m). The remainder of the drop is an extremely steep cascade with some free-falling sections.

With a total height of 26 feet (7.9 m), an 8-foot-wide (2.4 m) crest and a 23-foot (7 m) base, the Falls at Clarendon is at its best in the spring or after a period of heavy rain. Developed in the Gasport Dolostone Member of the Lockport Formation, the waterfall faces east. The dolostone is bluish gray and dates from the Early Silurian Period, making it roughly 432 million years old.

The waterfall was discovered in 1810 by Eldridge Farwell, while he was out looking for his brother's horse, which had strayed. Recognizing the potential water power of the falls, Farwell returned early the next year and built a sawmill and, a couple of years later, a gristmill. Clarendon was originally known as Farwell's Mills, but the name was changed when Orleans County was established in the 1820s.

In the 1870s and 1880s, Ogden Miller and Walter Pettengill owned a sawmill and gristmill at the falls. They also started a stave mill and developed a groundbreaking cider-evaporator process, eventually moving the business to Holley for better access to the railroad. In 1937, Morris Brackett donated land for a community park at the falls, though Brackett's dream didn't become a reality until 1965.

Geologists have detected a major earthquake fault about 0.5 mile (0.8 km) west of the ridge over which the falls plunges. Known as the Clarendon-Linden Fault, it has been traced north and south of Clarendon for roughly 60 miles (97 km) in each direction. The last major quake to be felt in the area occurred at 6:30 a.m. on August 12, 1929. No damage was reported in Clarendon, but the village of Attica, 25 miles (40 km) to the southwest, reported that hundreds of chimneys were toppled.

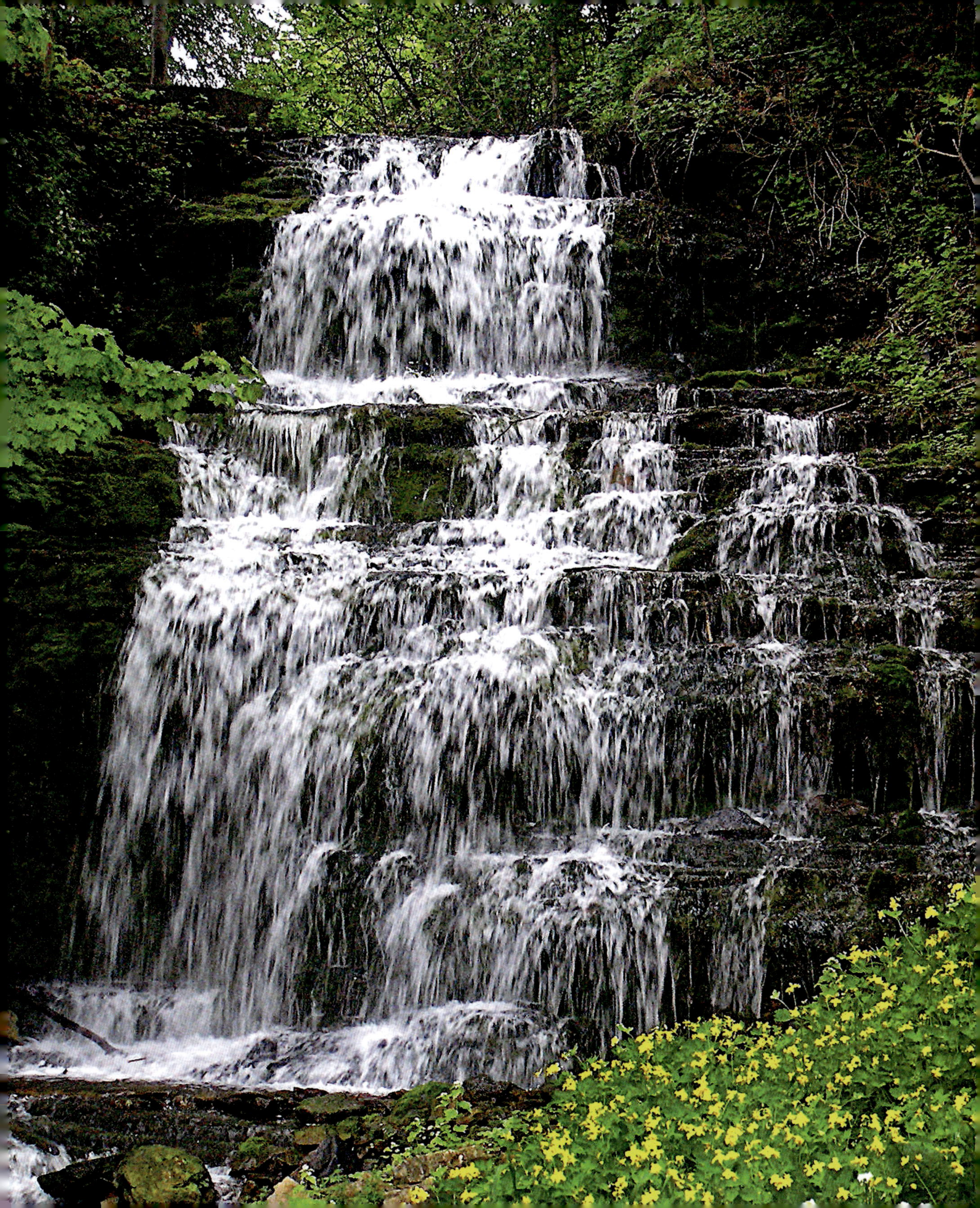

Holley Falls

From the intersection of NY 31A and NY 237 in Clarendon, follow NY 237 (Holley Byron Rd.) north for 2.8 mi (4.5 km) to Holley. Drive under the railroad bridge, and turn right onto Batavia St. After about 500 ft (153 m), turn left onto Mechanic St. (NY 31). One block later, turn right onto Frisbie Terr. (the cross street is Thomas St.). On the left, you'll pass a supermarket and a large, green Department of Public Works garage. On the right, a road leads downhill to Falls Park, less than 0.2 mi (0.3 km) away. At the end of the road, there is a parking area; the falls are plainly visible to the southeast. The park has picnic tables and a pavilion and is open year-round from sunrise until 10 p.m. (Facing page: Photo © Scott A. Ensminger)

COUNTY: Orleans

TOWNSHIP: Murray

PLACE: Holley

WATERWAY: overflow from the Erie Canal

TYPE: ribbon cascade

HEIGHT: 34 ft (10.4 m)

TRAIL: grass; easy

WALKING TIME: 5 min

PEAK ACTIVITY: May-Oct.

LATITUDE: 43.2250

LONGITUDE: –78.0183

With a 15-foot-wide (4.6 m) crest, Holley Falls plunges vertically for 6 feet (1.8 m), finishing the rest of its dramatic 34-foot (10.4 m) drop with a steep cascade. Once known locally as Glen Falls, the waterfall today is also called Holley Canal Falls. The purplish red rock beneath the water is Grimsby, or Medina, Sandstone. Its color comes from small amounts of iron found in the sediments from which it formed. It dates from the Early Silurian Period, roughly 427 million years ago.

When the sandstone was discovered in the early 1800s, several quarries opened in the area, and the Erie Canal was used to ship the sandstone out to the world. Thanks to its durability and magnificent color, the rock became a much-sought-after building material, locally and internationally, and was used in the New York State Capitol, Buckingham Palace and, more modestly, as street curbing. Once it was replaced by concrete as a construction material, however, sandstone was no longer quarried extensively in the area.

An excellent trail system connects the falls with the Erie Canal and the village of Holley, but there aren't many signs directing pedestrians to the area above the falls and canal. To reach the canal from Falls Park, cross the bridge over Sandy Creek and head toward the picnic pavilion. Follow the trail to the right for about 300 feet (9.5 m) until it curves northeast. You'll pass another trail heading south, and in roughly 650 feet (198 m), after passing a short loop trail to your right, you'll encounter the spillway gate for the Erie Canal. This spillway is the major source of the water that passes over Holley Falls.

The village, established in 1850, was originally named Saltport but was renamed to honor Myron Holley, a former commissioner of the Erie Canal. The falls probably came into existence around 1913, when the canal was widened and straightened, creating surplus water from the canal. After passing over the falls, the water flows into the East Branch of Sandy Creek, which then flows under the canal. This section of the canal is drained from November to May, and the flow over the falls may be rather low at this time.

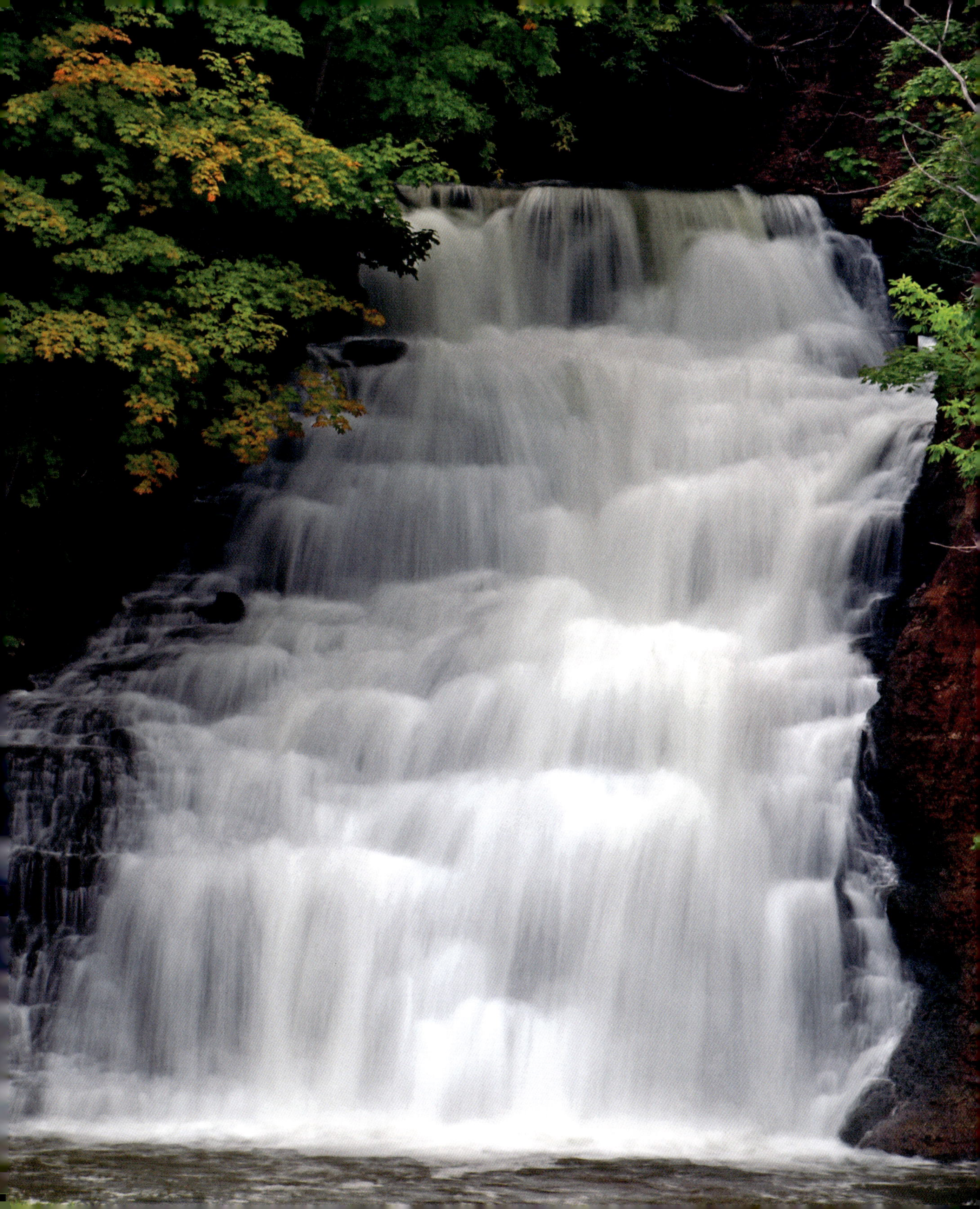

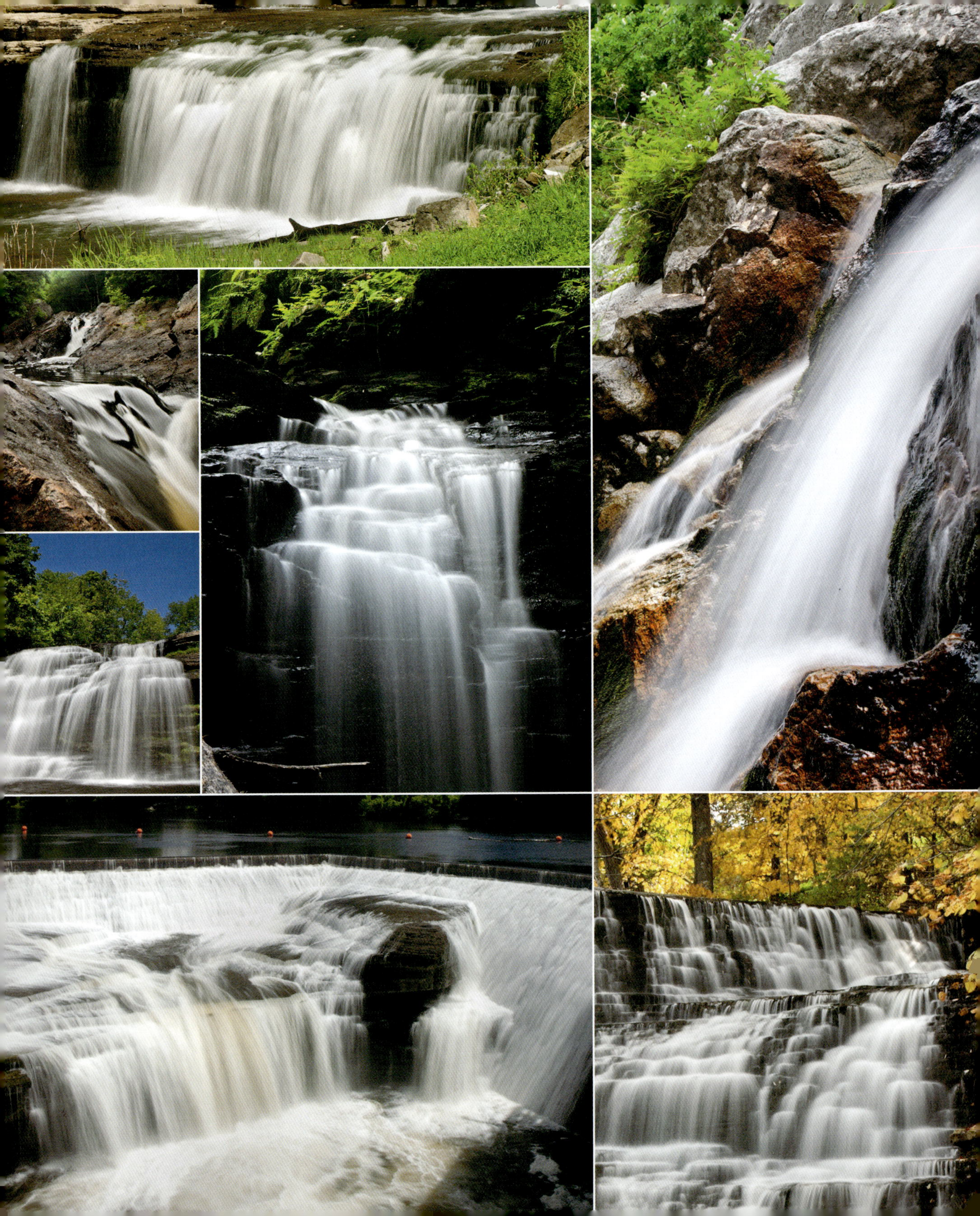

WATERFALLS OF NEW YORK STATE

North Country

Bordered on the west by Lake Ontario, on the north by the St. Lawrence River and the international border with Canada, on the east by Lake Champlain and Vermont and on the south by the Mohawk River valley, the North Country is the largest geographical region of New York State. It is also the most sparsely populated. It is dominated by the Adirondack Mountains and Adirondack Park, described as a 6-million-acre (2.4 million ha) "patchwork of public and private lands" by the Department of Environmental Conservation, which oversees 2.6 million acres (1.1 million ha) of the park as protected forest preserve.

Winters in the North Country are legendary: It is not unusual to have snowfall at least seven months of the year. Thanks to this climate, two Olympic Winter Games have been hosted here in Lake Placid, in 1932 and 1980. Only two other cities — St. Moritz, Switzerland, and Innsbruck, Austria — can make that claim.

When spring does arrive, the melting snow rushes through a vast network of rivers and streams. The area boasts hundreds, if not thousands, of waterfalls — from 300-foot (91.5 m) cascades to 10-foot (3 m) slides. Although many carry official monikers, the majority of them are known only by local names or by the waterways on which they occur. The North Country Region is a waterfall lover's paradise.

This section has been set up to provide a relatively systematic tour of the area. Starting with Salmon River Falls, the most south-westerly site listed, you can follow the waterfalls, traveling clock-wise, around the top of the state, ending at Auger Falls, just north of the Capital Region.

LEGEND

1. Salmon River Falls, p158
2. Pixley Falls, p160
3. Talcottville Falls, p162
4. Lyons Falls, p164
5. Whetstone Falls, p166
6. Whitaker Falls, p168
7. Kilbourn Falls, p170
8. Deer River Falls, p172
9. King Falls, p174
10. Burrville Falls, p176
11. Talcott Falls, p178
12. Black River Falls, p180
13. Glen Park Falls, p182
14. Pleasant Creek Falls, p184
15. Fullerville Falls, p186
16. Browns Falls, p188
17. Butter Tub Falls, p190
18. Chipmunk Falls, p192
19. Basford Falls, p194
20. Sinclair Falls, p196
21. Twin Falls, p198
22. Bulkhead Falls & Adrenaline Falls, p200
23. Rainbow Falls, p202
24. Copper Rock Falls, p204
25. Lampson Falls, p206
26. Harper Falls, p208
27. Cascade Falls & Rushton Falls, p210
28. Allen Falls, p212
29. St. Regis Falls, p214
30. High Falls on the Salmon River, p216
31. High Falls on the Chateaugay River, p218
32. Ausable Chasm, p220
33. Alice Falls, p222
34. Jay Falls, p224
35. High Falls Gorge, p226
36. Bog River Falls, p228
37. Rainbow Falls (AMR), p230
38. Roaring Brook Falls, p232
39. Christine Falls, p234
40. Auger Falls, p236

Please note that all waterfall locations are approximate. Visitors should consult regional maps for more specific information on roads and communities.

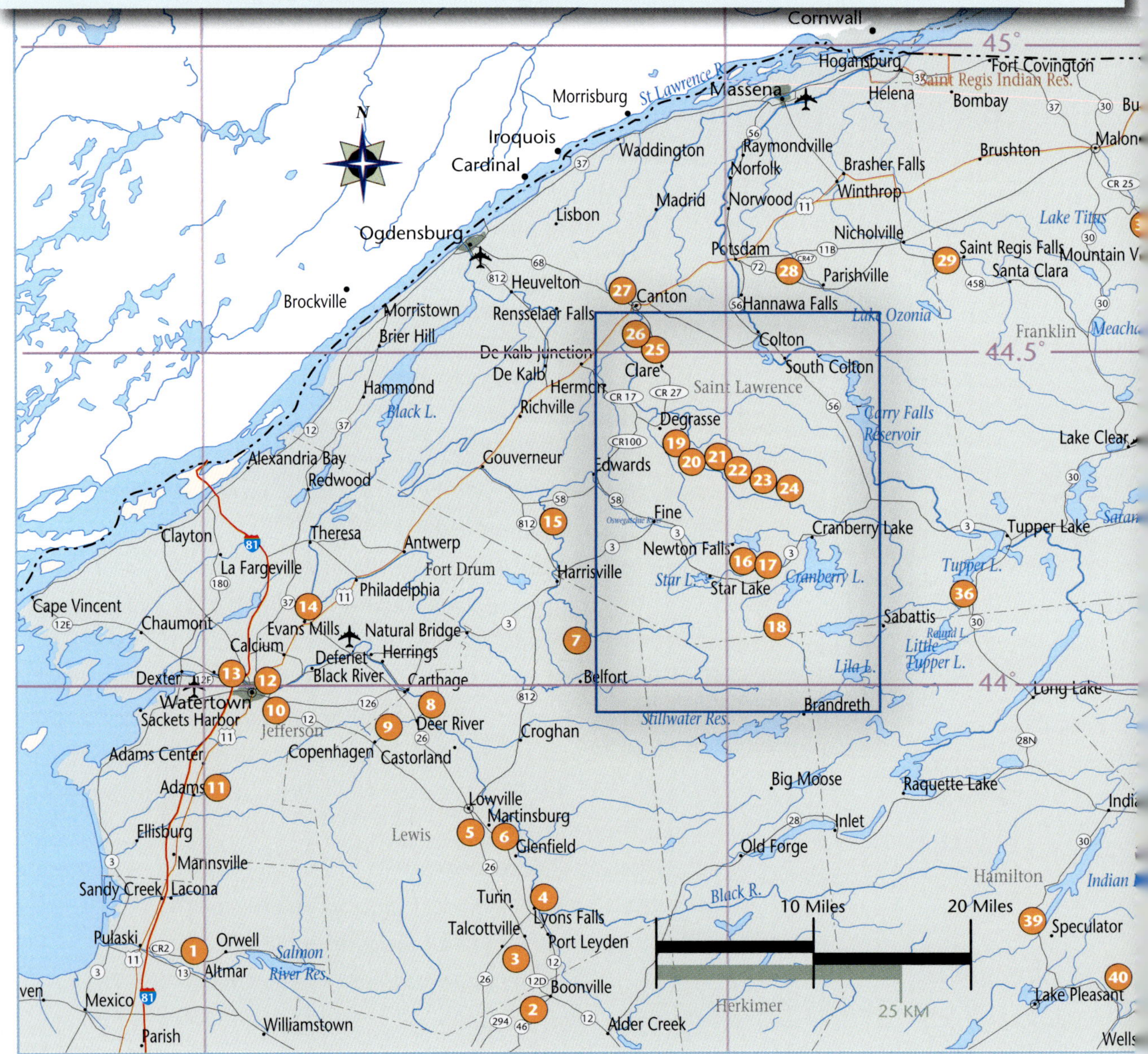

North Country Region

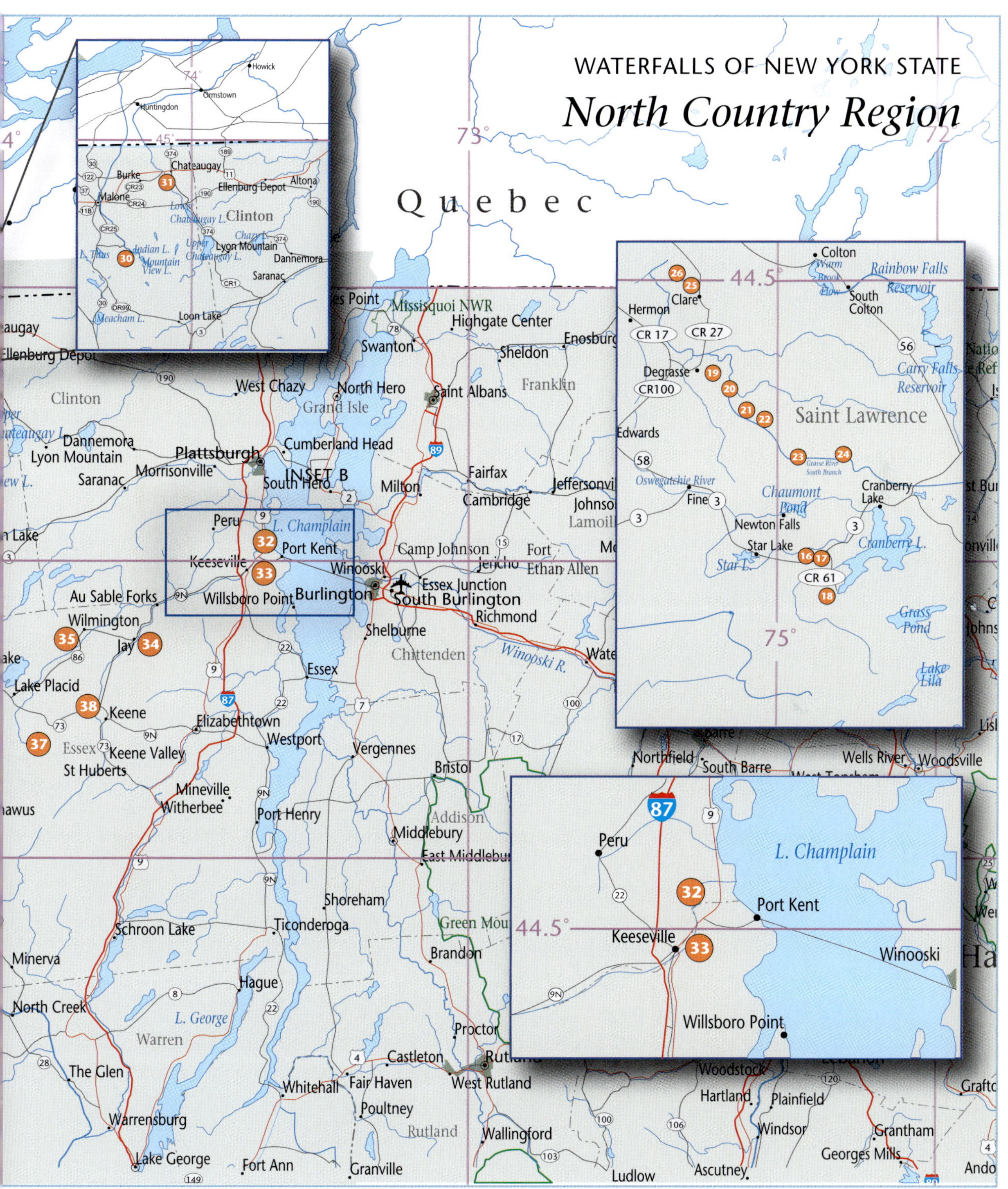

NORTH COUNTRY REGION

Salmon River Falls

From the north, on I-81, take exit 36 (Pulaski) and drive east (a left at the end of the ramp) on CR 2.

From the south, take a left at the ramp on NY 13 and follow the I-81 North signs through the village to CR 2.

Take CR 2 to the hamlet of Orwell. Just past Orwell, turn right onto Oswego CR 22 south. In a little over 2.5 mi (4.0 km), take a sharp left onto Falls Rd. Drive for about 1.5 mi (2.4 km). Salmon River Falls is on the right. It's a popular area attraction and is clearly marked.

COUNTY: Oswego

TOWNSHIP: Orwell

PLACE: Orwell

WATERWAY: Salmon River

TYPE: curtain falls

HEIGHT: 110 ft (33.5 m)

TRAIL: crushed limestone; easy

WALKING TIME: 10 min

PEAK ACTIVITY: May-Sept.

LATITUDE: 43.5474

LONGITUDE: –75.9405

Located in the Salmon River Falls Unique Area on the Falls Road in the town of Orwell, Salmon River Falls is by far the largest and most popular waterfall in Oswego County. This free-admission area is well maintained by DEC, and there are several information kiosks along the less than 300-yard (275 m) trail that leads from the parking lot to the upper overlook area. The 6-foot-wide (1.8 m) wheelchair-accessible trail has an average slope of 2 percent. Indeed, at no point is the slope greater than 5 percent, which makes this a leisurely walk.

There are excellent views into the gorge below the waterfall all along the trail, but shortly after the trail's start, there is an overlook. A wire railing marks the route to the upper overlook area, where, from a fenced observation platform, you can gaze down on the crest of the falls. For the slightly more adventurous, a set of wooden steps just beyond the upper overlook leads to the riverbed above the falls. You can actually walk out on the riverbed and look down over the falls. There are no railings or fences, however, so use extreme caution as you approach the crest. (For safety reasons, this area is closed during high water.)

More experienced hikers might like to attempt the Gorge Trail, which descends from the main trail to the river below. This trail is a combination dirt path and stone steps, many of them occurring naturally. The descent is moderate, but the return to the top will wind many hikers. For those willing to make the extra effort, though, the view looking up at the falls is awe-inspiring.

At 300 feet (91.5 m) wide and 110 feet (33.5 m) high, Salmon River Falls is considered a curtain falls. In the spring, the water flowing over these falls covers the width of the river, but as the year progresses, the flow decreases to a point where there are two or three separate ribbon falls across the span.

In the winter, the falls freeze over. In fact, ice climbing is allowed for those who register to do so. For the rest of us, the view of the frozen falls is magnificent enough.

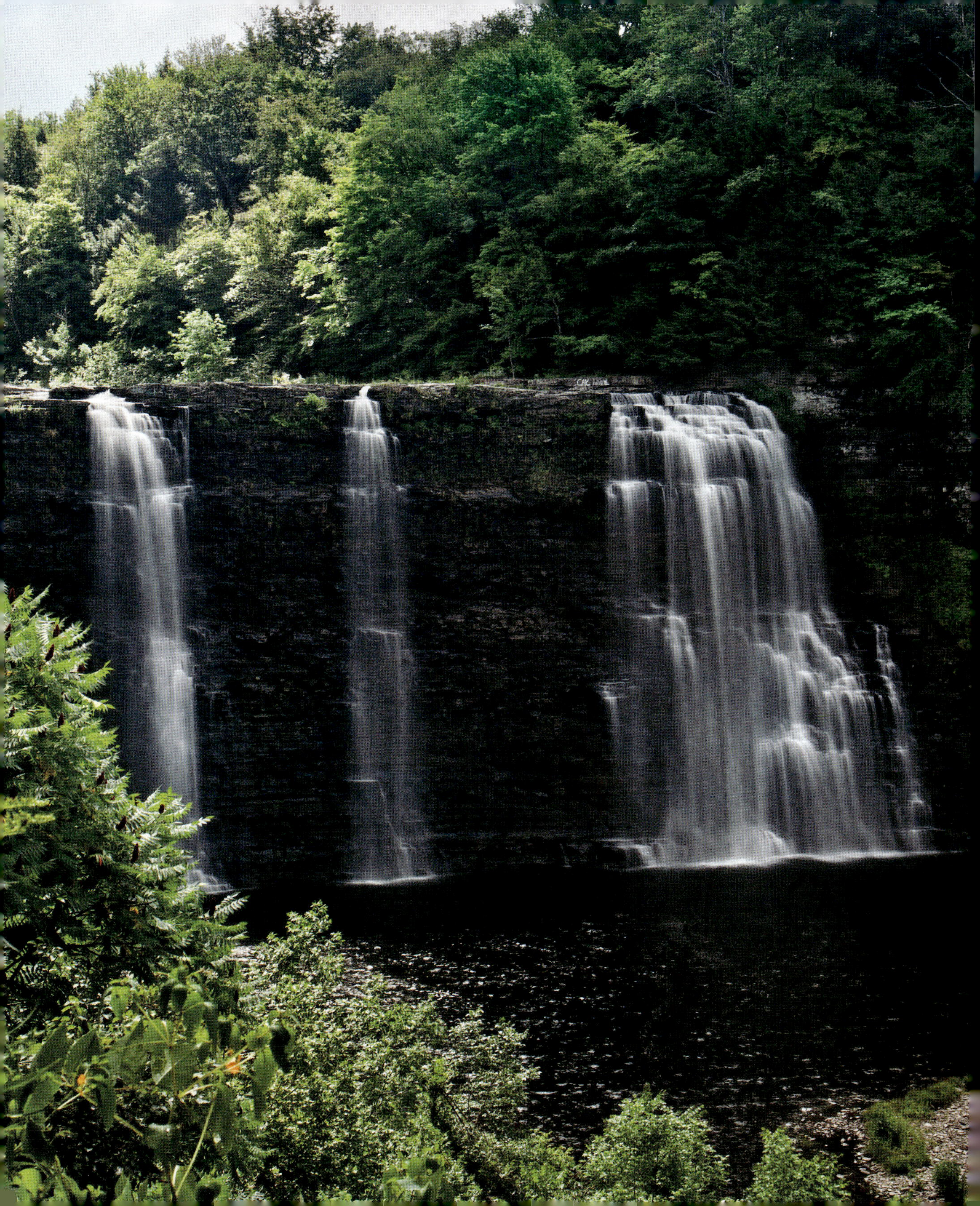

NORTH COUNTRY REGION

Pixley Falls

If you are using GPS, simply enter "11430 State Route 46" in Boonville, and proceed accordingly. Otherwise, take NY 46 south out of Boonville, and after about 6 mi (9.7 km), look for signs forPixley Falls State Park.

From the south, the state park is about 18 mi (29 km) north of downtown Rome on NY 46. It is well marked.

COUNTY: Oneida	
TOWNSHIP: Boonville	
PLACE: Boonville	
WATERWAY: Lansing Kill	
TYPE: classical falls	
HEIGHT: 50 ft (15.3 m)	
TRAIL: dirt and stone; easy	
WALKING TIME: 5 min	
PEAK ACTIVITY: May-Oct.	
LATITUDE: 43.4028	
LONGITUDE: –75.3444	

Most waterfalls are located on rivers and creeks, but Pixley Falls occurs on what is known regionally as a kill — specifically, the Lansing Kill.

The word kill derives from the Middle Dutch word *kille*, meaning "water bed" or "river channel"; the modern Dutch word is *kil*. Defined in dictionaries today as a channel, creek, stream or river, the term is especially common in Delaware, Pennsylvania and New York, the three present-day states where early Dutch colonists primarily settled.

Pixley Falls is the main attraction in Pixley Falls State Park, a very pleasant, well-maintained little park that is also known as Boonville Gorge State Park. Open all year, the park features a nature trail that winds through the woods and past the falls. In 2011, it became a day-use-only area, so camping is no longer allowed. The park is still available for picnics, hiking and other outdoor activities. On our last visit, the daily admission between the Memorial Day and Labor Day weekends was under $10 per person; in the off-season, there is no admission charge.

As you enter the park and cross the bridge, follow the road until it turns to the right. Shortly after, bear left at the fork, and continue to the upper area. The trail on the right leads to the bottom of the falls.

When viewing the falls from the bottom, note the layers of rock jutting out like balconies from the edge of the drop. Pixley Falls has an almost vertical 50-foot (15.3 m) plunge, and at its base, you're so close, you can feel the mist that forms as the falls meet the waterway. Here, you'll also notice an unnamed feeder stream. Just upstream, there is at least one other small, unnamed waterfall.

Known as the Lansing Kill Gorge, this particular section of the stream was originally part of the Black River Canal, which was built between 1837 and 1855 to create a water route between the Erie Canal and the Black River. When completed, the canal boasted 109 locks — still a world record. Although the canal has been out of service for decades, the remains of several of the locks can still be seen throughout the area. A number of nearby hiking trails follow the old canal towpath.

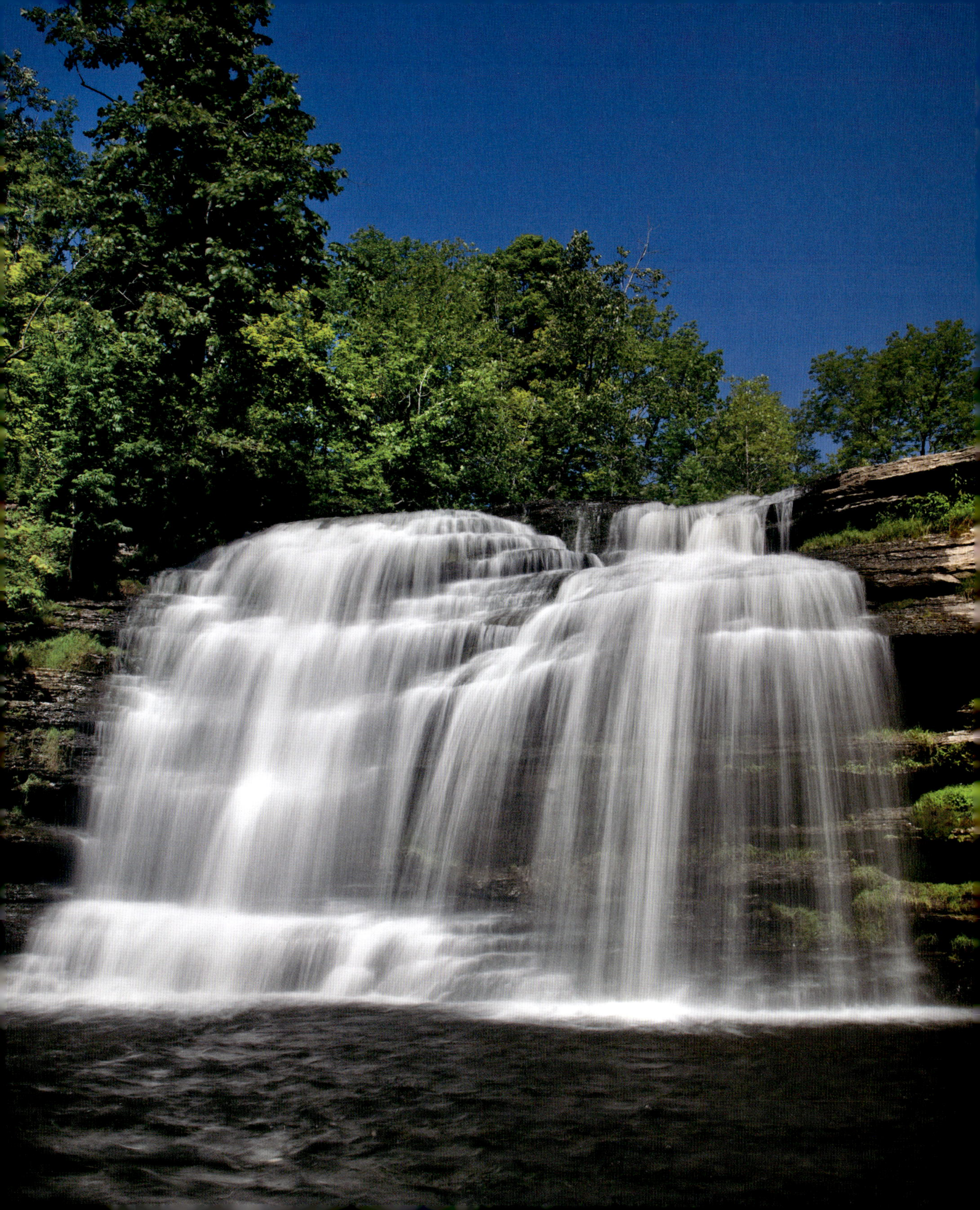

Talcottville Falls

Talcottville is on NY 12D. From the south, take NY 12 to Boonville. Bear left on Main St. and proceed to the end. Turn left onto E Schuyler St. and then right, which will take you to Post St., also called NY 12D. Talcottville is about 2 mi (3.2 km) north.

From the north, follow NY 26 south out of Lowville. Just south of Turin, you'll come to an intersection. Continue going straight. The road becomes NY 12D, and Talcottville is only a couple of miles ahead.

COUNTY: Lewis
TOWNSHIP: Leyden
PLACE: Talcottville
WATERWAY: Sugar River
TYPE: curtain falls
HEIGHT: 60 ft (18.3 m)
TRAIL: stone and dirt; easy
WALKING TIME: 5 min
PEAK ACTIVITY: April-Oct.
LATITUDE: 43.5354
LONGITUDE: –75.3679

As with hundreds of other waterfalls in northern New York, the waterfall near Talcottville is technically unnamed. In fact, it is not even indicated on topographical maps — a bit of a surprise, given its size and popularity. It is sometimes referred to as Sugar River Falls, but since there are several waterfalls on the Sugar River, it is perhaps most helpful to refer to it as Talcottville Falls (not to be confused with Stony Creek's Talcott Falls, one of the two most popular falls in nearby Jefferson County).

The hamlet of Talcottville is about 2 miles (3.2 km) north of Boonville. Named after Hezekiah Talcott, who moved there in the late 1780s, Talcottville was the first settlement in Lewis County. The Talcott family built a home, a gristmill and a stone quarry just above the falls. Many generations later, the property became the summer home and refuge of Edmund Wilson, the legendary 20th-century writer and critic. Wilson named this home "The Stone House" and made it famous in his book *Upstate: Records and Recollections of Northern New York*. Wilson died in 1972, but the house is known as the Edmund Wilson House to this day.

The falls are very easy to find. As you cross the bridge over the Sugar River, they are in sight off the west side of the highway. Fairly close to the highway, you'll see a small waterfall that is as large as or larger than some named waterfalls in northern New York. This, however, is not Talcottville Falls, which is about 300 yards (275 m) farther upstream.

In the southbound lane, just past the guardrails, is a path that leads to the falls. Bear left on the path. Within a couple of minutes, you'll arrive at a rock platform just below the falls that forms natural rock steps to the river. Use caution, as there are no railings or fences here and the rocks are wet and slippery with the spray from the waterfall. If you are visiting early in the day, the sun will be behind the falls as you view it. Often, small rainbows form in the mist.

The Sugar is a relatively small river. Just a few miles downstream, it empties into the Black River, a major northern New York waterway that flows into Lake Ontario.

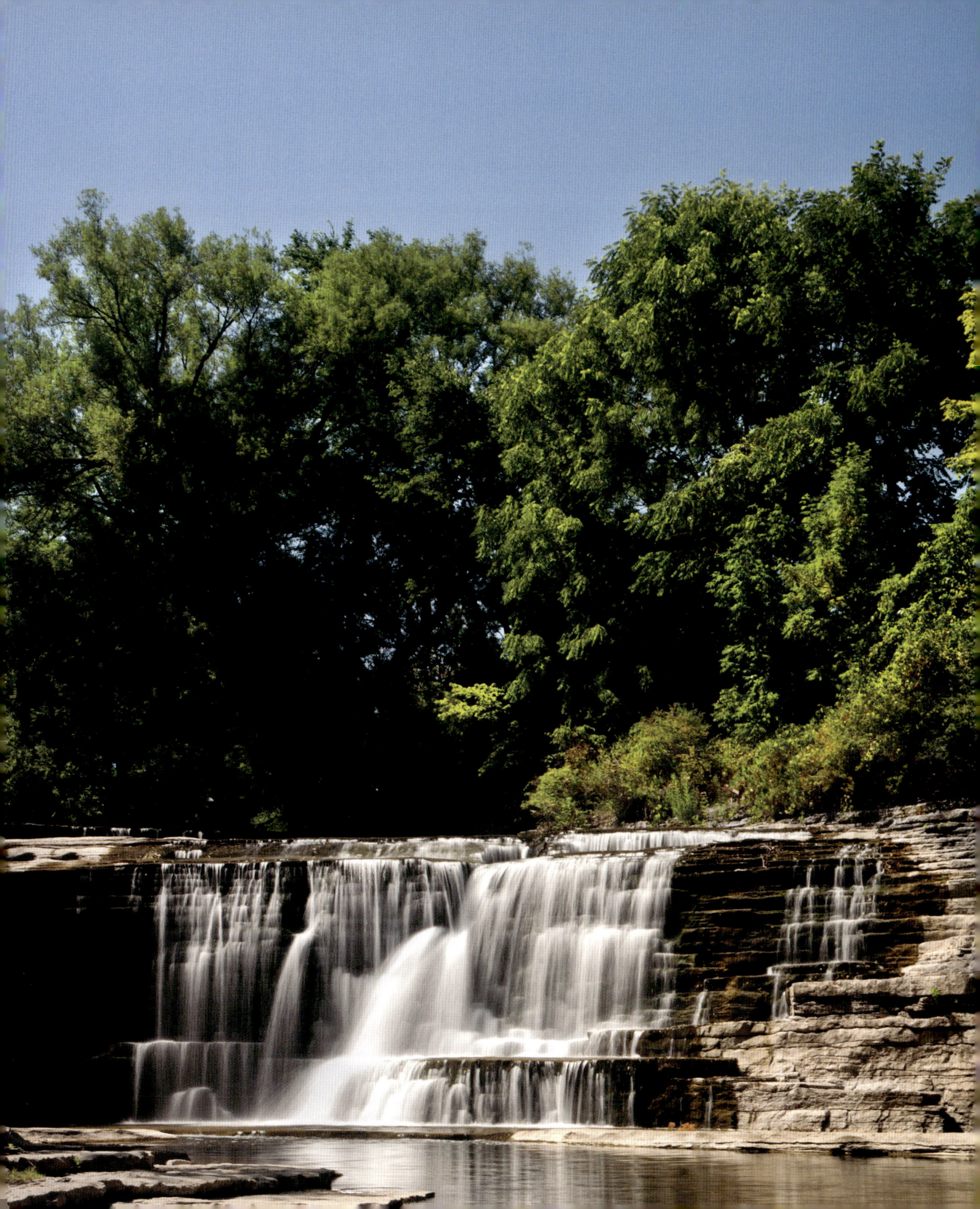

NORTH COUNTRY REGION

Lyons Falls

The village of Lyons Falls is located on NY 12. From the intersection of NY 12 and 12D, proceed into the village. Take a right at Center St., which becomes Franklin St. Take the first left, and cross the bridge over the Black River, then take the first left onto Lyons Falls Rd. Almost immediately, you'll cross the Moose River; the falls are just ahead, on the left.

Alternatively, follow the boat launch signs to the upper or lower parking area.

COUNTY: Lewis

TOWNSHIP: Lyonsdale and West Turin

PLACE: Lyons Falls

WATERWAY: Black River

TYPE: curtain cascade

HEIGHT: 63 ft (19.2 m)

TRAIL: stone road; easy

WALKING TIME: 1 min

PEAK ACTIVITY: June-Aug.

LATITUDE: 43.6180

LONGITUDE: –75.3579

Lyons Falls is one of the more popular waterfalls in Lewis County, perhaps because it is one of the highest and most easily accessed. Although a power dam was built on the Black River just above the falls many years ago, the waterfall is still impressive, drawing its power not only from the Black River but from the Moose River, a major tributary that enters the Black River upstream, almost within sight of the dam.

To reach the waterfall, follow the signs to one of two boat launches, either above or below the falls. If you park in the upper area, the walk down to the riverbank takes only a few minutes. There, you'll see the crest and the dam above the falls. If you park in the lower area, you'll see the waterfall as you drive in. There are no fences or railings here, and the riverbank is fairly level.

Timber and the pulp-and-paper industry drove the economy in this area for years. While the dam is still functional, the adjacent Lyons Falls Pulp and Paper Mill closed in 2001, and from the looks of the exterior, it has fallen into a serious state of disrepair.

The village of Lyons Falls is on the border of the town of Lyonsdale, which was settled in 1819. Both places were named after town founder Caleb Lyon, who is said to have built one of the first bridges across the Moose and Black rivers.

Although NY 12 is a major north-south connector, the area east of Lyons Falls quickly becomes remote and wild. Just south, at Alder Creek, NY 28 traverses almost 65 miles (105 km) of the Adirondacks before it reaches NY 30, the first state highway that offers either north or south access. To the north of Lyons Falls, it's an hour's drive to get to NY 3, the next easterly route to the mountain area. In this section, the beauty of New York State is at its finest. The abundant wildlife and Class V white-water rapids are popular with people who love and appreciate everything nature has to offer in this much-loved part of the country.

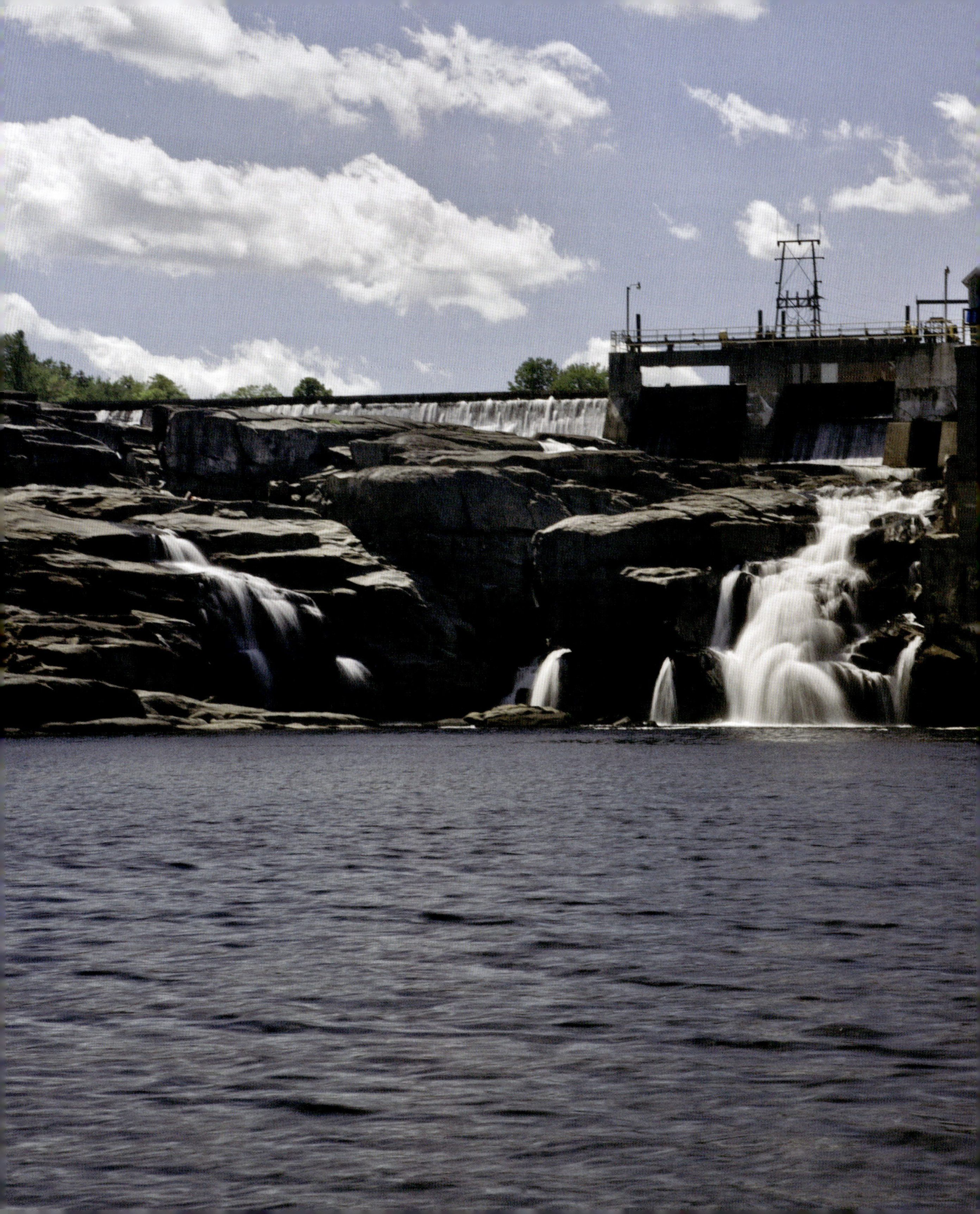

Whetstone Falls

Driving west from Martinsburg on Cemetery Rd., take a left at Alger Rd. As you cross West Rd., Alger Rd. becomes Corrigan Hill Rd. Continue along this road until you cross a bridge over Whetstone Creek. Just past this bridge is a parking area.

To reach the parking area from the east, take NY 26 to Houseville. Go west on Houseville Gulf Rd. The first right is Corrigan Hill Rd.

COUNTY: Lewis
TOWNSHIP: Martinsburg
PLACE: Martinsburg
WATERWAY: unnamed tributary to Whetstone Creek
TYPE: ribbon falls
HEIGHT: 50 ft (15.3 m)
TRAIL: dirt and stone; moderate
WALKING TIME: 15 min
PEAK ACTIVITY: June-Aug.
LATITUDE: 43.6930
LONGITUDE: –75.4997

Whetstone Creek descends through a three-mile (4.8 km) gorge in Whetstone Gulf State Park. The balance of this waterway is a rocky brook, but the upper end contains a number of small, pretty waterfalls.

The highlight of the area is a dramatic 50-foot (15.3 m) cascade. Also referred to as Whetstone Gulf Falls or Whetstone Creek Falls, this waterfall doesn't actually occur on Whetstone Creek but, rather, at the end of a small feeder stream that plummets from the top of the gorge to the creek below.

Our preferred route to the main waterfall is to park in the area described in the directions sidebar, at left. Use caution on the rough, unpaved road in. During the summer, the ride isn't bad, but in the soggy early-spring months, a four-wheel-drive vehicle with ample clearance is your best bet. On your return, your vehicle will probably look as if you have been mud bogging.

At the parking area, there are two clearly identified trails on opposite sides of the creek. The north-ridge trail leads directly to the falls. The south-ridge trail offers a view across the gorge. Both trails are well maintained, and each is a moderately difficult 15-minute walk. The foliage is quite heavy, even more so during the summer, and as a result, the views may be obscured and photo opportunities limited, especially of the smaller waterfalls. Stay well away from the edge, as there are very few fences or retaining devices and it is a long way down.

There are also two options for reaching the falls from the park end of the gorge. These involve a day-use or camping fee. Option one is the 5-mile (8 km) ridge trail loop, which ends at the parking area. Option two is for the truly hardy: Drive to the end of the campground, and walk the trail up the creek. At certain times of the year, this route may not be an option, because it involves walking some creek sections. During heavy runoff, the volume of water can become so great that you just won't be able to get through. During dry periods, you may be able to access some of the waterfalls in the gorge, but the feeder creek containing the main falls may dry up, shutting down that waterfall.

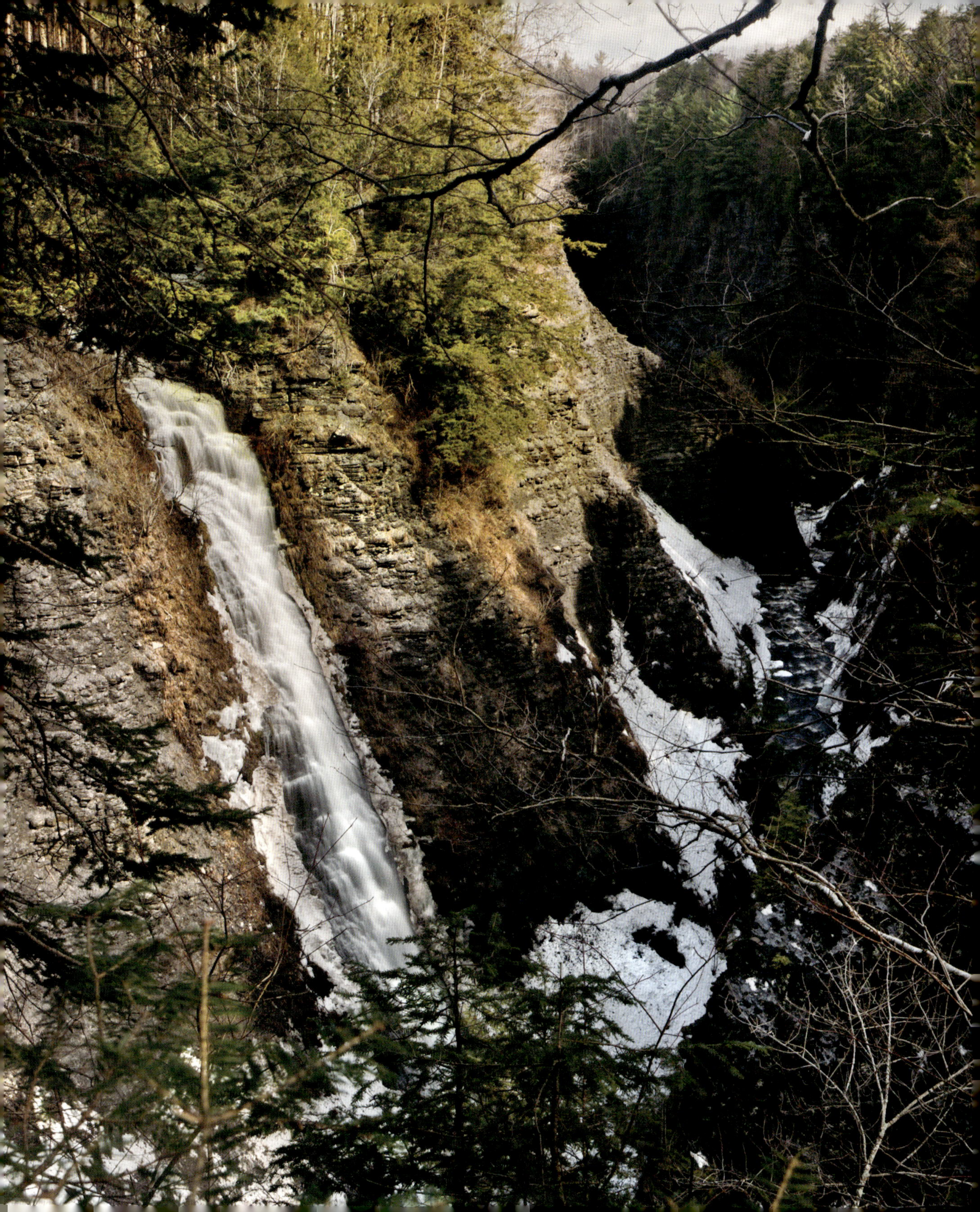

Whitaker Falls

Follow NY 26 south out of Lowville to Martinsburg, and take a left at Glendale Rd. A short distance up this road on the left is Whitaker Falls Park.

If you're driving from the south on NY 12, Glendale Rd. is on the left, just after the turn for Glenfield.

Enter the park, and drive straight through the first intersection to the buildings at the back of the park, where you'll find the parking area.

If you're a camper and have set aside more than a day for your waterfall adventure, consider making Whitaker Falls the last stop of the afternoon. The falls are located in Whitaker Falls Park, a nice little park that offers a view of the Black River valley as well as campsites, hot showers, picnic sites and a couple of pavilions that are a perfect setting for a family reunion. While there is no set charge to use the park or to visit the falls, the town of Martinsburg gratefully accepts donations, which are used for park improvements.

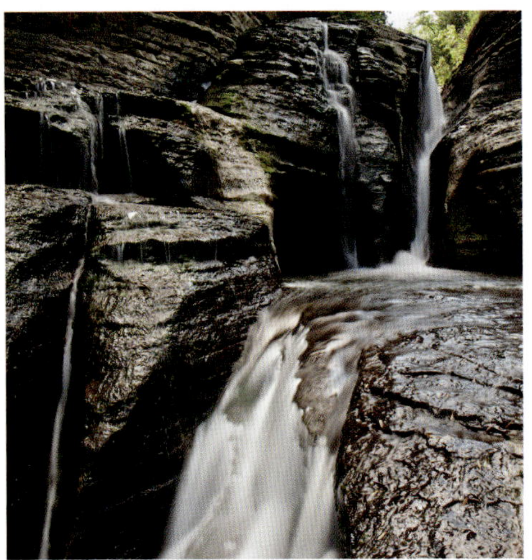

To reach the falls, follow the road between the parking lot and one of the pavilions. After about 500 feet (153 m), you'll see a wooden fence on the right that runs along the top of the embankment. A caution sign marks the descent to the river, which is the only part of this hike that even borders on strenuous.

A product of countless years of erosion, this beautiful waterfall descends through several drops. Here, we've classified it as a complex cascade, but in fact, the waterfall exhibits characteristics of different waterfall types. At one drop, for instance, it may be a ribbon cascade; at the next, a curtain falls. During spring runoff, the falls may span the entire width of the river, but by midsummer, the riverbed is dry enough to allow access through a series of natural rock steps.

While the Whitaker family (spelled with a single "t") donated the land for the park, a double "t" has crept into the spelling over the years in a variety of print and online references. To make things even more confusing, there is another Whitaker Falls, on the west branch of the St. Regis River, farther north in St. Lawrence County.

COUNTY: Lewis
TOWNSHIP: Martinsburg
PLACE: Martinsburg
WATERWAY: Roaring Brook
TYPE: complex cascade
HEIGHT: 40 ft (12.2 m)
TRAIL: dirt and stone; easy to moderate
WALKING TIME: 15 min
PEAK ACTIVITY: June-Aug.
LATITUDE: 43.7344
LONGITUDE: –75.4456

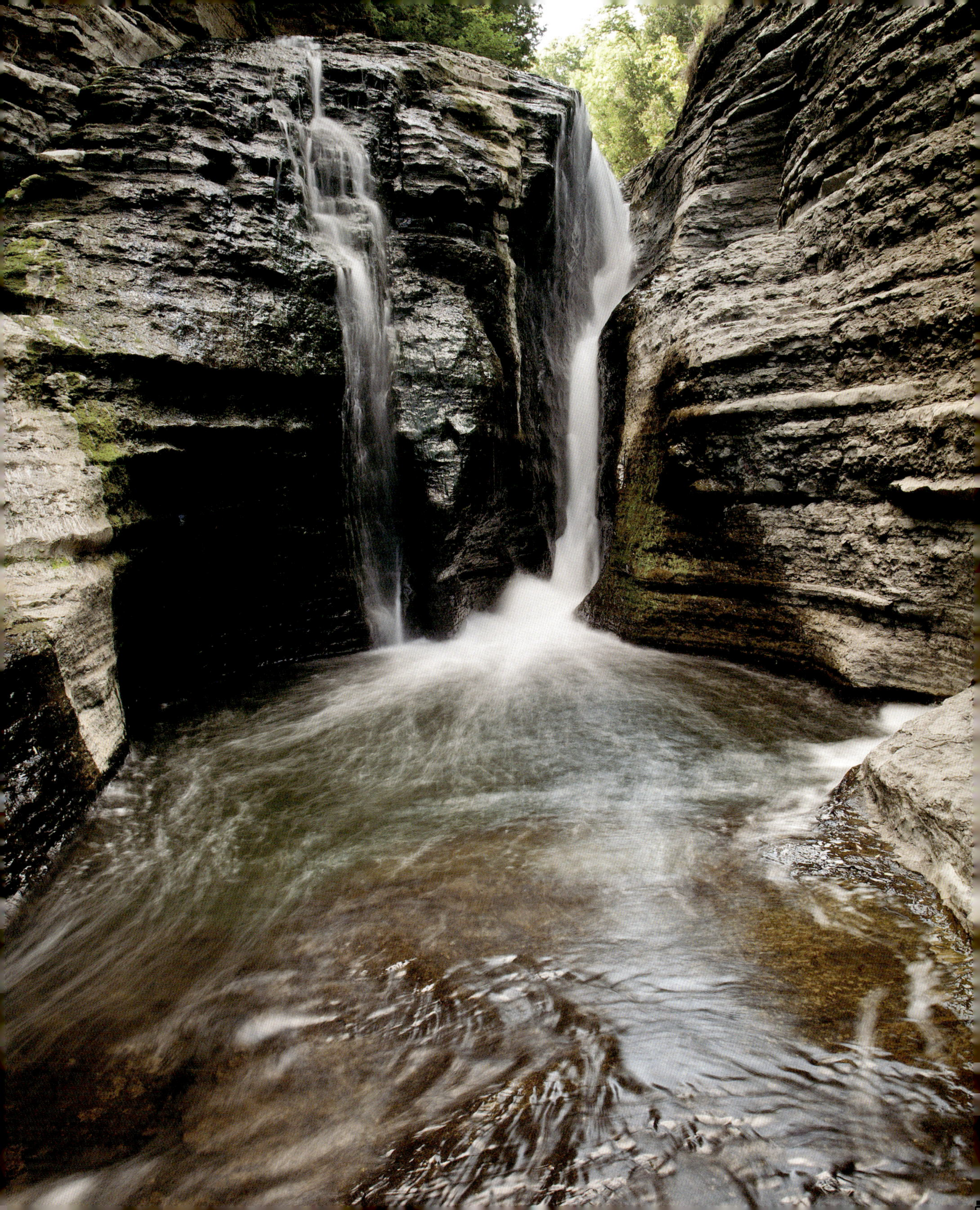

Kilbourn Falls

From the village of Croghan, take Belfort Rd. to Belfort. When Belfort Rd. meets Long Pond Rd., turn right. Follow Long Pond Rd., and turn left onto Bisha Rd. After a short distance, there is a fork in the road. Bear left onto Kilbourn Rd. After about 0.5 mi (0.8 km), you'll pass the intersection of Carthage Reservoir Rd. In 0.5 mi (0.8 km), make a left turn. In about 530 ft (160 m), turn right, following the "Public Fishing Access" signs. Park in the anglers' parking lot.

COUNTY: Lewis

TOWNSHIP: Croghan

PLACE: Belfort

WATERWAY: Oswegatchie River, West Branch

TYPE: classical cascade

HEIGHT: est. 35 ft (10.7 m)

TRAIL: dirt; easy

WALKING TIME: 15 min

PEAK ACTIVITY: May-Sept.

LATITUDE: 43.9882

LONGITUDE: –75.2925

The hike to Kilbourn Falls over a well-marked 0.4-mile (0.6 km) trail is fairly easy. As the river comes into sight, though, take a little time to look around and make some mental notes. From here on, the trail isn't quite as clear, and you'll want to feel confident about retracing your steps.

Once you reach the river, bear left and head downstream. From this location, there are pleasing views of the bottom of the falls as well as good photo opportunities. Then head back upstream, where you'll find a well-built footbridge that gives you direct access to the waterfall.

Above the falls, the river is deceptively calm, but anyone paddling downstream in a canoe or kayak had better know what lies ahead. The serene and quiet of the forest area might lull a paddler into a false sense of security. Then, suddenly, a rock outcropping narrows the channel to about 3 feet (1 m) and the water plunges an estimated 10 feet (3 m). Following a stretch of white water as the river descends slightly under the bridge, the waterfall takes its main drop of 35 feet (10.7 m) or so.

Like many waterfall locations in northern New York, the area around Kilbourn Falls can look very different in July or August than it does in April or May. The Oswegatchie, a major waterway in this area, has several branches that feed the main channel. They all start in the Adirondacks, where winter snowfalls are significant. As a result, spring runoff is serious business. While you can walk out onto the rocks and almost touch the waterfall during the summer, the rocks may be completely obscured when the river carries snowmelt down to the St. Lawrence River each spring.

There are no picnic tables or other facilities here, but don't let that discourage you from making this a family-picnic destination. Bring your fishing gear, or simply relax and enjoy the solitude.

Some of the roads leading to Kilbourn Falls are unpaved. Depending on the time of year, you might consider driving a truck or at least an SUV with adequate clearance.

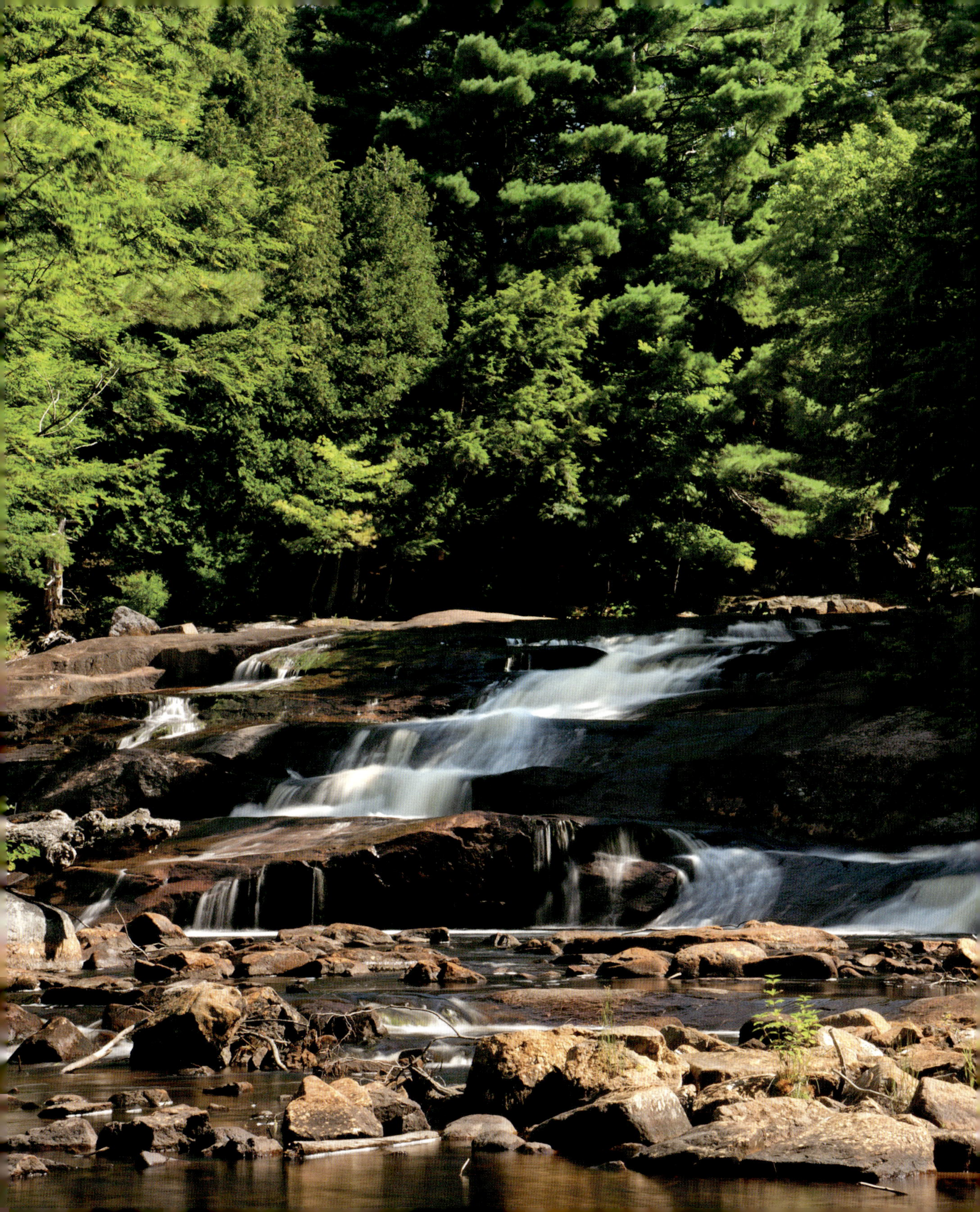

Deer River Falls

From West Carthage, take NY 26 south for roughly 3.5 mi (5.6 km). When you reach the community of Deer River, cross the bridge; the falls are on the right.

From the south, proceed north on NY 26 for a little over 11 mi (17.7 km). The falls are to the left of the bridge. Parking on the shoulder of the road is allowed, but there are also parking lots in Deer River.

COUNTY: Lewis
TOWNSHIP: Denmark
PLACE: Deer River
WATERWAY: Deer River
TYPE: curtain falls
HEIGHT: 15 ft (4.6 m)
TRAIL: stone; easy
WALKING TIME: 1 min
PEAK ACTIVITY: June-Aug.
LATITUDE: 43.9308
LONGITUDE: –75.5909

The hamlet of Deer River is located on the Deer River, a tributary of the Black River, one of northern New York's significant waterways. The Deer River is regarded as medium-sized by the standards of this part of the state. There are two major named waterfalls a few miles upstream from this little community, though its own waterfall is officially unnamed. For obvious reasons, it is known locally as Deer River Falls.

Over the years, the hamlet itself has had a number of different names, most notably French's Mills, after an early mill owner named Abel French, and later Myers Mills, after Richard Myers, who built a stone mill at this site in 1824. A postcard from an earlier era, labeled "Deer River Falls, near Carthage, N.Y.," appears, at first glance, to depict an entirely different location. It shows a dam immediately above the falls that is at least double the height of the present-day waterfall. Once you remove the dam in your mind's eye, however, the waterfall is instantly recognizable. Sometime in the 1960s, this dam was, indeed, removed.

During winter's deep freeze, Deer River Falls has no noticeable flow, but as the snow in the Adirondack Mountains melts each spring, the waterfall spans the width of the river. For the rest of the year, the falls is a pleasant piece of nature, easily accessible and ready to enjoy.

That said, take a reasonable amount of care when viewing this waterfall. Whether you park on the shoulder of the highway or in a nearby parking lot, you have to walk up the shoulder of the road to reach the bridge. The pedestrian walkway on the bridge faces downriver, away from the falls. On both sides of the road, there are guardrails, but they are relatively high, so the less athletic might want to walk around the rail on the walkway side of the bridge. On the falls side, due to the riverbank, you really can't get any closer to the falls, even if you were to climb over the guardrail. Still, you'll be close enough to view the falls and to take photographs from the roadway. Fortunately, this area doesn't see a lot of traffic, but use caution in any case.

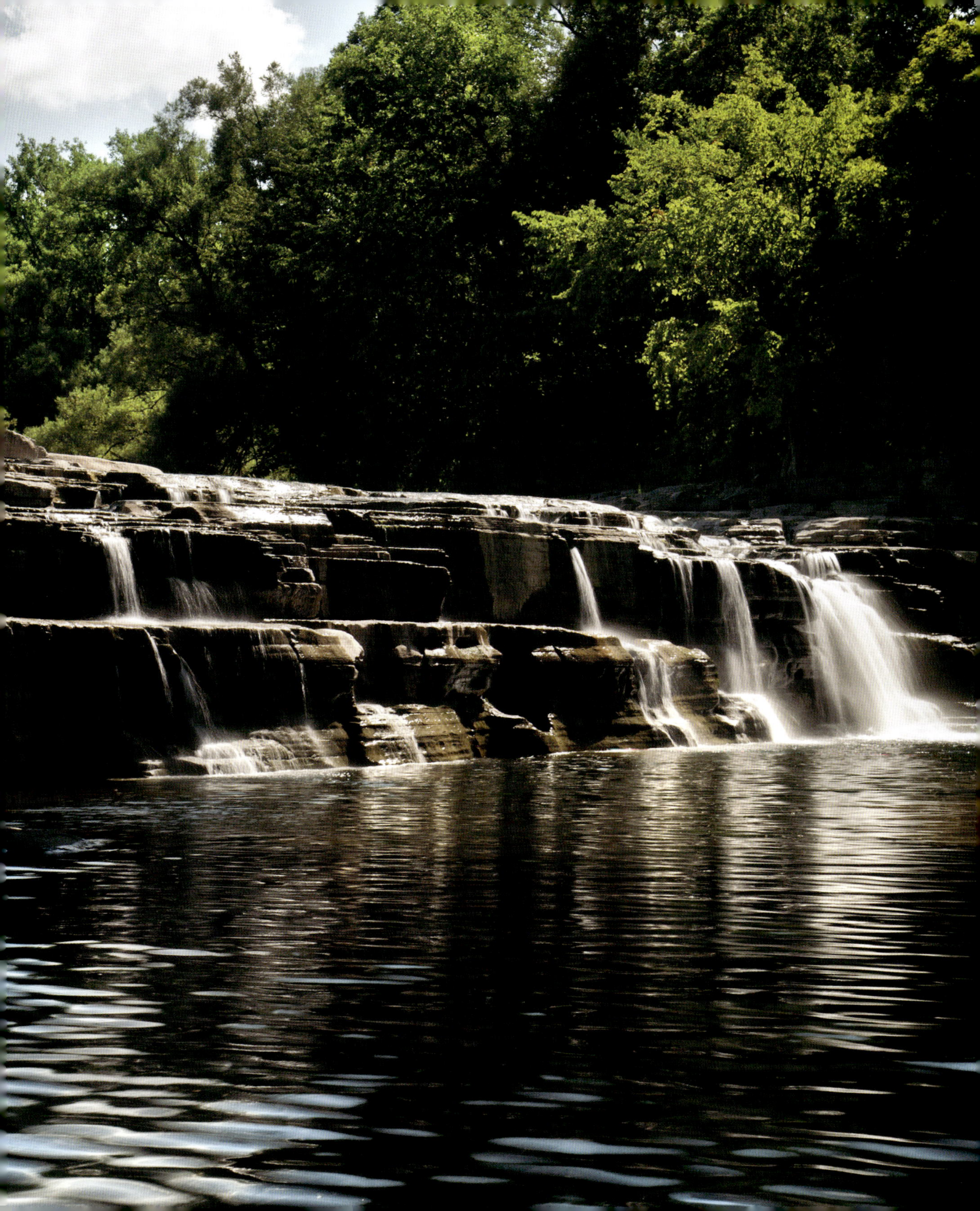

King Falls

Head south on NY 12 from Copenhagen, and take the first left onto Roberts Rd. Less than 0.25 mi (0.4 km) past Vorce Rd., there is a dirt road on the left. An entrance gate sits a short distance from the road, with a parking area just outside of it.

From Deer River, take Roberts Rd. toward Copenhagen. You'll find the access road less than 0.25 mi (0.4 km) after the Old St. intersection.

COUNTY: Lewis

TOWNSHIP: Denmark

PLACE: Copenhagen

WATERWAY: Deer River

TYPE: classical cascade

HEIGHT: est. 25 ft (7.6 m)

TRAIL: dirt and stone; easy

WALKING TIME: 20 min

PEAK ACTIVITY: June-Aug.

LATITUDE: 43.9168

LONGITUDE: –75.6334

Northwestern New York's Lewis County boasts the rolling Adirondack foothills in the east, the Tug Hill Plateau in the west and, as a result, an abundance of waterfalls. It isn't easy to pick the most popular falls in this county, but three have an almost cultlike following. Lyons Falls is the highest and undoubtedly the easiest to reach, and Whitaker Falls is an extremely popular destination for many families. But if local folklore has any merit, King Falls, one of Lewis County's most impressive sites, wears the crown. Stories about these falls — a popular hiking, picnic and party area — have circulated for decades.

Some sources state that King Falls is not accessible to the public. Although the land on the other side of the river is private, there is a hydro dam just upstream from the falls. By virtue of a DEC regulation that guarantees access at any hydroelectric facility, this area is open to anyone who wants to visit, with the exception of military personnel housed at nearby Fort Drum, for whom the area is restricted.

After you've parked, the walk in on a dirt road is less than 0.75 mile (1.2 km). Just before the fenced power plant is a cleared section that leads down to the area below the falls. To reach the area above the falls, including the dam, follow the fence to the right. In low water, you can go out on the riverbed from either of these locations. To get from one level to the other, climb up or down the adjacent stairlike rock formation.

Over time, the Deer River has carved a "throne" out of the layers of rock, thus the waterfall's name. It has also worn deep, narrow channels down both sides of the throne. Significant from a geological standpoint, the layers of limestone here can be easily differentiated in the exposed cliff wall. The water cascades about 15 feet (4.6 m) to a flat table below and then makes another roughly 10-foot (3 m) drop into the pool below, before eventually feeding into the Black River.

Thousands of people travel NY 12, one of northern New York's main north-south travel corridors, but remain unaware of this county's natural beauty, just a few miles off their chosen path.

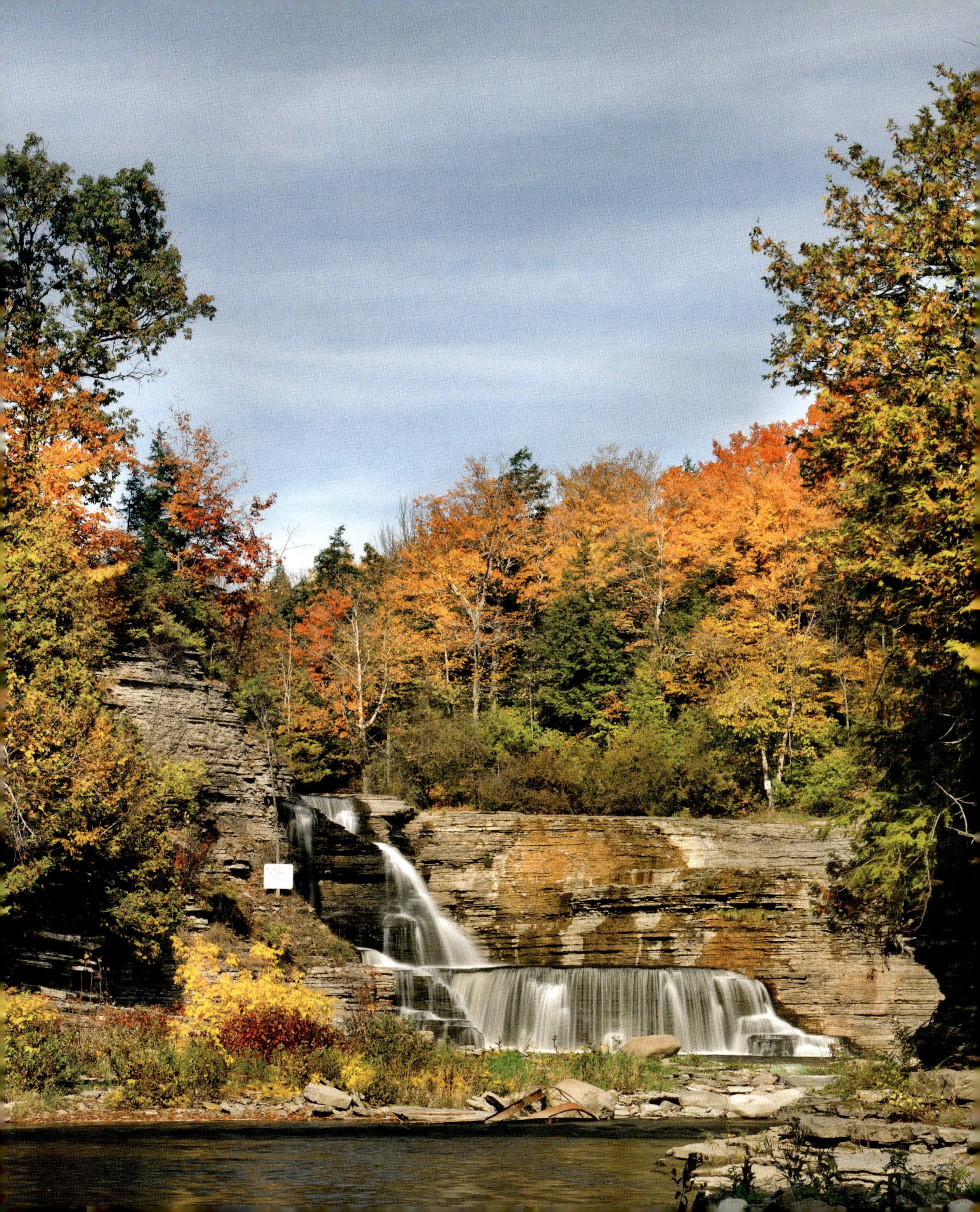

Burrville Falls

From Watertown, take NY 12 south. After a fairly long uphill stretch, the terrain levels out, and there is a sweeping left-hand curve just before you reach Burrville. Turn right onto Plank Rd. The Burrville Cider Mill is on the left. The waterfall is visible from the bridge or from the grounds of the mill.

COUNTY: Jefferson

TOWNSHIP: Watertown

PLACE: Burrville

WATERWAY: Jacobs Creek

TYPE: classical cascade

HEIGHT: 30 ft (9 m)

TRAIL: concrete walk and wooden steps; easy

WALKING TIME: 1 min

PEAK ACTIVITY: Sept.-Nov.

LATITUDE: 43.9301

LONGITUDE: –75.8592

One of the two most popular falls in Jefferson County, Burrville Falls is also the most visited, thanks to its location by the Burrville Cider Mill. Every autumn, people come from far and wide to taste the landmark mill's legendary cider and cider doughnuts and to view the falls. It's an annual ritual that is right up there with the running of the bulls in Pamplona, Spain.

This mill is one of the oldest buildings in the county. The structure was built in 1801, then purchased the following year by John Burr. Originally a sawmill and gristmill, it was converted to cider in the 1940s. The hamlet and mill were once named Burr's Mills, and the falls were referred to as Burr's Mills Falls. While today the waterfall is technically unnamed, it is known locally as Cider Mill Falls, although some sources call it Jacobs Creek Falls, a deceiving reference, since there are three other waterfalls upstream on Jacobs Creek, all on private property. Another source refers to it as Boynton Creek Falls, also a misnomer, since Boynton Creek joins Jacobs Creek about 0.25 mile (0.4 km) upstream from this location. There is, in fact, a 90-foot (27 m) waterfall on Boynton Creek, also on private land.

Burrville Falls is on private property as well, but when the cider mill is in operation, the owners encourage visitors to stroll around, enjoy the falls and the ambience of the old mill and look in on the cider- and doughnut-making process. There are viewing decks and stairs behind the mill, complete with handrails. There is no charge for viewing this beautiful waterfall, though when you catch the scent of the cider and doughnuts, it's hard to resist a visit inside to make a purchase.

The owners have no objection to people viewing the falls from the mill property during the winter, but they do stress that it is done at your own risk and that you refrain from using the deck, which can be treacherous when snow-covered.

Note that a bird's-eye view of the waterfall in the off-season is possible from CR 156, on which the mill is located.

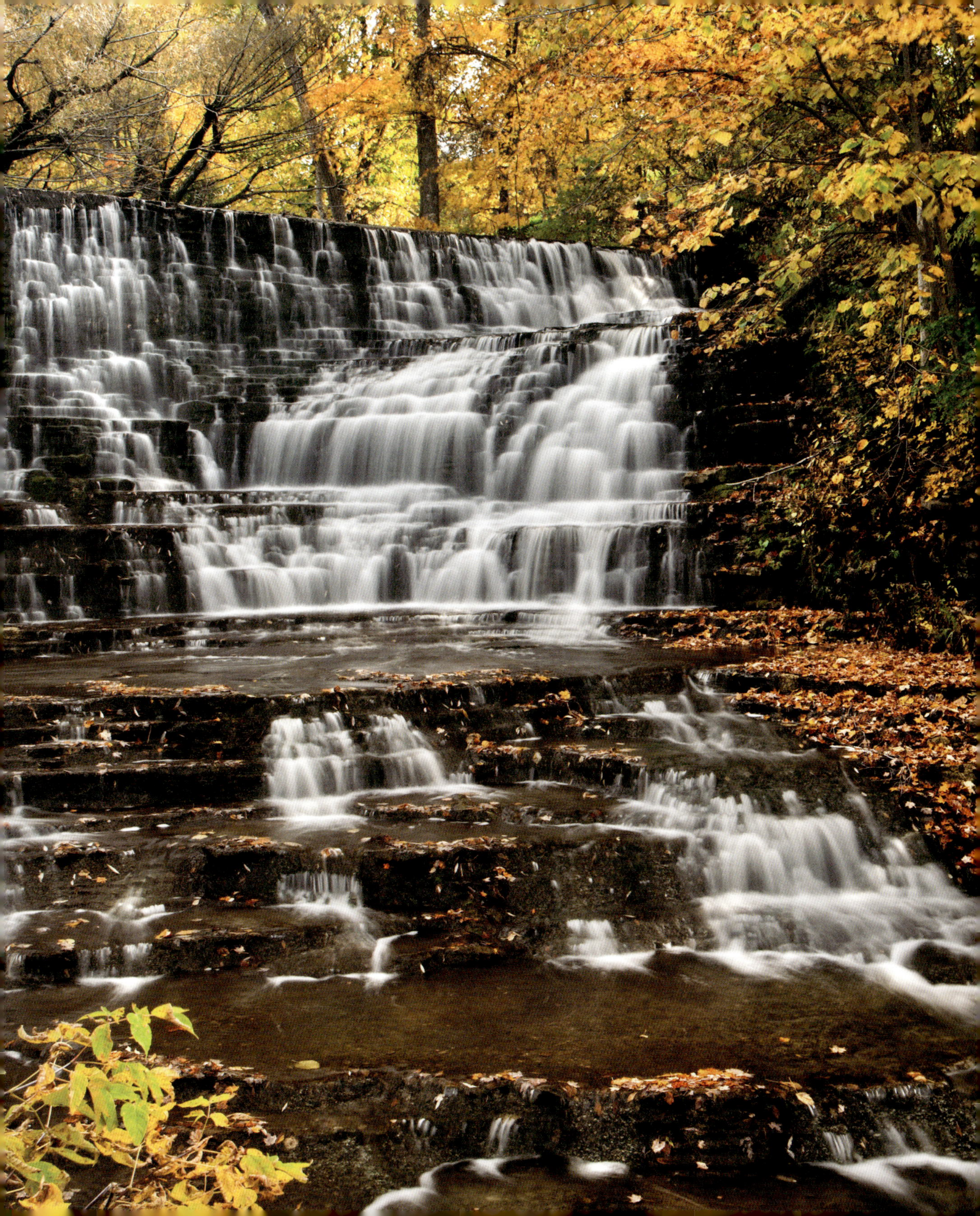

Talcott Falls

From I-81, take exit 43, commonly referred to as the Kellogg Hill exit, and head east. Shortly after, this road ends at US 11. The north- and southbound lanes are split by a large rock outcropping. Go straight across the southbound lane, bear left, and merge into the northbound lane. Move into the right-hand lane. The falls are roughly 0.5 mi (0.8 km) along the road on your right. There are signs as you approach. Park north of the falls.

COUNTY: Jefferson
TOWNSHIP: Adams
PLACE: Adams Center
WATERWAY: Stony Creek
TYPE: ribbon cascade
HEIGHT: est. 70 ft (21.3 m)
TRAIL: stone; easy
WALKING TIME: 1 min
PEAK ACTIVITY: March-Nov.
LATITUDE: 43.8919
LONGITUDE: –75.9792

Named after Daniel Talcott, who settled in the area in 1804, Talcott Falls is one of the two most popular waterfalls in Jefferson County — and probably the most consistently viewed. It is within sight of US 11, a few miles south of Watertown.

This waterfall is on private property, but the highway right-of-way provides ample viewing and photo opportunities. In fact, it is fairly common to see people stopped here — you don't even have to get out of your car to enjoy the falls or take photographs. If you do exit your car, though, please use caution. This is a well-traveled major highway. The safest option is to park on the northbound shoulder, on the side facing the falls. You'll notice a worn path to the riverbank; again, remember that this is not public land and respect the landowner's property.

Due to the lake effect off the eastern end of Lake Ontario, a snowfall in this area is often measured in feet rather than inches. Talcott Falls is frozen in winter, with little or no flowing water. But as the snow melts on the nearby Tug Hill Plateau, spring runoff turns the falls into a classical cascade, with the crest roughly the same size as the drop. As the volume of water slows over summer and autumn, the falls are reduced to a ribbon cascade. For that reason, some feel the best time to see Talcott Falls is in the spring. Still, the rich greens of summer make for pleasant viewing, and when the foliage turns in autumn, the colors framing the falls are truly spectacular. Indeed, summer and autumn scenes of Talcott Falls are popular subjects for many local artists.

The majority of the waterfalls in northern New York are on waterways that flow into Lake Ontario or the St. Lawrence River. A significant number empty into Lake Champlain, while others find their way into the Hudson River and, eventually, the Atlantic Ocean. Stony Creek is one of the smallest waterways that feature a waterfall and flow directly into Lake Ontario. From higher elevations within a mile or so of this site, you can even catch a glimpse of the lake.

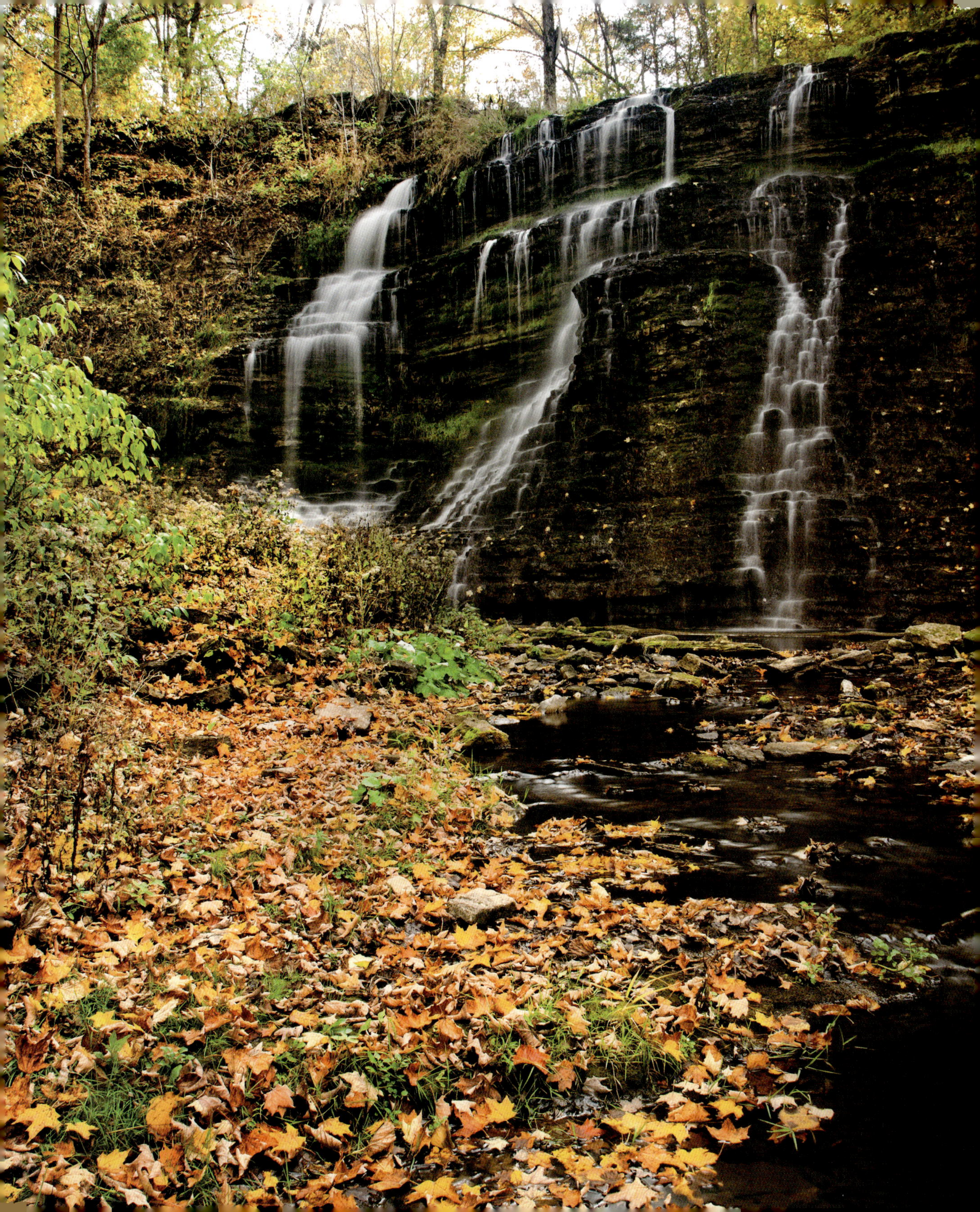

Black River Falls

If you're already in downtown Watertown, the falls are on Mill St., about a block away from Public Square.

From outside Watertown, take exit 47 from I-81, and drive into the city on Bradley St., which ends at West Main St. Turn left onto West Main St., and at the third traffic light, turn right onto Mill St. After the first traffic light, you'll cross a bridge. Park in the auto-parts store parking lot, and walk back to the bridge on the other side of the street to get a view of the falls.

COUNTY: Jefferson
TOWNSHIP: Watertown
PLACE: Watertown
WATERWAY: Black River
TYPE: curtain cascade
HEIGHT: est. 35 ft (10.7 m)
TRAIL: concrete sidewalk; easy
WALKING TIME: 1 min
PEAK ACTIVITY: June-Aug.
LATITUDE: 43.9767
LONGITUDE: –75.9068

Watertown was named for the abundant waterpower delivered by the 125-mile-long (200 km) Black River, which gets its start in the Adirondack Mountains in Herkimer County. Over the years, power dams have been built at several locations in and around Watertown, but Black River Falls, located a few hundred yards from Public Square and the downtown business district, was the community's largest waterfall.

While Black River Falls is the most popular name for this waterfall, it is also known as Watertown Falls and Great Falls. Just upstream from Watertown is the Village of Black River, which features a small, unnamed waterfall that locals have dubbed the Black River Village Falls, not to be confused with the falls we're discussing here.

Because the cement walls lining the bridge over the river are high, it's not possible to see this waterfall from your car. To enjoy the view, simply park nearby and take a stroll up the sidewalk on the east side of Mill Street. You'll notice that the street is almost always damp, and there is often mist in the air.

Settled around 1800, Watertown is the county seat of Jefferson County. Frank W. Woolworth, credited with launching the five-and-dime, was raised in Rodman, not far from Watertown. When he developed his groundbreaking business concept, Woolworth was working as a clerk in a local business.

Today, Watertown is a commercial hub whose economy is fueled by nearby Fort Drum, home to the 10th Mountain Division of the U.S. Army. It is also the headquarters of the Car-Freshner Corporation (manufacturer of the storied Little Trees), host of the longest continuously operating county fair in the United States and home to the Red & Black football franchise, the oldest semi-professional team in the country. It boasts Thompson Park, designed by Frederick Law Olmsted, the landscape architect of New York City's Central Park. The Paddock Arcade, an 1850 structure located on Public Square and listed on the National Register of Historic Places, is considered to be America's oldest continuously operating enclosed mall.

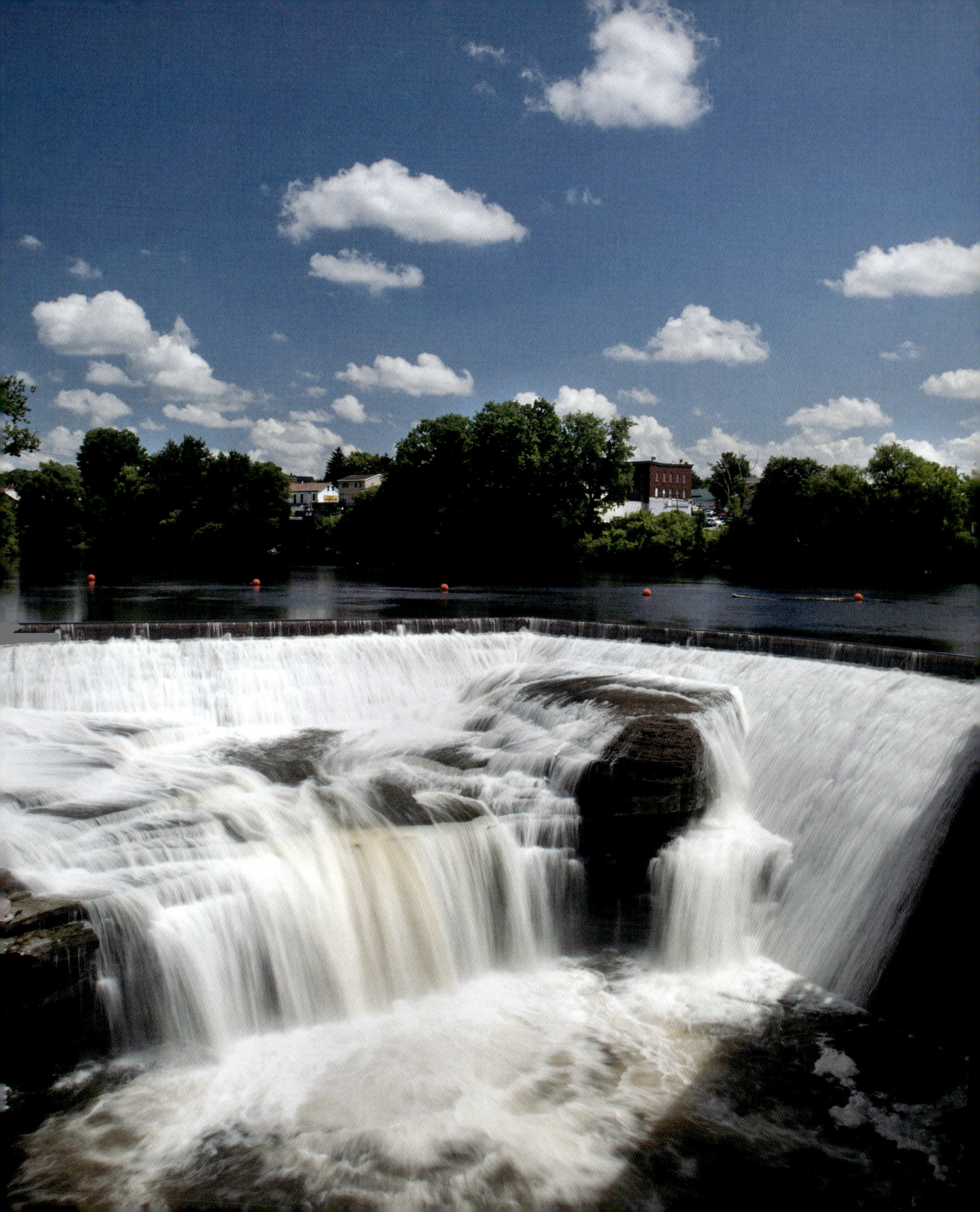

Glen Park Falls

From I-81, take exit 46 west onto Coffeen St., which becomes NY 12F. Proceed west to Paddy Hill, take a right, and cross the Black River into Brownville. Take another right onto Main St. (you are now heading back toward Watertown). Past the Brownville Elementary School, there is a dome structure on the right that houses the power plant, then a fenced-in area surrounding Glen Park Hydro. Park on the grass in front of the facility. Access to the waterfall is restricted to those registered with a white-water tour company.

During the 1950s and 1960s, parents in the Watertown area warned their children to steer clear of the Black River. Over a 10-mile (16 km) stretch, the river's vertical descent is 500 feet (153 m), creating several waterfalls and multiple sets of rapids. If a child were to venture too close, it was feared, he or she would be swept away.

Located west of I-81, in the village of Glen Park, Glen Park Falls is right in the middle of this drop and marks the beginning of a segment known as Black River Canyon. Today, this section is a white-water rafting and kayaking paradise.

This is private property, owned by the Glen Park Hydroelectric Project. While there are agreements in place for weekend activities such as fishing and white-water rafting, the area is completely off-limits to the public throughout the week. In fact, when the hydro facility is in operation, the water is diverted into the hydro channel and the main channel barely runs.

Between 11 a.m. and 4 p.m. on weekends, plant production is cut back and the river returns to its normal flow. The only legal way of viewing the falls is to register with one of the approved tour companies allowed access. If you and your group arrive just before the "switch is flipped," you'll hear the warning siren. The water level can rise up to 5 feet (1.5 m) in five minutes — you can literally see the water coming up.

The waterfall itself drops in two distinct steps. The first drop of 4 feet (1.2 m) is followed a short distance later by another plunge of 12 feet (3.7 m). Because of all the white-water activity here, you'll almost certainly see and be able to photograph marine daredevils paddling over the falls in their kayaks. In addition to the main falls, large rocks and other landmasses create an island of sorts, and there is a smaller waterfall, or slide, on the shore nearest you.

COUNTY: Jefferson

TOWNSHIP: Brownville and Hounsfield

PLACE: Watertown

WATERWAY: Black River

TYPE: curtain falls

HEIGHT: 16 ft (4.9 m)

TRAIL: dirt and rock; easy

WALKING TIME: 2 min

PEAK ACTIVITY: May-Oct.

LATITUDE: 43.9965

LONGITUDE: –75.9522

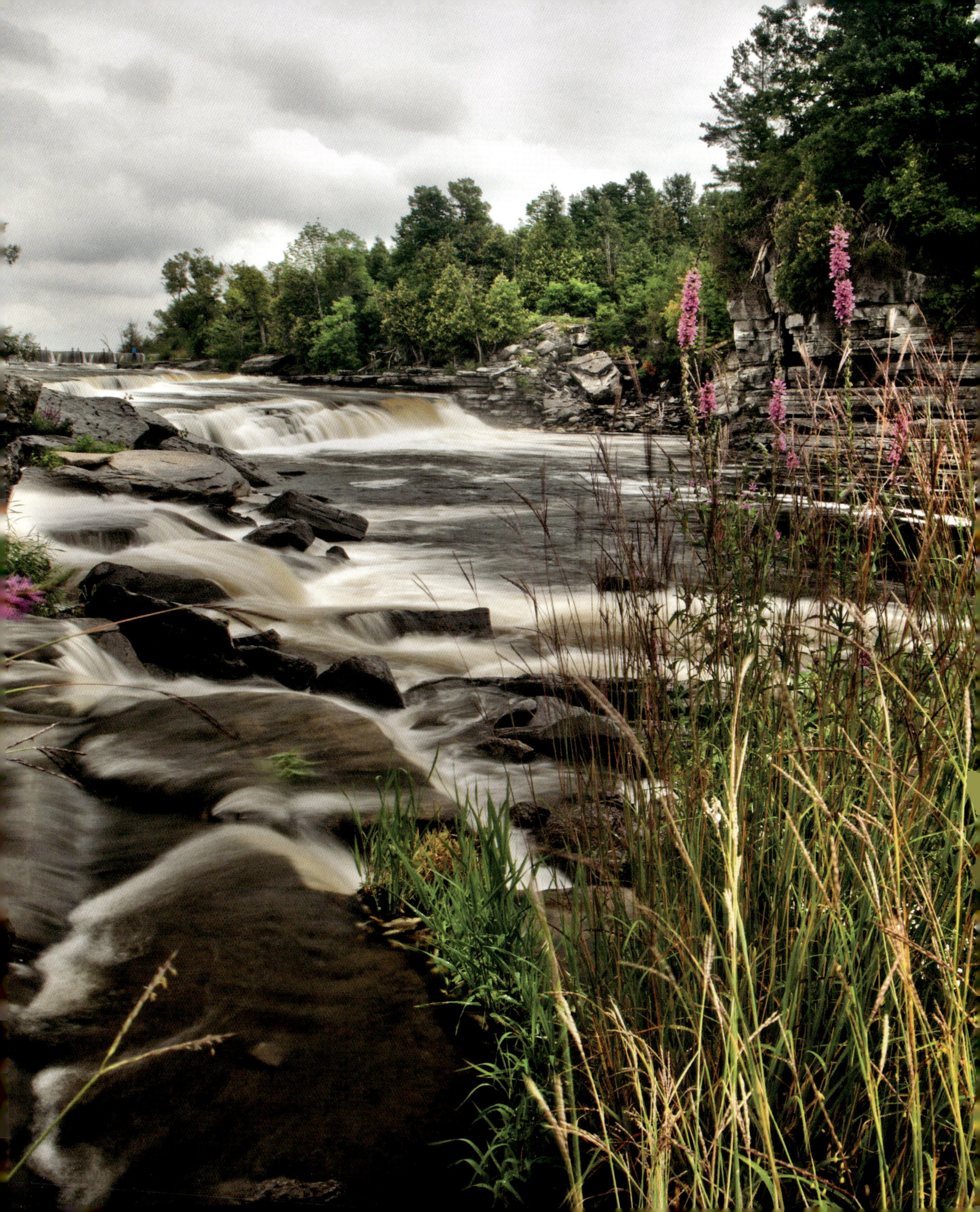

Pleasant Creek Falls

Evans Mills is north of Watertown on US 11. Turn left onto Leray St. (CR 46) and enter the village. As you cross the first main intersection, there is a building on the right that houses the library, town hall and museum. Turn right here. The walkway on the building's left leads to the falls.

If you turn left at the main intersection, there are also viewing opportunities. The bridge is a short distance from this corner. Street parking is available at both locations.

COUNTY: Jefferson
TOWNSHIP: Le Ray
PLACE: Evans Mills
WATERWAY: Pleasant Creek
TYPE: curtain cascade
HEIGHT: est. 20 ft (6.1 m)
TRAIL: concrete sidewalk; easy
WALKING TIME: 1 min
PEAK ACTIVITY: June-Aug.
LATITUDE: 44.0885
LONGITUDE: –75.8069

One of the hundreds of falls in northern New York that are technically unnamed, Pleasant Creek Falls is located on Pleasant Creek in the village of Evans Mills. It has been known variously as Evans Mills Falls and The Falls at Evans Mills; a postcard, circa 1911, which promotes the waterfall with a view from downstream, is labeled "The Falls, Evans Mills, N.Y."

Evans Mills was founded in the early 1800s, although the mills weren't built for a few years. In the mid-1800s, the community was known for a short time as Evansville, after an early settler, Ethan Evans. As was typical of the era, the mills probably drew their power from this waterfall.

The falls are nestled under a bridge, and because of the height of the bridge's concrete walls, they cannot be seen from a vehicle. Thousands of people have probably driven right over the falls without knowing it. In fact, when we were researching this waterfall, we spoke with a number of people who had once lived in the area but had neither seen nor even heard of Pleasant Creek Falls.

The waterfall steps down in three drops. The best views are afforded from behind the town hall, although from this vantage point, you can see only the lower two steps. The uppermost drop is hidden under the bridge. If you walk up the street and around the corner, you can look down on the waterfalls from the bridge. If you look over the east side of the bridge, you'll see the first drop. Unfortunately, maintenance is not consistent here, and tree limbs and other debris are often trapped at this juncture. The other two drops can be seen from the west side of the bridge.

Pleasant Creek Falls is a pretty sight, made more so by the sheer volume of water that flows over the crest, impressive when one considers that this creek is a very small waterway.

Evans Mills is close to the main entrance of Fort Drum, home to the U.S. Army's 10th Mountain Division, which drives a large part of the local economy. The community is also home to a well-known northern New York State auto-racing facility, one of the few area tracks that has an asphalt surface rather than dirt.

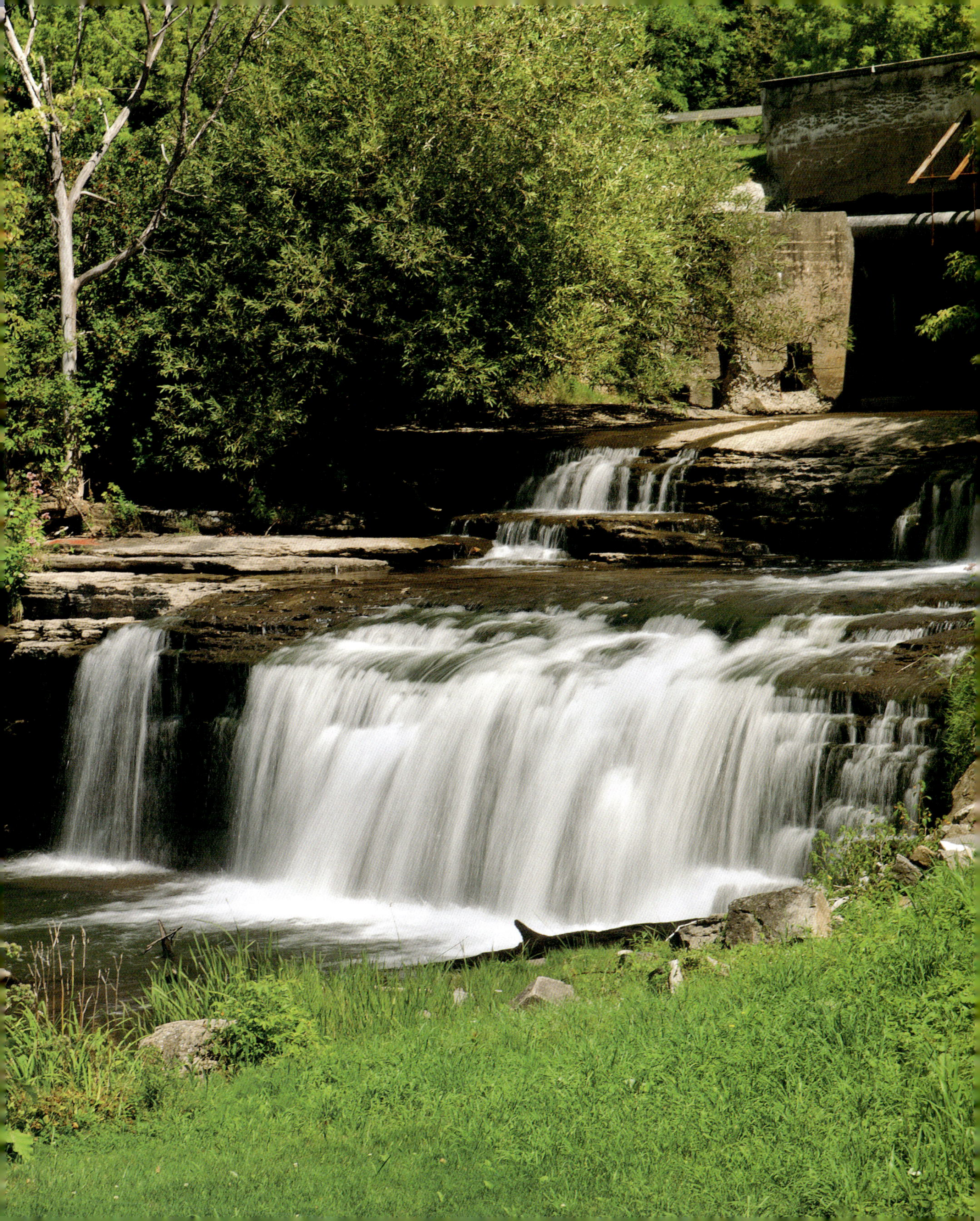

Fullerville Falls

From Gouverneur, proceed on NY 58 east toward Edwards. Just after passing the Edwards town-line sign, turn right onto CR 24. You'll come to a bridge that crosses the river. The falls are visible on your left, just upstream.

From Harrisville and points south, take NY 812 toward Gouverneur. In Balmat, turn right onto CR 24. Just past Fullerville, there is a bridge, with ample parking on the shoulder of the road.

COUNTY: St. Lawrence
TOWNSHIP: Fowler
PLACE: Gouverneur
WATERWAY: Oswegatchie River, West Branch
TYPE: curtain falls
HEIGHT: est. 12 ft (3.7 m)
TRAIL: within view of hwy.
WALKING TIME: 1 min
PEAK ACTIVITY: April-Nov.
LATITUDE: 44.2654
LONGITUDE: –75.3429

Not only is this waterfall technically unnamed, it isn't even marked on topographical maps. Due to its proximity to the hamlet of Fullerville, we have dubbed it Fullerville Falls.

This is a "see it from the car" waterfall. It has two sections separated by a small island. The banks of the Oswegatchie River are not easy to walk without getting wet, but you really don't need to get any closer to this waterfall to appreciate it. If you stroll along the roadside here, you'll be able to view the falls from several angles.

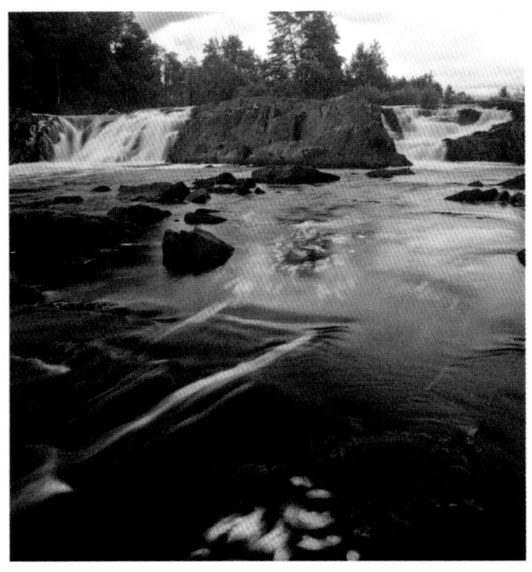

Fullerville was named after four brothers from Vermont — Sheldon, Stillman, Heman and Ashbel Fuller — who founded the once-thriving village and built and ran several businesses, including a gristmill and a blast furnace.

The area is also a popular fishing and canoeing destination. If you are a waterfall enthusiast who prefers getting closer to the falls from the water, there is an easy put-in point here. In fact, a few miles upstream, there are several other waterfalls as well as significant stretches of rapids that would be difficult to access other than from the river.

Locally, this section of highway is known as the Russell Turnpike. A compilation of many roads, the highway dates back to the early 1800s, when the United States and Britain were battling for control of the St. Lawrence River. It was built to help move troops and supplies from central New York to the river, and its construction led to the settlement of many communities in its path, including Fullerville, Edwards and Russell. The surnames on the document legalizing the road's construction read like a "Who's Who" of towns and communities in St. Lawrence, Jefferson and Lewis counties.

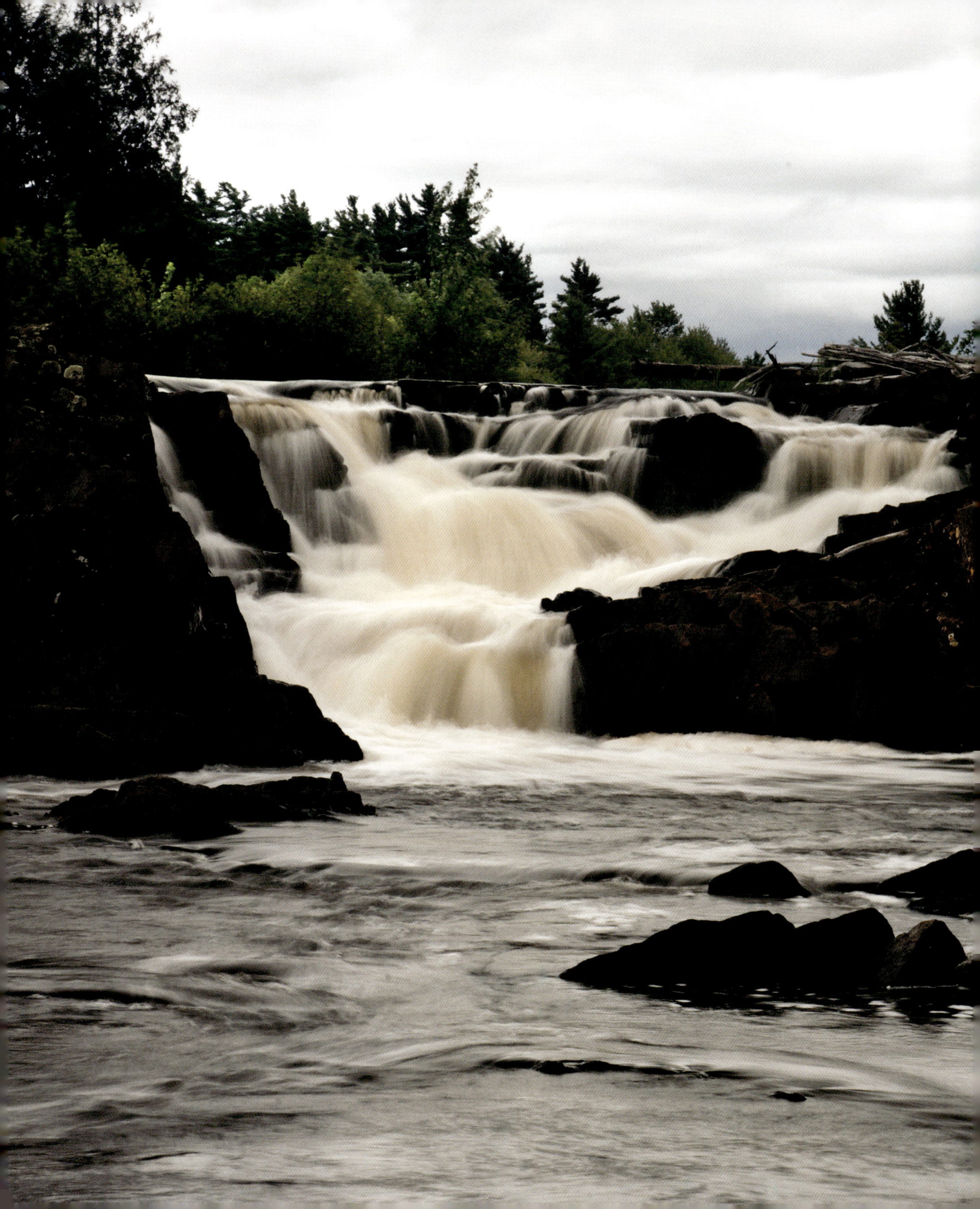

NORTH COUNTRY REGION

Browns Falls

From the intersection of NY 58 and NY 3 in the town of Fine, drive about 5 mi (8 km) west on NY 3 until it intersects with Browns Falls Rd. Turn left, and drive northeast for roughly 1.2 mi (1.9 km), until you come to a bridge. There is no parking lot per se, but there is very little traffic here. Park on the right shoulder of the road, and walk across the bridge.

If you are coming from Star Lake, drive east on NY 3 about 3 mi (4.8 km) and turn left onto Browns Falls Rd.

COUNTY: St. Lawrence

TOWNSHIP: Clifton

PLACE: Star Lake

WATERWAY: Oswegatchie River

TYPE: curtain cascade

HEIGHT: est. 25 ft (7.6 m)

TRAIL: dirt; moderate

WALKING TIME: 15 min

PEAK ACTIVITY: May-Sept.

LATITUDE: 44.2146

LONGITUDE: –75.0477

While many area residents are aware that the Browns Reservoir Dam is located down Browns Falls Road, few seem to know that the road also leads to this waterfall. In fact, this is a lovely stretch of the Oswegatchie River, and Browns Falls is a very attractive waterfall. Near your parking spot on the shoulder of the road, you'll find a trail that leads upstream.

The waterfall is in an undeveloped part of the Adirondack foothills, and the 0.5-mile (0.8 km) trail in is not well defined or maintained. The hike is neither long nor strenuous, but fallen trees lie across parts of it, and there are a few short but fairly steep grades. When you reach the river, be careful — there are no fences or railings.

Browns Falls descends in several steps or slides and covers a fairly long segment of the river. You can walk out onto the rocks anywhere along and around the falls, but these tend to be slippery, so use caution.

Just as interesting as the waterfall are the nearby remnants of a long-abandoned mill. The crumbling foundation can be seen, as can the concrete cradle that held its original penstock — a vast pipe that carried water from the river to a dam in the area. A small amount of water still flows through it much of the year, but this penstock was dismantled around the time of the First World War.

A few hundred yards farther inland, a new penstock that was built in the early 1970s carries much of the water from the Oswegatchie River to the Browns Reservoir Dam, a mile or so downstream. One can only imagine what Browns Falls would look like if this dam weren't there.

The waterfall is named for Amasa Brown. Not much is known about this early settler, but in land records, the entire area is described as the "John Brown Tract." This is *not* the abolitionist John Brown, who famously raided the federal arsenal at Harpers Ferry in 1859.

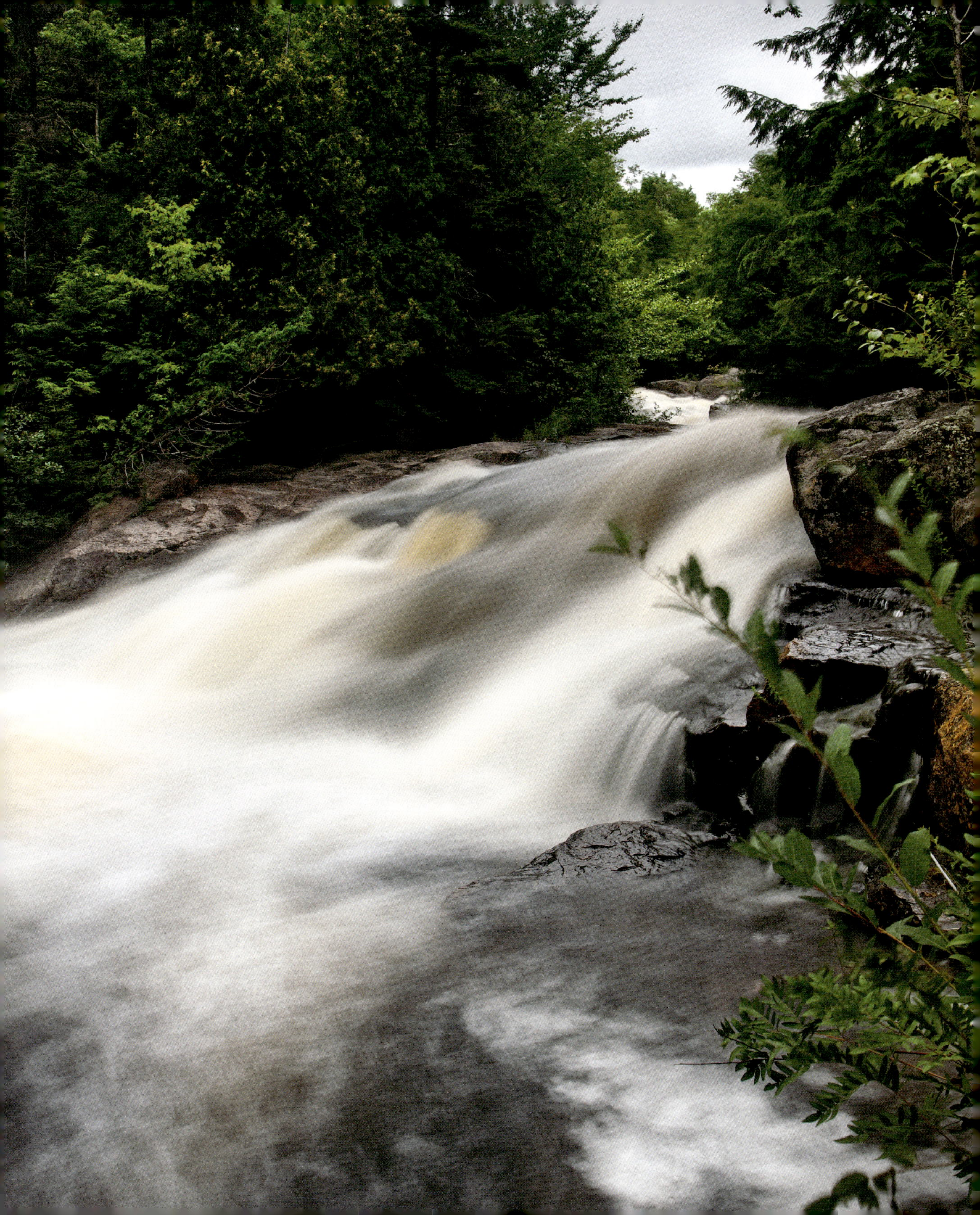

NORTH COUNTRY REGION

Butter Tub Falls

From the intersection of NY 58 and NY 3 in the town of Fine, drive about 5 mi (8 km) west on NY 3 until it intersects with Browns Falls Rd. Turn left, and drive northeast for roughly 1.2 mi (1.9 km), until you come to a bridge. There is no parking lot per se, but there is very little traffic here. Park on the right shoulder of the road, and walk across the bridge.

If you are coming from Star Lake, drive east on NY 3 about 3 mi (4.8 km), and turn left onto Browns Falls Rd.

Once you've reached Browns Falls, it's another 15-minute walk to Butter Tub Falls.

COUNTY: St. Lawrence

TOWNSHIP: Clifton

PLACE: Star Lake

WATERWAY: Oswegatchie River

TYPE: complex ribbon cascade

HEIGHT: est. 50 ft (15.3 m)

TRAIL: dirt; difficult

WALKING TIME: 30 min

PEAK ACTIVITY: May-Sept.

LATITUDE: 44.2143

LONGITUDE: –75.0428

After enjoying Browns Falls, continue upstream for about 0.25 mile (0.4 km) to Butter Tub Falls, which appears to be an even better-kept secret than is Browns. As with the hike in to the first waterfall, this trail is not maintained. Reaching Butter Tub Falls is a challenge (you're sure to encounter a few more fallen trees), but it will be well worth the effort. This lovely stretch of little-known wilderness is within a 15-minute walk of Browns Falls.

At the end of the trail is a fairly high ridge overlooking the river. Walk along the ridge until you see a selection of paths down to the water. As the embankment is quite steep, each is a bit of a scurry. Pick one that suits you.

Butter Tub Falls has three sections. The first is a pretty waterfall that sends water down into what looks a little like a natural waterslide. Today, the Oswegatchie River runs at only a fraction of its potential strength because most of the water is diverted around these falls to the Browns Reservoir Dam below. The exposed rocks in this middle section have been worn smooth over time, which suggests that at one point, they were entirely submerged under fast-running water. Here, too, is a series of tublike holes for which the falls is named, likewise carved from the rock over centuries.

On the south side of the channel is a second, smaller waterfall, and beneath the smooth central region, Butter Tub Falls finishes up with a final waterfall.

Consider taking an alternative route back to your vehicle. Climb up the embankment, and continue to the very top. There, you'll find the right-of-way for the buried penstock, easily identified by a raised mound along the ground. Follow the tree line that borders the river.

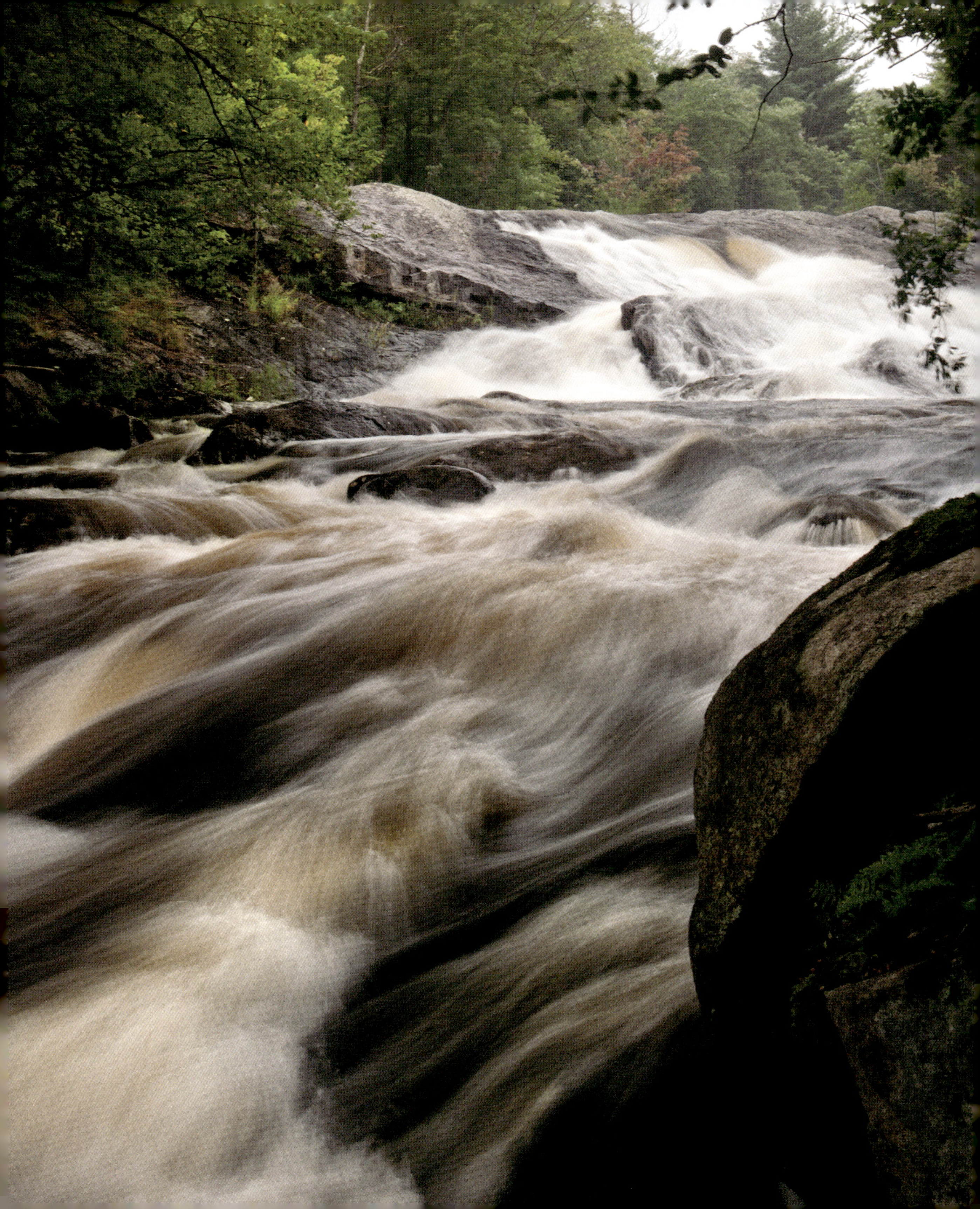

NORTH COUNTRY REGION

Chipmunk Falls

In the hamlet of Star Lake, turn onto the Oswegatchie Trail where it meets NY 3 (the Clifton-Fine Central School campus on the corner serves as a landmark). Continue on until you see the Clifton-Fine Hospital, then take a left at Lake Rd. After about 0.5 mi (0.8 km), there is a dirt road on the right. Drive until you reach a gate and a parking area.

COUNTY: St. Lawrence

TOWNSHIP: Fine

PLACE: Star Lake

WATERWAY: Little River

TYPE: ribbon cascade

HEIGHT: est. 25 ft (7.6 m)

TRAIL: dirt; easy

WALKING TIME: 8 min

PEAK ACTIVITY: June-Aug.

LATITUDE: 44.1441

LONGITUDE: –75.0582

As with hundreds of other falls in northern New York, this waterfall is not marked on maps and so is technically unnamed. Nevertheless, Chipmunk Falls — largely unknown to outsiders — has been a popular fishing and recreation spot with locals for years.

The Chipmunk Falls moniker dates back over a century, but no one seems to know its origin. The falls are also known in these parts as Schuler Falls. For many years, the Andrew Schuler family owned a 4,500-acre (1,820 ha) tract in the area. Originally from around Rochester, the Schulers made their name and fortune in the potato chip industry with an extremely popular snack called Schuler's Potato Chips. In fact, a portion of the family's estate was dedicated to growing potatoes. In 1975, the land was sold to the state and became part of the Aldrich Pond Wild Forest.

From the parking area, walk down the dirt trail until you reach a fork in the path. Bear right. You'll hear the roar of the falls as you approach Little River. Chipmunk Falls descends in two steps. The first drop is about 5 feet (1.5 m) and occurs a few feet upstream from an outcropping, where the stream narrows to 2 or 3 feet (0.6–1 m) and takes its second and final plunge.

Many families enjoy the year-round beauty and calm of nearby tiny Star Lake, which is named for its shape. Known as "the gem of the Adirondacks," Star Lake is definitely an outdoor enthusiast's paradise, and hunting and fishing opportunities abound. Unlike some of the larger and more popular Adirondack lakes, such as Saranac Lake, Lake Placid and Tupper Lake, this area has been spared being overwhelmed by tourists and related commercialism.

While it enjoys a significant flow for most of the year, Little River is almost completely frozen in the dead of winter. The area experiences significant winter weather.

Note that there are two Little Rivers in St. Lawrence County. This one empties into the Oswegatchie River, which flows to the St. Lawrence River in Ogdensburg. The other, in the Canton area, is a tributary of the Grasse River, which enters the St. Lawrence in Massena.

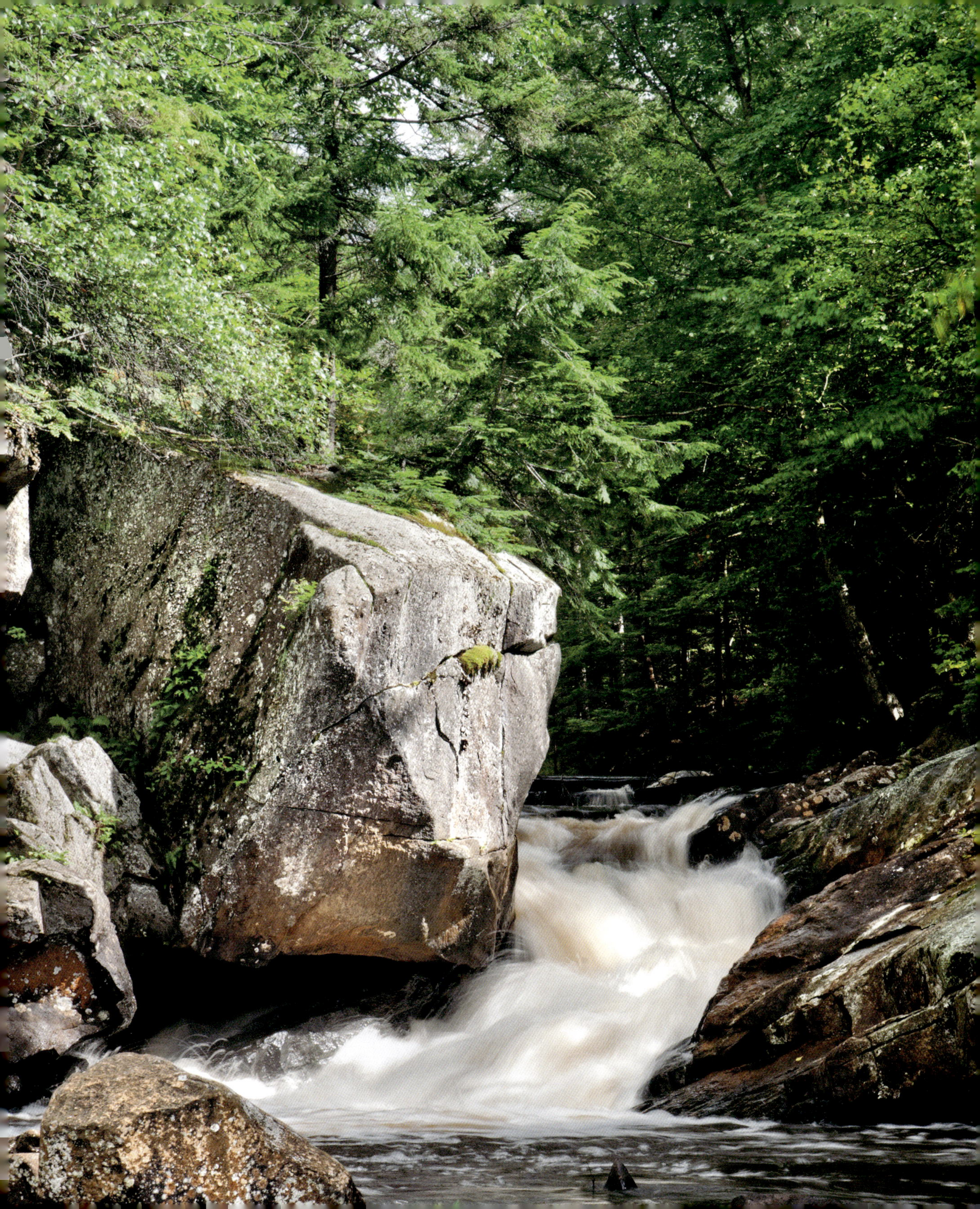

Basford Falls

Just north of Degrasse, CR 27 leads to the Tooley Pond Rd. junction. Travel for about 1.4 mi (2.3 km); the trailhead is on your right. Look for two red gateposts with a boulder between them that restricts motor-vehicle access. It is safe to park on the roadside as the road is not well traveled.

If you're driving from the south, Tooley Pond Rd. intersects with NY 3 just west of the hamlet of Cranberry Lake.

COUNTY: St. Lawrence

TOWNSHIP: Clare

PLACE: Degrasse

WATERWAY: Grasse (Grass) River, South Branch

TYPE: curtain cascade

HEIGHT: est. 15 ft (4.6 m)

TRAIL: dirt; moderate

WALKING TIME: 7 min

PEAK ACTIVITY: May-Sept.

LATITUDE: 44.3401

LONGITUDE: –75.0579

On Tooley Pond Road, there are seven waterfalls that are accessible to the public. Like many of these, Basford Falls is on DEC-maintained state land on the South Branch of the Grasse River. Consider planning a trip to see all seven falls at once. As it happens, this area is not far from both Lampson Falls and Harper Falls, and all nine sites can easily be seen in a day.

Tooley Pond Road links CR 27 in the hamlet of Degrasse to NY 3 near Cranberry Lake. Much of the road is unpaved, and navigating it in the winter can be a challenge. If you're starting out from Degrasse, Basford is the first waterfall you'll encounter. The trailhead is easy to find, and the trail is fairly well maintained. In addition to the landmarks mentioned in the directions sidebar, at left, there should be a white DEC sign on a tree with the name Basford Falls on it. It's not a particularly solid-looking sign, however, and there's no guarantee it will still be there for your visit.

Degrasse is perched at the northwestern edge of the Adirondack State Park region in the Adirondack foothills and is only about 260 feet (79 m) above sea level. The seven-minute walk in to the falls is not overly demanding. It's a great walk for a family outing, one even young children can negotiate without too many "are we there yets?"

Basford Falls is quite long and has a number of steps, one of which is a drop of about 15 feet (4.6 m). The others are less profound. The top step occurs at a small turn in the river where there are a number of good-sized boulders in the stream. The main drop is next, followed by several descending steps and slides, until the water empties into a pool. There, the river turns again and continues its flow toward the St. Lawrence.

This area is sparsely populated, and hunting and fishing are popular outdoor activities. You might be wise to avoid it during deer season, from October to November. Otherwise, bring your gear if you're keen on fishing. Geocaching (a scavenger hunt using GPS) is also popular, and this entire stretch of river is extremely attractive to white-water kayakers, who have named this section "Lights Out."

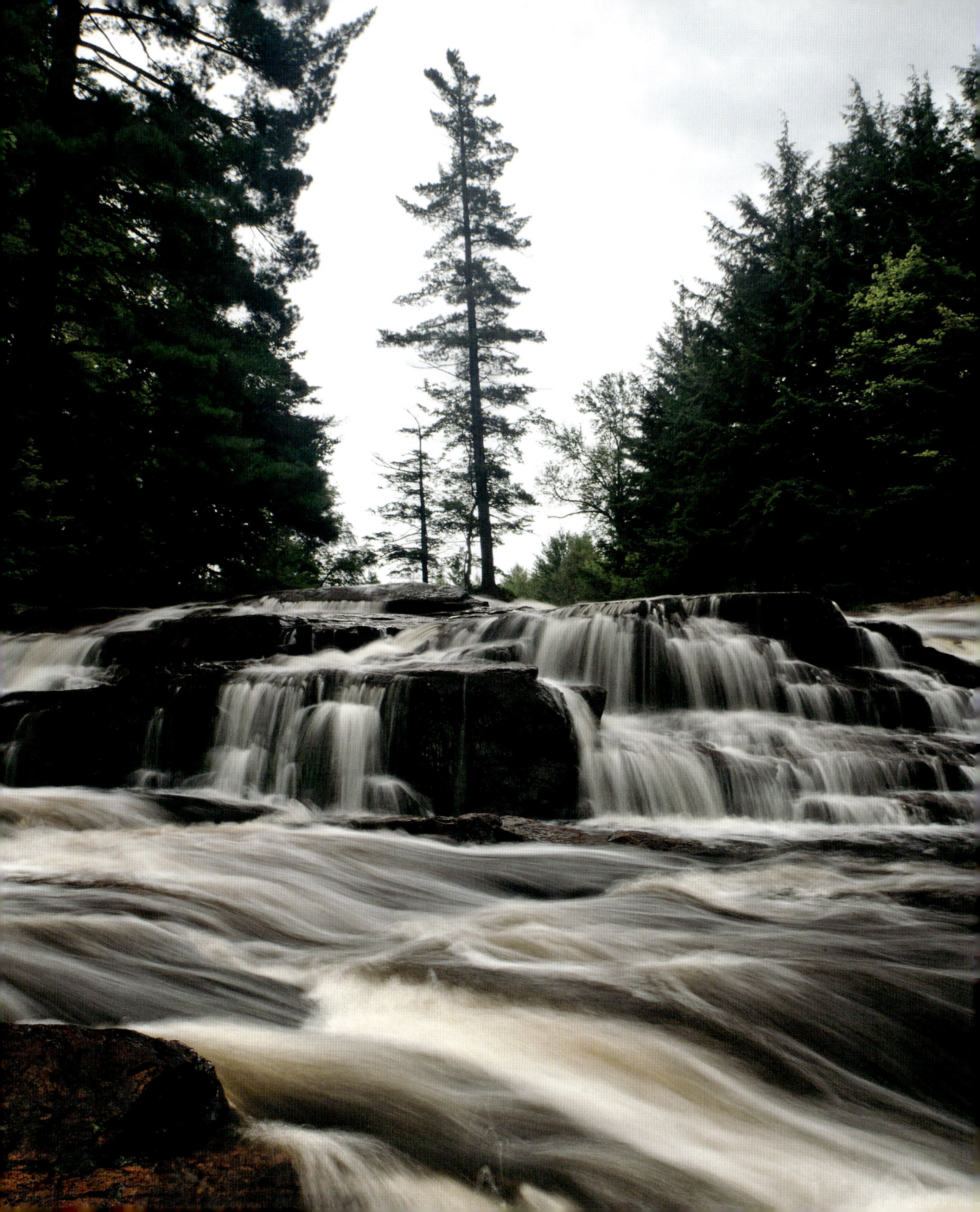

Sinclair Falls

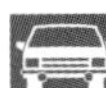

Just north of Degrasse, CR 27 leads to the Tooley Pond Rd. junction. Drive for about 2 mi (3.2 km); the trail-head is on your right. There is a sign-in kiosk just before the Lake George Rd. corner. You can park here or around the corner on Lake George Rd.

If you're driving from the south, Tooley Pond Rd. intersects with NY 3 just west of the hamlet of Cranberry Lake.

Sinclair Falls is another of the seven waterfalls on the South Branch of the Grasse River that is fairly easy to access from the Tooley Pond Road. It is the second waterfall you'll come to from the Degrasse end. For those visiting the falls on Tooley Pond Road in order, this is about 0.6 mile (1 km) beyond Basford Falls.

Like many of the falls on this road, Sinclair Falls is on DEC-maintained state land and accessible to the public. It is situated closer to the road than the other falls and, unlike the others, has a kiosk where people register before heading to the waterfall, which is easily in sight of the road. Not only does this sign-in allow the DEC to determine the number of visitors, but it is also a way of ensuring that those who go in actually come out. It's not clear why this service is offered only at Sinclair Falls.

There is a path from the kiosk to the waterfall, but we suggest that you walk or drive down the road to the corner of Lake George Road. A short distance along this side road is a clearly marked trail on which you can take a leisurely stroll to the falls. In fact, there is a DEC sign on a tree at this point that marks the entrance to Sinclair Falls.

If you had a bird's-eye view of this waterfall, you'd see that it has an almost question mark shape. The river bends to the right here, takes its first sliding drop and then makes a second, more pronounced plunge as the river wraps around to the left. From there, the next 300 feet (91.5 m) or so downstream is quite shallow.

While planning your trip to Sinclair Falls, make note of the other six falls on the Tooley Pond Road, as well as Lampson Falls and Harper Falls, which are in the area. All nine of these falls can easily be visited in a day. Remember, too, that all these waterfalls are in a natural, noncommercial setting, so if you carry it in, carry it out.

COUNTY: St. Lawrence
TOWNSHIP: Clare
PLACE: Degrasse
WATERWAY: Grasse (Grass) River, South Branch
TYPE: curtain cascade
HEIGHT: 25 ft (7.6 m)
TRAIL: dirt; easy
WALKING TIME: 5 min
PEAK ACTIVITY: May-Sept.
LATITUDE: 44.3380
LONGITUDE: –75.0459

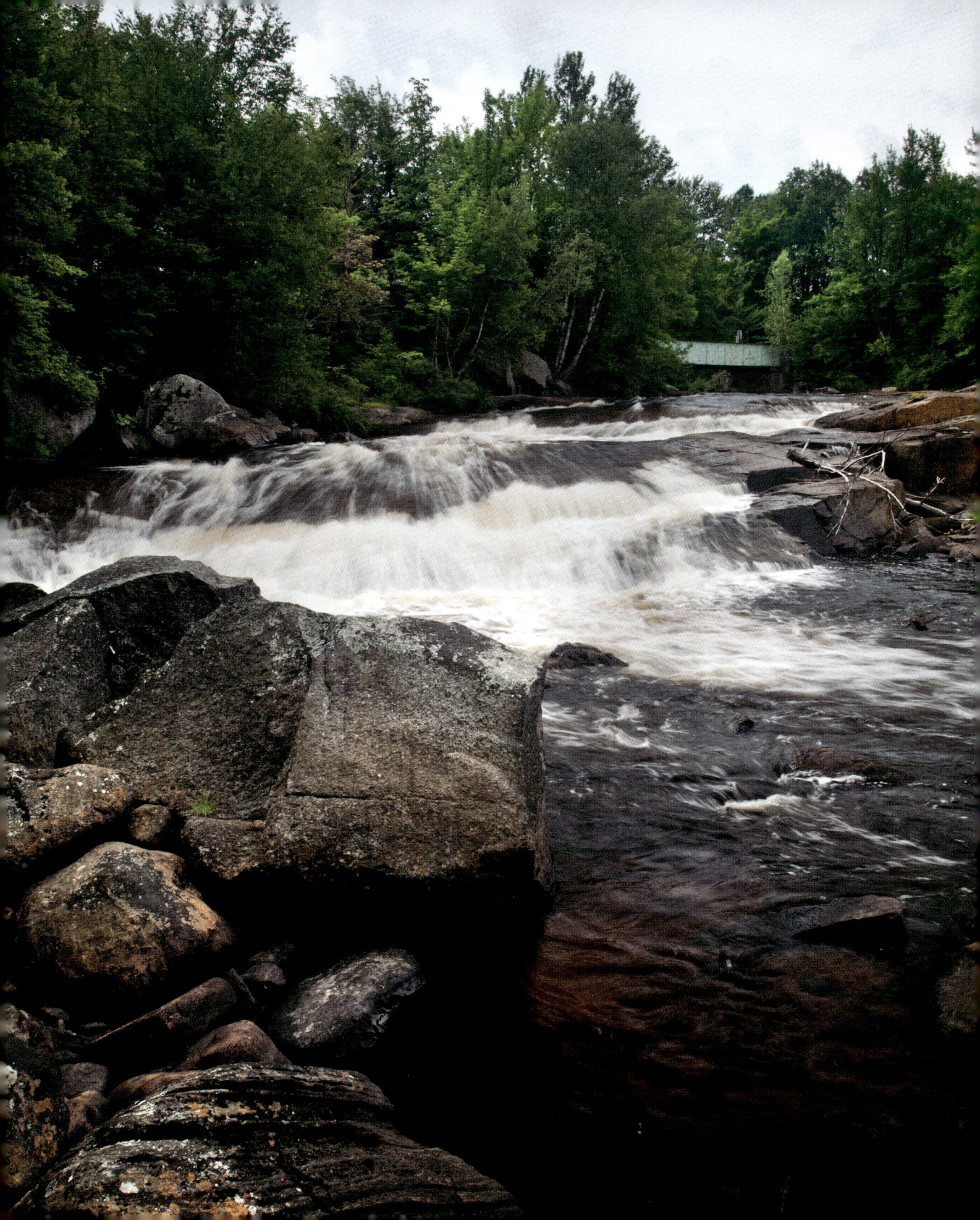

Twin Falls

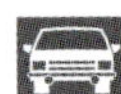

Just north of Degrasse, CR 27 leads to the Tooley Pond Rd. junction. After about 3.5 mi (5.6 km) on Tooley Pond Rd., you round a curve. As you come up the hill, the river and the smaller of the Twin Falls are visible on the right. A fallen tree trunk spans the channel. Park on the roadside.

Twin Falls, the third waterfall on Tooley Pond Road from the Degrasse end, is just over 1 mile (1.6 km) past Sinclair Falls. As its name suggests, this waterfall has two parts, created where a good-sized island divides the Grasse River.

The slender northern channel is visible from the road, as is the top of the smaller falls, a ribbon cascade. Its water dances down the rocks as it slides into a little pool below. The river narrows again downstream as it flows around a point of land and continues on.

To view the second, larger waterfall, you must walk across the channel to the island. Water shoes or boots are recommended. Cross at the shallow point where the river starts its drop. On the island, trails bear off to the right. You can take one of these to the base of the smaller cascade or hike the short distance across the island to view the larger falls.

The Grasse River is quite long and has several branches. It carries melting Adirondack snow to the St. Lawrence River, and during spring runoff, this waterfall is intense. Indeed, large volumes of water plunge over these falls even into the autumn. As a result, the larger channel ends in a roaring 55-foot (16.8 m) curtain cascade.

You can't see both sides of Twin Falls at once from the island; that view is possible only from private land or downstream, from a kayak or canoe. In fact, this is one of just two segments of land in the area that are privately owned. A couple of miles upstream is a private hunting club, which completely encompasses Flat Rock Falls, the only one of the eight waterfalls on Tooley Pond Road that cannot be viewed from public land.

COUNTY: St. Lawrence

TOWNSHIP: Clare

PLACE: Degrasse

WATERWAY: Grasse (Grass) River, South Branch

TYPE: classical cascade

HEIGHT: 55 ft (16.8 m)

TRAIL: dirt and water; easy

WALKING TIME: 5 min

PEAK ACTIVITY: May-Sept.

LATITUDE: 44.3324

LONGITUDE: –75.0269

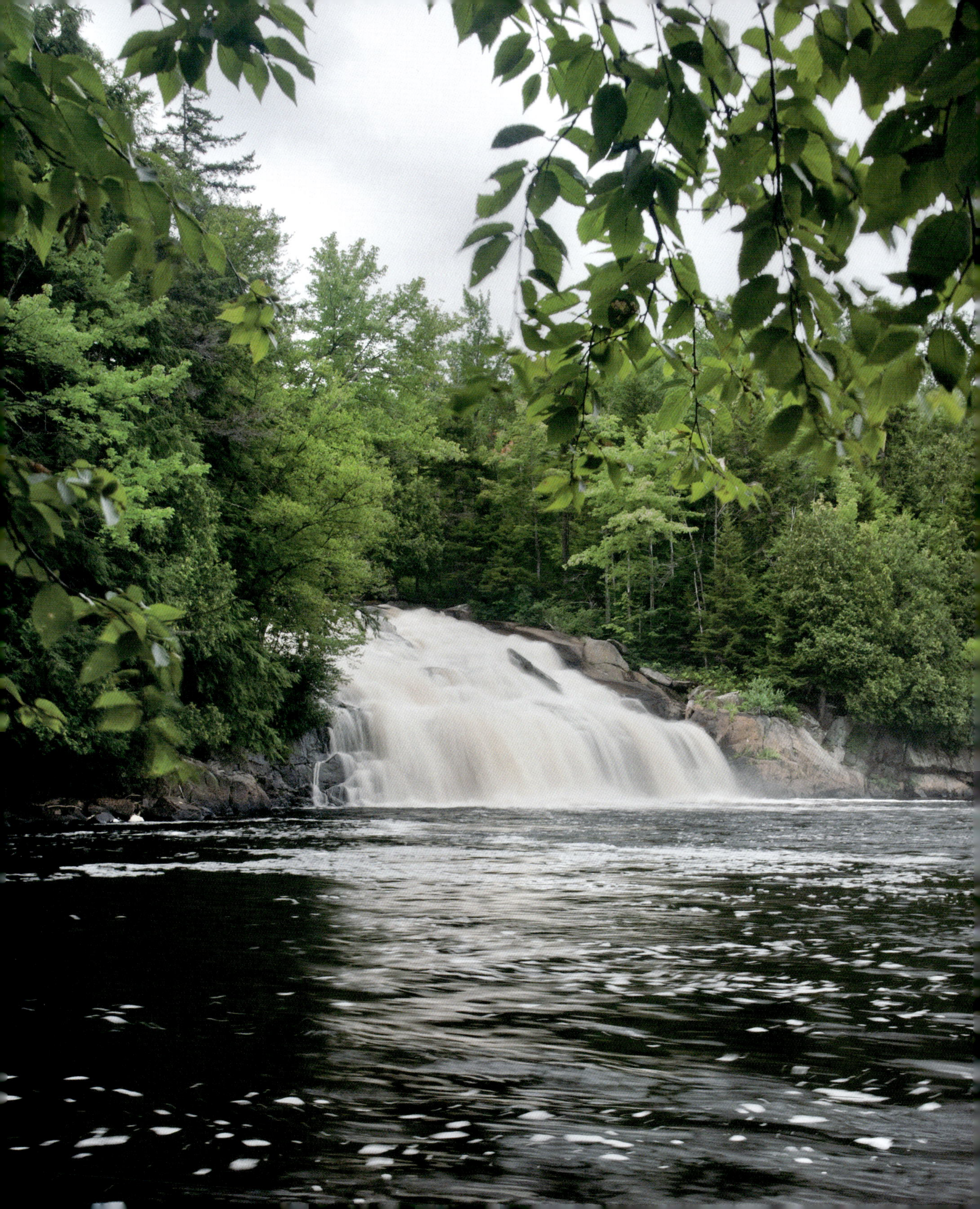

Bulkhead Falls & Adrenaline Falls

Just north of Degrasse, CR 27 leads to the Tooley Pond Rd. junction. After roughly 3.5 mi (5.6 km) on Tooley Pond Rd., there is a large bend in the river. (This occurs about 0.4 mi/0.6 km beyond Twin Falls.) There should be a yellow sign on a tree stating "No Motor Vehicles Allowed Beyond This Point." This is the trailhead. (Note your mileage, as there are several similar signs in the area.)

COUNTY: St. Lawrence

TOWNSHIP: Clare

PLACE: Degrasse

WATERWAY: Grasse (Grass) River, South Branch

TYPE: ribbon cascade

HEIGHT: 25 ft (7.6 m)

TRAIL: dirt; moderate

WALKING TIME: 8 min

PEAK ACTIVITY: May-Sept.

LATITUDE: 44.3303

LONGITUDE: –75.0182

On the way to Bulkhead Falls, you'll encounter another small waterfall. At 3.3 miles (5.3 km) from the beginning of Tooley Pond Road (0.2 mile/0.3 km beyond Twin Falls), the river takes a large turn. This stretch is commonly referred to as Stewart Rapids, but the 12-foot (3.7 m) drop is also known as Adrenaline Falls. There are no signs posted, but it is easy to find the trail to the river.

After you've visited Adrenaline Falls, continue along Tooley Pond Road for another 0.2 mile (0.3 km). At the 3.5-mile (5.6 km) point from the beginning of Tooley Pond Road, you'll find the trailhead for Bulkhead Falls. During our last visit, there was a sign posted that read "No Motor Vehicles Allowed Beyond This Point," but from the looks of the tree on which it was posted, there is no guarantee the sign will have survived the winter — or even a good wind. There are a number of these signs along this stretch, so be sure to stop at the one closest to the 3.5-mile (5.6 km) mark.

Bulkhead Falls is on DEC-maintained state land and is accessible to the public. If you come in on a trail by the aforementioned tree and sign, you'll arrive at the bottom of the falls. A bit farther down the road is another trail that will bring you to the middle of the stretch of falls, but there are no markings for that trail on the roadside.

This waterfall has several drops. At the first, the river narrows to about one-third of its width and enters a chutelike channel. It rushes through two or three more steps until the main drop, which occurs as the river widens again. Below this spot is a final small plunge into a pool, where the river then bends to the right.

As the water roars through the narrow channel at the main drop, it looks as if it is going over a wall or a bulkhead. Since there is no written record of how Bulkhead Falls came by its name, perhaps this is as good an explanation as any.

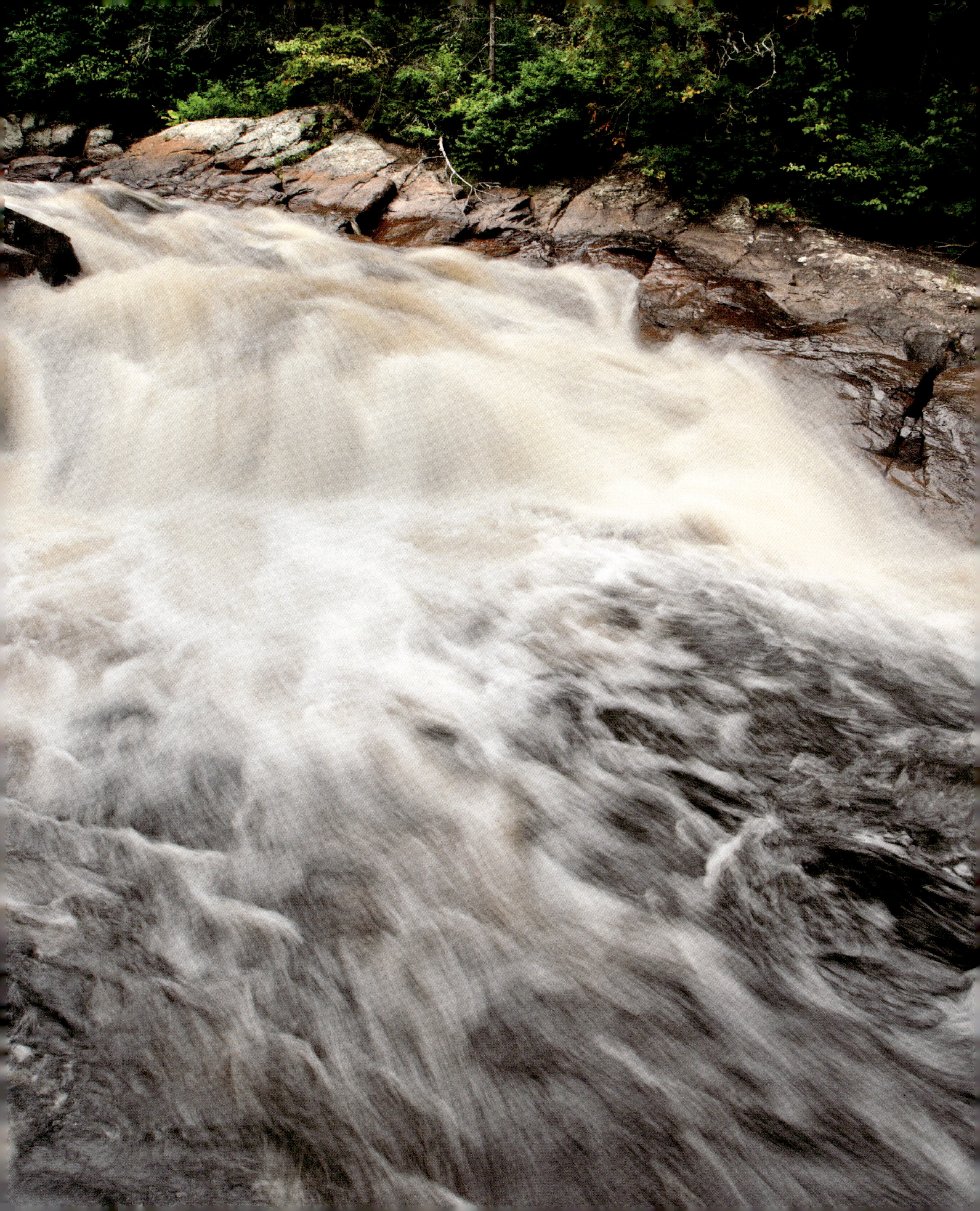

Rainbow Falls on the Grasse River, South Branch

Just north of Degrasse, CR 27 leads to the Tooley Pond Rd. junction. Travel for about 6.1 mi (9.8 km), and on your right, you'll see a white sign on a tree for Rainbow Falls. (Rainbow Falls is 2.6 mi/4.2 km beyond Bulkhead Falls.) A few boulders block access to an old road and an unused parking area. The other end of this road intersects NY 3 near the hamlet of Cranberry Lake. If approaching from that direction, watch for these landmarks.

COUNTY: St. Lawrence

TOWNSHIP: Clare

PLACE: Degrasse

WATERWAY: Grasse (Grass) River, South Branch

TYPE: classical cascade

HEIGHT: 35 ft (10.7 m)

TRAIL: dirt; moderate

WALKING TIME: 6 min

PEAK ACTIVITY: May-Sept.

LATITUDE: 44.3066

LONGITUDE: –74.9989

There is no shortage of waterfalls named Rainbow Falls in northern New York. In fact, there are at least six in the region; two of these are in St. Lawrence County. The falls described here (known as "Large Marge" to the white-water community) are the sixth of the seven waterfalls that can be accessed from Tooley Pond Road if you're traveling from the Degrasse end. Although not the largest waterfall in this region, Rainbow Falls is perhaps the most impressive of the Tooley Pond Road waterfalls.

Rainbow Falls is on DEC-maintained state land and is accessible to the public. The trailhead is clearly marked, and the walk in is not overly challenging. After about five minutes on the trail, you'll reach a wooden footbridge that crosses a narrow channel created by an island. A set of rapids runs down this stretch, and there is a small waterfall several yards downstream.

Cross the bridge and continue walking on the path until you see Rainbow Falls. This powerful, awe-inspiring waterfall drops into a narrow but fairly deep gorge, and if the breeze is just right, you can't avoid the spray created as the water pours over the crest. On sunny days, rainbows form in the mist, earning the falls its name.

Several paths on the island lead to the area downstream from the narrow channel, where you can view the smaller waterfall. At about 15 feet (4.6 m), it is as large as some other named falls in the area.

Use care while you are at this site. You are in the Adirondack foothills and experiencing nature at its finest. No fences or handrails separate you from the waterway, and some of these drops are a long way down. Keep a tight grip on your children.

This beautiful location is well worth the drive and casual hike in. When planning your trip to Rainbow Falls, make note of the other six falls on the Tooley Pond Road, along with Lampson Falls and Harper Falls, which are nearby. All nine of these waterfalls can easily be seen in a day, and all operate on a carry-in, carry-out policy.

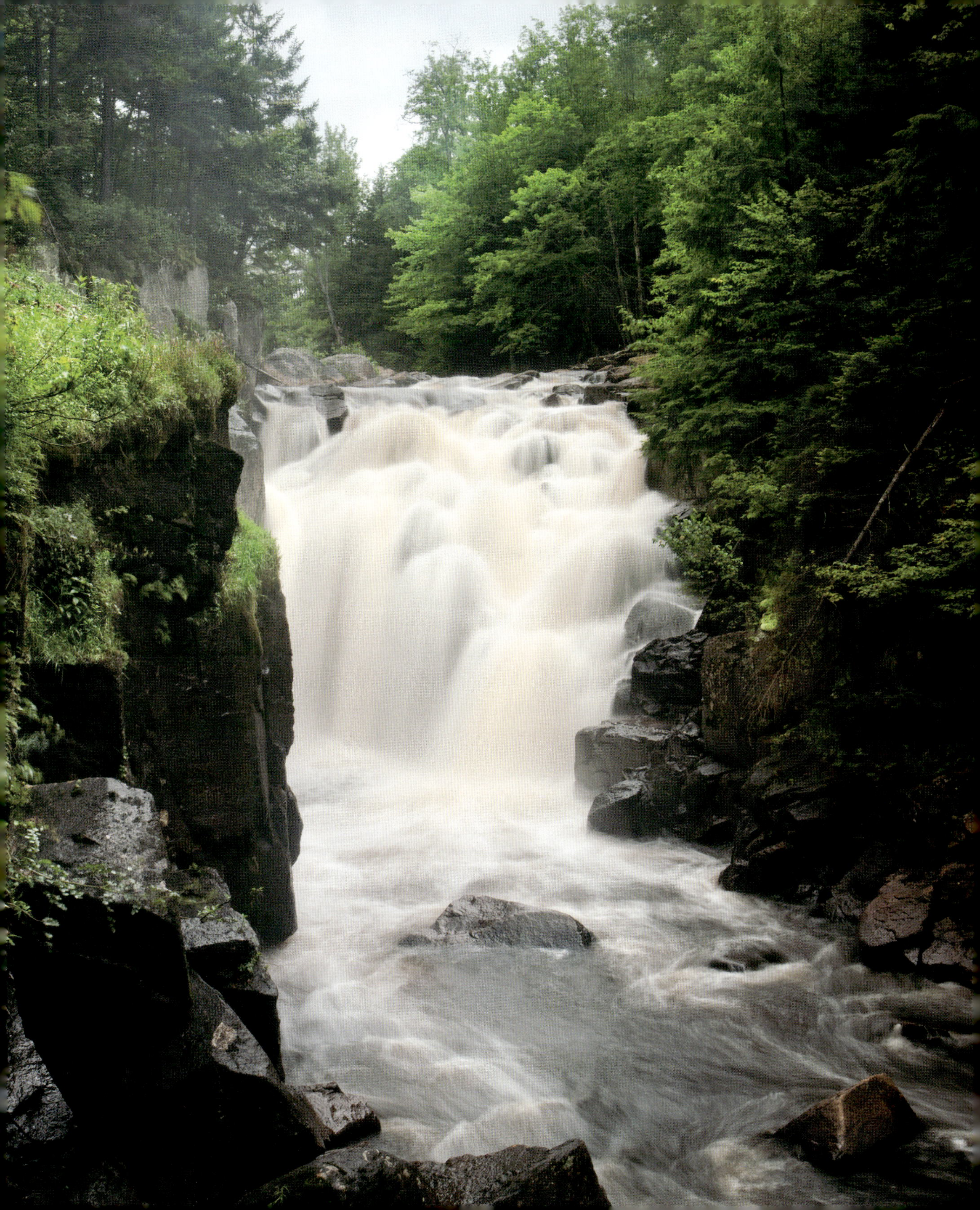

NORTH COUNTRY REGION

Copper Rock Falls

Just north of Degrasse, CR 27 leads to the Tooley Pond Rd. junction. Copper Rock Falls is about 8.9 mi (14.3 km) from Degrasse or 2.8 mi (4.5 km) past Rainbow Falls. The trailhead is clearly marked with a yellow sign that reads "Forest Preserve Wild Forest." Underneath is a white sign for Copper Rock Falls.

If you are driving from the south, Tooley Pond Rd. intersects with NY 3 just west of the hamlet of Cranberry Lake. Copper Rock Falls is the only waterfall on this road with the trailhead on the left as you approach from Degrasse.

COUNTY: St. Lawrence

TOWNSHIP: Clare

PLACE: Degrasse

WATERWAY: Grasse (Grass) River, South Branch

TYPE: curtain cascade

HEIGHT: 10 ft (3 m)

TRAIL: dirt; moderate

WALKING TIME: 5 min

PEAK ACTIVITY: May-Sept.

LATITUDE: 44.2886

LONGITUDE: –74.9597

Copper Rock Falls is the last of the seven waterfalls on Tooley Pond Road that are accessible to the public. It is about 8.9 miles (14.3 km) from the Degrasse end and 2.8 miles (4.5 km) past the trailhead for Rainbow Falls. It is the only waterfall on the road that is on your left as you travel in this direction. A bridge just before the trailhead takes you over the South Branch of the Grasse River.

Like many of the falls on this road, Copper Rock Falls is on DEC-maintained state land. Signs clearly mark the trailhead. While the five-minute hike in to the falls is not particularly challenging, the trail itself is not well maintained. As the trail reaches the river's edge, you'll see a set of rapids. Bear right, and follow the river upstream to the falls.

The Grasse River has many branches, all of which start in the Adirondack Mountains. During spring runoff, it's a roaring torrent. Once the ice starts to melt, the entire width of the river at the waterfall's crest may be covered with water. (In fact, depending on the severity of the winter, chunks of ice are sometimes spotted flowing through in May.) At that time, the waterfall is best classified as a curtain cascade.

As summer approaches and the volume of water diminishes, the river forms an S-shaped chute. The water drops in three steps or, more accurately, slides. One look at the waterfall at this time makes the inspiration for its name self-evident: The rocks in its path have large spots of copper coloring. When the flow is reduced and the rocks become more visible, the water appears to be almost copper-colored as well.

This is a very pretty stretch of the Grasse River's South Branch and well worth a visit. The hike in to Copper Rock Falls is moderate, and it's an extremely pleasant destination for a family outing.

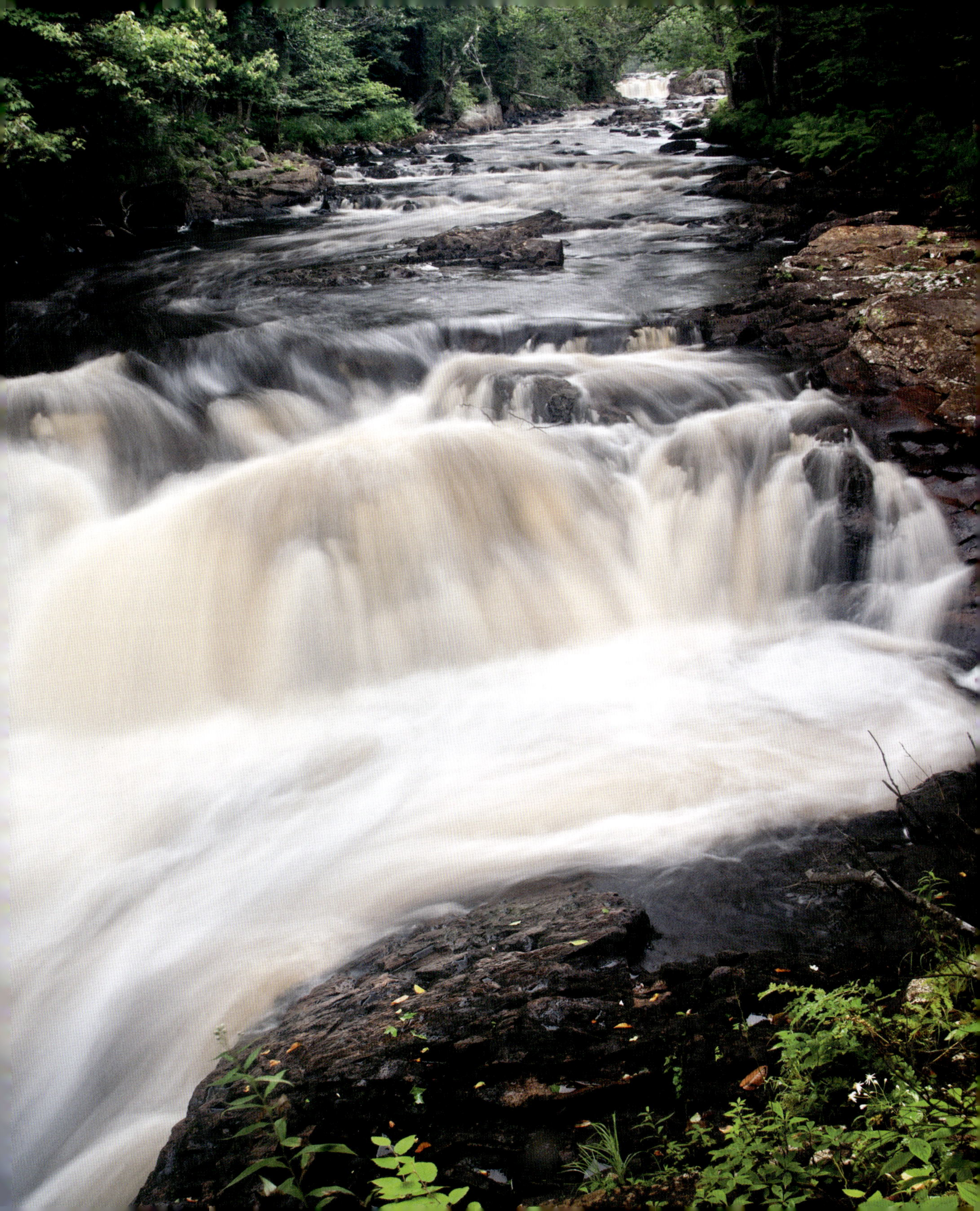

Lampson Falls

From the south, proceed north on CR 27 from the junction of CR 17 and CR 27 in Degrasse for 4.6 mi (7.4 km). Just before you reach the falls, you'll pass an airstrip. Watch for DEC signs for the Grasse River Wild Forest and Lampson Falls.

From the north, drive southeast out of Canton on Park St., which becomes CR 27, and through Pierrepont. After entering Clare, watch for a sign for Lampson Falls on your right. There is paved parking at the side of the road.

COUNTY: St. Lawrence

TOWNSHIP: Clare

PLACE: Clare

WATERWAY: Grasse (Grass) River

TYPE: curtain cascade

HEIGHT: 40 ft (12.2 m)

TRAIL: dirt; easy

WALKING TIME: 10 min

PEAK ACTIVITY: May-Sept.

LATITUDE: 44.4055

LONGITUDE: –75.0671

Lampson Falls is probably the most popular waterfall in St. Lawrence County, not only with locals and students from area colleges but with kayakers from northern New York, New England and Canada. On any given day during the summer, four or five vehicles may be parked in the paved parking area on the shoulder of the road where the trail begins.

That's not to say you'll be fighting a crowd. This is, after all, rural St. Lawrence County. It's not very commercialized, and there is no fee to visit the waterfall.

This state-owned land is maintained by the DEC, and the 0.5-mile (0.8 km) trail to the waterfall is well maintained and easy to walk. On your way in, you'll see a bulletin board and a registration kiosk, where visitors are expected to sign in upon entering and leaving.

As you reach the falls, there's a trail to the left that goes to the area just above the crest of the falls. It includes a wheelchair-accessible segment that allows for a close view. Other trails lead downstream, and there is a small picnic area off the bay below the falls. From here, you can continue around the bay to a small point where you can view the falls from downstream.

Best classified as a curtain cascade, Lampson Falls comprises two drops. The first is a very short distance upstream from the main drop. While there are many vantage points for this waterfall, be sure to use caution wherever you stand, as there are no railings or fences.

Like most of the waterfalls in this county, Lampson Falls is nature at its finest. For the die-hard hiker, Lampson is accessible even in the colder months. With the snow and ice formations, this is a delightful wintertime destination. Even so, while you may run into an occasional cross-country skier or snowshoer, you'll most likely be enjoying the scenery in solitude.

Remember, no matter what season you visit, this is a carry-in, carry-out area, so whatever you bring, make sure you take it with you when you leave.

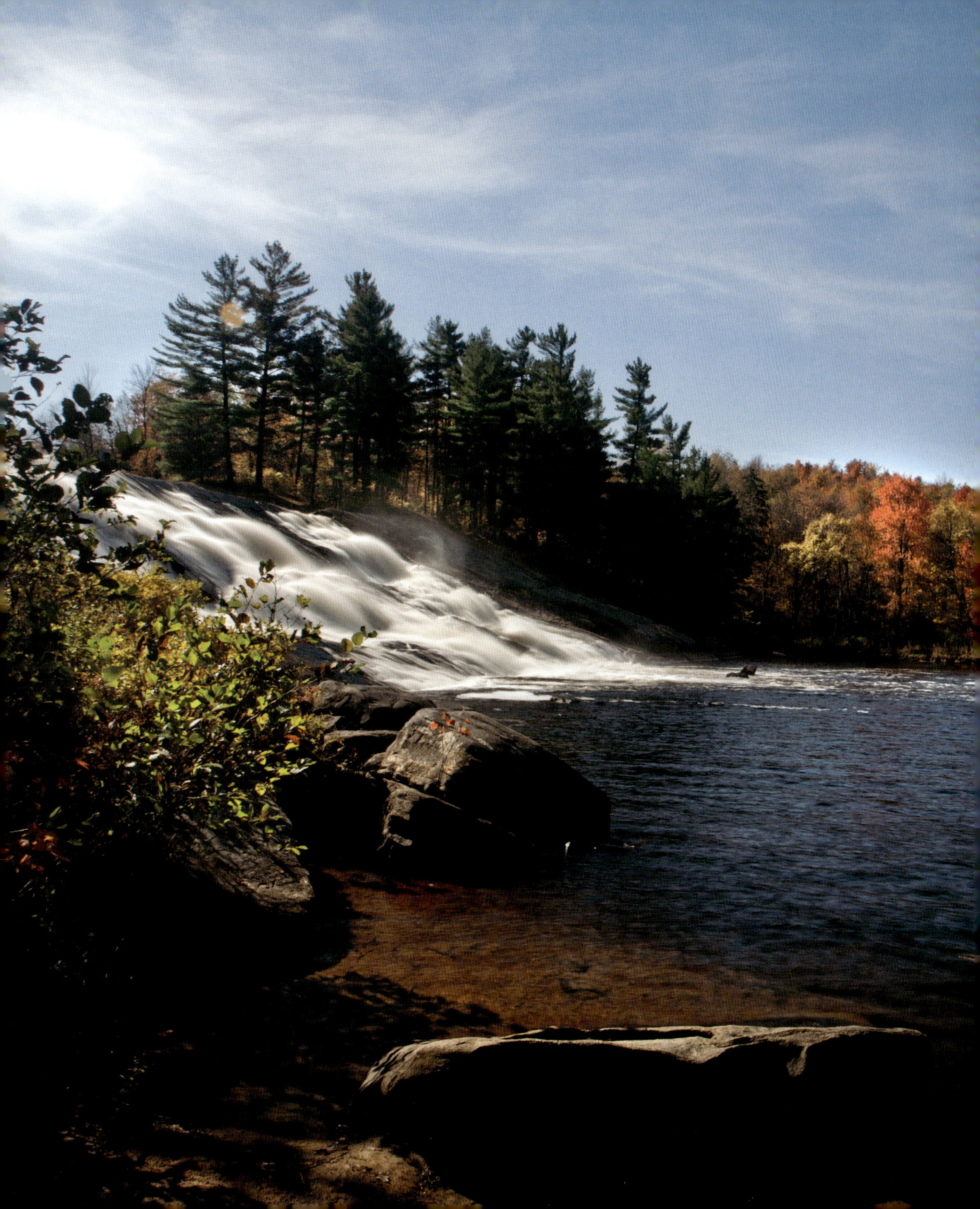

Harper Falls

At the junction of CR 17 and CR 27 in Degrasse, proceed north on CR 27 for 7.4 mi (11.9 km). Downerville Rd. is 0.5 mi (0.8 km) past the Clare Town Barn, on your left.

From the north, drive southeast out of Canton on Park St. As you exit the village past the St. Lawrence University campus, Park St. becomes CR 27. Drive through Pierrepont, and shortly after you enter Clare, Downerville Rd. is on your right. The trailhead is about 0.5 mi (0.8 km) up this road.

COUNTY: St. Lawrence

TOWNSHIP: Clare

PLACE: Degrasse

WATERWAY: Grasse (Grass) River, North Branch

TYPE: ribbon cascade

HEIGHT: 60 ft (18.3 m)

TRAIL: dirt; moderate

WALKING TIME: 12 min

PEAK ACTIVITY: May-Sept.

LATITUDE: 44.4354

LONGITUDE: –75.0751

Located just a few miles from Lampson Falls, Harper Falls is on the North Branch of the Grasse River. While it's possible to access these falls from the other end of Downerville Road, on the north side of Russell, that route can prove challenging at certain times of the year. In the spring, water sometimes floods the road in the lower, swampy areas, so approach from the south. (Don't even attempt this road in the winter.) For year-round hikers, the waterfall is only about 1 mile (1.6 km) from CR 27. The trail can be navigated on snowshoes, but you'll probably discover that the falls is one big icicle once you arrive — this area gets some serious winter weather.

The road's actual name is a bit of a mystery. Local signs are for Downerville Road, but some sources list it as Donnerville Road.

When you reach the trailhead, there is a well-maintained trail of moderate difficulty. At less than 15 minutes, the hike in to Harper Falls is longer than the hikes to the other waterfalls we've described in this area.

Apart from the company of a few small woodland animals, you may very well be on your own on this walk. Harper Falls is very close to several other popular falls, but it is not nearly as well publicized, perhaps because of the time factor. But for those accustomed to hiking an hour or more to see a waterfall, it's a stroll in the park.

The waterfall itself is somewhat V-shaped — the base width is less than one-third the width of the crest. The upper part flows around a boulder that is not quite as visible during spring's high water. As the channel narrows, the water takes a somewhat corkscrew plunge with significant force.

All nine waterfalls — Harper Falls, Lampson Falls and the seven publicly accessible waterfalls on Tooley Pond Road — can easily be visited in one day.

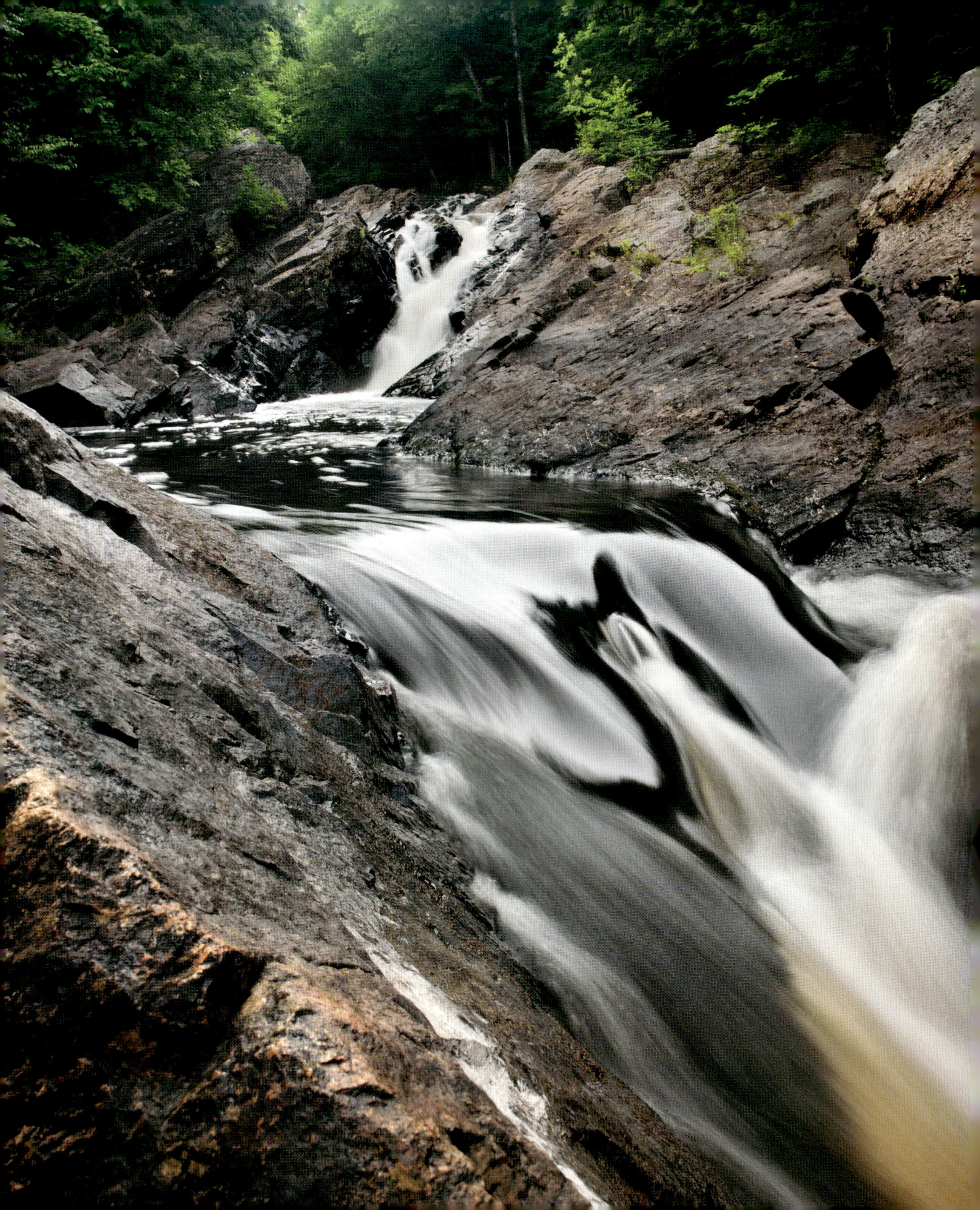

Cascade Falls & Rushton Falls

In Canton's downtown, you'll have no problem finding Cascade Falls. Just after the intersection of US 11 from the south and US 68 from the west, a bridge crosses the Grasse River. Keep in the left lane, then turn left into the parking area of a village-run park.

Coming from the north on US 11, drive through the business district. The parking area is on the right after the first set of traffic lights (before the bridge).

COUNTY: St. Lawrence

TOWNSHIP: Canton

PLACE: Canton

WATERWAY: Grasse (Grass) River

TYPE: curtain cascade

HEIGHT: 10 ft (3 m)

TRAIL: paved walkways; easy

WALKING TIME: 2 min

PEAK ACTIVITY: June-Aug.

LATITUDE: 44.5958

LONGITUDE: –75.1755

Typically, when a river's flow is interrupted by an island and two waterfalls are created on either side, they are given one name. In the case of Cascade Falls and Rushton Falls, we have a two-for-one special.

To view these two falls, park in the parking area on Willow Island in the village of Canton and cross the footbridge to Falls Island. Grasse River Heritage has done a tremendous job developing this park. Several strategically placed kiosks provide information on the history of the area with pictures and maps. Well-maintained paths allow you to stroll comfortably around the island, and a few well-placed benches offer a comfortable spot to take a break.

Bear left on Falls Island, and you'll reach Cascade Falls on the west side. A gristmill once stood on this side of the channel, while a second mill stood on the opposite side, now the site of the Cascade Inn. Cascade Falls itself is a two-part waterfall. The water flowing down the west channel forms the larger part, with the water flowing from the east channel between the two islands making up the rest.

The water continuing down the east channel on the other side of Falls Island forms Rushton Falls. Take any of the paved paths to the other side of the island to see this waterfall. Although it has the same descent as Cascade Falls, Rushton spans a greater horizontal distance and more closely resembles a set of rapids.

On the mainland side of the east channel, a memorial plaque shows that the falls is named in honor of J. Henry Rushton (1843–1906), a famed canoe builder and local legend. Born in the nearby town of Edwards, Rushton made Canton his home. His lightweight cedar canoes became popular not just in the neighboring Adirondacks but nationwide and internationally. By the late 1800s, his Canton shop produced canoes as well as other vessels, including rowboats, Adirondack guide boats and sailboats. Today, his boats are collectible treasures, and the Rushton Memorial Canoe Races, inaugurated in 1962, are held every May in Canton.

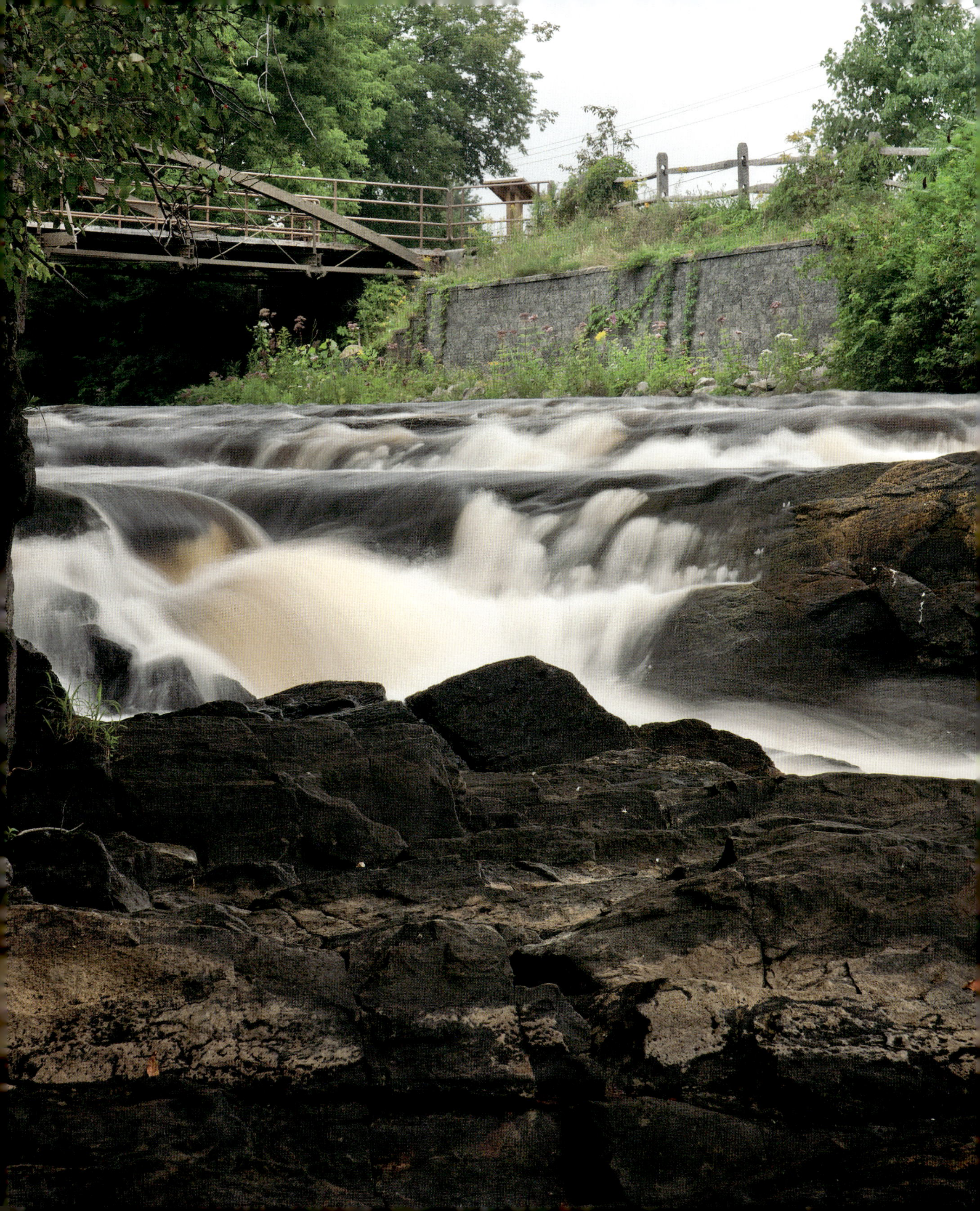

Allen Falls

NY 11B is a major travel route between Potsdam and Malone. Take it to Southville, and turn onto St. Lawrence CR 47. Turn right at Allen Falls Rd., the first crossroad. As an alternative route, take CR 47 from NY 72 in Parishville. Take a left at the first crossroad, which is Allen Falls Rd. You'll reach a bridge, with a parking area on the left side of the road.

COUNTY: St. Lawrence

TOWNSHIP: Parishville

PLACE: Parishville

WATERWAY: St. Regis River, West Branch

TYPE: curtain cascade

HEIGHT: 35 ft (10.7 m)

TRAIL: dirt; moderate

WALKING TIME: 7 min

PEAK ACTIVITY: May-Sept.

LATITUDE: 44.6551

LONGITUDE: –74.8502

Allen Falls (referred to in some sources as Allen's Falls) may be the second most popular waterfall in St. Lawrence County, after Lampson Falls, in the town of Clare.

Across from the parking area is a small clearing, from which a path leads downstream. The path is not officially maintained, but foot traffic keeps it well worn. The hike in is less than 450 yards (412 m), and the path takes you to the edge of the river, just where the waterfall crests.

Roughly 200 feet (60 m) upstream from the falls, the river begins its descent. From this point, you can see the rapids and the churning water of the first couple of small drops, before the river takes a final steep plunge that is close to three times as wide as it is high. A large rock outcropping just past the midpoint splits what would otherwise be a wall of cascading water.

Nearby, up a small rise, you'll find a place where you can scramble down some 40 feet (12.2 m) or so to the level of the river. The best views of the falls are from this vantage point.

Allen Falls forms at the base of the channel on one side of an island. Walk along the riverbank until you can see the smaller falls at the bottom of the other channel. If you want to reach it, however, you'll probably have to do some wading.

As with most waterfalls in northern New York, there is usually snow on the ground until after mid-April.

In the early 1800s, much of this region was owned by Jacques-Donatien Le Ray de Chaumont. In neighboring Jefferson County, the town of Le Ray and the village of Chaumont are both named after him. The son of a Frenchman of the same name, James Le Ray, as he was known in America, owned vast tracts of land. David Parish bought this piece in 1808, and the town of Parishville was named after him. The waterfall itself was named for William Allen, a long-time town supervisor in Parishville in its early years.

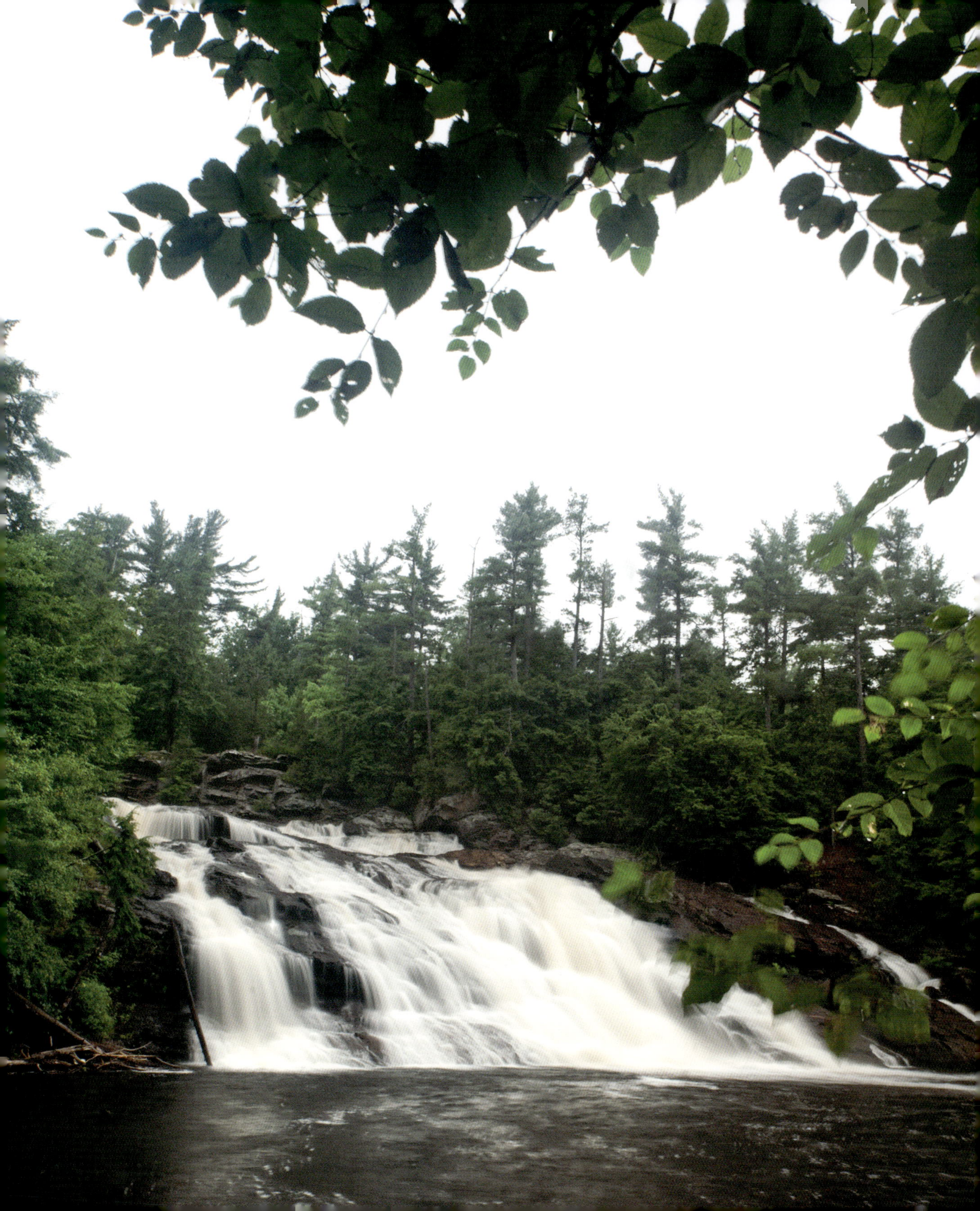

St. Regis Falls

From Potsdam, head east on NY 11B. Past Hopkinton, take a right on NY 458. You are now in Franklin County. Just after crossing the bridge over the St. Regis River, as you enter the village of St. Regis Falls, the entrance to the St. Regis Falls Scenic Campsite is on your left. Drive past the campground office; the river is on your left.

COUNTY: Franklin
TOWNSHIP: Waverly
PLACE: St. Regis Falls
WATERWAY: St. Regis River
TYPE: curtain cascade
HEIGHT: 30 ft (9 m)
TRAIL: dirt; easy
WALKING TIME: 5 min
PEAK ACTIVITY: May-Sept.
LATITUDE: 44.6733
LONGITUDE: –74.5505

The St. Regis River is a good-sized waterway that gets its start near the Adirondack community of Paul Smiths, not far from the very popular Saranac Lake. The river has an East Branch that joins the main channel a few miles upstream from St. Regis Falls and a West Branch that meets the main channel a number of miles downstream, in the hamlet of Winthrop. Like the main channel, both branches originate in the Adirondack heartland, where there are more lakes, ponds, rivers and streams than you can shake the proverbial stick at. The St. Regis River joins the St. Lawrence River in Quebec, just downstream from Malone.

St. Regis Falls is located in a campground and picnic area operated by the Town of Waverly. Visitors can rent RV sites, tents and cabins, but there is no charge for viewing the waterfall, which is located behind the campground office.

The waterfall can be viewed from two different locations. If you park near the entrance and walk behind the office, you'll find an overlook built right next to the falls. While the view is intimate, it doesn't allow you to see the face of the waterfall.

Alternatively, continue down the hill, by foot or by car, and take the first left past the St. Regis Pavilion. There is a 150-foot-long (46 m) footbridge on the left; from here, the view is unobstructed, if a little distant. With a zoom lens, you can still get some good photos. The bridge also provides access to a number of hiking trails on the other side of the river.

For those who bring their water shoes or waders, there is a third option. Between the falls and the bridge, the riverbank is accessible at several points. It is a popular fishing stream and not too deep just below the falls, so the water route might be a choice for the more adventuresome.

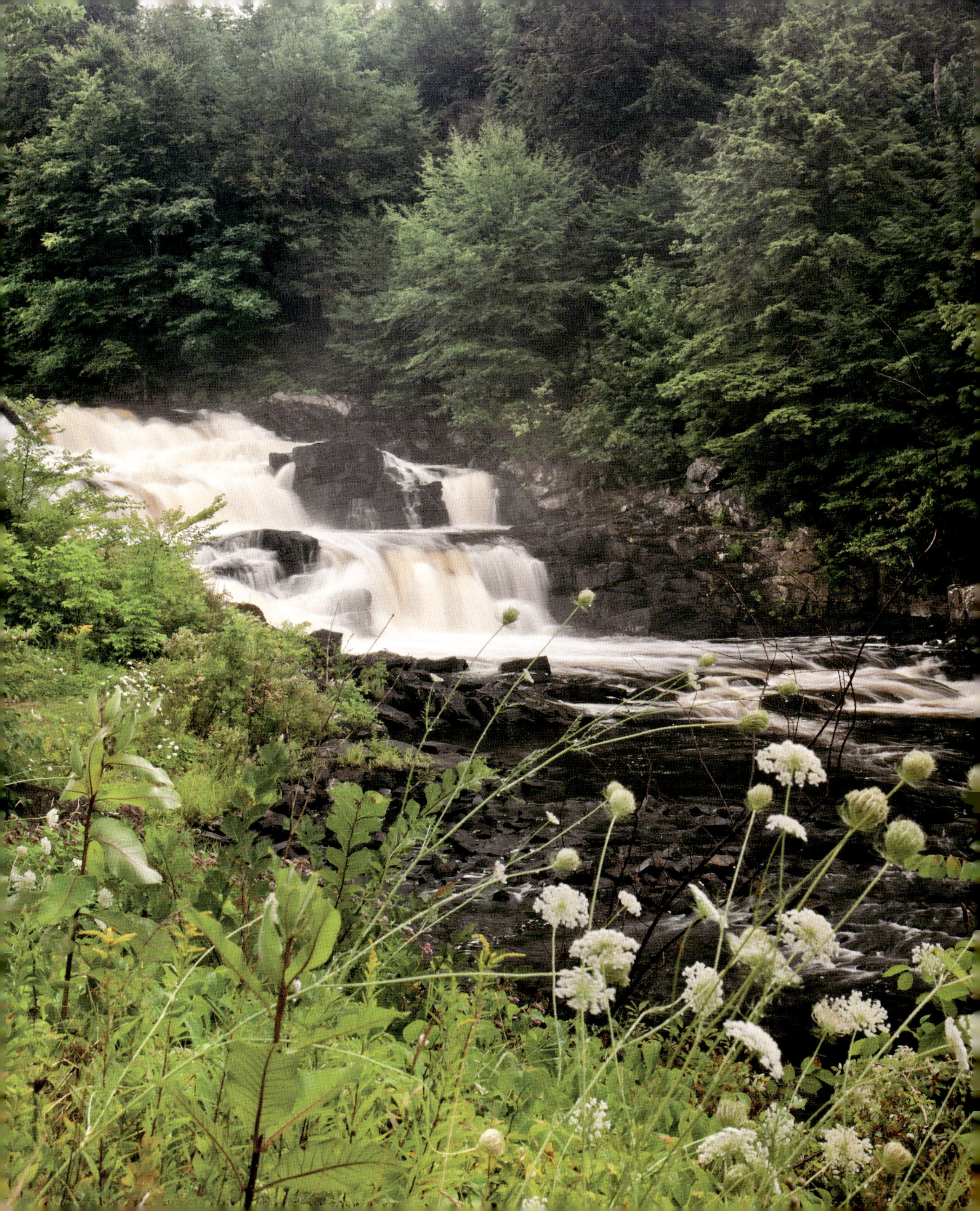

NORTH COUNTRY REGION

High Falls on the Salmon River

Duane St. in the village of Malone becomes Franklin CR 25. Continue to the hamlet of Chasm Falls, and turn left on CR 27. After a few miles, Barnesville Rd. is on the right. At the corner, you'll see a sign for the Big Salmon River Public Fishing Stream. (The Trailside Bar and Restaurant is just beyond on the left, so if you pass it, you have gone too far!) This dirt road is full of bumps and rocks, so use caution. After 0.75 mi (1.2 km), there is a sign for the Titusville Mountain State Forest and High Falls. Park on the side of the road, which is slightly wider here. It's a low-traffic area.

COUNTY: Franklin
TOWNSHIP: Bellmont
PLACE: Mountain View
WATERWAY: Salmon River
TYPE: curtain cascade
HEIGHT: 30 ft (9 m)
TRAIL: dirt; moderate
WALKING TIME: 15 min
PEAK ACTIVITY: May-Sept.
LATITUDE: 44.7100
LONGITUDE: –74.1729

There are more waterfalls named High Falls in northern New York than there are waterfalls by any other name. This particular waterfall on the Salmon River is in one of the more remote locations we've included in *Waterfalls of New York State.*

Because the site is out of the way, you may arrive after having spent some time in the car. Rather than pausing to snack or eat your lunch roadside, fill your backpack with food and start the hike in. The trail from the parking area (basically just a widening in the road) is about 0.75 mile (1.2 km) and should take roughly 15 minutes. This area is maintained by DEC, and the trail is fairly well tended and marked.

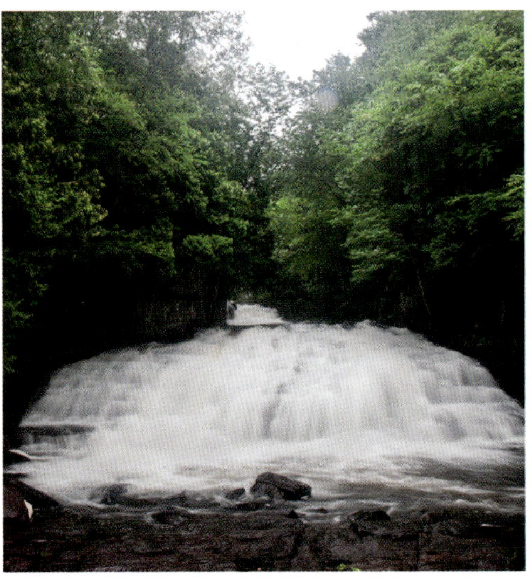

As you hike, you'll pass a small waterfall that is just upstream from High Falls, a sign that you're getting close. Once you reach the waterfall, there are plenty of rocks that can serve as makeshift chairs. Get comfortable, and enjoy your picnic as you relax to a chorus of chirping birds against the background roar of the falls. A mix of protective tree canopy and open area allows you to choose between basking in the rays of the sun or kicking back in the shade.

Once you start to explore, you'll discover that the river channel upstream narrows and begins its gradual descent over several hundred feet. As the flow picks up speed, the waterway levels for a brief span and widens just before a bend in the river. Then it makes its central 30-foot (9 m) plunge. The natural beauty of this waterfall is enhanced by the curious combination of the water's power and the peaceful calm of the surroundings.

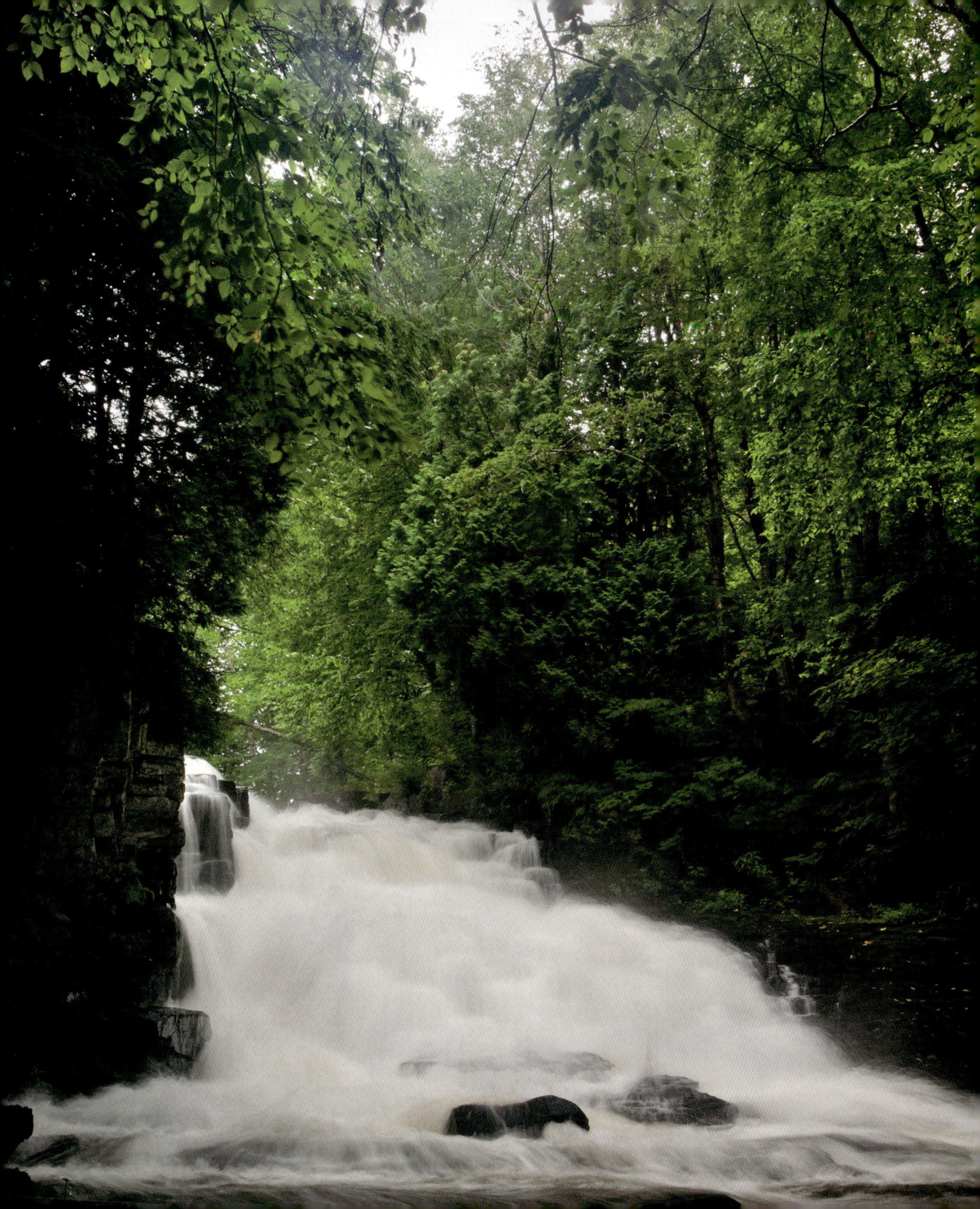

High Falls on the Chateaugay River

West of the village of Chateaugay, on US 11, a bridge crosses the Chateaugay River. The first left after the bridge is Franklin CR 22. Almost immediately, Cemetery Rd. is the first left. This short road ends at a T-junction. Turn left, and follow the road as it makes a sweeping curve to the right. The entrance to High Falls Park is on the left. Drive straight through, and park by the camp store.

COUNTY: Franklin
TOWNSHIP: Chateaugay
PLACE: Chateaugay
WATERWAY: Chateaugay River
TYPE: ribbon falls
HEIGHT: 120 ft (36.6 m)
TRAIL: dirt, rock, wood and steps; easy to moderate
WALKING TIME: 10 min
PEAK ACTIVITY: May-Sept.
LATITUDE: 44.9092
LONGITUDE: –74.0870

As we've said, High Falls is an extremely popular name for waterfalls in northern New York. The waterfall on the Chateaugay River is the second High Falls in Franklin County alone.

This particular High Falls was almost certainly named for its height. While there is an upper trail from which you can see the top of the falls and the dam upstream, the best views are, without a doubt, from the base: this four-step, 120-foot (36.6 m) waterfall is nothing short of beautiful. Through countless years of erosion, the river has cut a path that reveals a spectacular cross-sectional view of the ground we walk on. Walls of layered rock line a narrow gorge, framing the waterfall and enhancing its beauty.

The Chateaugay is one of the smaller rivers in New York and one of the most northerly. Its source is just a few miles upstream in neighboring Clinton County, but the river officially begins in Franklin County. Generally flowing north after High Falls, the Chateaugay enters Quebec, where it is known as Rivière Châteauguay. High Falls may have the distinction of being the North Country waterfall that is closest to Canada.

It's also one of only a handful of waterfall destinations in northern New York where visitors must pay an admission fee. Located in a privately owned campground, the waterfall can currently be viewed for $2 for adults and $1 for students and seniors. After paying your admission at the camp store, you are about 350 yards (320 m) from the falls. Much of the walk is on a fairly level, well-maintained dirt path. The last 350 feet (107 m) or so takes you down more than 200 wooden and stone steps. The walk down isn't bad, but the energy required to climb back up might wind even the seasoned hiker.

Just imagine trying to descend into this gorge without the stairway, and you'll appreciate the modest admission charge. This private park is open from May 1 through October 15 or later, if the weather permits.

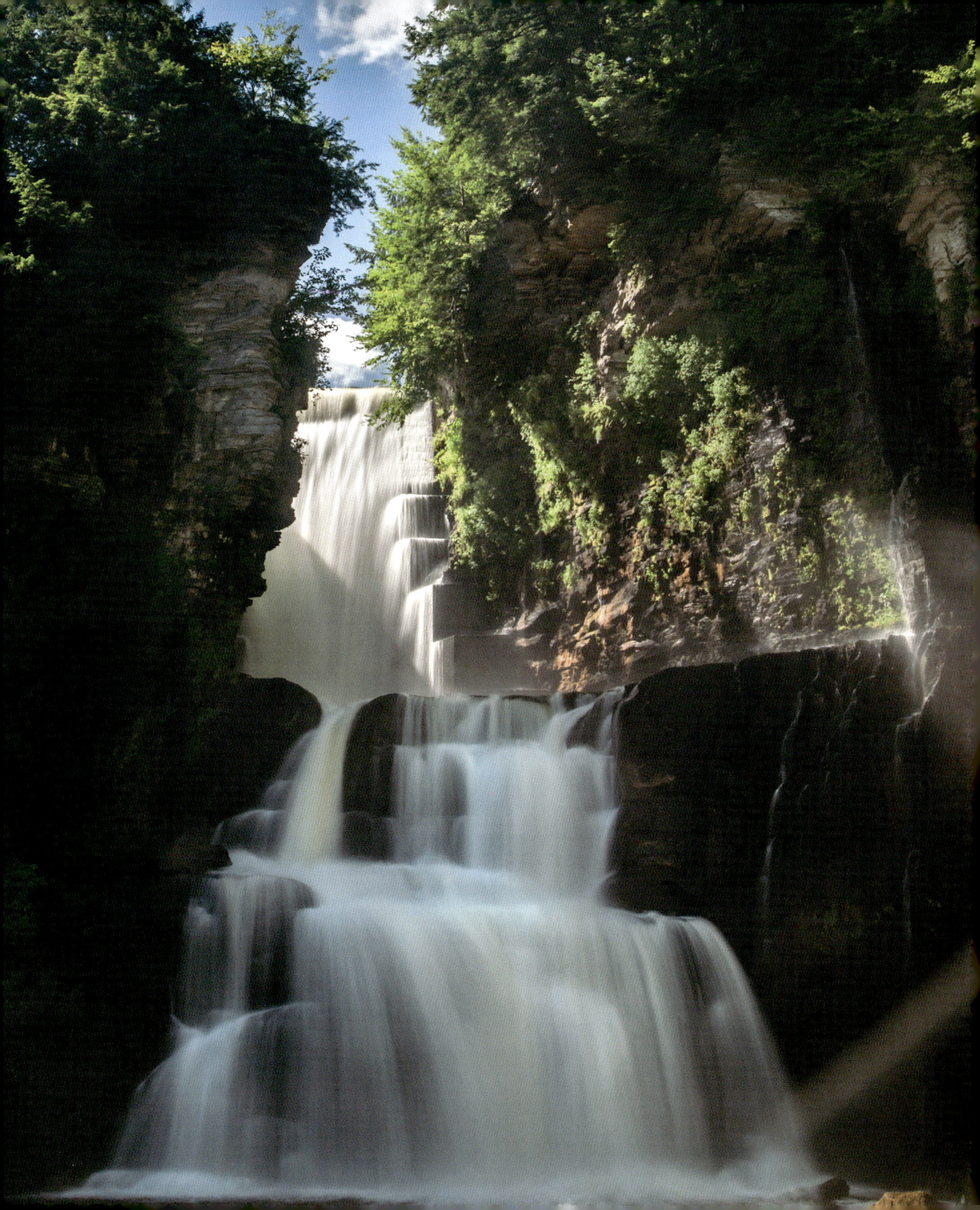

Ausable Chasm

Head north on NY 9 from Keeseville. You'll have no problem finding this very popular and heavily commercialized scenic attraction. On the south side of the river, there are parking areas on both sides of the road. If you park here, you'll have to walk across the bridge to the welcome center and gift shop. There is also a parking lot on the northeast side of the river, near the welcome center.

COUNTY: Clinton and Essex

TOWNSHIP: Ausable and Chesterfield

PLACE: Keeseville

WATERWAY: Ausable River

TYPE: classical falls

HEIGHT: 80 ft (24.4 m)

TRAIL: dirt and rock; moderate

WALKING TIME: varies

PEAK ACTIVITY: May-June

LATITUDE: 44.5236

LONGITUDE: –73.4602

Dubbed the "Grand Canyon of the East," the 2-mile-long (3.2 km) gorge on the Ausable River is billed by the area's promoters as the "oldest and largest natural attraction in the Adirondacks."

There are seven waterfalls at the Ausable Chasm, and the scenic attraction is a "pay-per-view" facility. The price of admission buys access to the grounds and any of three hiking trails, from which you can view the three larger waterfalls: Rainbow, Horseshoe and Lower Horseshoe. For additional fees, there are scheduled guided tours of differing lengths, including the Cave & Waterfall Hike, which takes hikers down to river level for a look at six waterfalls. There are also opportunities for rafting and tubing.

The main attraction is 80-foot (24.4 m) Rainbow Falls, located just upstream from the welcome center. This waterfall is typically active, but water flow is governed by the production schedule at the dam and hydro facility upstream. During dry spells, there may not be enough water to support both the hydro plant and the waterfall.

The trail map that comes with the price of admission identifies only Rainbow Falls and Horseshoe Falls. Located between Rainbow Falls and the bridge on NY 9, Horseshoe Falls can be seen from directly above, on the pedestrian walkway on the upstream side of the bridge. You can also get a clear but rather distant view of Rainbow Falls from this vantage point. A table map on display at the welcome center names Lower Horseshoe Falls. Just downstream from Horseshoe, this waterfall is almost directly under the bridge. These two waterfalls combine for an additional 11-foot (3.4 m) drop. The other four falls at this site remain unnamed.

While the Ausable Chasm grounds are accessible year-round, the facility is not. We have listed the peak activity period as May to June simply because of the greater likelihood that there will be water over Rainbow during this time.

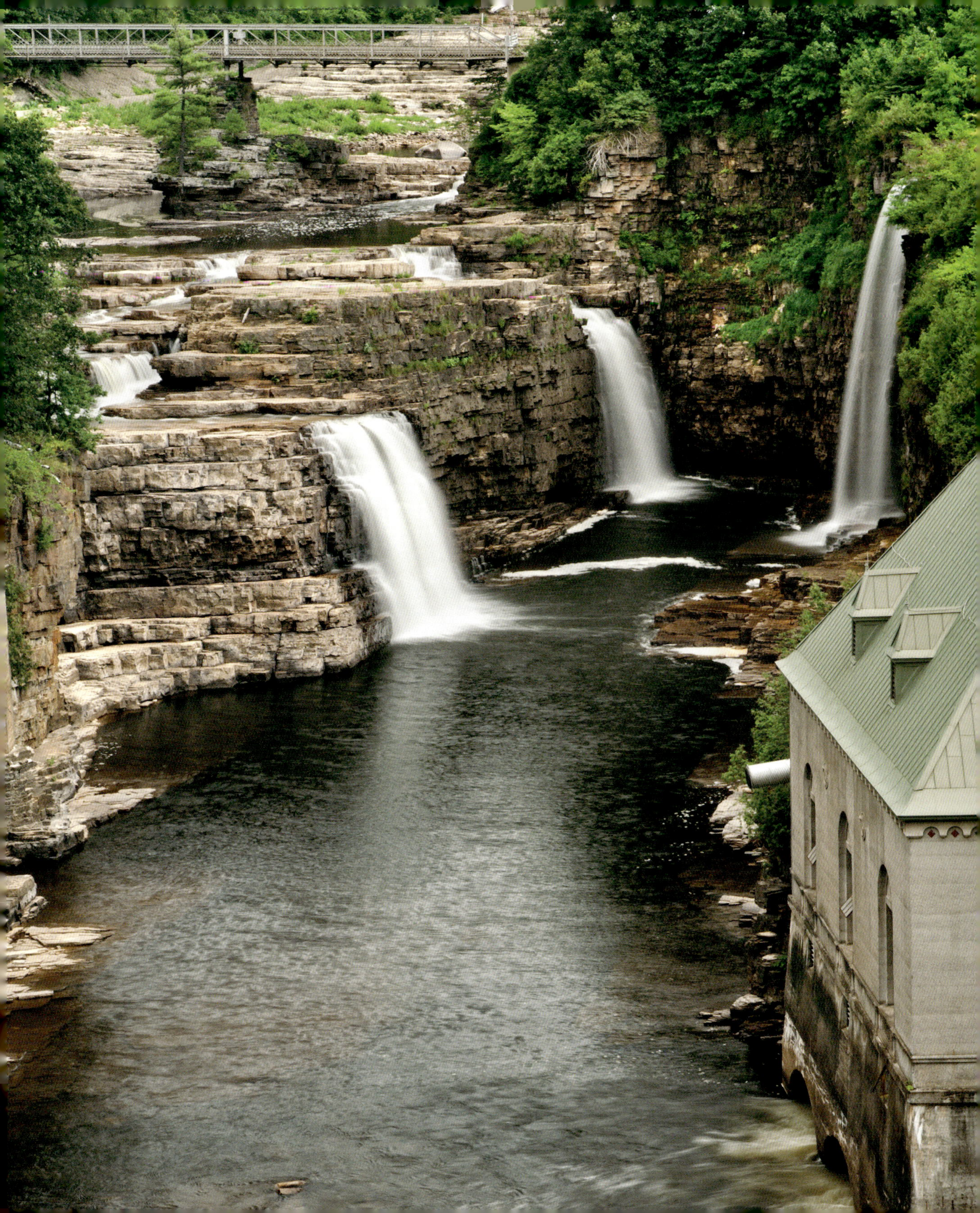

NORTH COUNTRY REGION

Alice Falls

From the south, head north on NY 9 from Keeseville. Keep an eye out for the signs for Alice Falls Hydro Project on the right. They are a short distance in from the road and somewhat obscured and can be easily missed.

From the north, this point is only 0.3 mi (0.5 km) past the Ausable Chasm attraction. Proceed past the hydro facility on the right and a trailer on the left to a parking area.

COUNTY: Clinton and Essex

TOWNSHIP: Ausable and Chesterfield

PLACE: Keeseville

WATERWAY: Ausable River

TYPE: classical falls

HEIGHT: 35 ft (10.7 m)

TRAIL: dirt and rock; easy

WALKING TIME: 1 min

PEAK ACTIVITY: May-Oct.

LATITUDE: 44.5193

LONGITUDE: –73.4637

Beautiful Alice Falls is only about 500 feet (153 m) off NY 9, just north of Keeseville. Signs near the parking area direct visitors to a fishing spot. At the bottom of a hill, a natural rock stairway leads to a level area at the base of the falls.

The waterfall is almost half the width of the river, sharing the space with an adjacent hydro facility. This section of the Ausable River effectively serves as the county line between Clinton and Essex. A purist might argue that the waterfall is actually in Essex County, while the hydro plant is in Clinton. We won't split hairs on this issue, but we will say it is a captivating area. Even in late summer, when the water flow is slower, this waterfall is gorgeous.

During spring runoff, however, the water volume is intense. Located just a few miles inland from Lake Champlain, this stretch of river receives everything that the East and West branches send its way. Ausable's East Branch starts not far from Mount Marcy, the state's highest point. The West Branch originates in the Mount Van Hoevenberg area, home to the 1932 Winter Olympic bobsled event and the 1980 Olympic bobsled, luge, cross-country skiing and biathlon events. We're in the Adirondack heartland, where winter snow is legendary, and each spring, the Ausable carries much of its meltwater away.

At Alice Falls, the river makes an almost vertical descent over the layers of rock that are typical of this area. As you view the falls from downstream, you can almost count the layers. You'll also notice that the geological structure is exactly like that of the natural stairway leading to the riverbank as well as the bordering riverbanks.

The Alice Falls site is no more than 0.25 mile (0.4 km) upstream from the Ausable Chasm tourist attraction, home to the region's most popular waterfalls. Obscured by the shadow cast by the chasm's high profile, this area is almost unknown to nonresidents. Hundreds, if not thousands, of people drive right by the entrance to Alice Falls on their way to Ausable Chasm without even knowing Alice Falls is here.

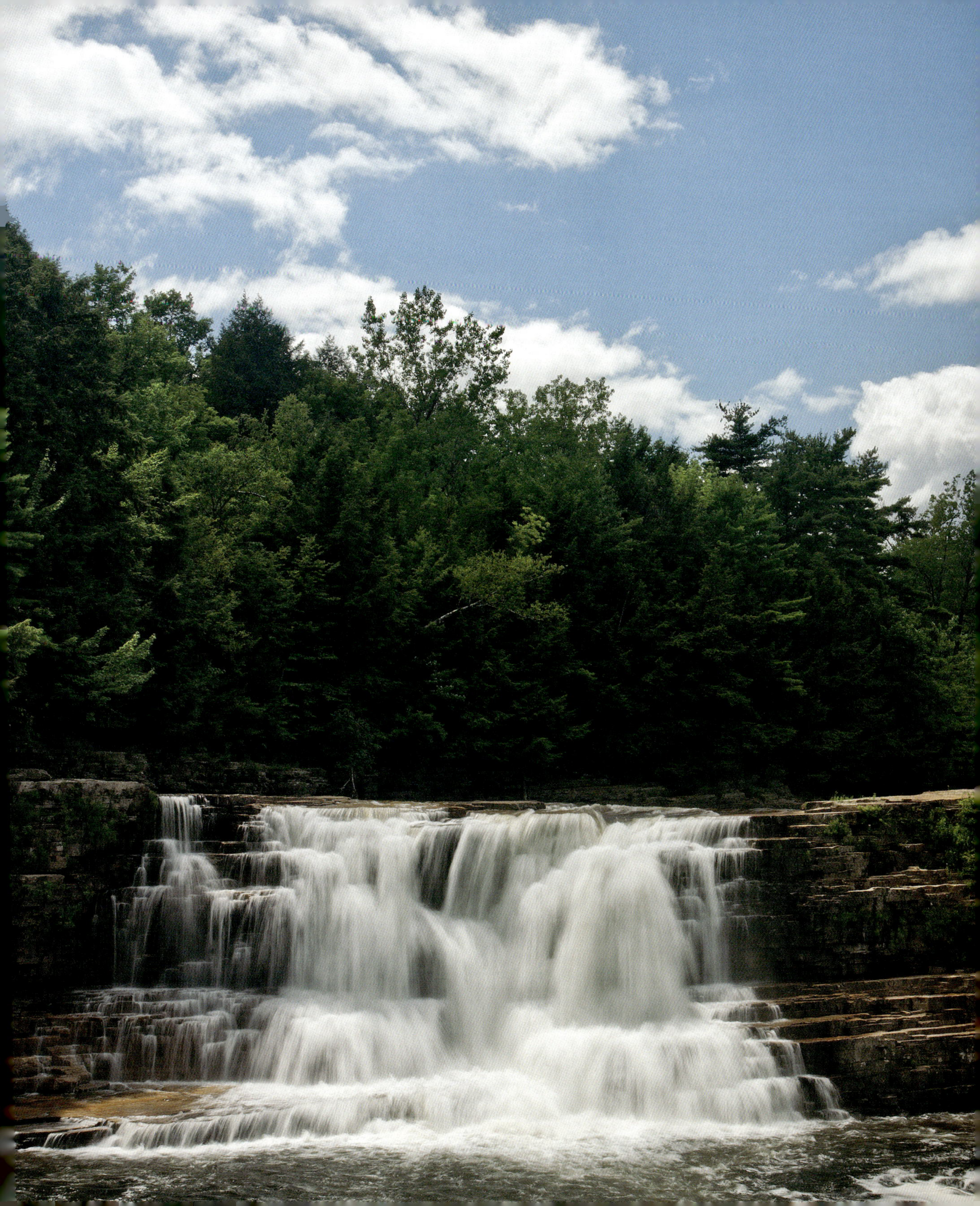

NORTH COUNTRY REGION

Jay Falls

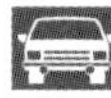

Jay is on NY 9N in the extreme northern section of Essex County. Across from NY 86, at the intersection of NY 86 and NY 9N, take John Fountain Rd. to the bottom of the hill. Brick Store Lane is on the right, and within a few feet, there is a parking area for the covered bridge and waterfalls. Another parking area at the other end of the bridge is accessible from NY 9N south of the river.

COUNTY: Essex

TOWNSHIP: Jay

PLACE: Jay

WATERWAY: Ausable River, East Branch

TYPE: curtain cascade

HEIGHT: 10 ft (3 m)

TRAIL: pavement; easy

WALKING TIME: 1 min

PEAK ACTIVITY: May-Sept.

LATITUDE: 44.3727

LONGITUDE: –73.7262

Named for former state governor John Jay, the hamlet of Jay is one of hundreds of small villages and communities in northern New York that is rich in history and tradition. Originally, the lumber industry drove its economy, and from the early 1800s on, the Ausable River provided a route for logs being transported down to Lake Champlain. Just west of Jay is Lake Placid, host to the 1932 and 1980 Winter Olympics and a renowned winter wonderland.

The region is also the source of the Ausable River's East Branch. Jay Falls is not large, but it occurs at a section of the riverbed that is effectively a natural rock waterslide. During the high water caused by melting Adirondack snow in spring, the water bubbles and churns in a curtain cascade that covers the entire width of the river. Ice jams commonly result in flooding. At other times of the year, vast slabs of the underlying rock are exposed and the waterfall is reduced to a pair of ribbon cascades emerging from two of the lower openings in the rock. Depending on the time of year, you may see either of these two radically different views — or something in between.

The site is also home to the Jay Covered Bridge. Many covered bridges in the state have been built privately, but today, only about two dozen historic covered bridges survive. Most were constructed in the 1800s and are listed in the National Register of Historic Places. Built in 1857 and restored in 2006, the Jay Covered Bridge is one of only two or three located at a waterfall location. According to a sign near the landmark, this bridge is "the sole remaining wooden Howe Truss Bridge in the Adirondack Park."

A pleasant little park has been built beside the bridge, which is closed to motor vehicles but open to bicycles; brick paving stones allow easy access. The river edge is fenced to allow a safe and unobstructed view of the falls, and kiosks post pictures and information about the area. It's only a short stroll to the other side and an opportunity to enjoy a view of the river and waterfall from another perspective. Both parking areas provide a roadside view of the bridge and falls, and the area is wheelchair-accessible.

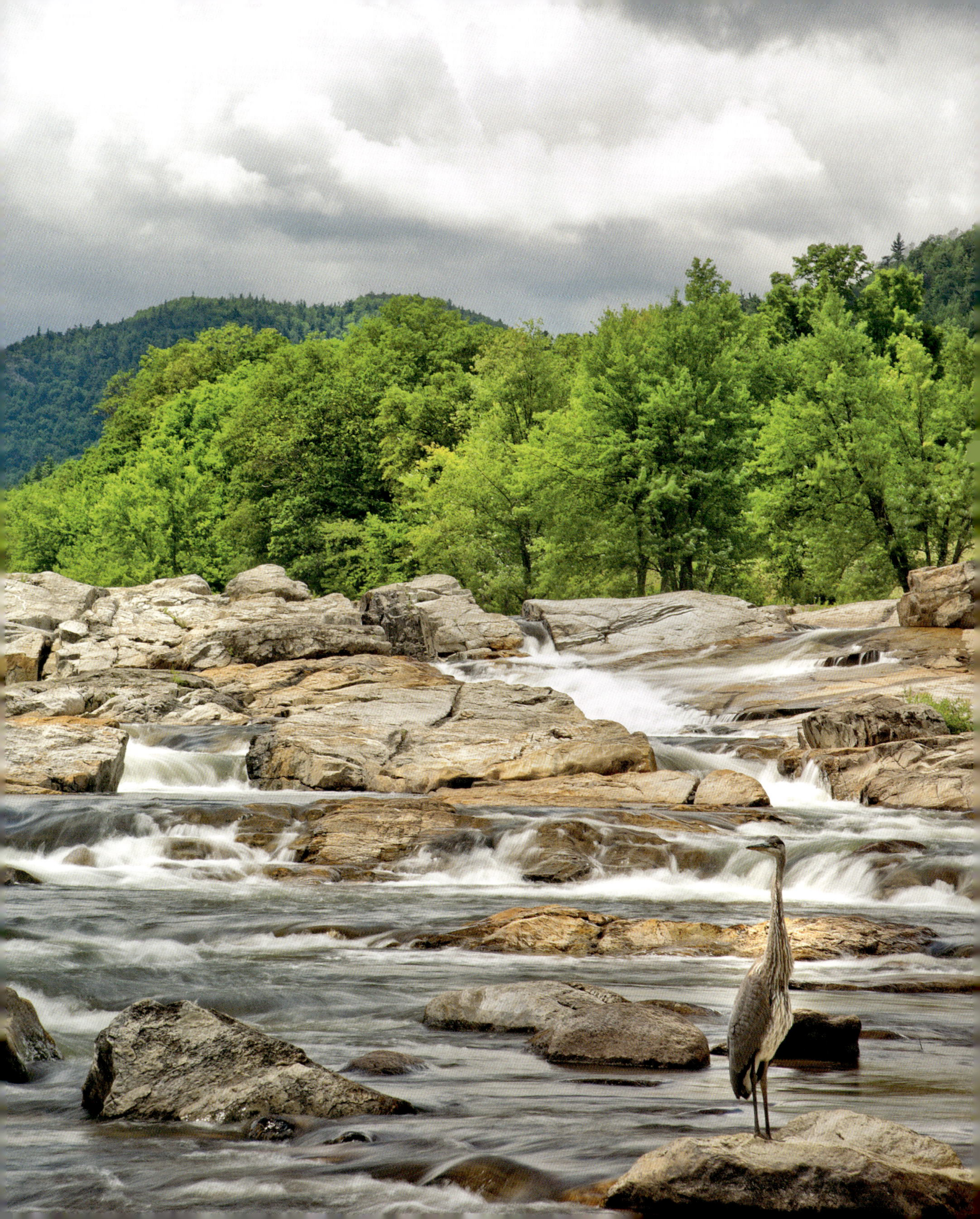

NORTH COUNTRY REGION

High Falls Gorge

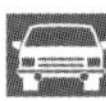

High Falls Gorge, located on the north side of NY 86 between Wilmington and Lake Placid, is well marked. Depending on your starting point, head northeast from Lake Placid or southwest from Wilmington. If you use a GPS, simply enter 4761 State Highway 86 in Wilmington, New York.

COUNTY: Essex

TOWNSHIP: Wilmington

PLACE: Wilmington

WATERWAY: Ausable River, West Branch

TYPE: ribbon cascade

HEIGHT: 80 ft (24.4 m)

TRAIL: dirt, rock, wooden paths and stairs; moderate

WALKING TIME: 30 min

PEAK ACTIVITY: May-Sept.

LATITUDE: 44.3487

LONGITUDE: –73.8745

Ironically, although this popular tourist destination in the Adirondack Mountains is called High Falls Gorge, not a single one of its four waterfalls is named High Falls. In fact, these waterfalls comprise four continuous steps through the gorge, flowing one into the next, separated by small pools or very short connecting streams. They could almost be considered one waterfall but have been named Main Falls, Mini Falls, Rainbow Falls and Climax Falls.

Enter through the gift shop to pay the admission fee to the gorge itself. (In 2011, the adult admission was $10.95, with a reduced rate for children.) Access is limited to business hours, which vary depending on the time of year and the day of the week. Be sure to check the High Falls Gorge facility's schedule before making the trip. The 0.5-mile (0.8 km) round-trip self-guided tour takes roughly 30 minutes over well-maintained trails, stairs and bridges. Signs posted on the way describe gemstones, fossils, arrowheads and the area's geology; there are descriptive color brochures about the waterfalls themselves at the gift shop. Skis, snowboards and snowshoes can be rented or purchased, as can hiking maps and other outdoor items.

While the complimentary trail map highlights three waterfalls — Main, Mini and Climax — several other area brochures mention Main, Rainbow and Climax. Staff members confirm that there are four waterfalls here. The first is Main Falls. With a 35-foot (10.7 m) drop, this waterfall flows almost immediately into the 5-foot (1.5 m) Mini Falls. A small pool separates that waterfall from 20-foot (6.1 m) Rainbow Falls. Just below Rainbow is the final drop, Climax Falls, also about 20 feet (6.1 m).

High Falls Gorge is one of the few waterfall facilities in northern New York that charge admission, but it is undoubtedly worth the trip and the cost. The terrain is so extreme that reaching the falls would be dangerous, if not impossible, had the facility not developed the wooden paths and bridges that ensure your visit is relaxed and secure and your views of the falls clear and unobstructed.

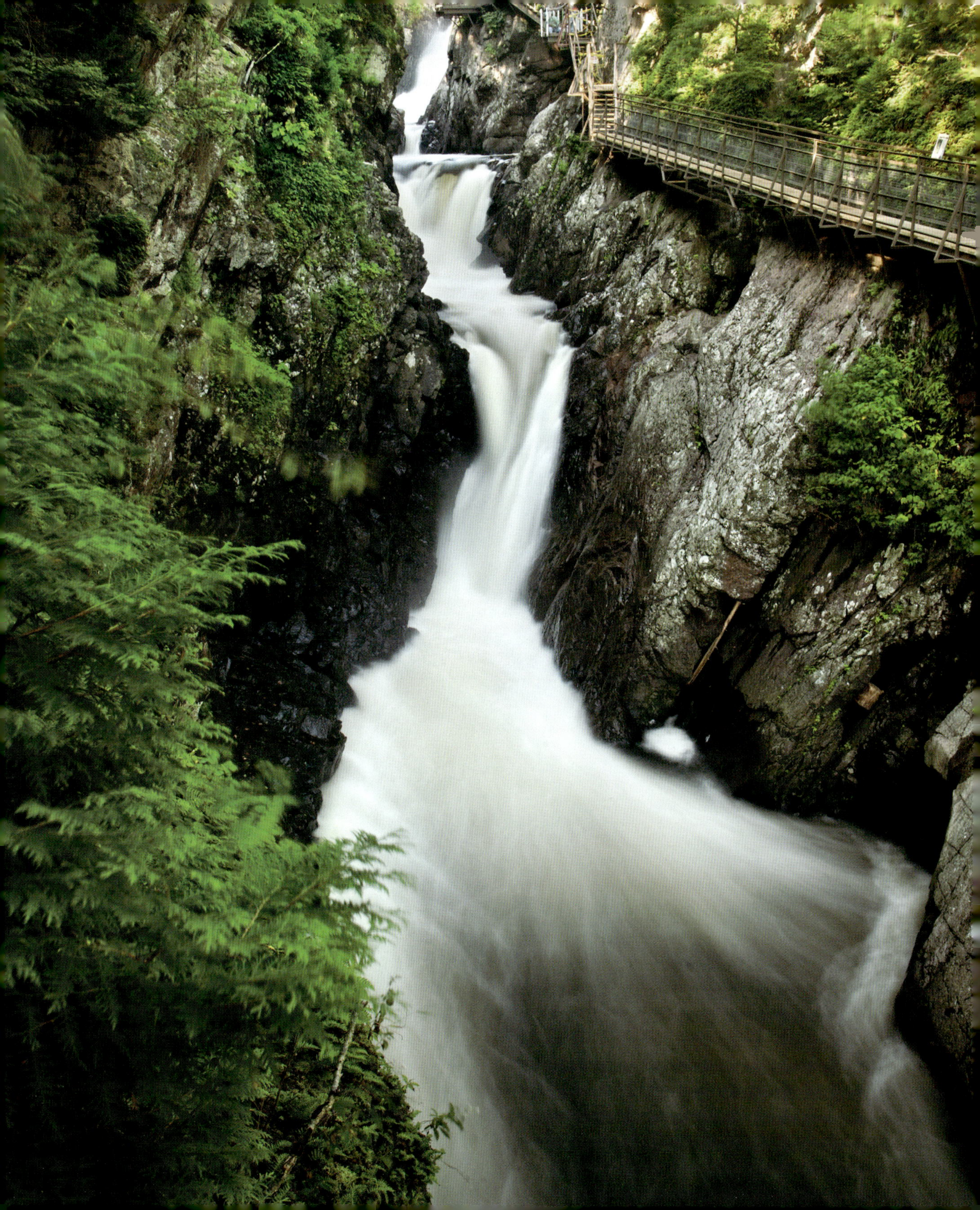

NORTH COUNTRY REGION

Bog River Falls

From the north, take NY 30 south from the town of Tupper Lake. Approximately 8 mi (12.9 km) past the Adirondack Medical Center, take the CR 421 exit on the right.

From the south, take NY 30 north from Long Lake. The CR 421 exit is about 1.5 mi (2.4 km) beyond the Franklin County line sign. In a little over 0.5 mi (0.8 km), CR 421 bends to the left and crosses the river via a bridge. Just beyond the bridge, a widened section of the road allows for parking.

COUNTY: St. Lawrence
TOWNSHIP: Piercefield
PLACE: Tupper Lake
WATERWAY: Bog River
TYPE: curtain cascade
HEIGHT: est. 30 ft (9 m)
TRAIL: stone; easy
WALKING TIME: 1 min
PEAK ACTIVITY: May-Sept.
LATITUDE: 44.1289
LONGITUDE: –74.5454

Although Bog River Falls is in the Adirondack heartland, it is not at all hard to find. It's situated within sight of (and literally under) a county road.

Interestingly, Bog River Falls empties directly into a lake, distinguishing it from most waterfalls, which typically occur on a river or creek somewhere upstream from the outlet.

From the bridge across the Bog River, there is a lovely view of the upper section of this two-part waterfall, which is a roughly 8-foot (2.4 m) drop created where the river splits around a tiny island studded with evergreen trees. A path to the riverbank offers a closer look.

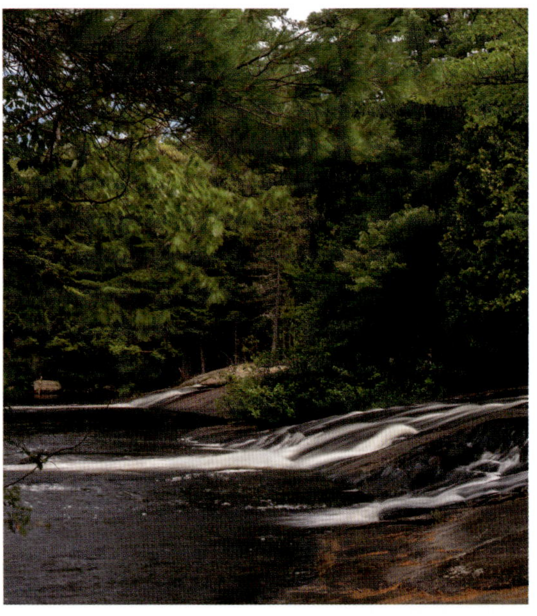

The bottom section makes up the balance of the waterfall's entire 30-foot (9 m) descent as it enters Tupper Lake. Easily viewed from the bridge, it can also be appreciated at lake level, thanks to a path from the parking area to the water's edge.

These paths might not be visible when the snow is on the ground, which is usually from October through April and occasionally even into May. That should tell you something about the heartiness of the people who live in this region and why snowmobiles, snowshoes, skiing and ice fishing are so popular.

While you might make this trip just to see the waterfall, once you're standing on the banks of Lake Tupper, you'll find yourself well situated for big views of impressive sunsets, sunrises and all kinds of weather.

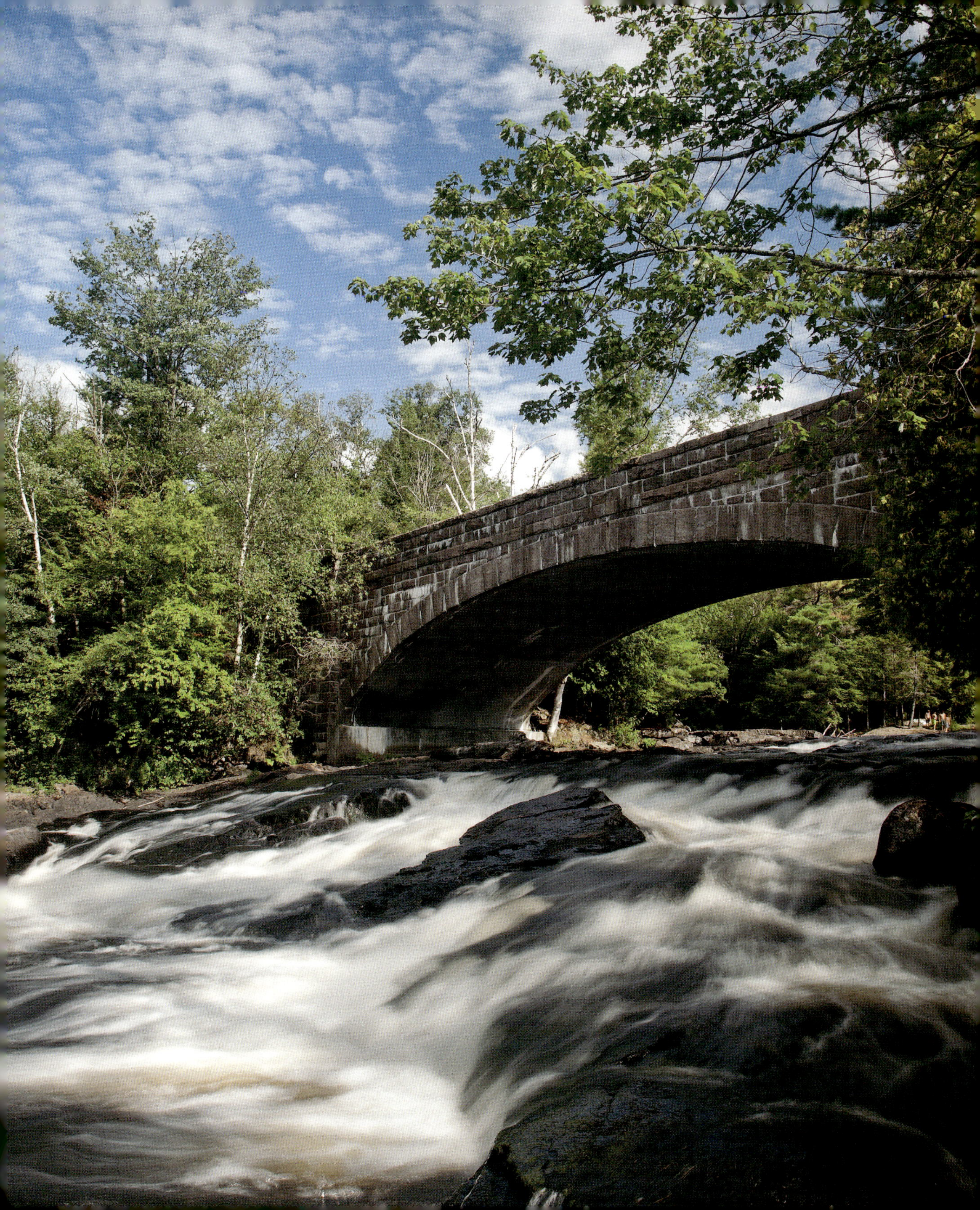

NORTH COUNTRY REGION

Rainbow Falls in the Adirondack Mountain Reserve

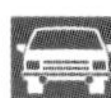 From I-87, take exit 30 and turn north onto US 9 toward Keene Valley (Lake Placid). After 2.2 mi (3.5 km), keep straight on NY 73 west for 5.3 mi (8.5 km). Turn left onto Ausable Club Rd., and you'll see parking on the left.

Located in the 7,000-acre (2,830 ha) Adirondack Mountain Reserve (AMR), Rainbow Falls is a spectacular waterfall that is accessible courtesy of a well-maintained trail system. The round-trip hike to and from the base of the falls is just under 10 miles (16.1 km), depending on the route you choose, and it is entirely on property owned by the AMR and the Ausable Club.

After parking at the end of Ausable Club Road, walk up the dirt road until you reach Lake Road on the left. The intersection is just before the historic St. Hubert's Inn, built in 1890 on the site of the Beede House, which burned to the ground earlier that year. The inn is now the clubhouse for the Ausable Club. The road is well marked as private, but members of the public are allowed to use it to gain access to the trail system leading to Rainbow Falls.

A large wooden gate restricts vehicle traffic to the dirt road beyond. After signing the guest book, proceed past the gate and follow the road for just over 3 miles (4.8 km), until you reach the dam at the end of Lower Ausable Lake.

As you hike, you'll find that there are plenty of opportunities to visit other major waterfalls in the valley. The trails are interconnected to allow you to travel from waterfall to waterfall with little trouble. Some require a bit of a hike off the main trail, but they are all well worth the detour. Take your time and explore.

At the dam, a series of signs guide you to Rainbow Falls. Cross the bridge over the outlet to the lake. The signs lead you straight into the woods and eventually into a very deep ravine and to the base of this 150-foot (46 m) waterfall. As you gaze ahead, you'll notice that the ravine soon disappears into the face of the cliff beside the falls. There is no other way in or out of this spot.

The hike is considered moderately easy, but you should still take proper equipment with you. (The bus that travels back and forth from the lake is for Ausable Club members only.) Remember that the club does not permit dogs on its trail systems. Since the property is private, please respect this rule and others posted on the trails. You are welcome on this property at the Ausable Club's discretion.

COUNTY: Essex

TOWNSHIP: Keene

PLACE: Keene Valley

WATERWAY: Cascade Brook

TYPE: ribbon falls

HEIGHT: 150 ft (46 m)

TRAIL: gravel roadway and rock; easyto moderate

WALKING TIME: 2 hr

PEAK ACTIVITY: May-Sept.

LATITUDE: 44.1184

LONGITUDE: –73.8296

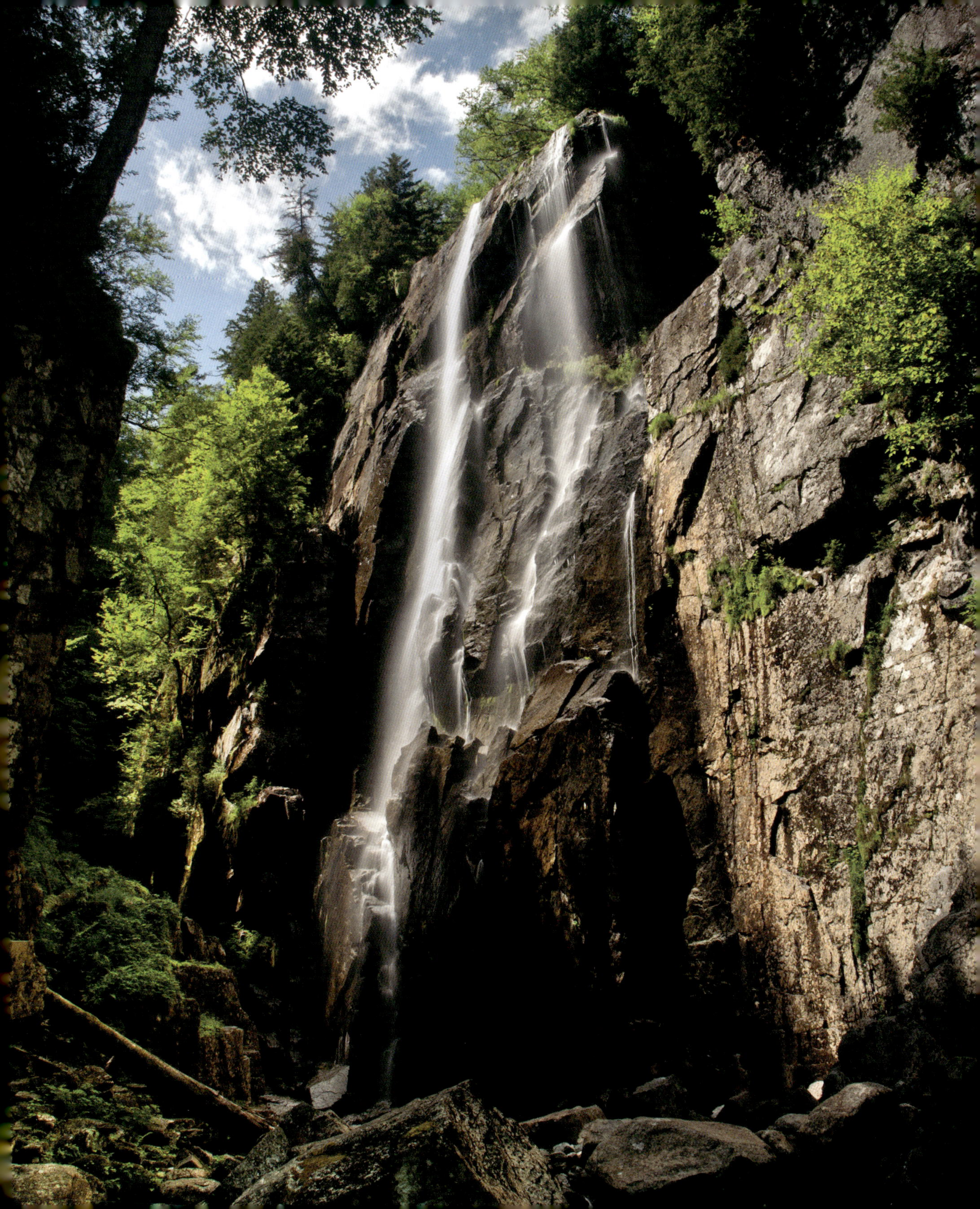

NORTH COUNTRY REGION

Roaring Brook Falls

NY 73 runs north-south through the Adirondack heartland between Keene and I-87 (also known as the Adirondack Northway). In the north, it runs concurrently with NY 9N and becomes NY 9 in the south. Just south of St. Huberts, there is a parking area on the east side of the highway that is well marked by signs for the Giant Mountain Wilderness Area. This is about 3 mi (4.8 km) south of Keene Valley and 1.25 mi (2 km) north of Chapel Pond.

COUNTY:	Essex
TOWNSHIP:	Keene
PLACE:	Keene Valley
WATERWAY:	Roaring Brook
TYPE:	ribbon falls
HEIGHT:	300 ft (91.5 m)
TRAIL:	dirt; moderate
WALKING TIME:	10 min
PEAK ACTIVITY:	May-Sept.
LATITUDE:	44.1501
LONGITUDE:	–73.7611

Located just east of 5,344-foot (1,629 m) Mount Marcy, the state's highest point, Roaring Brook Falls is especially impressive in spring, thanks to runoff from the area's heavy snowfall. Although Roaring Brook doesn't get water directly from Marcy, it is one of many small streams that carry away the snowmelt. The waterfall's drop measures anywhere from 290 to 325 feet (88.4–99 m), depending on which reference you consult, and that results in an extremely dramatic sight when the water is high.

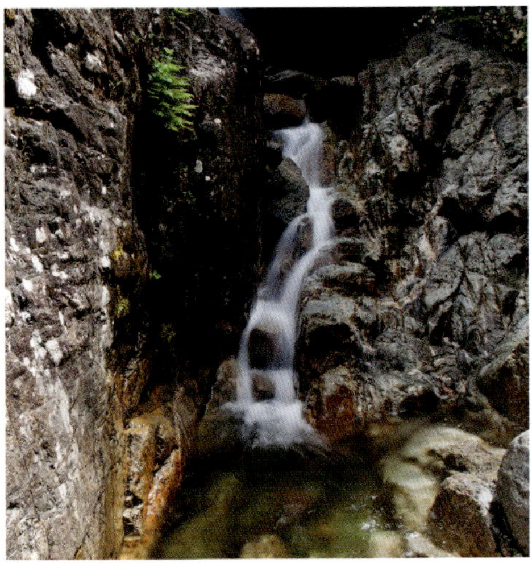

At other times of the year, Roaring Brook doesn't roar much at all: "Babbling Brook" might be more accurate. During a dry summer, you may even be able to step across the rocks in the stream without getting wet. As you look up, however, it's easy to envision what this falls might have looked like just a few weeks earlier.

From the Giant Mountain Wilderness Area parking lot, it's a mere 0.3 mile (0.5 km) to Roaring Brook Falls. The dirt trail leading to the base of the falls is well marked, well maintained and easy to follow.

Roaring Brook Falls plummets in two steps — the upper drop covers about two-thirds of the total relief, while the lower portion takes up the remaining third. As you gaze up from the base, you may not be able to see the upper drop, as it is set back slightly from the lower section. Once you move downstream a little, however, the entire cascade comes into view. If you turn left as you exit the parking area to head back down NY 73, there is a roadside pull-off where you can enjoy the falls from a distance. Some claim Roaring Brook is the highest waterfall in the Adirondacks that is visible from the road.

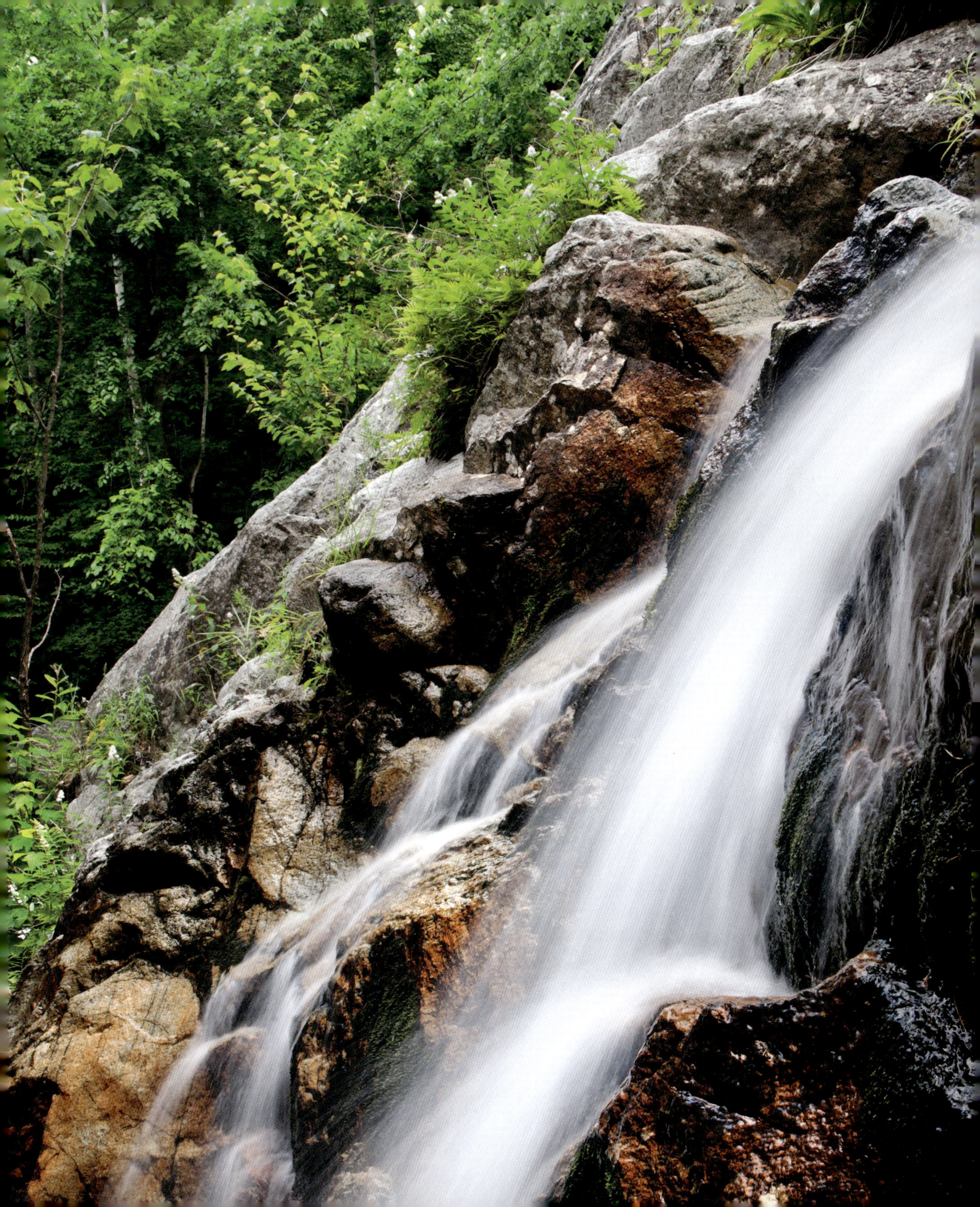

Christine Falls

About 3 mi (4.8 km) east of the intersection of NY 8 and NY 30 in Speculator, you'll come to Old Route 30 on your left. In another 0.3 mi (0.5 km), just beyond a sweeping left-hand curve in the road, there is an opening in the wire guardrails. Enter here, and drive down an incline to the parking area. With your back to the highway, the trailhead is in front of you and to the right.

From the south, this spot is about 6 mi (9.7 km) from where NY 30 and NY 8 join in Wells.

COUNTY:	Hamilton
TOWNSHIP:	Wells
PLACE:	Speculator
WATERWAY:	Sacandaga River
TYPE:	classical cascade
HEIGHT:	20 ft (6.1 m)
TRAIL:	dirt and stone; easy
WALKING TIME:	5 min
PEAK ACTIVITY:	May-Sept.
LATITUDE:	43.5131
LONGITUDE:	–74.3090

To reach Christine Falls, take a slight right from the parking area and hike over a small knoll and down the embankment to the river. Downstream, you'll see a building at the end of the channel on the left side of the river, just before it opens into a pool. Walk a short distance downstream, and you'll find a two-tiered drop of about 20 feet (6.1 m). Welcome to Christine Falls.

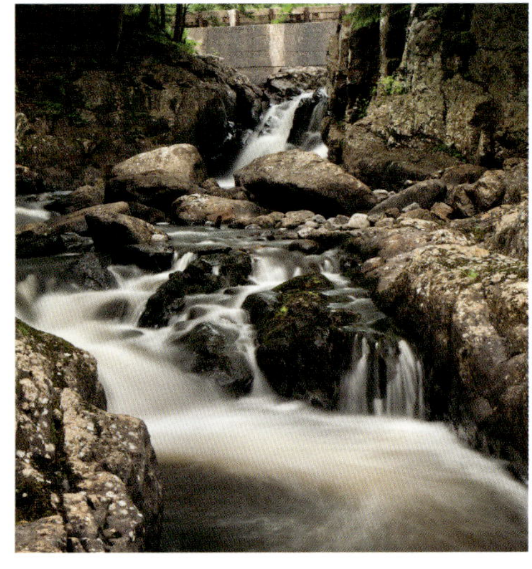

The waterfall is a fairly vertical plunge at the top, followed by a very short level section, and then a gentle slide takes it home. We've classified this waterfall as a classical cascade, but when the two parts are viewed separately, the upper portion is a classical falls, while the lower section is a classical cascade.

After enjoying the waterfall, take a stroll upstream. As an added treat, there are two other small plunges there. As you proceed up the river's edge, you'll pass a set of rapids several hundred feet long. In the middle of this stretch is a drop that could be considered a small waterfall. Continue to the upper section, where you'll see a 10-foot (3 m) cascade through a narrow section of the river between rock outcroppings on both sides. Above, you can see rapids and the retaining dam at a hydro plant to your right.

As with so many waterfalls in the Adirondacks, this site is a great place to enjoy a family picnic. As you sit with your snack taking it all in, it's easy to forget that you are less than 0.25 mile (0.4 km) from a major state highway. In fact, this section of just under 10 miles (16 km) is two highways in one. NY 30 is the primary north-south route through the center of the Adirondacks, and NY 8 is the major east-west route across the southern portion of the park.

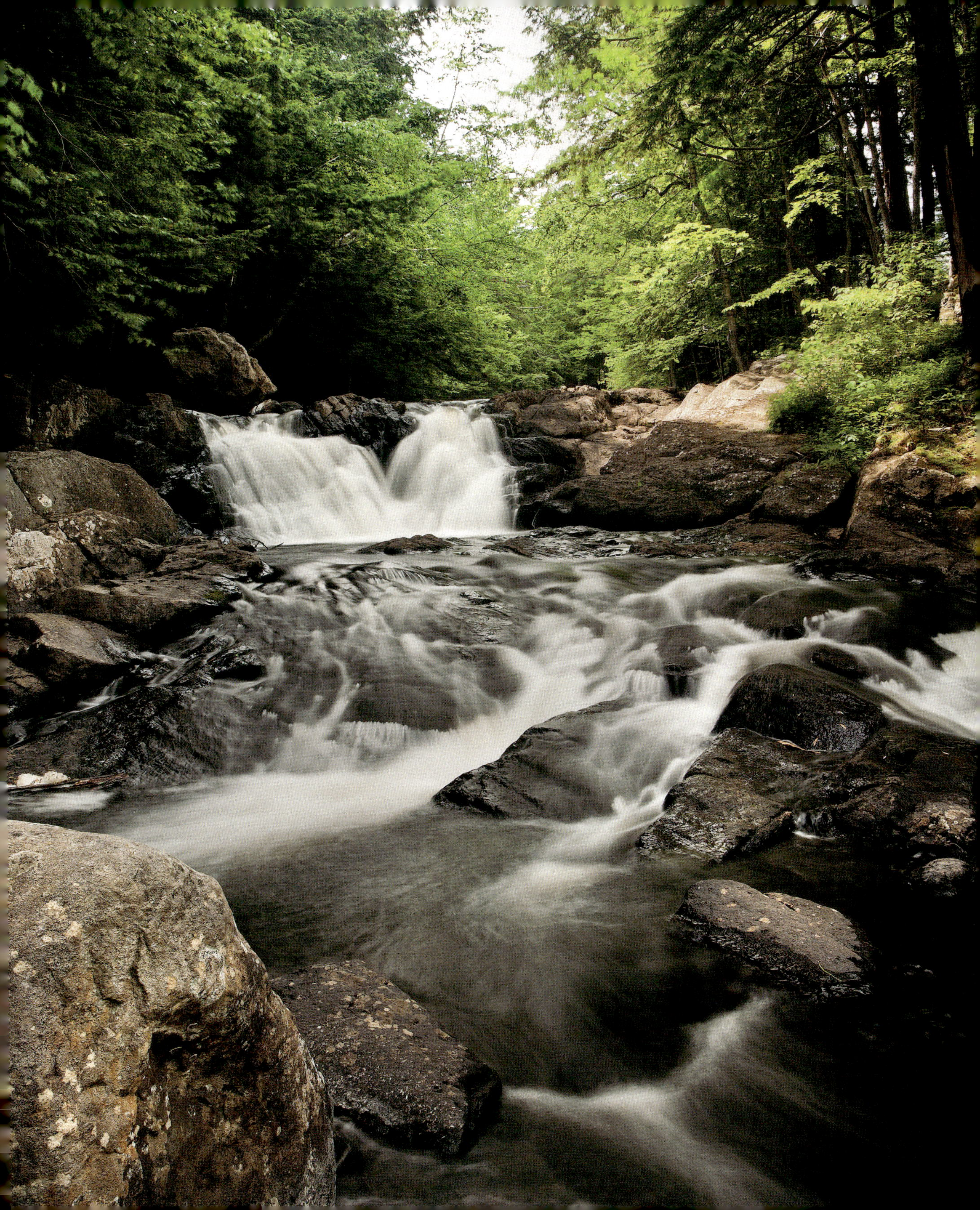

Auger Falls

Between the hamlet of Wells and the village of Speculator is a stretch of highway where NY 8 and NY 30 run together. About 1.7 mi (2.7 km) north of the intersection in Wells, a dirt road exits on the east side of the highway, then splits into two parts that head in opposite directions. The waterfall can be reached from either of these, but the right fork is the shorter and easier route. This 0.2-mi (0.3 km) dirt road ends in a small parking area, where the trailhead is readily found.

The Sacandaga River flows south from northern New York, making its way through several lakes before joining the Hudson River in the town of Lake Luzerne, just west of Glens Falls. Auger Falls is one of the more popular destinations in a region that is rich in waterfalls. There is a much-loved local swimming hole just above the top of the falls.

There are a few theories as to how these falls were named. One is that the twisting, rolling action of the water resembles the shape of a drill or an auger. Another is that the S-shaped walls of the gorge appear to have been carved out by an augerlike device. Yet another is that several potholes in this section, usually visible only when the water is low, look as though they have been drilled into the rocks.

A short distance from the trailhead in this DEC-maintained area, you'll encounter a registration kiosk. The registration system helps to justify state funding and provides a record of visitors in the event of an emergency.

Follow the well-marked trail to the river, but once there, use caution. The rocky, boulder-strewn terrain overlooking the gorge is often wet and slippery from the mist of the waterfall, and there are no fences or other retaining devices. The waterfall drops through the gorge in three sections. The upper section comprises two small falls in rapid succession that total roughly 10 to 15 feet (3–4.6 m). A short, fairly level portion anticipates the middle section — a 40-foot (12.2 m) vertical drop. The lower section is a longer stretch of smaller drops and rapids. The overall relief in the area is about 100 feet (30.5 m) over approximately the same distance.

COUNTY: Hamilton
TOWNSHIP: Wells
PLACE: Wells
WATERWAY: Sacandaga River
TYPE: ribbon cascade
HEIGHT: 100 ft (30.5 m)
TRAIL: dirt; easy
WALKING TIME: 10 min
PEAK ACTIVITY: May-Sept.
LATITUDE: 43.4673
LONGITUDE: –74.2465

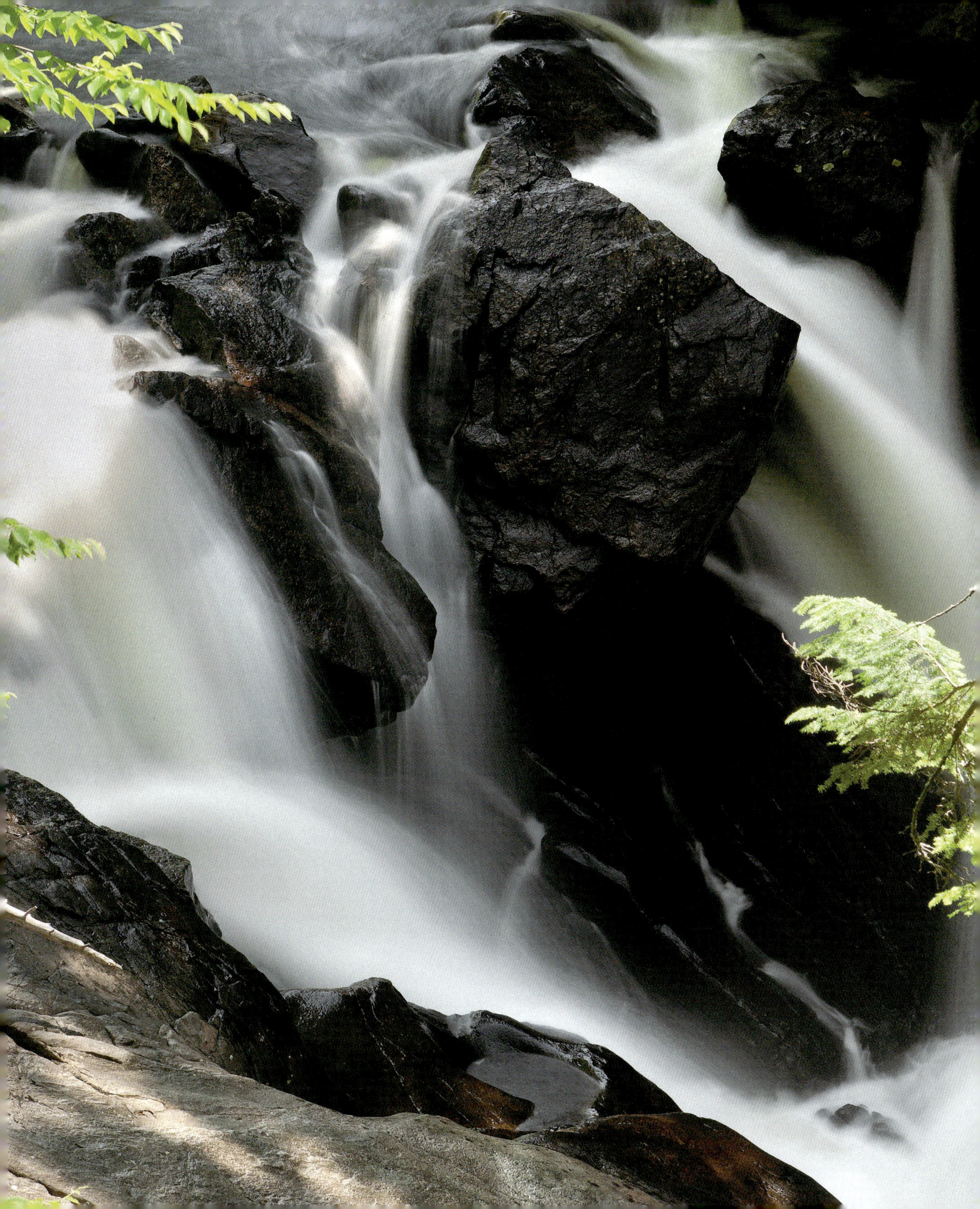

About the Authors

SCOTT A. ENSMINGER

A resident of western New York, Scott A. Ensminger has a long-standing interest in waterfalls. Over the past 25 years, he has written a number of books about the waterfalls of New York, including *The Caves of Niagara County, New York; A Waterfall Guide to Letchworth State Park; Finger Lakes Falls*; and *Niagara's Sisters*. In 1991, Ensminger initiated the Western New York Waterfall Survey. Visit his website at **falzguy.com**.

DAVID J. SCHRYVER

David J. Schryver was born and raised in northern New York. A native of Watertown, in Jefferson County, he has lived the past 34 years in St. Lawrence, the state's largest county. A high school math teacher for 33 years, Schryver has always had an interest in waterfalls, and around the time of his retirement in 2006, he started to visit and research the dozens of falls in his home area. This passion and his sideline of web development led to the website **nnywaterfalls.com**.

EDWARD M. SMATHERS

Interested in photography since he was young, Edward M. Smathers has taught himself the technical aspects of camera systems, gradually honing his skills and learning the fine art of photo editing. Capturing the essence of the natural world and waterfalls has become almost an obsession for Smathers, who spends much of his time searching out new locations and beautiful subjects to photograph. A native New Yorker, Smathers has traveled all over the world but is confident that his perfect shot will be taken right here in New York State. Visit his waterfall website at **digthefalls.com** and his professional website at **edwardsmathers.com**.

REFERENCES

Dunn, Russell. *Mohawk Region Waterfall Guide*. New York: Black Dome Press Corp., 2007.

_________. *Hudson Valley Waterfall Guide*. New York: Black Dome Press Corp., 2005.

_________. *Catskill Region Waterfall Guide*. New York: Black Dome Press Corp., 2004.

_________. *Adirondack Waterfall Guide*. New York: Black Dome Press Corp., 2003.

WEBSITES

To research state park conditions and find out visiting hours, go to the website of the New York State Office of Parks, Recreation & Historic Preservation at **www.nysparks.com**

To learn more about publicly managed land, visit the website of the Department of Environmental Conservation at **www.dec.ny.gov**.

NOTES

Throughout *Waterfalls of New York State*, the acronym DEC is used to refer to the Department of Environmental Conservation. Please note that in the driving directions that accompany each entry, CR stands for County Route and NY stands for New York Route.

Index of Waterfalls